2nd edition

Babies and Young Children

Book 1: Early Years Development

Marian
Beaver

Jo
Brewster

Pauline
Jones

Anne
Keene

Sally
Neaum

Jill
Tallack

Stanley Thornes (Publishers) Ltd

First published in 1994 by:
Stanley Thornes (Publishers) Ltd
Ellenborough House
Wellington Street
CHELTENHAM
GL50 1YW
United Kingdom

Second edition 1999

99 00 01 02 03 / 10 9 8 7 6 5 4 3 2 1

A catalogue record for this book is available from the British Library.

ISBN 0 7487 3974 2

Illustrations by Phil Ford and Oxford Illustrators
Typeset by Columns Design Ltd, Reading
Printed and bound in Italy by Vincenzo Bona, Turin

Contents

Introduction

This book has been written for both child-care students and practitioners with the intention of providing a comprehensive guide to all aspects of the development of children from birth to 8 years. The book relates to the syllabus requirements of the CACHE Certificate in Child Care and Education and the CACHE Diploma in Nursery Nursing as well as the BTEC National Diploma in Early Childhood Studies. The book also covers the requirements for underpinning knowledge for NVQ awards in Child Care and Education. Students on any of the many other courses that require a knowledge and understanding of child development will also find the book useful. Child-care establishments may find the book a valuable addition to their reference shelves and helpful in supporting in-service training.

The book is divided into a number of parts, each part containing a number of chapters covering an area of development. All aspects of child development are presented in a way that is accessible to the reader and the responsibilities of the child-care worker and their role in promoting children's development are emphasised. Case studies help the reader to relate theoretical points to real-life situations and throughout the chapters there are questions and tasks to recall knowledge and develop understanding.

Although the book is complete in itself, some references are made to chapters in the companion volume, *Babies and Young Children 2: Early Years Care and Education*, 2nd edition, so that readers can extend their understanding of a particular point, perhaps relating it to the context of care and education. The index also contains full page referencing to the companion volume.

Since the first edition, the book has been substantially revised. Every chapter has been examined and extended or updated as necessary and there are some additional chapters. A number of new features have been introduced to help readers relate theory to practice and to check and develop their own learning. Throughout the book there are cross-referenced exercises and tasks which provide the reader with opportunities to gather evidence for Key Skills at level 2 in Communication, IT and Application of Number.

About the authors

Marian Beaver has worked in social work, teaching and early years care and education. She has taught for many years on child-care courses in FE. She continues to work in FE at New College Nottingham, Basford Hall and as an external verifier for CACHE, as well as writing and inspecting nursery provision for Ofsted.

Jo Brewster has practised as a nurse, midwife and health visitor. She has taught for many years on child-care courses in FE at New College Nottingham, Basford Hall, as well as writing, inspecting nursery provision for Ofsted and working as an external verifier for CACHE.

Pauline Jones worked in residential child care and as a social worker before lecturing in FE, including Doncaster College for the Deaf. She developed the Diploma in Nursery Nurse Training for profoundly deaf students. She now manages the Child, Health and Social Care curriculum area at West Nottinghamshire College.

Anne Keene comes from a background of nursing, midwifery and Health Visiting. Until June 1998 she managed child-care programmes at Basford Hall College. She has recently established MTW International, a child-care training and recruitment agency, which aims to recruit high quality child-care workers for families, child-care establishments, out-of-school clubs and playschemes, as well as businesses seeking to meet child-care needs of their employees.

Sally Neaum has taught in nursery classes and across the infant age range. She has taught a range of child-care courses in a college of FE. She now works freelance, writing, teaching and as an Ofsted inspector of nursery provision.

Jill Tallack has taught in schools across the whole primary age range. She has worked for some years in a college of FE, teaching on child-care programmes. As well as writing, she also inspects nursery provision for Ofsted.

How to use this book

The new edition of this book and its companion volume, *Babies and Young Children Book 2*, have been written and designed to be even more effective and informative than their enormously popular first editions. The features have been changed to update their relevance. The design has been altered to make the books more open, and a second colour added to make each page more attractive and easy to use. The range of features used in both books is described below.

Introduction to each part

Both books are divided into a number of parts, each of which has a title and comprises several chapters linked by a common theme.

Chapter introduction

Every chapter begins with a summary of its contents, and a list of other chapters that may be relevant for additional reading.

Definitions

Students can be surprised by some of the technical language included in what they read. Where significant new words are introduced in the text, you will find a clear definition of each word in a box in the margin alongside.

Case studies

New case studies have been developed, showing how an issue can be dealt with in a practical environment. Each is followed by two or three questions to give you practice in problem-solving.

Do this!

These are activities that require you to do something. Each one is numbered and by looking up the number in the Key Skills grids on pages x–xi you will find out the Key Skills evidence that may be generated if you complete the activity.

Think about it

These are ideas for thought and reflection. You may wish to think these through on your own, or discuss them with others. Many make ideal subjects for whole class discussion.

Progress check

At the end of each major section within a chapter you will find a short list of questions. Answering these will confirm that you have understood what you have read.

Key terms

At the end of each chapter you will find a list of all the words that appear in the definition boxes throughout the text. You can read through to check that you understand each one.

'Now try these questions'

Each chapter finishes with a number of short-answer questions. If you answer these, you will show that you understand the key concepts in the chapter and are able to write about them in your own words.

Glossary

At the end of the book you will find a comprehensive glossary. It explains all the key terms used both Books 1 and 2 of *Babies and Young Children*.

Index

Like the glossary, the index covers both Books 1 and 2. If a word has an entry in both books, then both page references will appear, with the references to this book in blue, and to the companion volume in black.

Key skills

Many students studying child care also need to demonstrate their competence in Key Skills. You will find guidelines to five of the level 2 Key Skills on pages vi–ix (more detailed coverage will be available from your tutor, assessor or supervisor). The *Do this!* activities in these books provide evidence for the Key Skills units Communication, Number and Information Technology. You will also find a grid on pages x–xi showing you which *Do this!* activities provide evidence for which Key Skills units and elements.

This book and its companion has been written to support a variety of CACHE, City and Guilds, Edexcel (BTEC), RSA early years education, child-care and health awards at level 2 and level 3. It aims both to provide knowledge and understanding and to enhance practical skills for a range of workers including NVQ candidates and DNN (NNEB) students. We are sure that you will like it – and wish you good luck in your studies.

Key skills guidelines

Communication

Effective communication is at the heart of good working practice. There are many ways in which we communicate at work, through conversations, discussions and presentations. These may be direct, over the telephone, by fax, letter or e-mail. They may involve colleagues, managers, children, their parents and others in the community. When you are caring for children what you say and what you understand can have serious consequences for children's well-being. Communication includes each of the following areas.

Taking part in discussions

Child-care workers need to be able to speak clearly and listen carefully. In any discussion it is helpful to:
- keep to the subject
- express yourself clearly (and say if you do not!)
- keep the discussion moving forwards.

Discussions take many forms: informal conversations with colleagues, formal meetings such as staff meetings, planned presentations to groups of people or telephone conversations with, for example, a child's parent or carer.

Producing written material

The benefit of written communication is that the opportunity for misunderstanding may be reduced and accurate records kept. Information can also be shared between several people when direct contact is not possible. Once something is written down, however, it is more difficult to amend. Written information needs to be accurate, legible, easy to understand and in a suitable format.

There are many ways in which written material can be produced. You may need to complete a child's record card, send a letter to a parent, produce a report for a nursery manager, apply in writing for a job as a nanny or complete surveys and questionnaires when helping to set up a local playgroup. Spelling, grammar and punctuation should be checked to ensure accuracy.

Using images

You have probably heard the saying that a picture is worth a thousand words. There will be many opportunities in your work in early years care to use pictures and images to communicate.

Choose clear images that are relevant to what you want to say and:
- suited for those who will need to understand them
- recognise and value diversity
- promote equality of opportunity and anti-discriminatory practice.

Images may be nursery floor plans, illustrations for a monthly newsletter for parents, graphs and charts of attendance for use in an annual report or eye-catching photographs for advertising your facilities. Images can equally well be used to clarify a point in one-to-one or group discussion.

Reading and responding to written materials

We are surrounded by written materials: magazines, reports advertisements, timetables, signs, books and leaflets – the list is endless. It is important to be able to choose the right source of material for your purpose and to be able to get the information you want from it. Once you have chosen your source you need to be able to extract the relevant information, check that you understand it and are able to summarise it.

As a child-care worker you need to understand documents such as the important written policies and procedures of your workplace, the timetable for the children's day, letters from parents or the statutory bodies and agendas and minutes for meetings. You also need to be able to interpret any pictures and images accompanying written information.

Application of number

It may surprise you how often you will be dealing with numbers, data and mathematical problem-solving in your work with children. Dealing with numbers is more straightforward when you understand why you are doing it. Accuracy is important. Application of number includes the following areas.

Collecting and recording data

Data is numerical information; you need to be able to collect and record such information. Once you know what kind of information you need, you will have to decide how you are going to collect it, conduct your tasks in the right order and record your results clearly and accurately. You may wish to record information from parents at an enrolment interview or record attendance levels at a nursery over a period of weeks. You may need to plan a new home corner, measure up the space available and draw up an accurate plan of your proposals. You may be involved in collecting money from parents and keeping accurate records of how much has been paid to you.

One question you do need to ask yourself when collecting data is how precise you need to be. If you are surveying the arrival times of children at a nursery you may need to be precise only to the nearest five minutes. If you are collecting money from parents, you cannot afford any mistakes at all!

Tackling problems

From time to time you will come across problems at work which will need to be solved using numerical techniques. It is important to choose the correct technique to start with and to make sure that you do everything in the right order. Any calculations need to be accurate and you should check your work to make sure that there are no errors and that your results make sense.

You may need to:
- work out amounts of disposable materials such as paper, paints or clay that will be required for an activity
- account for how money has been spent during a certain period
- help in conducting local surveys for the opening of a new nursery.

All these require their own techniques and the results of each need to be presented appropriately.

Interpreting and presenting data

Large amounts of data are impossible to understand unless presented clearly; just as a picture can speak a thousand words, so a graph can present a thousand numbers. It is almost certain that you, or someone else, will be making decisions based on the information you present, so the graphs, charts, tables, pictograms, plans, diagrams or drawings used should be clear and appropriate. You should outline the main features of your data, ensure appropriate axes or labels are clear and explain how your results are relevant to the problem.

The outcome of a nursery survey may best be presented in graphs, charts an tables, while proposals to change the use of nursery space, for example, will probably use plans and diagrams.

Information technology

Most information is now stored electronically, on an information technology (or IT) system. The strength of such systems is that they can also reorganise, manipulate and provide information and (in theory at least!) reduce the amount of paper used in the workplace. Information technology includes the following areas.

Preparing information

Output information is only as good as the information put in, so all information should be accurate. It is important to plan carefully so that the information you put in is in an appropriate form, and once entered, can easily be edited. You should also save all your information in well organised files and folders and make back-up copies in case something goes wrong with your centrally stored files.

The names, addresses and postcodes of parents, for example, should be organised so that the information can be easily used for mailings; survey and questionnaire findings should be carefully recorded so that they can be transferred to a spreadsheet and source information for a termly newsletter (text, pictures, tables or graphs) entered so that it can be electronically merged into a single file.

Processing information

Entering information onto a system is not, in itself, particularly useful. It is the computer's power to access and select information in different ways, to combine information from different sources and to provide user-friendly output that makes it such a useful tool. Finding, retrieving, editing, combining and reorganising information will help you shape raw data to your needs.

Once properly organised, parental addresses can be used, for example, for mail shots, individual letters, reaching the parents of children within a specific age range or within a particular postal district. The raw data from the survey can be processed into graphs, charts or tables and the individual parts of the newsletter put into an appropriate format.

Presenting information

Presenting information clearly and professionally is in your own interest as well as your employer's. Even the best ideas may go unnoticed if poorly presented; people may simply not understand your point. A professional approach is particularly important in working with children, as you may need to win the approval, confidence and support of parents, the local authority and the wider community – and your employer.

You should be able to present your processed information in an appropriate way and choose the most effective software to do so. Consistency is important and you should always save your finished work in carefully organised files and make regular back-ups.

You will develop a reputation for thoroughness and professionalism by doing the following:

- consistently and accurately fulfilling and updating your mailings
- producing surveys and other reports in a recognisable form in a common format
- publishing your newsletters to the same high standard every term.

Evaluating the use of information technology

It is important that you know when information technology can make your life easier – and when it cannot! It is also important to understand the range of software available to you and what its functions and limits are.

A computer and its software is like any other machine. It needs to be carefully maintained, and faults and problems logged so that they can be dealt with. It is also important that your working practices are healthy and safe and that you protect yourself and your machine by correctly positioning the keyboard and screen, keeping cables tidy, keeping food and drink away from where you are working and storing equipment away from sources of heat and other electrical equipment.

Improving own learning and performance

We all have strengths and weaknesses, and to improve our own learning and performance it is important that we can identify them. Setting targets and reviewing progress will help you to focus more clearly on what you need to do. Improving own learning and performance includes the following areas.

Identifying targets

You should be able to identify your strengths and weaknesses and provide evidence to support what you say. You will also need to be able to help in setting short-term targets for your own improvement, in conjunction with your teacher, assessor or workplace supervisor. When targets have been set, make sure that you understand what is required of you!

Following schedules to meet your targets

Once your targets for improvement are agreed, you should be able to follow them without close supervision, within the specified time scale. You will, of course, receive support in your work and you should know how to put this to good use in improving your work and meeting your targets.

Being SMART!

Be	**S**pecific in setting your targets and schedules!
Tackle learning in	**M**anageable chunks!
Make sure your targets are	**A**chievable!
Keep your targets	**R**elevant.
Track progress so you are on	**T**ime in meeting your targets!

Working with others

When you work in child care, you are unlikely to work alone. Learning with other people can be a great challenge, but also bring great rewards. Working with others includes the following areas (see also Book 2, Chapter 3, *The nursery nurse in employment*).

Identifying collective goals and responsibilities

When you work with others you need to be able to identify and agree group goals. You also need to be clear about who is responsible for what and how you are going to organise working together.

Working to collective goals

Once you understand your responsibilities you should set about organising your work so that you will be able to achieve your goals on time. You will need to stick to the working methods agreed by the whole group.

When working in a group communication is important, so you should keep others informed of your progress. You may also encounter difficulties, or circumstances may change. When that happens it is crucial that you let others know – it is possible that their work will be affected as well as yours.

Key skills grid

The following grid indicates key skills coverage provided by *Do this!* activities in this book.

Do this!	Communication				Information Technology				Application of Number		
	2.1	2.2	2.3	2.4	2.1	2.2	2.3	2.4	2.1	2.2	2.3
1.1									x		
2.1		x									
3.1		x	x						x		
3.2		x	x								
3.3		x									
3.4		x	x								
3.5		x									
3.6	x										
3.7	x										
3.8	x										
3.9	x										
3.10									x		
4.1		x		x							
4.2		x		x							
4.3	x	x	x	x							
5.1		x	x	x						x	x
6.1		x	x	x	x	x	x				
6.2			x	x					x	x	x
6.3		x	x	x							
7.1	x	x	x								
8.1		x									
8.2					x	x	x				
8.3		x		x							
8.4							x		x	x	
8.5	x										
8.6			x								
8.7		x		x							
8.8		x		x							
8.9		x		x							
8.10							x				
9.1	x	x									
9.2		x									
9.3		x			x	x	x				
9.4		x									
9.5		x		x							
9.6	x		x	x							
10.1									x	x	x
10.2		x			x						
10.3		x									
10.4									x		x
10.5		x		x							
11.1					x	x	x				
12.1	x	x									
12.2	x	x			x	x					
12.3	x				x	x	x				
12.4		x									
12.5					x	x	x				
12.6	x			x		x	x				
13.1		x									

Do this!	Communication				Information Technology				Application of Number		
	2.1	2.2	2.3	2.4	2.1	2.2	2.3	2.4	2.1	2.2	2.3
13.2					x	x	x				
13.3		x									
13.4		x									
14.1		x									
14.2		x									
14.3		x									
14.4				x							
14.5		x	x								
14.6		x									
14.7	x										
14.8	x	x									
14.9	x										
14.10		x									
14.11	x										
14.12			x		x		x				
15.1	x										
15.2			x	x							
15.3	x	x									
15.4	x	x									
15.5	x			x							
15.6		x					x				
15.7	x										
15.8	x										
15.9	x	x		x				x			
15.10				x				x			
16.1				x							
16.2	x										
16.3					x	x	x				
16.4		x	x								
17.1	x										
17.2		x		x							
18.1	x								x		
19.1	x										
19.2		x									
19.3	x			x							
19.4	x	x		x							
19.5		x	x								
19.6		x		x	x		x				
20.1	x			x							
20.2		x		x							
20.3	x			x							
20.4	x			x							
20.5		x		x			x		x		
21.1	x	x					x				
21.2			x	x							
21.3	x	x	x	x			x				
21.4		x	x								
21.5		x									
21.6	x	x					x				
22.1	x			x							
22.2				x							
22.3		x		x							

Acknowledgements

The authors and publishers would like to thank the following people and organisations for permission to reproduce photographs and other material:

Dr S Lingam, Royston Westgarth/BDA, Guardian Newspapers Ltd, Ward Lock Educational; Val Jackson, Juliette Khan, Jean Reed, Jane Rigg and Sterling Associates for the cover photograph.

Every effort has been made to contact copyright holders and we apologise if any have been overlooked.

Part 1: Physical Development

Each child is a unique individual and all the areas of development are interlinked and dependant upon each other. Children's development is a continual process in which they develop through a series of stages at their own pace. One skill must be accomplished and practised before a child progresses to the next, more complex, achievement.

Although no two children are the same, there are recognised patterns to human growth and development. Children's progress is measured against their previous achievements, the average achievement for their age group and established developmental 'norms'.

To be able to stimulate children's development, it is necessary for all child-care workers to know the developmental stages and to understand the factors that influence development.

All child-care workers must have a sound knowledge of child development so that:

- they can plan activities which will help the children in their care to progress to the next stage of development
- their expectations of the child are realistic
- they can identify children who are not making progress.

1 Physical growth

This chapter includes:

- **Physical growth**
- **Bone development**
- **Measuring physical growth**
- **Factors affecting physical growth**

Physical growth begins at conception and follows a recognised pattern. Within this pattern, each child grows and develops in their own particular way. Physical growth and physical development are very closely linked. Development of physical skills will only be achieved if children develop their bones and muscles and learn to balance and co-ordinate their bodies. Child-care workers need to know the pattern of physical growth and how to measure and record it. They need to understand how to apply this knowledge when they care for children.

Physical growth

Physical growth is the increase in size that takes place as the child develops. The adult human is composed of many cells, but begins life as a single cell, the fertilised egg. The fertilised egg divides into two cells then into four, eight, sixteen, and so on. This process of cell division is the basis for human growth.

 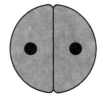 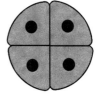

What happens when a cell divides

One cell divides into two ...   the two cells divide again ...   and so on

At first the new cells are smaller than the original parent cell, but they soon grow to full size. For this to happen, they must have food to provide the material for growth. Eventually these cells will turn into different types of cell. For example, some cells will become muscle cells, some brain cells, some nerve cells. The process by which cells become specialised like this is called **differentiation** and it plays a vital part in forming the adult human (see the diagram on page 4).

In a growing child, cell division takes place in all parts of the body and the child gets steadily larger. Some parts of the body grow more quickly than other parts. This process alters the proportions of the body as the

differentiation
The term used to describe how cells in the body develop and take on different functions

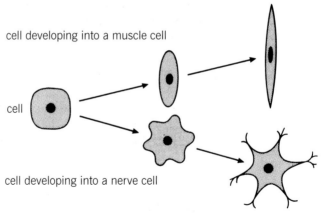

How different cells are formed

child gets bigger. The head grows quickly in the early stages of development and then slows down, whereas the legs and arms grow slowly at first and speed up later.

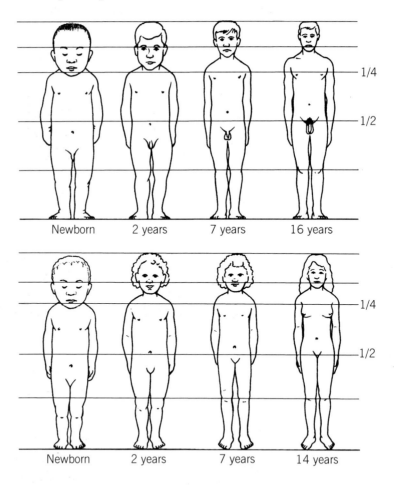

Changing body proportions

The growth of different parts of the body at different rates is closely linked to development:

■ The head grows quickly in fetal life because the brain is developing rapidly.

- The neck lengthens and strengthens after birth to support the head and enable it to turn; this takes place as the baby develops the ability to see things further away.
- The chest becomes broader and stronger as the lungs develop and the child becomes more active in sitting and standing.
- The arms lengthen and the hands increase in size and strength as the child develops the ability to manipulate objects.
- The legs and feet increase in size and strength as the need to balance, walk, run, jump and climb develops.

The head

The growth of the head is affected by the structures within it, such as the eyes, teeth, nose, sinuses and brain. As the head grows, the baby chubbiness disappears and the face lengthens to give a more angular appearance. The jawbone becomes bigger and stronger, and teeth appear. These changes are linked with the child's developing ability to chew food and develop speech.

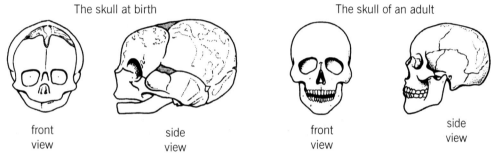

The skull at birth   The skull of an adult

front view   side view   front view   side view

The developing skull

The hands

The hands at birth are chubby and the bones in the ends of the fingers are tiny seeds of cartilage. As the child grows and develops, the bones grow harder and lengthen, the layer of protective fat disappears and the hands develop more strength for lifting and manipulating objects.

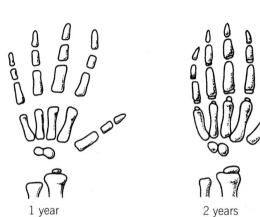
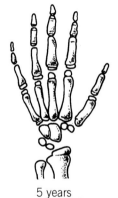

The developing bones of the hand

1 year   2 years   5 years

Progress check

1 What proportion of the newborn baby's total length is the head?
2 What proportion of the total length of the adult is taken up by the legs?
3 Why does this change in proportions happen?
4 What areas of development are influenced by the growth of the head?

Bone development

The body framework is provided by the skeleton – a collection of bones, each designed to perform a particular function.

The functions of the skeleton are to:

■ support the body framework, for example, the neck supports the head
■ protect vital organs, for example, the skull protects the brain
■ manufacture red blood cells
■ store calcium and other minerals.

The development of the bones of the skeleton begins before birth, in fetal life, when some of the body cells specialise and form bone cells. There are different types of bones:

■ long bones, for example the bones of the legs and arms
■ flat bones, for example the bones of the skull
■ irregular bones, for example the bones of the spine
■ sesamoid bones, for example the bones of the kneecap, ankle and wrist.

Fully developed bones are hard and strong so that they can do the job of supporting the body and protecting its organs. Bones begin, however, as softer materials from which harder bone develops. These are:

■ cartilage, from which bone cells form long bones
■ membrane, from which bone cells form flat bones.

In fetal life, much of the skeleton is composed of cartilage and membrane. Cartilage and membrane have a very important function. They are capable of growing; but because they are soft and without much strength, the cartilage and membrane in the bones must gradually become harder to give the bones the strength they need to support the body. This process of changing from the soft cartilage and membrane to the hard bone is called **ossification**.

ossification
The process by which the bones become hardened

Long bones

The long bones of growing children are made up of cartilage and ossified (hardened) bone. This is because the cartilage part of the bone can grow, while the ossified part gives the bone its strength. Ossification is a very gradual process and takes 18 to 20 years to complete.

Long bones begin in fetal life as a rod of cartilage

Centres of ossification appear in the middle and each end of the long bone

As the long bones grow, the area of ossified bone increases, leaving a narrow neck of cartilage at each end of the bone, allowing continued growth

A bone becomes fully ossified when growth is completed, usually by 18–20 years

The ossification of the long bones

Flat bones

The bones of the baby's skull are flat bones. They are made up of membrane, cartilage and ossified bone. The brain grows very rapidly while the baby is developing before birth. To enable this to happen, there are gaps between the bones of the skull called **fontanelles** (see the diagram on page 8). The fontanelles also allow the shape of the baby's head to alter during labour (this is called **moulding**) so that the birth of the head is easier. There are two fontanelles that you need to know about. They are:

- the anterior fontanelle, at the front of the head
- the posterior fontanelle, at the back of the head.

Both fontanelles are covered by tough membrane, which protects the brain. The membrane is very strong and there is no danger of inflicting any damage during normal handling or when washing the baby's hair. The anterior fontanelle is quite noticeable at birth but gradually becomes smaller as the bones of the skull grow together and ossification takes place. It is usually closed by the time the baby is 18 months old. The posterior fontanelle is much smaller and closes up soon after birth.

Children's bones are continually growing and are not fully ossified. These are the important things to remember when you are caring for them:

- Handle babies and small children carefully. Support a small baby's head when you pick them up. Support babies when they are learning to sit and walk.
- Remember that as the bones ossify they will gradually grow strong enough to take the baby's full weight.
- Make sure that shoes and clothes allow room for fingers, toes and limbs to grow and move; the cartilage part of the bone is soft and will easily be deformed by poorly fitting socks, shoes and clothes.

fontanelles
The areas on the baby's head where the skull bones have not joined together

moulding
The process during birth where the shape of the baby's head is changed to make the birth easier

■ Provide children with a diet that will encourage the bones to grow properly.

■ See that children have the opportunity to take suitable exercise and have adequate rest.

These points are vital if the bones are to grow and develop properly.

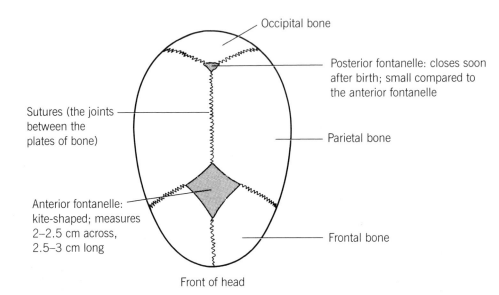

The top of the head of a newborn baby

Occipital bone

Posterior fontanelle: closes soon after birth; small compared to the anterior fontanelle

Sutures (the joints between the plates of bone)

Parietal bone

Anterior fontanelle: kite-shaped; measures 2–2.5 cm across, 2.5–3 cm long

Frontal bone

Front of head

 Progress check

1 What is the process of the hardening of the bones called?
2 What is the essential function of cartilage?
3 What is the essential function of membrane?
4 What is the essential function of hardened bone?
5 By what age are the long bones fully hardened?

Measuring physical growth

Physical growth in children can be measured in different ways. It is important to remember that there can be a wide variation in measurements and that such variations are quite normal. Average measurements are often useful as they provide a guide when measuring children.

Centile charts

The best way to record a child's growth is to use a **centile** (or **percentile**) **chart**. When measuring physical growth there are centile charts for:

percentile charts/centile charts
Specially prepared charts that are used to record measurements of a child's growth. There are centile charts for weight, height and head circumference

- weight
- height
- head circumference.

Study the charts below and the explanation which follows to make sure that you know how to interpret the information centile charts provide.

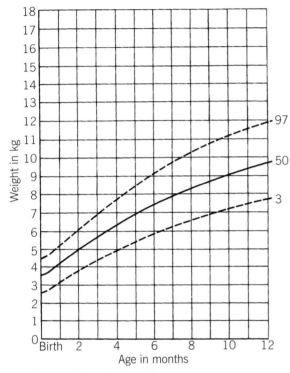

A centile chart for weighing girls

A centile chart for weighing boys

Look at the centile chart for weighing girls (above). You will see that the age of the baby is shown along the bottom of the chart; while the weight in kilograms is shown along the left-hand side of the chart.

There are three lines marked on the chart. The bold line, marked 50 on the right-hand side of the chart, represents average weights for girls. The other dotted lines (marked 3 and 97 on the right-hand side of the chart) show a range of measurements above and below the average.

For example, the dotted line marked 97 (the 97th centile) shows weights of girls who are heaviest within their age group. If a girl aged 6 months weighs 9 kg, her weight will be plotted on the dotted line marked 97. This means that 97 per cent of girls will weigh less than she does and 3 per cent will weigh more.

The dotted line marked 3 (the 3rd centile) shows the weights of girls who are lightest in their age group. If a girl aged 6 months weighs 6 kg, her weight will be plotted on the dotted line marked 3. This means that 97 per cent of girls will weigh more than she does and 3 per cent will weigh less.

Recording a child's measurements regularly on the correct centile chart will produce a new line on the chart especially for that child. The new line will show the progress of this particular child. It will also show the relationship of this particular child's measurements to other children of the same age and sex.

 Progress check

1 What measurements can be recorded on a centile chart?
2 Which centile line on the charts represents average measurements?
3 Are there different charts for girls and boys?
4 If you plot the weight of a child and it falls on the 97th centile, what is the relationship of this child's weight to other children of the same age and sex?

Think about it

Why is using a centile chart to record measurements more meaningful than making a list of those measurements?

Do this!   1.1

You now know that there are centile charts for recording weight, height and head circumference. There are also separate charts for girls and boys.

1 Use the centile charts to find out the average weights of (a) a girl and (b) a boy at:
   i)   birth
   ii) 5 months
   iii) 12 months.

2 Look at this list of ages and weights. They are for a girl at:
      birth   3.5 kg
      1 month   4.0 kg
      2 months   4.5 kg
      4 months   5.0 kg
      6 months   6.0 kg.
   You can see that the baby's weight is gradually increasing. Plot the information on the correct centile chart. Note your results. What do you think is happening to the baby's weight?

3 Use the correct centile charts to record the measurements of a child you are studying over a period of time. You can link this task with the child study in Chapter 3, page 64.

Case study: Using a centile chart

Lindon is 6 months old. His mother, Clare, had a normal and uneventful pregnancy and gave birth to Lindon at full term. The delivery was normal and Lindon was a healthy baby weighing 3.5 kg. Lindon thrived and gained weight steadily; his weight remained at or around the 50th centile. When he was 5 months old, Clare returned to her work on a part-time basis and Lindon was looked after at the local nursery where he has settled in happily. However, since he started nursery Lindon has had two bad colds, and he is also teething. When he was weighed recently, at age 6 months, his weight was 6 kg exactly. Clare is now worried about Lindon – he is not eating well and she feels his weight gain is not satisfactory.

1 Plot Lindon's weight on the correct centile chart.
2 Which centile is his weight on?
3 How does this compare with the centile his weight was on at birth?
4 What do you think the reason for this change might be?

Factors affecting physical growth

Children are individuals and the way they grow varies. There are many influences on the way in which a child grows, but these factors can be broadly divided into three main groups:

- **antenatal** factors: occurring before birth
- **perinatal** factors: occurring during the birth
- **postnatal** factors: occurring after the birth.

All of these factors are discussed in detail in Chapter 6, *Factors affecting physical development*. The following information provides a summary of antenatal and postnatal factors.

Antenatal factors

The following factors can all have a profound influence on the growth of the unborn baby. The harmful influence of many of them can be minimised by good **preconceptual** and antenatal care.

Heredity

A child **inherits** genes from both parents and these will decide, for example, the maximum height to which a child will grow and the shape and size of the body. A more detailed explanation of **heredity** is given in Chapter 6, *Factors affecting physical development*.

Multiple pregnancies

Two or more babies growing in the uterus at the same time may mean that one or more will be lighter than the average birth weight. Modern diagnosis with an ultrasound scan enables twin or multiple pregnancies to

---

antenatal
The period of time from conception until the baby is born

perinatal
The period of time during birth

preconceptual
The time between a couple deciding they would like to have a baby and when the baby is conceived

heredity
The transmission of characteristics from one generation to the next

inherit
The passing of a characteristic or set of characteristics from one generation to the next

be discovered much earlier. This means that with careful management of the pregnancy the babies have a much better chance of growing well in the uterus.

Illness of the mother

Women who are known to have a medical condition, such as diabetes, will need extra care and careful monitoring during their pregnancy, as such a condition may affect the growth of the **fetus** (the unborn baby). Illnesses in pregnancy may mean that the mother's diet is not sufficient to sustain fetal growth. Good care at this time will enable early detection of illness so that any adverse effects of the mother's illness or medical condition on the fetus can be kept to a minimum.

fetus
The term used to describe the baby from the eighth week after conception until birth

Diet in pregnancy

The growth of the fetus is closely linked to the amount and quality of food that the mother is eating. Good antenatal care will provide women with the information to help them understand the importance of a good quality diet to the growth of the fetus. Good food can be expensive and people on low incomes may find it difficult to provide a high quality diet. They may need extra help and advice from their midwife or health visitor to help them select a good diet, while keeping the cost within their budget.

Smoking in pregnancy

Smoking in pregnancy by the mother or those around her slows down the growth of the fetus. Giving up smoking is strongly encouraged. If at all possible, both partners should make this decision well before they decide to have a baby.

Postnatal factors

postnatal
Describes the period of time after the birth

Diet

The right amount of food containing the correct nutrients is essential for growth. Breast milk provides exactly the right nutrients for the growing baby. Formula (bottle) feeds also provide all the correct nutrients for the baby to grow well. It is very important that formula feeds are made up correctly using the correct quantities of water and powder. Close attention to hygiene when making up feeds prevents any contamination that might lead to infection. Once a baby is weaned onto solid food, a good diet enables satisfactory growth and muscle development to take place. Adults need to provide, and encourage children to select and eat, a healthy balanced diet. Poverty or famine means that food is in short supply or that the food consumed is not supplying the right balance of nutrients. This restricts normal healthy growth.

Exercise

Exercise helps muscle and bone development. The adult needs to provide safe opportunities for the child to take suitable exercise. It is important to make sure that the exercise takes account of the child's stage of bone development. Children who cannot exercise by themselves because they are ill, or have restricted movement because of a disability, will need an adult carer to help them exercise their bodies. Physiotherapists are the professionals who will help the adult to understand how to do this effectively.

Illness

Severe illness may slow the rate of growth but this is usually temporary and children soon catch up. It is important that children avoid getting infections. Good standards of hygiene and immunisation against childhood diseases will help to protect young children from infection.

Smoking

Smoking in a child's environment may slow the rate of growth. Recent research that shows that passive smoking is harmful to babies and young children.

Hormones

hormones
Chemical messengers produced in endocrine glands and carried in the bloodstream to their target organ to stimulate a specific action

Hormones are chemicals made by the endocrine glands. The testes, ovaries and pituitary glands produce hormones which influence growth. Hormones affect the body shape. As puberty approaches, the sex hormones cause the typical feminine and masculine outlines to develop.

Seasons

Growth is faster in the spring and slower in the autumn.

Environment

Our environment is our total surroundings and experiences. Growth depends on the provision of a healthy, hygienic environment, but it also depends on the child feeling secure loved and wanted. Consistent, loving care is an important factor in the normal growth and development of babies and young children.

Variations in growth rate

Growth is a continuous process, but there are spurts in the rate of growth. Growth is individual and is controlled by genetic information. Children will achieve different heights, weights and proportions as they move towards maturity. Growth and physical development are very closely linked. As children grow, develop their bones and muscles and learn to balance and co-ordinate their bodies, they will move through the stages of acquiring physical skills. They will do this at their own pace. A baby of 3 months will not be able to sit or walk because the bones and muscles are not sufficiently developed to support the weight of the body. The proportions of the body are still top heavy and the legs need to grow longer and stronger to take the child's full weight. Physical skills, like sitting and standing, will not be achieved until the body reaches the stage in growth required to support the skill.

Progress check

1 Why is it important for the mother to have a good diet in pregnancy?
2 How can smoking in pregnancy affect the fetus?
3 What influence does the environment have on the child after birth?
4 Why is exercise important to the developing child?
5 How do hormones affect growth after birth?

Key terms

You need to know what these words and phrases mean. Go back through the chapter to find out.

antenatal
differentiation
fetus
fontanelle
heredity
hormones
inherit
moulding
ossification
percentile/centile chart
perinatal
preconceptual
postnatal

Now try these questions

1 Describe how the proportions of the body change as a child grows. How is the change in proportions linked to physical development?

2 What are the functions of the skeleton?

3 Describe the process of ossification. How is ossification of the bones linked to physical growth and development?

4 Why is using a centile chart the best way to record a child's physical growth?

5 Why is good antenatal care important to ensure the healthy growth and development of the fetus?

2 Development from conception to birth

This chapter includes:

- **The male and female reproductive organs**
- **The menstrual cycle**
- **Development of the ovum**
- **Fetal growth and development**
- **The importance of preconceptual and antenatal care**

Growth and development of the baby begins well before the actual birth. Preparation by the prospective parents and good preconceptual care has a strong influence on future growth and development. Growth and development begins in the uterus at conception and continues throughout the 40 weeks of pregnancy and proceeds according to a set timetable. During this time there are many good and harmful influences that can affect growth and development. Good antenatal care helps to ensure the health of the mother and the unborn baby.

You may find it useful to read this chapter in conjunction with:

▶ **Book 1, Chapter 6**   Factors affecting physical development

The male and female reproductive organs

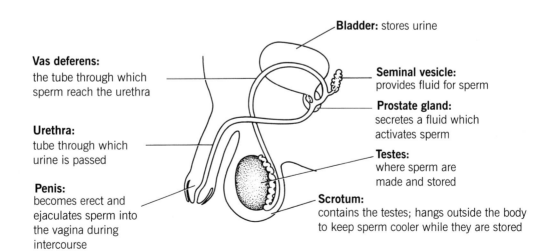

Vas deferens: the tube through which sperm reach the urethra

Urethra: tube through which urine is passed

Penis: becomes erect and ejaculates sperm into the vagina during intercourse

Bladder: stores urine

Seminal vesicle: provides fluid for sperm

Prostate gland: secretes a fluid which activates sperm

Testes: where sperm are made and stored

Scrotum: contains the testes; hangs outside the body to keep sperm cooler while they are stored

The male reproductive organs

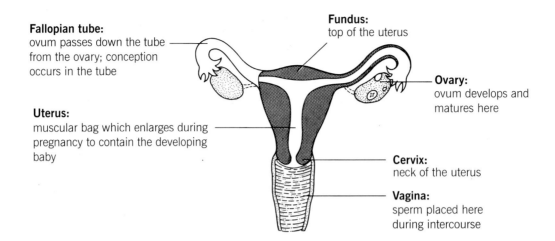

Fallopian tube: ovum passes down the tube from the ovary; conception occurs in the tube

Fundus: top of the uterus

Ovary: ovum develops and matures here

Uterus: muscular bag which enlarges during pregnancy to contain the developing baby

Cervix: neck of the uterus

Vagina: sperm placed here during intercourse

The female reproductive organs

menstrual cycle The process of ovulation and menstruation in sexually mature, non-pregnant women

ovum Egg produced by the ovary

uterus Part of the female reproductive tract; the womb

sperm (spermatozoa) The mature male sex cell

conception Occurs when a sperm fertilises a ripe ovum

oestrogen A hormone produced by the ovaries

progesterone A hormone produced by the ovaries

✔ *Progress check*

1 What is the name of the narrow opening between the uterus and vagina?
2 What is the function of the prostate gland?
3 Where does the ovum develop?
4 What is contained in the scrotum?
5 Where does conception take place?

The menstrual cycle

The **menstrual cycle** concerns the production of a ripe **ovum** by the ovary and the preparation of the **uterus** to receive it. If the ovum is fertilised, by a **sperm**, after it has been released from the ovary then **conception** takes place. The menstrual cycle usually takes about 28 days to complete, but this will vary from woman to woman. The menstrual cycle is controlled by two hormones (chemical messengers) called **oestrogen** and **progesterone** which are produced by the ovary. The first part of the cycle (called proliferation) is stimulated by oestrogen: the **endometrium** (the lining of the uterus) is reconstructed. The second part of the cycle (known as secretion) is stimulated by progesterone and the endometrium becomes thickened and **vascular** (well supplied with blood vessels) in order to nourish the fertilised ovum. In the premenstrual phase (called regression) the endometrium stops growing 5–6 days before menstruation.

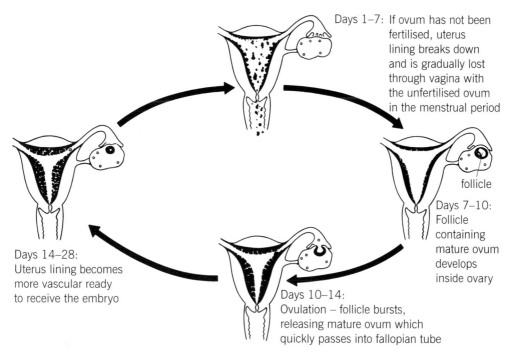

Days 1–7: If ovum has not been fertilised, uterus lining breaks down and is gradually lost through vagina with the unfertilised ovum in the menstrual period

follicle

Days 7–10: Follicle containing mature ovum develops inside ovary

Days 14–28: Uterus lining becomes more vascular ready to receive the embryo

Days 10–14: Ovulation – follicle bursts, releasing mature ovum which quickly passes into fallopian tube

The menstrual cycle

---

endometrium
The lining of the uterus

vascular
Well supplied with blood vessels

The influence of the ovarian hormones

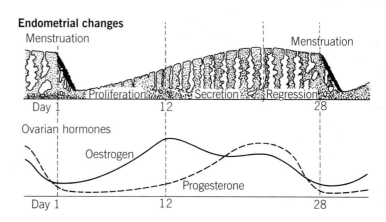

Endometrial changes

Menstruation

Menstruation

Proliferation   Secretion   Regression

Day 1   12   28

Ovarian hormones

Oestrogen

Progesterone

Day 1   12   28

 Progress check

1 What is a hormone?
2 Which two hormones does the ovary produce?
3 When, in the menstrual cycle, does ovulation take place?
4 What happens to the endometrium if the ovum is not fertilised?
5 Where does the ovum develop?

Development of the ovum

At around day 12 of the menstrual cycle, a woman's ovaries release one ripe ovum. The ovum quickly passes into the fallopian tube. During intercourse mature sperm from the male are deposited at the **cervix** in the female. The sperm are contained in a fluid called semen. If intercourse takes place around the time the ovum is released, the first active sperm to reach the ovum in the fallopian tube will penetrate the outer shell and fertilise the ovum. Conception will have taken place. As soon as this happens the outer shell of the ovum becomes resistant to any other sperm so that only one sperm is allowed to fertilise the ovum.

When the ovum and sperm unite at fertilisation, genetic information from both partners combines to create a new individual. The fertilised ovum immediately begins to divide, first into two cells then into four. It continues to divide in this way as it passes down the fallopian tube to arrive in the uterus. The uterus lining has been preparing to receive it. The ball of cells settles into the uterine lining. This is called **implantation** and happens at around day 21 of the menstrual cycle.

> **cervix**
> The narrow entrance to the uterus from the vagina

> **implantation**
> Occurs when the fertilised ovum settles into the lining of the uterus

Implantation

The stages leading to implantation

Once it has implanted into the lining of the uterus, the fertilised ovum continues to divide and develop. The number of cells increases and an **embryo** forms. Besides producing the embryo, the fertilised ovum also gives rise to the **placenta**, **umbilical cord** and **amnion**. These structures are developed for the support of the baby and they leave the uterus with the baby at birth.

> **embryo**
> The term used to describe the developing baby from conception until eight weeks after conception

> **placenta**
> The structure that supports the baby as it develops in the uterus

- The developing baby until eight weeks after conception is called the embryo.
- The developing baby from eight weeks after conception until the birth is called the fetus.

umbilical cord
Contains the blood vessels that connect the developing baby to the placenta

amnion
The membranes that make up the sac containing the developing baby

Case study: Becoming pregnant

Rosa and Damon have a stable relationship and would like to have a baby. Rosa has a normal menstrual cycle lasting about 28 days. Rosa has not, so far, become pregnant but this month she has missed her normal menstrual period and is now two weeks past the date that this should have happened.

1 Is it likely that Rosa is pregnant?
2 Describe what has been happening to the ovum since it was released from the ovary.

The placenta

The life-support system of the embryo and the fetus is the placenta. The placenta has finger like projections called **villi**. The villi fit closely into the wall of the uterus. The placenta is joined to the fetus by the umbilical cord. Inside the cord are an artery and a vein. The artery takes the blood supply from the fetus into the placenta, and the vein returns the blood to the fetus.

In the placenta are **capillaries** filled with the blood of the fetus. In the wall of the uterus are large spaces filled with the mother's blood. The blood of the fetus and the mother's blood do not mix; the wall of the placenta separates them, but they are brought very close together. The wall of the placenta is very thin. This allows oxygen and nutrients to pass from the mother to the fetus and waste products to be passed back to the mother for disposal.

villi
Finger-like projections of the placenta that fit into the wall of the uterus

capillaries
Very small blood vessels

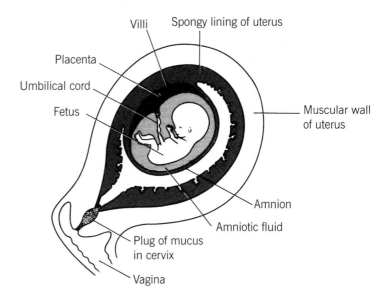

The developing fetus

Progress check

1 What does the ovum do immediately after fertilisation?
2 What is the term used to describe the developing baby until eight weeks after conception?
3 What is the term used to describe the developing baby from eight weeks after conception until birth?
4 How does the fetus exchange oxygen and nutrients with the mother?
5 What is the function of the umbilical cord?

Fetal growth and development

The growth and development of the embryo and fetus take place over the 40 weeks of pregnancy. The timetable of growth and development for all babies follows the same pattern. Any harmful influences during this time can result in abnormalities in growth or development. These are antenatal factors affecting growth and development and are explained in details in Chapter 6, *Factors affecting physical development*.

4–5 weeks after conception

neural tube
Cells in the embryo that will develop into the baby's spinal cord

Five weeks after conception is the time when most pregnant women are beginning to think that they are pregnant. Yet already the nervous system in the embryo is beginning to develop. Cells fold up to make a hollow tube, called the **neural tube**. This will become the baby's brain and spinal cord, so the tube has a head end and a tail end. At the same time the heart is forming and the embryo already has some of its own blood vessels. A string of these blood vessels connect the mother and the embryo and will become the umbilical cord.

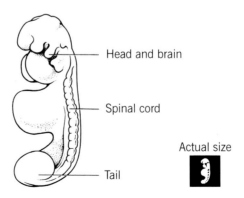

The embryo 5 weeks after conception

6–7 weeks after conception

The heart is beginning to beat and this can be seen on an ultrasound scan. Small swellings called limb buds show where the arms and legs are growing. At seven weeks the embryo is about 8 mm long.

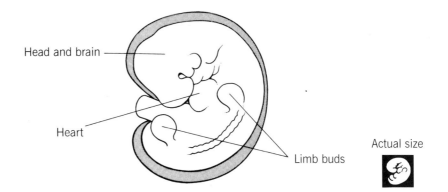

The embryo 6–7 weeks after conception

8–9 weeks after conception

The developing baby is now called the fetus. The face is slowly forming. The eyes are more obvious and there is a mouth with a tongue. The major internal organs (the heart, brain, lungs, kidneys, liver and intestines) are all developing. At nine weeks the fetus is about 17 mm long from head to bottom.

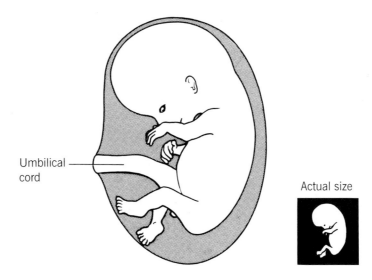

The fetus 8–9 weeks after conception

10–14 weeks after conception

Twelve weeks after conception the fetus is fully formed. From now on it has to grow and mature. The fetus is already moving, but the mother cannot feel these movements. By about 14 weeks the heartbeat is very strong and can be heard using an ultrasound detector. The heart rate is very fast – about 140 beats per minute. At 14 weeks the fetus is about 56 mm long from head to bottom.

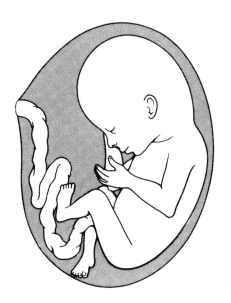

The fetus 10–14 weeks after conception

15–22 weeks after conception

The fetus is now growing quickly. The body has grown bigger so that the head and body are more in proportion. The face looks much more human and the hair is beginning to grow as well as the eyebrows and eyelashes. Finger and toe nails are now growing. The lines on the skin are now formed and the fetus has its own fingerprints. At about 22 weeks the fetus becomes covered in fine downy hair called **lanugo**. At about 18–22 weeks movements are first felt by the mother. If this is a second baby, movements are often felt earlier, at about 14–16 weeks after conception. At 22 weeks the fetus is about 160 mm long from head to bottom.

lanugo
The fine hair found on the body of the fetus before birth

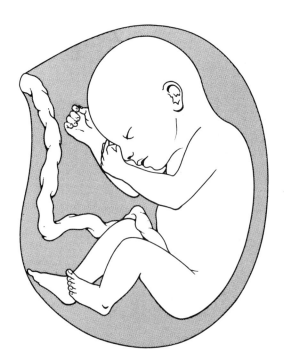

The fetus 15–22 weeks after conception

23–30 weeks after conception

The fetus is now able to move around and responds to touch and sound. The mother may be aware that the fetus has its own times for being quiet and being active.

The fetus is covered in a white creamy substance called **vernix**, which is thought to protect the skin as the fetus floats in the amniotic fluid. At about 26 weeks the eyes open. At 28 weeks the fetus is **viable**, which means that it is now thought to have a good chance of surviving if born. Many babies born before 28 weeks do survive, but often have problems with their breathing. Specialised care in special care baby units (SCBUs) helps more babies born early to survive. At 30 weeks the fetus is about 240 mm long from head to bottom.

31–40 weeks after conception

During the last few weeks the fetus grows and puts on weight. The skin, which was quite wrinkled, is now smoother and the vernix and lanugo begin to disappear. It is important that the fetus moves into the head-down position, which is the safest position for the birth.

vernix
White creamy substance found on the skin of the fetus

viable
Capable of surviving outside the uterus

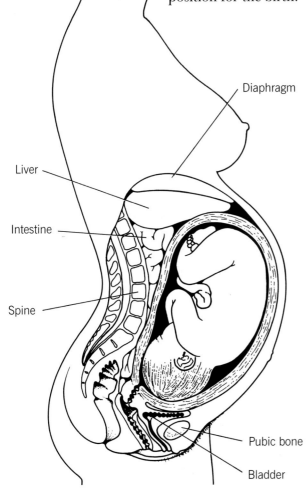

Diaphragm

Liver

Intestine

Spine

Pubic bone

Bladder

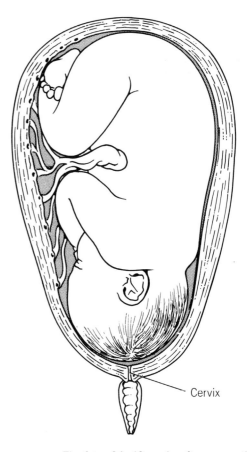

Cervix

The fetus 31–40 weeks after conception

Progress check

1 What will the neural tube eventually become?
2 Name the fluid in which the fetus floats.
3 How long is the fetus at nine weeks?
4 When is the fetus fully formed?
5 What is:
   a) lanugo?
   b) vernix?
6 When does the mother first feel the fetus move?
7 When does the fetus respond to sound?
8 When do the eyes of the fetus open?
9 What is the best position for the fetus to be in ready for the birth?

Do this!   **2.1**

1 Write an account of the development of the young human from conception to birth. Include these words in your description:

    ovum   conception   embryo
    sperm   implantation   fetus

2 If possible, obtain and watch a video about fetal development. Summarise the main points. There are many videos to choose from. Ask your tutor or health visitor for advice about this

The importance of preconceptual and antenatal care

The health of the mother and that of the developing fetus are very closely linked. To give the fetus the best chance of developing and growing normally, a good system of antenatal care is needed. Preconceptual advice and care may also be available.

Preconceptual care

Preconception is the term used to describe the time between a couple deciding they would like to have a baby and when the baby is conceived. This is the time when future parents can make sure they are in the best of health so that their child has the greatest chance of growing and developing normally. In some places it may be possible to attend preconceptual care clinics for help and advice. These clinics may be part of the local maternity services or part of the general practitioner service.

Antenatal care

Throughout pregnancy regular check-ups at hospital, antenatal clinic, by a general practitioner or a combination of these carers, will make sure that the mother and the developing fetus are both fit and well. The health of the mother can be maintained or improved. Checks can be made on the growth and development of the fetus and any problems, large or small, can be identified early. Pregnancy and delivery can be planned by the parents to suit their needs. The prime aim of antenatal care is to help the mother to a successful delivery of a live healthy infant.

Case study: Antenatal care

Rosa and her husband Damon planned to start a family and they have worked together to make sure their baby will have the best possible start in life. Rosa is now 13 weeks pregnant. She has had an uneventful pregnancy so far, and plans to carry on working for as long as she can. She has been attending the antenatal clinic at her GP's surgery regularly and last week she went to the maternity hospital for a regular antenatal appointment. Rosa is trying to do everything she can to make sure her baby will be born fit and healthy, and her husband Damon has supported Rosa all through her pregnancy.

1 What steps could Rosa and Damon have taken before Rosa became pregnant to try to give their baby a good chance of growing and developing normally?
2 What important point in its development would Rosa's baby have reached at her last antenatal visit?
3 Describe the growth and development of Rosa's baby from now until the baby is born.
4 Why are regular antenatal checkups important?

Think about it

1 Think of all the things, positive and negative, that might affect the baby during pregnancy.
2 Think of things that the parents need to be aware of to make sure that their baby has a good chance of growing and developing well.

Key terms

You need to know what these words and phrases mean. Go back through the chapter to find out.

amnion
capillaries
conception
embryo
endometrium
implantation
lanugo
menstrual cycle
neural tube
oestrogen
ovum
placenta
progesterone
sperm
umbilical cord
uterus
vascular
vernix
viable
villi

Now try these questions

1 Copy this diagram of the male reproductive organs and label the following parts:
   vas derefens
   scrotum
   penis
   prostate gland
   testes
   urethra

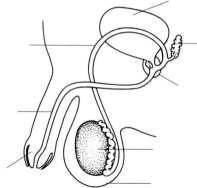

The male reproductive organs

2 Copy this diagram of the female reproductive organs and label the following parts:
   vagina
   fundus
   uterus
   fallopian tube
   cervix
   ovary

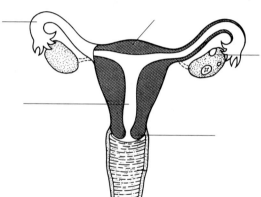

The female reproductive organs

3 Describe the development of the fertilised ovum, from conception until implantation in the wall of the uterus.

4 What are the important points in the timetable of fetal development?

5 Why are good preconceptual care and good antenatal care important to the development of the fetus?

3 *Physical development*

This chapter includes:

- **An introduction to physical development**
- **Physical development (1): Birth to 18 months**
- **Physical development (2): 2 to 7 years**

In the first year of life physical and cognitive development are closely related, and the achievement of landmark skills are thought to be an indication of the child's intellectual maturity. Delay in the development of physical skills at this age can indicate learning difficulties. As the child gets older, physical development continues at a slower pace, but the achievement of skills is still dependent upon maintaining health and preventing illness. This chapter includes a brief introduction to physical development, followed by detailed descriptions of the average physical achievements to be expected at various ages.

You may find it useful to read this chapter in conjunction with:

- ▶ **Book 1, Chapter 1**   Physical growth
- ▶ **Book 1, Chapter 5**   Measuring and recording physical development
- ▶ **Book 1, Chapter 6**   Factors affecting physical development

An introduction to physical development

- *Physical* means anything to do with the body and can be used in a wide range of contexts, from how people look physically to how they move physically.
- *Development* means a change in performance and is usually associated with progression, becoming more complicated or skilful. It could also be defined as an increase in complexity.

With these two definitions you can see that the phrase *physical development* means the way that the body increases in **skill** and becomes more complex in its performance. This will involve movement. The progress of muscular movement is called **motor development**.

Developmental norms

There is a recognised pattern of physical development which it is expected that children will follow. These are known as the developmental **norms**. Norm should not be confused with normal, a word which is not encouraged when describing physical development because there is such a

skill
An ability that has been practised

motor development
The process of muscular movements becoming more complex

norm
Developmental skill achieved within an average time-scale

wide range of normal (i.e. acceptable or satisfactory) development. It is dangerous to assume that children are abnormal if they do not all progress in exactly the same manner. Variations will always exist, since each child is an individual developing in their own unique way.

A likely expectation is that babies will be mobile (rolling, crawling, creeping, bottom-shuffling or walking) by the time they reach their first birthday. However, a baby may have been concentrating on acquiring **fine motor skills**, social skills or language skills and may have advanced beyond the average in one or more of these developmental areas. In the development of **gross motor skills**, they may not have progressed beyond sitting, but have been absorbing huge amounts of information from the world around them. Examining only their lack of mobility could make the examiner assume that their development was delayed, but the overall picture is of a child who has not yet seen the need for mobility but can do many other things in advance of their age.

Nevertheless, knowledge of these patterns of expected development does help us to look at the child as a whole, and to measure their progress as an individual and as a member of the human species.

> **fine motor skills**
> Hand–eye co-ordination

> **gross motor skills**
> Whole body movements

Human attributes

The human animal (we are all animals) has several biological attributes, different from most other animals, which make it easy to separate the different areas of development:

- the ability to stand on two legs and walk, leaving the hands free for more complicated tasks – a gross motor skill
- the use of the hands and flexible fingers in co-ordination with the eyes – fine motor skills
- possession of a spoken language, and the ability to translate non-verbal messages, allowing communication between people
- the evolution of complicated social structures for the benefit and protection of all individuals.

The first two human characteristics are relevant to the study of physical development because they concern movement, so it is necessary to look at them separately and in more detail.

Gross motor skills

The ability of the human animal to use two legs and walk involves the whole body. These whole-body movements are described as gross motor skills. Sometimes they are referred to as **posture** and large movements. These terms have the same meaning and cover the stages a child goes through in developing control of the body:

> **posture**
> Position of parts of the body

- learning to support the head
- rolling over
- sitting
- crawling
- pulling to stand

- walking
- running
- climbing the stairs
- hopping
- playing football
- skipping
- riding a tricycle and a bicycle
- standing on one leg
- swimming
- climbing.

There are many more examples of gross motor skills. They all require strength, stamina and suppleness to increase co-ordination, balance and judgement.

Crawling   Sitting from lying down   Bear-walking

Walking with two hands held   Walking with one hand held   Walking alone

Example of gross motor skills involved in the development of walking

Fine motor skills

The second human characteristic is the use of the hands in co-ordination with the eyes. This allows human beings to perform very delicate procedures with their fingers, with the eyes influencing the precise movements of the fingers. These manipulative aspects of physical development are called fine motor skills, and include aspects of vision and fine and delicate movements.

The role of those who monitor the physical development of children is to know whether a child can easily perform a certain skill or whether it is a new skill for them and they require further practice.

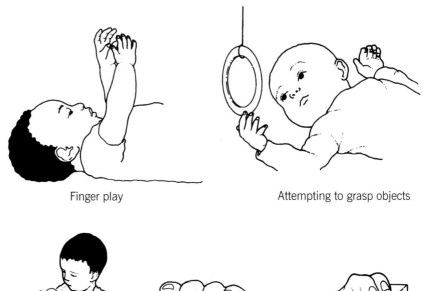

Finger play

Attempting to grasp objects

Holding and exploring objects

Palmar grasp using whole hand

More delicate palmar grasp involving the thumb

Development of manipulation (fine motor skills)

Primitive pincer grasp

Exploring with the index finger

Delicate/mature pincer grasp

✓ *Progress check*

1 What does motor development mean?
2 Why should you beware of using the word 'normal' in describing development?
3 What are the four characteristics which make humans different from most other animals?

Do this!   **3.1**

Try to do up some buttons, eat your lunch, fit shapes in a shape-sorter, thread a needle, tie up shoelaces with your eyes shut or with a blindfold on. You will realise how important this hand–eye co-ordination is. Watch a child using fine motor skills, for example a baby using a spoon, a child tying a shoelace or any other activity requiring hand–eye co-ordination. Look for concentration, perseverance, frustration. How can you help them in this area of development?

Write an information sheet highlighting the specific assistance that can be given to children to encourage their fine motor development. Use illustrations/photographs to reinforce your points.

Physical development (1): Birth to 18 months

Terminology used in studying physical development

The following terms are in common use in assessing physical development and it is important that you are familiar with them and understand what they mean:

- prone – lying face down
- supine – lying on the back
- ventral suspension – held in the air, face down
- head lag – the head falls back when pulled to sit
- reflex – involuntary response to a stimulus
- neonate – a newborn baby
- stimulus – something that arouses a reaction
- posture – position of parts of the body
- symmetrical – balanced movements both sides of body
- asymmetrical – jerky, unco-ordinated movements.

The following pages describe the average physical achievements to be expected from birth to 18 months.

The neonate

The newborn baby in the first month of life is often called the **neonate**, which means newly born.

New babies have an attitude of flexion, which means that they are curled up, with arms and legs bent inwards towards the body. They maintain this fetal position (the position they were in inside the womb), but gradually extend (straighten) the arms and legs. A baby which was in the breech position may lie with the legs straight up, one each side of the face, if this was the position in the womb.

Descriptions of the typical postures of neonates are shown below.

neonate
A newborn baby

Gross motor development

Prone

- The baby lies with the head turned to one side-resting on the cheek.
- The body is in a frog-like posture with the bottom up and the knees curled up under the tummy.
- The arms are bent at the elbows and tucked under the chest with fists clenched.

prone
Lying face down

Supine

- The baby lies with the head to one side.
- The knees are bent towards the body, with the soles of the feet touching.
- The arms are bent inwards towards the body.
- Jerky, random, assymetrical kicking movements can be seen.

supine
Lying on the back

Ventral suspension

- The head and the legs fall below the level of the back, so the baby makes a complete downwards curve.

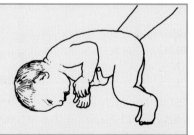

ventral suspension
When the baby is held in the air, face down

PHYSICAL NEEDS OF THE NEONATE

Neonates are entirely dependent on carers to provide for all their physical needs. Their only means of communicating their needs at this stage is by crying. They need food, warmth, clothing, shelter, high standards of hygiene and protection from infection, and to be physically safe. The opportunity to move the limbs without being restricted by nappies or clothing is also important for their physical development.

Neonates are sensitive to touch and pain. They enjoy being cuddled and all physical contact with the parent or carer which helps to increase their security and consistency of care.

Sitting

- When the baby is pulled upwards into a sitting position there is complete **head lag**. The head falls backwards as the body comes up and then flops forwards onto the chest.

- If the baby is held in a sitting position, the back is completely curved and the head is on the chest.

head lag
The baby's head falls back when pulled to sit

Fine motor development

- The fists are clenched
- The baby can focus 15–25 cm and stares at brightly coloured mobiles within visual range.
- The baby concentrates on the carer's face when feeding.

VISION

Neonates can focus on faces close to their own, and research shows that they prefer to look at the human face. They have skills of imitation and may try to copy facial expressions and movements, for example sticking the tongue out. These are not deliberate actions. Eye contact with parents helps to establish interaction. Babies also like to look at brightly-coloured objects – red, green, blue, yellow – rather than the pastel shades which are often used for nursery equipment. Flat pictures will not generate as much interest as three-dimensional, 'real' objects, such as toys and rattles with faces, mobiles and baby gyms.

The neonate

PRIMITIVE REFLEXES

A **reflex** action is an automatic, involuntary movement made in response to a specific **stimulus**. Testing the presence of reflexes in babies, children and adults can help doctors to assess the health of the **central nervous system** (CNS). Everyone should have a range of protective reflexes, like blinking, coughing and sneezing. New babies have a range of other survival reflexes, called the **primitive reflexes**, which are only present during the first few months of life. After this they are replaced by actions which the baby chooses to do – **voluntary actions**. The primitive reflexes are a reminder of how the human race has evolved over millions of years. They are:

- rooting reflex
- sucking reflex
- grasping reflex
- placing reflex
- walking reflex
- Moro (startle) reflex.

reflex
An involuntary response to a stimulus
stimulus
Something that arouses a reaction
central nervous system
The brain, spinal cord and nerves
primitive reflex
An automatic response to a particular stimulus in a neonate
voluntary action
An intentional act that a child chooses to do

Rooting reflex

- Stimulus: brushing the cheek with a finger or nipple.
- Response: the baby turns to the side of the stimulus.

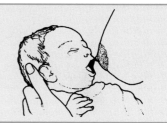

Sucking reflex

- Stimulus: placing nipple or teat into the mouth.
- Response: the baby sucks.

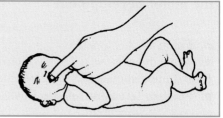

Grasping reflex

- Stimulus: placing object into baby's palm.
- Response: the fingers close tightly around the object.

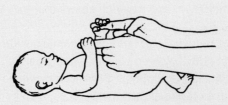
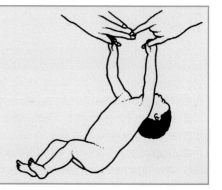

WHY PRIMITIVE REFLEXES ARE IMPORTANT

The presence or absence of these reflexes in a new baby can measure the maturity of the baby and the health of the central nervous system. For instance a baby born prematurely may not have developed full reflex action. If these reflexes continue for longer than the first few months of life, it can mean that the child has some form of developmental delay and should be examined by a paediatrician.

Placing reflex

- Stimulus: brushing top of foot against table top.
- Response: the baby lifts its foot and places it on a hard surface.

Walking reflex

- Stimulus: held standing, feet touching a hard surface.
- Response: the baby moves the legs forward alternately and walks.

Moro (startle) reflex

- Stimulus: insecure handling or sudden loud noise.
- Response: the baby throws the head and the fingers fan out; the arms then return to the embace posture and the baby cries.

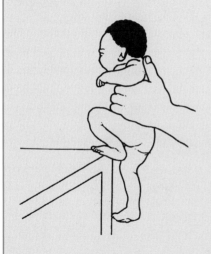

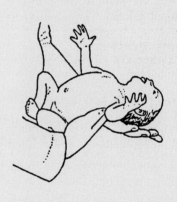

TESTING THE PRIMITIVE REFLEXES

Examination should only be performed by a qualified doctor, midwife or health visitor. The best time to observe and test these reflexes is when the baby is awake but not hungry, quietly lying with the eyes open and with or without arm and leg movements. A crying baby who is hungry, uncomfortable or unhappy, or a baby who is tired or drowsy, will not perform well. It may be possible to accompany a parent for the baby's 6-week check and observe the doctor testing the reflexes.

✔ Progress check

1 What is the posture of a neonate in prone and supine?
2 What does ventral suspension mean?
3 What is a reflex?
4 Describe the reflex, stimulus and response of six primitive reflexes.
5 Why are these reflexes important in assessing development?

1 month

The infant continues to sleep for long periods between feeds, but is wakeful for varying lengths of time. She enjoys being played with, physical contact and cuddles. Crying is still the main form of communication for letting carers know that the baby's needs must be met, for example hunger, thirst, discomfort due to position, temperature or a desire for physical contact. Making throaty noises of pleasure when being spoken to and enjoying caring routines and attention, the baby will begin to coo at 5–6 weeks. The baby maintains an attitude of flexion, but the limbs are beginning to extend, with large jerky movements. Support for the head when being carried, bathed and dressed is very important.

Gross motor development

Prone

- The baby lies with its head to one side but can now lift its head to change position.
- The legs are bent, no longer tucked under the body.
- The arms are bent away from the body, the hands usually closed.

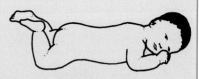

Supine

- The head is on one side.
- The arm and leg on the side the head is facing will stretch out.
- Both arms may be bent, with legs bent at the knees, the soles of the feet facing each other.

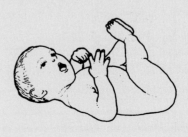

- Lots of facial and physical contact
- Respond to the baby's needs – unless the basic needs are met (food, warmth, safety, etc.), there will be very little progression.
- Talking and singing
- Massaging with baby oils or massage gels
- Mobiles with bright, shiny, primary colours
- Baby gym with toys with facial characteristics
- Wind chimes
- Take baby from room to room in a bouncing cradle, encourage family and social contacts, lots of gentle talking and touching

SAFETY FOR YOUNG BABIES

- Babies must always be cared for in a safe environment by carers who are aware of their vulnerability.
- Always place a baby on the floor, rather than on a table or other high surface.
- Lie a baby on the back to sleep.
- Dress the baby in clothing with safe fasteners, for example with poppers rather than ribbons or ties.
- Never prop a baby up to feed.

Ventral suspension

- The head is on the same level as the back and the legs are coming up towards the level of the back.

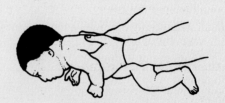

Sitting

- If the baby is pulled to sit the head will lag, falling backwards, but will remain steady for a moment as sitting position is achieved, then it will bob forwards again.
- The back is a complete curve when the baby is held in sitting position.

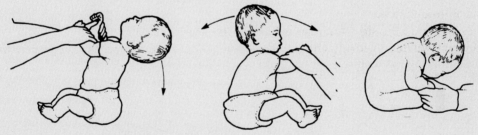

Note The head should be supported at all times.

OBSERVING BABIES AT 1 MONTH

At this age it is preferable to observe all-round development by asking the primary carer about the baby's routines and progress to date. To do this effectively, you must know about average development at 1 month. Some suggestions for situations and related purposes for observing development at this age are:

- *Bonding with primary carer* – How does the baby let the carer know their needs? How does the carer respond to the baby? At feeding time, look for eye contact with carer, physical contact, the process of winding and the baby's reaction to it, distractions, etc.
- *Physical progress* – Place the baby in prone and supine and observe their posture, ask the carer to gently pull them to sit and observe their head control, note their limb movements. Primitive reflexes may be observed at the 6-week check, and a parent may demonstrate the baby's placing or walking reflex and allow you to test rooting, sucking and grasping.
- *Reactions to noisy toys*, for example hold a rattle at about 20–30 cm from the baby's face, watch to see if the baby follows with their eyes. Note their limb movements.

1 month

- All the caring routines should enable the baby to progress physically, to explore their movement and to improve their co-ordination. For example, at changing times and bath times, give the baby space and opportunity to kick safely without nappies or clothing.
- Sensory experiences, such as gentle massage and stroking, help the baby to feel secure and to develop sensitivity to touch.
- Bouncing cradles to transport the baby from room to room with their carer encourage visual skills as they view the world around them. Small toys strung across the chair also increase visual focusing and hand–eye co-ordination.

Fine motor development

- The baby turns its head towards the light and stares at bright shiny objects.

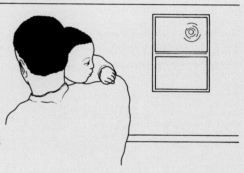

- The baby is fascinated by bright shiny objects and follows moving objects within 5–10 cm from the face.

✅ Progress check

1 Describe the typical position in prone of a baby aged 1 month.
2 Describe the typical position in supine of a baby aged 1 month.
3 What is meant by head lag?
4 At this age, how does the baby control its head when pulled to sit?
5 What is the position of the head in relation to the back in ventral suspension at 1 month?

TRAVELLING WITH A BABY

Babies must be kept physically safe at all times. It is especially important to ensure their safety in a car and on the move in a pushchair or pram. Equipment is available which will meet their safety needs if it is used correctly.

■ A rear-facing baby car seat protects the baby from injury during car journeys and can also be used as a first seat in the home.

■ Babies should never be placed on the back seat of a car in a carry-cot – in the event of an accident, they will be lifted from the cot and thrown at high speed.

■ Prams and pushchairs should comply with the British Standards Institute (BSI) safety regulations.

■ The baby gazes attentively at carer's face whilst being fed, spoken to or during any caring routines.

■ The baby grasps a finger or other object placed in the hand.

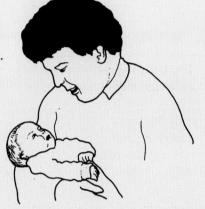

■ The hands are usually closed.

All the primitive reflexes are still present.

Do this! 3.2

Design and make a mobile for a young baby. Remember their preference for bright colours and three-dimensional shapes, and also their fascination with faces.

Evaluate the effectiveness of your design by using the mobile with babies of slightly different ages, for example 1 month, 3 months and 6 months. Observe their reactions to the mobile and record your findings.

3 months

THE BABY AT 3 MONTHS

By now, most babies are developing voluntary movements to replace the primitive reflexes. They are wakeful for longer periods of time and show awareness of familiar situations by smiling, cooing and by excited limb movements when, for example, they hear the bath water running or see the breast or bottle. Babies enjoy all the contact and stimulation of the caring routines of bathing, feeding and changing. They need support at the shoulders during bathing and dressing, even though head control should be fairly well established. They may hold objects briefly, but are unable to co-ordinate hands and eyes yet.

Gross motor development

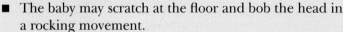

Prone

- The baby can now lift up the head and chest supported on the elbows, forearms and hands.
- The baby may scratch at the floor and bob the head in a rocking movement.
- The bottom is flat now, with the legs straighter and kicking alternately.

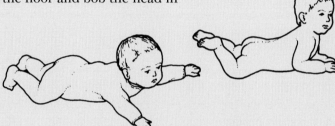

Supine

- The baby usually lies with the head in a central position.
- There are smooth, continuous movements of the arms and legs.
- The legs can kick strongly, sometimes alternating and sometimes together.
- The baby waves the arms symmetrically and brings hands together over the body.

Ventral suspension

- The head is now held up above the level of the back, and the legs are also on the same level.

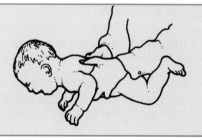

Sitting

- When the baby is pulled to sit, the head should come forwards steadily with the back.
- The head may fall forwards after a short time in the sitting position.
- There should be little or no head lag.

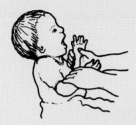

- When held in a sitting position the back should be straight, except for a curve in the base of the spine – the lumbar region.

Standing

- The baby will sag at the knees when held in a standing position.
- The placing and walking reflexes should have disappeared.

STIMULATING ACTIVITIES AT 3 MONTHS

- Offer toys that a baby can hold as well as look at, for example brightly coloured rattles made of light, safe materials which produce interesting sounds, or a chiming ball.
- Blowing bubbles fascinates babies at this age as they watch them float and pop.
- Sing songs with actions with the baby sitting on your knee, giving the baby the opportunity to bounce and find their feet.
- Toys attached to a baby gym or strung over the cot will stimulate the baby to reach out with their arms and provide the stimulus for grasping interesting objects.
- Provide the opportunity for exercise – let the baby lie safely on a floor mat without a nappy or clothing so that they can explore their movements and develop further their co-ordination skills. Place the baby in prone to help them to develop the strength to support their upper body on their forearms and to prepare for rolling their body over.

3 months

Fine motor development

■ Finger-play – the baby has discovered its hands and moves them around in front of the face, watching the movements and the patterns they make in the light.

■ The baby recognises the bottle or the breast and waves the arms around in excitement.

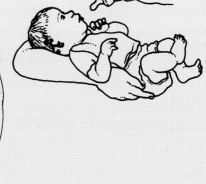

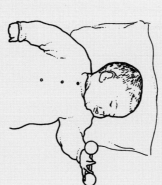

■ The baby holds a rattle or similar object for a short time if placed in the hand. Frequently hits itself in the face before dropping it!

 Progress check

1 What is the position of the baby in ventral suspension at:
   a) birth?
   b) 1 month?
   c) 3 months?
2 What are three major elements of gross motor development at 3 months?
3 Describe three fine motor achievements at about 3 months.
4 How can physical development be stimulated between birth and 3 months?
5 Which reflexes should have disappeared by 3 months?

■ The baby is now very alert and aware of what is going on around.

■ The baby moves its head to look around, and follows adult movements.

OBSERVING PHYSICAL DEVELOPMENT AT 3 MONTHS

A variety of methods can be used to observe physical development at this age, for example:

- a narrative description of what the baby is doing
- a development checklist (see below)
- photographs and video recordings.

DEVELOPMENT CHECKLIST

This method provides an opportunity to observe several babies of the same age to compare their developmental progress. It is possible to compile checklists for each age and area of development. A suggested format is shown below.

Aim: To observe a series of babies at 3 months

Purpose: To note the similarities and/or differences in their physical developmental achievements

Physical achievement	Baby A Age:	Baby B Age:	Baby C Age:	Comments
In prone, lifts head and chest supported on forearms				
Sags at knees when held standing				
Smooth, continuous movements of legs and arms				
In ventral suspension, head is held above the plane of the back				
No head lag when pulled to sit				
Holds rattle briefly when placed in the hand				
Finger-play				
Turns head to follow adult movements				

The observation should be evaluated in terms of:

- the babies' individual achievements
- a comparison of their development as a small group
- how they compare to theory.

6 months

THE BABY AT 6 MONTHS

The baby at 6 months is usually lively and sociable, not yet wary of strangers but welcoming of all friendly interest, usually responding with laughs and loud, tuneful vocalisations. Babbling with double syllables, for example *dada*, *nana*, begins accompanied by a developing understanding of commonly used words and phrases, for example 'No'. The routine screening hearing test is conducted from 6 months onwards. Physical skills are quite extensive and may include rolling and grasping.

Gross motor development

Prone

■ The baby can now lift the head and chest well clear of the floor by supporting on outstretched arms. The hands are flat on the floor.

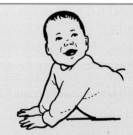

■ The baby can roll over from front to back.
■ She may pull the knees up in an attempt to crawl, but will slide backwards.

Supine

■ The baby will lift her head to look at her feet.

■ She may lift her arms, requesting to be lifted.

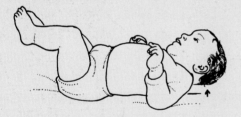

■ She may lift up her legs, grasp one or both and attempt to put them in her mouth, often successfully.

■ She will kick strongly, enjoying the exercise.

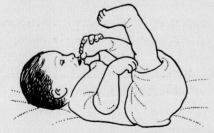

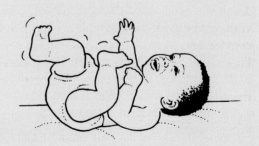

■ She may roll over from back to front.

OBSERVING BABIES AT AROUND 6 MONTHS

Suggestions for situations to observe:

■ *Baby sitting, with support if necessary, surrounded by different toys* – Look at the baby's posture, which toys are of the most interest and why, how the baby picks objects up, how they examine and explore them, what may distract them their stability, etc.

■ *Baby lying on the floor* – Observe their movements in prone and supine. Are they able to roll over? Do they play with their feet? Do they attempt to crawl? How do they attempt to get to objects just out of reach?

Remember to include in your observations the baby's facial expressions and all verbal and non-verbal communication they use.

Sitting

■ If pulled to sit, the baby can now grab the adult's hands and pull herself into a sitting position; the head is now fully controlled with strong neck muscles.

■ She can sit for long periods with support. The back is straight.

■ She may sit for short periods without support, but will topple over easily. She cannot yet put an arm out to break the fall.

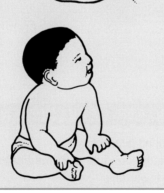

Standing

■ If the baby is held standing she will enjoy weight bearing and bouncing up and down.

■ The baby may also demonstrate the downward parachute reflex: when held in the air and whooshed down feet first, the legs will straighten and separate and the toes will fan out.

Case study: Physical development at 6 months

Jacob was born at term weighing 3.4 kg. He is now 6 months old, and the health visitor is very pleased with his progress. He completed his primary course of immunisations at 4 months. Weaning has commenced and, although he is taking an increasing variety of foods from a spoon and has begun to finger-feed, he still enjoys small breast feeds several times a day. At his recent hearing test, the health visitor conducted a routine developmental assessment and confirmed that he is achieving his physical milestones.

1 Which gross motor and fine motor skills do you think Jacob is displaying?
2 What sorts of activity will promote and extend these areas of development?

6 months

Fine motor development

■ The baby is bright and alert, looking around constantly to absorb all the visual information on offer.

■ She is fascinated by small toys within reaching distance, grabbing them with the whole hand, using a **palmar grasp**.

■ She transfers toys from hand to hand.

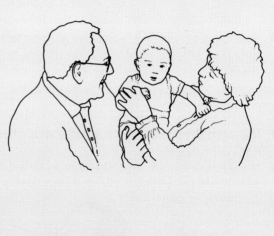

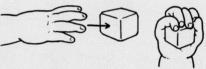

palmar grasp
Whole-hand grasp

ACTIVITIES TO STIMULATE FINE MOTOR DEVELOPMENT AT 6 MONTHS

■ Offer toys which nest and stack, for example round beakers.

■ Provide bricks to hold and bang together – adults building with the bricks will excourage the baby to copy the actions and experience delight as the tower falls.

■ Offer objects to grasp, for the baby to transfer from hand to hand and which are safe to put in the mouth.

■ Offer finger-feeding foods – *always* with supervision.

■ Allow the baby to experience the texture of their food with the fingers.

■ Provide sensory experience with the use of bean bags filled with different materials, such as rice or cornflakes.

■ Give the baby a plastic mirror to hold and recognise their reflection!

■ Encourage the baby to wave bye-bye.

■ Play clapping games and peek-a-boo.

■ Repeat finger rhymes, such as 'This little piggy'.

■ Look at picture books and point out familiar objects.

■ Encourage the baby to practise drumming, using upturned saucepans and wooden spoons.

■ She puts them in the mouth to explore them.

■ If a toy is dropped, the baby will watch where it falls, if it is within sight.
■ If a toy falls out of sight, the baby does not look for it. At this age the world ends where she can see it!

PLANS TO STIMULATE PHYSICAL SKILLS FROM 3 TO 6 MONTHS

■ Planning activities to promote physical development is essential for child-care workers who work with babies. Providing a range of suitable activities encourages gross and fine motor skills.
■ When planning for babies, it is always important to remember to meet individual needs, consider safety and anticipate the objectives (learning outcomes) of every activity.
■ Plans can be completed for each day within a broader weekly or monthly plan.
■ Detailed plans of some of the activities may be included in the plan. When planning each activity, include a note of the equipment required and the benefits of the activity (i.e. the objectives in terms of physical development).
■ Evaluate the plan as a whole in terms of whether the objectives were achieved and how the plan may be improved.

✓ *Progress check*

1 Describe the process of head control in the first six months of life.
2 When should the baby have developed a palmar grasp?
3 Describe the posture of the typical 6-month-old baby in supine and prone.
4 What is the downward parachute reflex?

9 months

THE BABY AT 9 MONTHS

Many babies are mobile by 9 months, with a desire to explore and an increasing curiosity about the world. Mobility does not include common sense, and babies at this age are unlikely to recognise danger. This means that constant vigilance is required to keep them safe. Now stable sitters, they are beginning to balance and develop increasingly complex fine motor skills as they examine objects and investigate their properties. Understanding has increased and the baby is beginning to recognise more words, including their own name.

Gross motor development

Prone

- The baby may be able to support his body on knees and outstretched arms.
- He may rock backwards and forwards and try to crawl.
- Moving backwards in the crawling position precipitates forward movement.

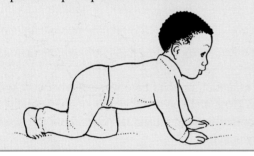

Supine

- The baby rolls from back to front and may crawl away, roll around the floor or squirm on his back.

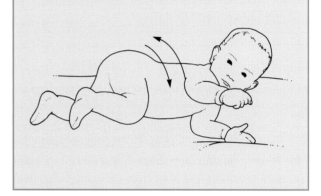

Standing

- The baby can pull himself to a standing position, supporting first on the knees.
- When supported by an adult he will step forward on alternate feet.
- He supports his body in the standing position by holding on to a firm object.
- He may begin to side-step around furniture.

- He cannot yet lower himself to the floor and falls backwards onto his bottom.
- He may begin to crawl upstairs but cannot get down safely.

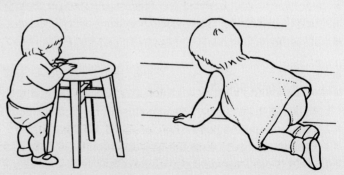

- The forward parachute reflex: when the baby is held firmly during a controlled forwards fall (head first), the arms will shoot out and straighten and the fingers will fan out.

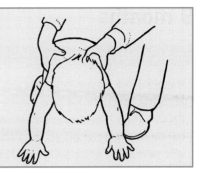

Sitting

- The baby is now a secure and stable sitter – he may sit unsupported for 15 minutes or more.
- He can keep his balance when turning to reach toys from the side.
- He leans forward to retrieve toys, returning to an upright sitting position.
- He puts out his arm(s) to prevent falling.
- Some babies may begin to bottom-shuffle, moving around the floor in the upright, sitting position using the legs to propel them.

SAFETY

As babies begin to move, their safety is of paramount importance. They will no longer remain safely in the place they were put. At all times, they require the watchful attention of a responsible adult who is aware of the stages of development.

Remember:

- A baby will put small items in their mouth and this is a potential choking hazard.
- Never leave a baby alone when they are eating finger foods.
- *Never* use a babywalker. They are dangerous and completely unnecessary – babies will learn to walk without them.
- When babies learn to crawl up the stairs, teach them how to come down safely backwards.
- Remove tempting dangers, for example hanging wires which may be pulled and saucepan handles projecting from the cooker.
- Make sure that fireguards and stairgates are fixed in position.
- When using a high chair, pram or pushchair, make sure that the baby is safely strapped in.
- A forward-facing baby car seat may be used if it is safely anchored in the car.

9 months

Fine motor development

- He uses the inferior **pincer grasp** with index finger and thumb.
- He drops objects or bangs them onto a hard surface to release them – he cannot let go voluntarily yet.
- He looks for fallen objects out of sight – he is now beginning to realise that they have not disappeared forever.

pincer grasp
Thumb and first finger grasp

ACTIVITIES AT 9 MONTHS

- Roll balls for the baby to catch as they sit.
- Strings attached to small wheeled toys will encourage a pincer grasp as the baby tries to pull the toy towards them.
- Provide bath toys that can be used to pour and squeeze.
- Offer toys and objects that have specific results so that babies begin to learn cause and effect, for example balls and wheels roll when pushed, bricks stack, some toys squeak when squeezed.

- Visually alert and curious, the baby is exploring objects before picking them up.

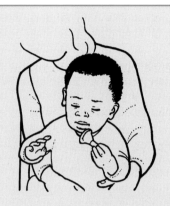

- He grasps objects, usually with one hand, inspects with the eyes and transfers to the other hand.

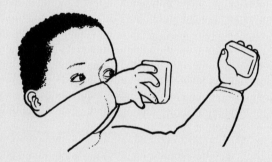

- He may hold one object in each hand and bang them together.
- He uses the index finger to poke and point; this finger starts to straighten and play a greater role.

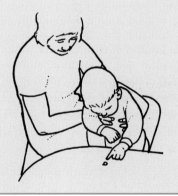

✅ *Progress check*

1 How can you stimulate a baby to develop a pincer grasp?
2 Name three ways in which a baby may be mobile at around 9 months.
3 What is the forward parachute reflex?
4 How could you ensure the safety of a baby of this age?

12 months

THE BABY AT 12 MONTHS

By 12 months, babies are transformed from the helpless creatures they were just a year before. They are usually mobile and use a delicate pincer grasp to pick up tiny objects from the floor as they travel! A preference for one hand may now be clear, and the baby can use both hands co-operatively, beginning to place objects down with increasing control. With a developing understanding of language, they are often able to say two or three recognisable words and make their needs known by sound and gestures.

Gross motor development

Sitting
- The baby can sit alone indefinitely.

- She can get into sitting position from lying down.

Standing
- The baby pulls herself to stand and walks around the furniture.
- She can return to sitting without falling.
- She may stand alone for a short period.

Think about it

Think of six activities to encourage gross motor skills from 6 to 12 months of age. Remember the variations in development between these ages.

STIMULATING GROSS MOTOR DEVELOPMENT AT 12 MONTHS

Provide the following:
- wheeled toys and trolleys to push and pull, to practise balance and increase strength. Later these toys will enable the development of steering and reversing around corners and obstacles.
- carts to sit on and propel with the feet
- small climbing frames to encourage the child to climb up and through the apparatus, to slide and roll, and to begin to develop **spatial awareness**
- large balls to throw or roll in the garden or park.

Many babies enjoy swimming and floating with inflatables.

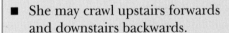

spatial awareness
A developing knowledge of how things move and the effects of movement

Mobility
- The baby is now mobile by crawling, bottom-shuffling, bear walking, walking alone or with one or both hands held.

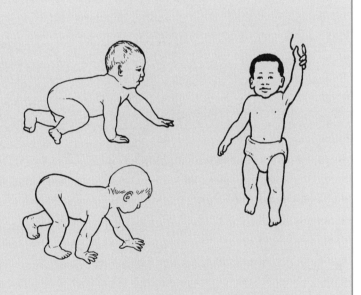

- She may crawl upstairs forwards and downstairs backwards.

OBSERVING BABIES AT 12 MONTHS

Observe a group of two or three babies of around 12 months.
- *Gross motor skills* – Compare and contrast their physical skills. Look at their mobility and posture, how they get into the sitting position from lying, how they stand, whether they can push a trolley, their climbing ability.
- *Fine motor skills* – Look at their ability to pick up small objects, their grasp of a crayon and how they let go of objects. Observe their posting skills and how they examine objects that are new to them – whether they continue to put them into the mouth, their visual examination of the object.

12 months

Fine motor development

- The baby looks for objects hidden and out of sight.

- She uses a mature pincer grasp and releases objects.

- She throws toys deliberately and watches their fall.

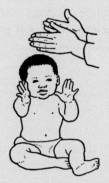

- She likes to look at picture books and points at familiar objects, for example cup, ball, teddy.
- She claps hands together in delight and in play.

STIMULATING FINE MOTOR DEVELOPMENT AT 12 MONTHS

The following equipment will provide suitable opportunities for developing fine motor skills:

- boxes and containers with small objects to put in and take out
- containers to post round shapes into
- stacking and nesting cups and boxes
- balls for throwing and rolling
- thick, non-toxic wax crayons to make marks on paper
- board books to point at pictures and turn pages
- bricks to practise building.

Remember:

At 12 months, babies are still at the oral phase and tend to put objects in their mouths. This is a choking hazard and babies should be supervised at all times.

Do this!   3.3

Make an article to stimulate fine motor development for a child in the first year of life.

Remember:
- All areas of development are interlinked and children learn a great deal through sensory experience, i.e. sight, touch, taste and sound.
- The article must be attractive to a baby. It should excite and encourage sensory areas.
- It must strong enough to withstand vigorous activity and be safe enough for a young baby to play with.

Write a report describing your:
- overall aims and objectives (why you chose this article and how it would encourage development)
- planning
- designs (including diagrams)
- how you made it.

Observe a baby using the article and assess (honestly and critically) how useful it is. Did you achieve your aims and objectives? Should any aspect of the item be adapted or changed to make it safer, more stimulating or more attractive?

Include this evaluation and your conclusions in your report.

- She points at desired objects, and may show a preference for one hand.
- The **primitive tripod grasp** is used: the thumb and first two fingers.

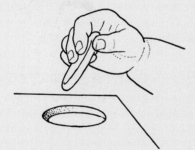
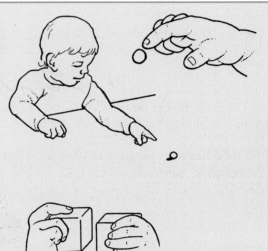

- She bangs cubes together.
- She recognises familiar people up to 10 metres away.

primitive tripod grasp
Thumb and two finger grasp

 Progress check

1 When should the pincer grasp be present and when could it be described as mature?
2 What aspects of gross and fine motor development are seen at 12 months of age?
3 When should a baby be mobile?
4 Note five elements of physical skills at 12 months of age.
5 By what age should all the primitive reflexes have faded?

15 months

The baby at 15 months is usually walking unaided, but has limited control of stopping and starting and falls over a lot. Supervision with steps and stairs is vital to prevent accidents. The desire to be independent is increasing at this age and feeding skills are improving. The child can usually try to use a spoon with some success. Throwing, trying to catch and throwing back balls, and pushing toys and trolleys are popular activities.

Gross motor development

- The baby walks alone, feet wide apart with arms raised to keep balance.

- He falls easily, sometimes after just a few paces, and usually on stopping; he cannot avoid obstacles on the floor.

- He can sit from standing by falling backwards onto the bottom or forwards onto the arms.

■ He gets to standing without help from people or furniture.

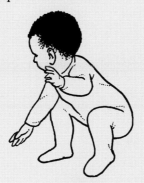

■ He kneels without support.

■ He may climb forwards into a small chair and turn to sit.

■ She can climb the stairs on all fours.

■ She can throw back a ball, but often falls over.

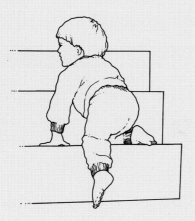

15 months

Fine motor development

■ The baby enjoys playing with small bricks.

■ She builds a two-brick tower.

■ She can put a button into the neck of a bottle.

■ He can hold a spoon, but puts it in the mouth upside down.

STIMULATING FINE MOTOR DEVELOPMENT AT 15 MONTHS

Provide:
■ large round and cuboid beads to thread with thick laces
■ small bricks for building
■ crayons and paintbrushes
■ books with familiar characters and pictures to point at
■ plastic bottles and jars with screw caps to remove and replace
■ small-world toys, such as Duplo
■ spoons and fork at mealtimes to practise feeding skills.

■ He enjoys brightly coloured picture books and turns several pages at once.

■ He points at familiar objects in the book and pats the page.

■ He uses the index finger constantly to demand drinks, food and toys out of reach.
■ He often stares out of the window for long periods watching and pointing at the activities outside with interest.

■ He holds a crayon in a palmar grasp, scribbles backwards and forwards over the paper.
■ He uses either hand but shows a preference for one.

Do this!   *3.4*

1 Write an account of physical development at 15 months.
2 How would you encourage a child to progress and achieve the skills usually seen at 2 years of age?

18 months

The 18-month-old child is extremely active, racing around at high speed to explore the environment. The child runs, with arms and legs apart, investigating corners and hurrying upstairs. Stopping and starting well, the child finds corners more difficult, but pulls large toys around and plays ball with whole-arm movements. Her world is one of 'here and now'. The child is self-willed and has yet to develop the ability to see others as people like herself.

Gross motor development

- The child walks confidently now, without using the arms for balance and is able to stop without falling.
- She may carry large toys.

- She squats to the floor to pick up toys.

- He climbs into an adult-sized chair forwards and then turns round to sit down.

- He tries to kick a ball, often with success.

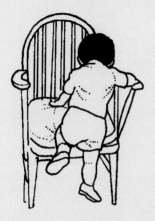

■ He runs but often falls as he is unable to co-ordinate movements to get around objects in the way.

■ He likes pushing brick trolley or similar wheeled toy.

■ She walks upstairs with hand(s) held.

■ She comes downstairs safely, either forwards on the bottom (one step at a time) or backwards crawling or sliding on the tummy.
■ She may walk downstairs with a hand held or holding onto the rail.

 Progress check

1 List four gross motor skills that are typical at 18 months.
2 Explain why small bricks are a valuable tool to enable young children to develop fine motor skills.
3 How could an adult ensure the safety of young children who need assistance to go up and down stairs?
4 How does an 18-month-old child usually get into a large chair?

18 months

Fine motor development

- The baby can now use a delicate, refined pincer grasp to put small objects through small spaces.

- The tripod grasp of crayon and pencil (using the thumb and two fingers in adult fashion) is developing.

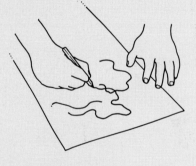

- She scribbles on paper to and fro and with random dots.

ACTIVITIES AT 18 MONTHS

Provide opportunities for:
- sand and water play – jugs for pouring, plastic pots to fill
- finger painting and hand and foot printing
- water painting with large brushes and buckets of water
- practising drawing skills with chalk and large crayons
- helping with domestic routines – dusting, vacuuming, etc.
- large piece jigsaws
- large piece construction toys with pieces to twist, to turn, to hammer and to push into place
- threading beads
- pushing and pulling toys.

■ She builds a tower of three cubes, and sometimes more.

■ He tries to thread large beads and sometimes succeeds.

■ She continues to enjoy picture books and points at known objects.

OBSERVATIONS AT 18 MONTHS

■ Observe a child with an adult who is reading a story. Look at:
  – their physical reactions to the story, for example facial expressions and body movements
  – how they attempt to turn the pages
  – whether they point at familiar pictures in the book
  – whether it is a familiar book, for example do they show recognition of the characters or try to tell the story?
■ Observe a child who is playing outside. Note their gross motor skills:
  – how they pick up objects from the floor
  – their posture when running
  – climbing skills
  – balance
  – co-ordination.

Do this! 3.6

1 Child development study

Completing a series of observations of a specific child will:

■ increase your knowledge of child development
■ heighten your awareness of variations in 'normal' development
■ enable you to make accurate recordings of child development
■ encourage your understanding of the factors which influence development.

Find a family with a baby aged 6 months or under, who will allow you to visit them at regular intervals (preferably monthly), at a mutually convenient time. Plan to make eight visits. Explain to the family the purpose of the study and assure them that confidentiality will be maintained.

Begin with a short history of the baby, including birth details and development since birth. Include some family details, for example brothers, sisters, position in the family, etc. *Do not* record names or addresses.

Make eight observations of the baby at monthly intervals. These observations should include all aspects of physical development. Ask the parents about any achievements since your last visit, as you may not see the baby demonstrate everything they are capable of at each visit.

Evaluate every observation by:
a) recording what you have seen the baby do and comparing this with what is expected at that age
b) comparing what the baby is doing at this visit with what they were capable of last time.

Include some ideas of how to help the baby extend their development.

Complete a development and weight chart to display the results of your research and compare this child's growth and development with what you have learnt about the developmental norms. Write an evaluation of your findings.

Choose one area of development to describe in detail to cover the first two years of life. Include references to your observed child. Aim to write 750–1,000 words.

2 a) Look at these pictures of babies at two developmental stages. Try to assess the ages of the babies in group A and those in B.

Group A

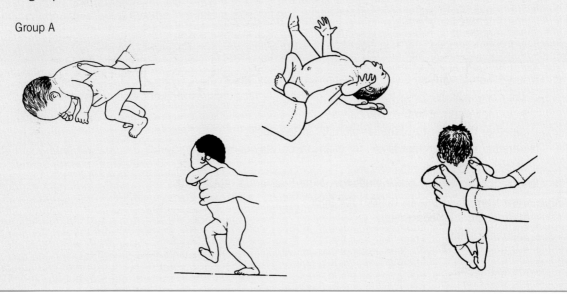

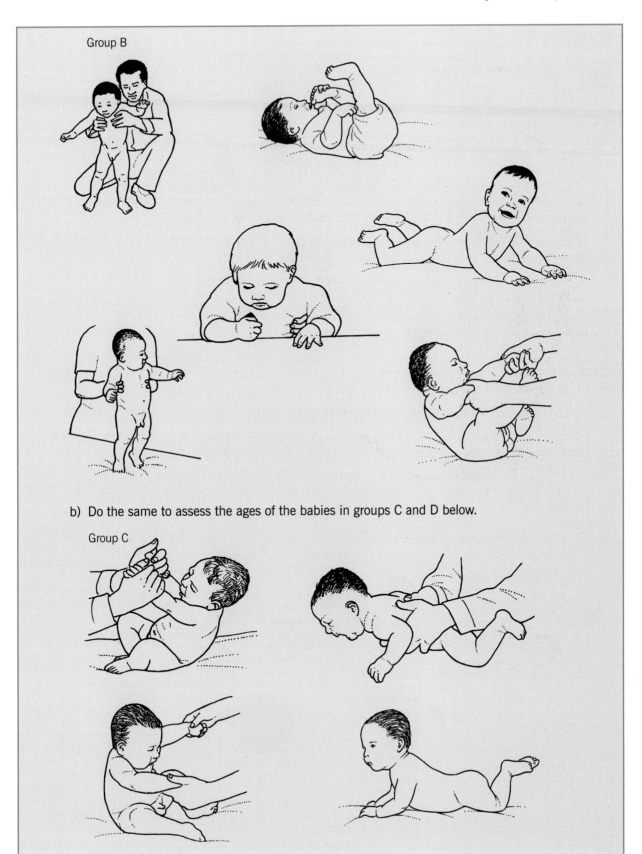

Group B

b) Do the same to assess the ages of the babies in groups C and D below.

Group C

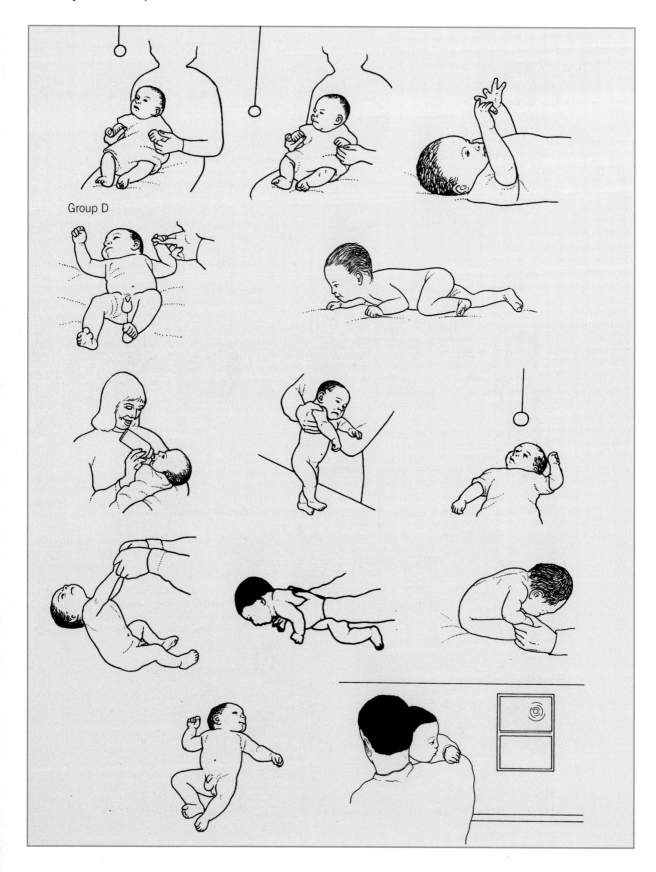

Group D

c) It is possible to see clearly the progression in development in areas of gross and fine motor skills. How would you expect a baby in C to proceed in:
   i) gross motor development?
   ii) fine motor development?
d) How would you expect a baby in D to proceed in:
   i) gross motor development?
   ii) fine motor development?

3 Look at the pictures of young children below and give the approximate age by which each skill shown should have been accomplished.

a)

b)

c)

Looks for objects hidden and out of sight

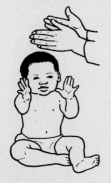
d) Claps hands in play

e) Holds crayons in palmar grasp and scribbles backwards and forwards

f) May carry large toy

g) Enjoys picture books and points at familiar objects

h) Pushes and pulls wheeled toy

i) Climbs into adult-sized chair

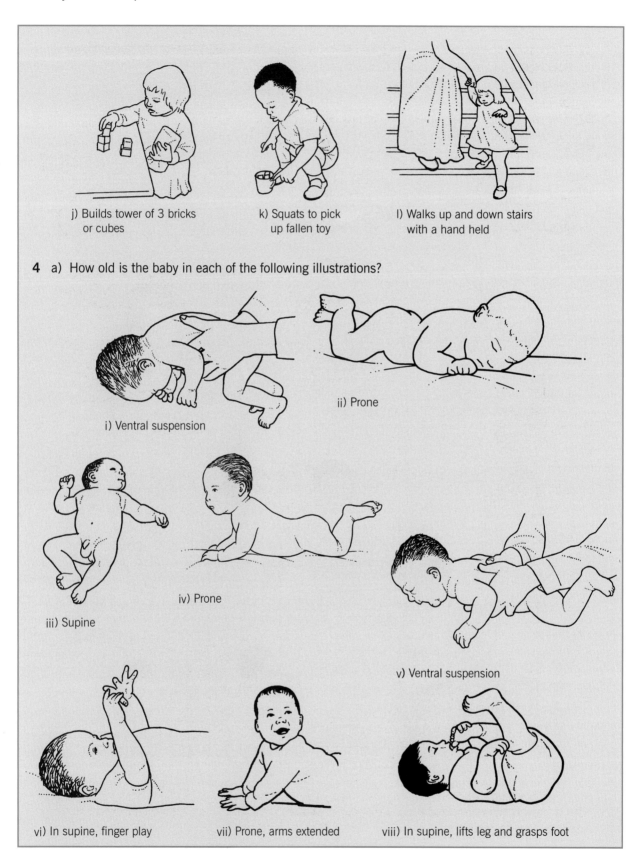

j) Builds tower of 3 bricks or cubes

k) Squats to pick up fallen toy

l) Walks up and down stairs with a hand held

4 a) How old is the baby in each of the following illustrations?

i) Ventral suspension

ii) Prone

iii) Supine

iv) Prone

v) Ventral suspension

vi) In supine, finger play

vii) Prone, arms extended

viii) In supine, lifts leg and grasps foot

b) Study the following diagrams which show the progress of gross motor skills at various stages. Label them and put them in the correct sequence.

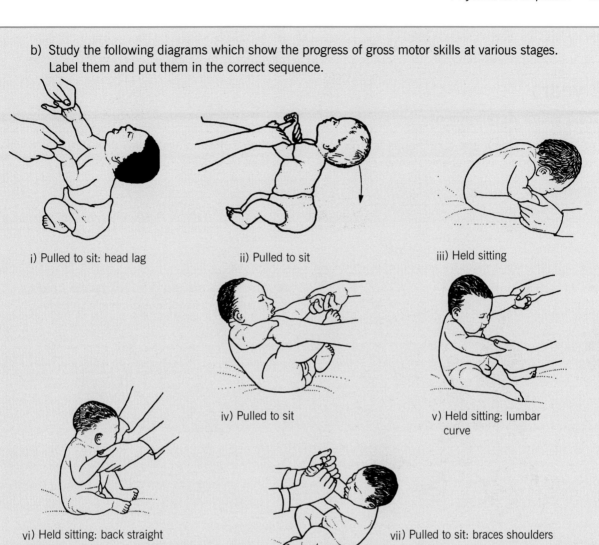

i) Pulled to sit: head lag

ii) Pulled to sit

iii) Held sitting

iv) Pulled to sit

v) Held sitting: lumbar curve

vi) Held sitting: back straight

vii) Pulled to sit: braces shoulders

c) How old is the baby in the following illustrations?

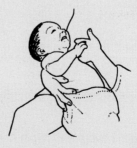

This work can all be included in a portfolio of evidence for National Vocational Qualifications in Early Years Care and Education.

Physical development (2): 2 to 7 years

The following pages describe the average physical achievements to be expected from 2 to 7 years.

2 years

Gross motor development

At 2 years children are very mobile and love exploring their surroundings. Their developing skills of **locomotion** and balance enable them to explore the environment by walking, running and climbing.

locomotion
The developing ability to move from one place to another, usually by crawling, walking, running

- The child runs safely.

- He stops and starts easily.
- He squats down steadily to play with or pick up a toy, and gets up again without using the hands.

- She walks up and down the stairs holding on; she puts two feet on every step.

- She pushes and pulls large wheeled toys; can pull along a small wheeled toy by the string and goes in the right direction.

Do this!   3.6

Plan two outdoor activities for children aged 2 years old that will help to develop their skills of locomotion and balance.

The activities should encourage the children to explore different ways of using equipment, while ensuring their safety and allowing them sufficient independence.

Say how you would adapt the activities for children who have difficulties in skills of locomotion and balance and for those who are less confident in these skills.

- He rides a small tricycle by pushing it along with the feet; he does not use the pedals.

- She tries to kick a ball but usually walks into it.

- He can climb up onto the furniture, usually to reach something or to see out of the window.

- She is beginning to show awareness of how she relates to other objects (spatial awareness).

OBSERVATIONS OF GROSS MOTOR SKILLS AT 2 YEARS

Observe several 2-year-old children at different activities that promote their gross motor skills. Make observations of children walking, running, negotiating obstacles, climbing and using a variety of outdoor equipment. Observe them moving forwards, backwards and sideways. Observe those who are just 2 and those who are nearly 3.

In your evaluation of what you have observed, comment on the differences in their skills.

Case study: Supporting the development of physical skills

Aaron is 2 years 3 months old and comes to the nursery every day. He has settled in well and enjoys playing outside. Although he is confident when riding the wheeled toys, he has not yet attempted to climb up the ladder and go down the slide. He has watched the other children with interest and on one occasion started to go up the ladder.

Today, Aaron approaches the slide as usual. Urmala, the nursery nurse, is nearby and encourages him, standing close to the ladder, helping him to place his feet and hands as he climbs. When he succeeds in climbing to the top, she praises him, helps him to sit on the slide and holds his hand as he slides down. When he arrives at the bottom, Aaron and Urmala clap their hands. Aaron immediately runs round to have another go and Urmala stands ready to support him.

1 Why does Aaron spend time watching the other children?
2 How did Urmala help Aaron to achieve his goal?
3 What did Aaron do after he successfully went down the slide?
4 Why is this important?

2 years

Fine motor development

At 2 years children enjoy pulling things apart, fitting things together, pushing in, pulling out, filling and emptying. The will still often test by touch and taste. The use of the fine pincer grip is well established. By now, a 2-year-old will use a preferred hand to hold a pencil, but both hands are used to perform complicated tasks.

- The child usually uses a preferred hand to hold a pencil; he draws circles, lines and dots.
- He can use a fine pincer grasp to pick up and put down tiny things.
- He can manipulate toys.

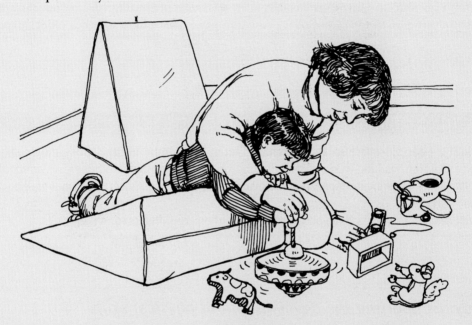

- She holds a pencil and draws circles, lines and dots.

■ He can use a fine pincer grasp with both hands to do complicated tasks, like peeling a satsuma.

■ He can match miniature toys on request.

■ He carefully builds a tower of six or seven bricks.

■ He likes picture books, enjoys recognising things in favourite pictures. He now turns the pages one at a time.

OBSERVATIONS OF FINE MOTOR SKILLS AT 2 YEARS

Observe 2-year-old children as they build with small bricks. Take a particular note of how they handle the bricks and how they use their eye to judge, measure and decide how to place the bricks. Notice what happens when they are building a tower of small bricks. How many bricks can be piled up? What happens when the tower falls over?

3 years

Gross motor development

At 3 years children's gross motor skills are developing well. They walk and run confidently, moving forwards, sideways and backwards, managing stairs easily. They use wheeled toys with skill and with an awareness of obstacles around them.

- The child can stand and walk on tiptoe.
- She walks forwards, sideways and backwards.

- She can kick a ball hard.

OUTDOOR PLAY

Playing outside:
- helps to use up energy and to release tensions. It is a place where it is acceptable to make more noise and to run around
- stimulates the appetite, aiding the digestion and the circulation, and develops the lungs
- promotes healthy sleep patterns
- helps to develop muscle tone, balance and motor control
- develops skills such as running, jumping, hopping, climbing, stopping and starting, pedalling, steering, crawling through and under and over equipment.

- She walks upstairs with one foot on each step.
- She walks downstairs with two feet on each step.

- She is now well aware of her own size in relation to things around her.

- She rides a tricycle using the pedals.

Do this! *3.7*

Plan two outdoor activities for children aged 3 years old that will help to develop their spatial awareness.

The activities should encourage the children to negotiate obstacles and to judge speed and distance using a variety of equipment.

Say how you would adapt these activities for those children who are less confident in these skills.

3 years

Fine motor development

At 3 years old children's hand–eye co-ordination is good. They can pick up small objects, such as pieces of collage material and place them with some accuracy. Three-year-olds enjoy painting pictures with a large brush and usually name them when they are finished. Their drawings of people show the head and one or two other parts. They enjoy simple conversations about the current activity, asking many questions. They listen eagerly to stories and enjoy finger rhymes and action songs.

- The child can now build a tower of nine or ten bricks.
- She can pick up small pieces of collage material using the thumb and first finger.
- He can co-operate in simple vision tests by recognising toys.

- He can thread large wooden beads onto a lace.

Case study: *Proving suitable equipment*

Sarah, aged 3, is new to the nursery. She joins in many of the activities, and seems to prefer activities like collage and box modelling. Jason, the child-care worker who is Sarah's key worker, has noticed that she doesn't use scissors very easily and often tears collage material to get the shape and size she wants.

Jason sat with Sarah and showed her how to use the scissors and she made some progress. Later, when Sarah was using a pencil, Jason noticed that she was using her left hand. When Sarah wanted to do a collage activity, Jason made sure that left-handed scissors were available and sat with Sarah while she used them. With Jason's help and encouragement, Sarah was able to progress with her cutting skills.

1 Why did the child-care worker intervene here?
2 What good practice enabled Jason to help Sarah effectively?

- She can cut with scissors.
- She may know colours.
- She matches two or three primary colours.
- She controls a pencil in the preferred hand, between the thumb and first two fingers.
- She enjoys painting with a large brush.

Do this!   3.8

You are preparing a collage activity for a group of children aged 3 to 3 years 11 months.

a) What would you provide?
b) Explain why you have selected each of the items.
c) What are the expected learning outcomes for the children?
d) What additional resources, if any, would you need?
e) What aspects of health and safety would you need to consider?
f) What aspects of equal opportunities would you need to consider and provide for?
g) What would be your role in the activity?
h) Evaluate the activity after you have carried it out.

4 years

Gross motor development

At 4 years children have developed good muscle control which helps with energetic climbing, jumping, hopping and tricycle riding. They are adept runners and climbers and enjoy any games that involve running and jumping. Four-year-olds are adding the skills of running on tiptoe. They are confident climbing over apparatus and, if they get the chance, up trees.

■ The child can stand, walk and run on tiptoe.

■ Keeping the legs straight, he can bend at the waist to pick up things from the floor.

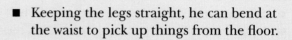

■ He climbs trees, ladders, play equipment.

■ She walks or runs up and down stairs, putting one foot on each step.

Do this! 3.9

Draw a plan to show how large equipment could be set out for *indoor* physical play activities.
a) Describe each piece of equipment and its purpose and value to children's development.
b) What safety procedures need to be carried out?
c) Describe modifications that would need to be made to take account of children of different ages and those with special needs.

■ He can catch, kick, throw and bounce a ball and hit it with a bat.
■ Rides a tricycle well, able to make sharp turns.
■ Children are confident at climbing over and through apparatus.

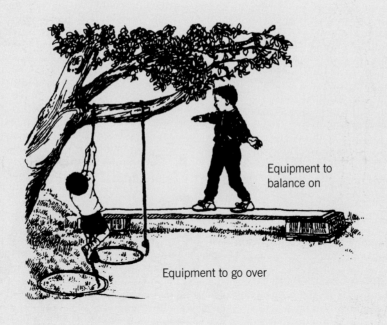

Equipment to balance on

Equipment to go over

Progress check

At what age would you expect a child to be able to do the following:
a) walk upstairs with one foot on each step, and down with two feet on each step?
b) walk up and down stairs with one foot on each step?
c) ride a small tricycle pushing it along with the feet?
d) be aware of their own size in relation to things around them?
e) bend at the waist to pick things up from the floor?

4 years

Fine motor development

At 4 years old children are becoming adept at tasks needing careful hand–eye control. They are not so confident or accurate in their skills of catching and hitting as they are in games of running and jumping. They enjoy building with small- and large-scale construction materials and are learning to be more skilful in using scissors. They learn the combination of visual and fine manipulative skills that are required to complete jigsaws.

■ He can build three steps with six bricks, after being shown how.

■ The child is able to build a tower of ten or more bricks.

■ They enjoy pouring, filling and emptying containers.

■ She can thread smaller beads than at 3 years.

- He grasps a pencil maturely and has good control
- He draws a person on request, showing head, legs and trunk.

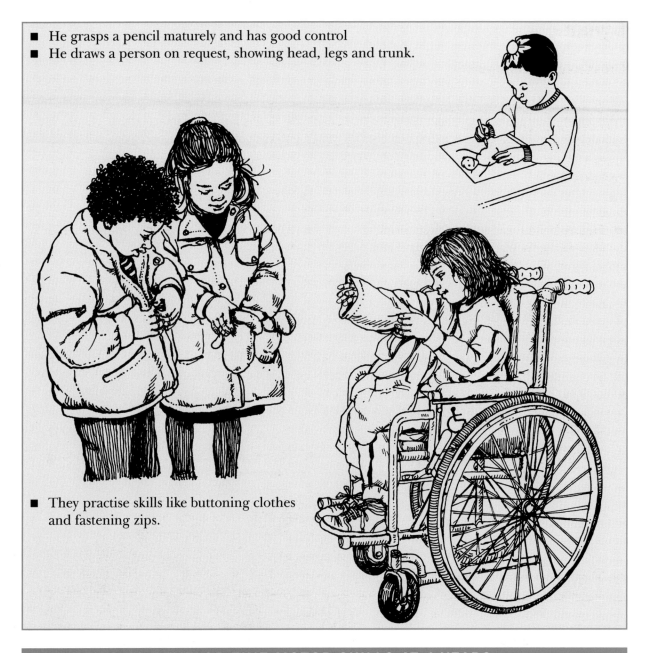

- They practise skills like buttoning clothes and fastening zips.

ACTIVITIES TO DEVELOP FINE MOTOR SKILLS AT 4 YEARS

- Malleable materials, such as clay, dough and plasticine – encourage the development of the muscles and control of the fingers as children roll, knead break up the materials
- Jigsaw puzzles with thick pieces – allow children to manipulate them
- Writing tools and paper, including pencils of various thicknesses
- Painting and collage activities
- Imaginative play, such as dressing up, where clothes are fastened and unfastened, and home play where meals are 'cooked' and tea is 'poured'.
- Sand and water play, with equipment for pouring, filling and emptying
- Small construction equipment and woodwork tools

5 years

Gross motor development

At 5 years children cope with most daily personal duties and are ready for the wider world of school. They run, climb, dance and jump about. Some children combine all this into some imaginataive 'stunts'. Most children will use these skills in hiding and chasing games with each other, often involving any willing adults!

■ She plays a variety of ball games quite well.

■ The child moves rhythmically to music.

■ He can hop and run lightly on the toes.

■ He can walk along a thin line, climb, dig, and use slides and swings.

Fine motor development

At 5 years fine skills are well co-ordinated and children can play games needing appropriate placing of objects. Five-year-olds will be able to manage most of the fastenings on their clothes, although they find tying laces difficult.

- He can draw a person with head, trunk, legs and eyes, nose and mouth.
- He matches 10 to 12 colours.
- He can sew large stitches.
- He may be able to thread a needle.

- She builds three to four steps with bricks from a model.

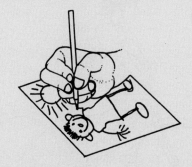

- There is good control of pencils and paintbrushes.

 Progress check

Which combination of equipment will best stimulate fine manipulative skills when used by a 5-year-old?

a) water, dry sand, dough
b) jigsaws, collage, sewing
c) hats, dolls, pushchairs
d) bicycles, trucks, tyres

6 years

Gross motor development

At 6 years the children have developed agility and strength. Six-year-olds become increasingly adept in climbing and jumping. They enjoy experimenting with their movements on the large apparatus, beginning to learn to suspend themselves by the arms and knees.

- He kicks a football a distance of 3–6 metres.
- He makes a running jump of approximately 100 centimetres.

- He rides a two-wheeled bicycle.

- She can make a vertical jump of about 10 centimetres.

Think about it

Allowing for individual differences, as children grow and develop they:
- gain increasing control of their own bodies
- naturally show particular skills and talents in their physical skills
- have different degrees of competence in these areas – some will have better skills of balance and some better skills of co-ordination
- vary in their levels of confidence when attempting physical activities – some need a lot of adult encouragement to try new physical activities and some appear fearless and full of confidence.

It is the role of the child-care worker to give children the opportunities to learn and practise physical skills in an environment where challenge is balanced with safety.

Fine motor development

At 6 years old children can use a pencil, crayon or brush to produce drawings of people and buildings with much more detail. In order to write, children need to move from a whole-hand grip to a finer hold involving the thumb and fingers holding the pencil nearer the point. Six-year-olds are adjusting their grip on the pencil, forming letters and getting their writing to flow.

- The child can carefully align cubes to build a virtually straight tower.

- He can catch a ball thrown from 1 metre with one hand.

- She grasps and adjusts the pencil as at 5 years.
- The writing hold is similar to that of an adult.
- Writing is confined to a small area of the paper.
- He draws recognisable pictures.

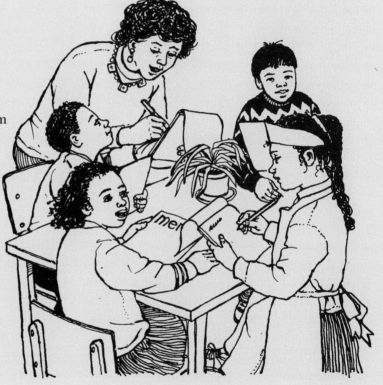

✔ Progress check

Which combination of skills best describes the fine motor skills of a 6-year-old?
a) build three steps with six bricks; thread small beads; copy a square
b) build a tower of nine or ten small bricks; cut with scissors; copy a circle
c) catch a ball; draw recognisable pictures; adult writing hold
d) draw a diamond; sew neatly with a needle and thread; tie shoelaces

7 years

Gross motor skills

At 7 years children's physical progress is consistently improving; they can balance and climb the apparatus with ease. Seven-year-olds become more able to experiment with the movements that they make and can deliberately vary their speed. These skills can be used in expressive movements, and children of this age enjoy dancing to music in various forms.

- The child can now ride a two-wheeled bicycle expertly.
- She can jump off the apparatus from about four steps high.

- He hops easily, keeping well balanced.
- They enjoy games and sports, and run around energetically.

- She can climb, balance and adapt physical skills to negotiate the

OBSERVATION OF GROSS MOTOR DEVELOPMENT AT 7 YEARS

Aim and purpose: To observe, evaluate and compare children's differing physical skills

The observation: Choose an area of gross motor development, for example hopping, and observe a number of children of the same age. Record:
- how many hops they can do on the spot, on the right foot and then on the left foot
- how far they can hop on the right foot and then on the left.

Construct a pie or bar chart to display your results.
Evaluate your findings by comparing the results.

Fine motor development

At 7 years children are generally learning to write. The skills of writing, forming and joining letters will only improve with a lot of practice. Children are beginning to get their writing to flow. Some children may also be aware that there are different scripts and different directions of writing. As with gross motor development, there will be differences in skill and confidence between individual children.

- She can build a tall straight tower with bricks.
- She can draw a diamond neatly.

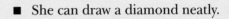

- She can sew neatly with a large needle.

- He writes most of the letters of the alphabet.

- He draws a person with originality, for example clothed and seated.

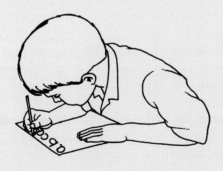

 Progress check

At what age would you expect a child to be able to do the following:
- a) thread large beads?
- b) match two or three primary colours?
- c) draw a person showing head, legs and trunk?
- d) build three or four steps after a demonstration?
- e) draw a diamond?

Variations in developmental progress

The development of a child is a progression through stages. Very often an age is attached to a stage of development, such as children walking at 15 months. In reality some children walk as early as 9 months and others as late as 18 months. This is perfectly normal. Development is not a line but an area or range. Although you need a working knowledge of the *average* age at which children achieve their developmental milestones, you will always need to remember the *range* of achievement.

Children progress through the stages of development at their own pace. There may be many reasons why some children do this more quickly or more slowly. Factors may include race: African and Caribbean children often achieve the stages of gross motor more quickly than the average, sitting, standing and walking early in the range. Children who have a condition such as cerebral palsy may achieve the stages more slowly. Progress is individual, but the child will move through the stages in the same order, for example gaining head control, sitting with support, sitting unaided, pulling to stand, walking with help, walking alone. What is important is that the child is making progress through the stages.

There are other broad principles which can be applied to physical development and these are more thoroughly explained in Chapter 4, *The principles of development*.

The role of the adult

The adult needs to provide a safe environment for babies and children to extend their physical skills. Children need room to move around freely and the opportunity to extend their range of movements in both gross motor and fine motor skills.

There are many toys that will help with this, and it is important to choose carefully with safety and the child's stage of development in mind. Many toys will be labelled as suitable for certain age groups, but bear in mind the stage the child is at and select accordingly.

Providing toys and activities which stimulate development needs to be carefully undertaken. Children usually need activities which will extend their abilities, but not so difficult or easy that they lose interest. However much children enjoy a challenge, they will always enjoy their favourite toys. Children will work at achieving a skill, practise it and then enjoy themselves using their new-found achievement.

Although bought toys can be good, there are plenty of things around the home, garden and park which can be used by adults to stimulate children's physical development: boxes to climb in and out of, saucepans and cupboards to explore, wooden spoons, buttons, cotton bobbins to sort, hideaways under the table with a long cloth. Outside in the garden or park there is room to move around; there are plants, insects, animals, mud and water to explore. All these things can be observed, experienced and explored with imaginative, sensitive, adult encouragement and supervision. It is up to the adult to recognise the stage of development the child has reached and to provide the encouragement needed to help the child move forward at the pace each one needs. This pace may well vary with each child and should reflect individual needs.

Exploring in the garden

 Progress check

At what age would you expect a child to be able to do the following:
a) ride a tricycle using the pedals?
b) walk up stairs and down stairs holding on and putting two feet on every step?
c) balance on the apparatus beam?
d) walk up stairs with one foot on each step, but down stairs with two feet on each step?
e) draw a recognisable person with head, body, arms, legs and possibly eyes, nose, mouth?
f) build a tower of ten bricks?
g) build a tower of six or seven bricks?
h) hold a pencil in the preferred hand?
i) stand, walk and run on tiptoe?
j) match and name four primary colours?

Do this! 3.10

1 Try out some simple developmental assessment for yourself. Use a set of small bricks and ask children of different ages to construct a tower.

   Devise a visual method to present your results and compare them with the norms.

2 Make a collection of children's drawings of people. Put them into the order of the developmental stages. Does this order correspond with the ages of the children?

3 Do 12 observations of children, one at each of the following ages: 2, 3, 4, 5, 6 and 7 years. Do six to show the progression of gross motor development and six to show the progression of fine motor development. You will be able to use these observations for your portfolio for the CACHE Diploma (NNEB) or as evidence for your NVQ Early Years Education award.

4 Look closely at the large apparatus and equipment which is used inside and outside at your school or nursery. Describe each item, if necessary drawing a diagram to make the explanation clearer. Evaluate each item saying how it helps to stimulate all areas of development. To do this you may need to refer to other chapters in this book.

5 a) Conduct a survey amongst the children you are working with. Find out what recreational activities they take part in outside the home, school or nursery and what the children think about these activities.

  b) Write about 250 words to say:

  i) how these activities help to extend physical development

  ii) why the children enjoy these activities.

6 Look at these pictures of young children and give the approximate age by which each skill shown should have been accomplished.

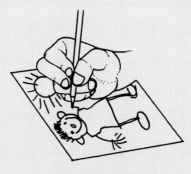

b) Draws a recognisable person with head, trunk, legs, arms and facial features

a) Builds 3 steps with 6 bricks after a demonstration

c) Sits and steers but cannot yet use pedals

d) Builds a tower of 9 or 10 bricks

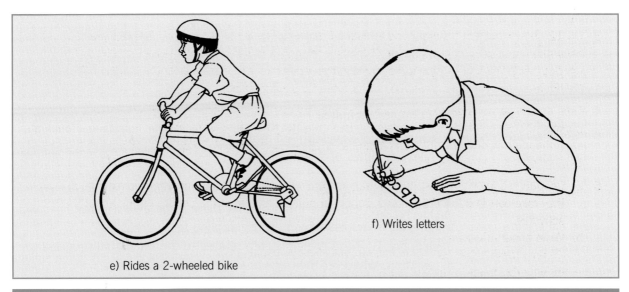

e) Rides a 2-wheeled bike

f) Writes letters

Think about it

Now you have made some observations and done some research of your own, think about developmental ages and stages.

From your own research, can you show that variations in achieving stages are acceptable and part of normal development? Can you produce some evidence from your research to support this?

Key terms

You need to know what these words and phrases mean. Go back through the chapter to find out.

central nervous system
fine motor skills
gross motor skills
headlag
locomotion
motor development
neonate
norm
palmar grasp
pincer grasp
posture
primitive reflex
primitive tripod grasp
prone
reflex
skill
spatial awareness
stimulus
supine
ventral suspension
voluntary action

Now try these questions

1 What are the stages in the development of locomotion?

2 Describe the stages in the development of fine manipulative skills.

3 What important points should adults be aware of when supporting children's physical development?

4 Discuss 'normal' and 'norms' in the context of development.

5 Describe the primitive reflexes present in the 'normal' neonate.

4 The principles of physical development

This chapter includes:

- ■ **Principles of development and children's progress**
- ■ **Five principles of development**

For child-care workers to develop an understanding of the process of development, it is important for them to be aware of the underlying principles which can be applied to all areas of development. These principles are related to the individual progress of all children, whatever their age or stage of development.

You may find it useful to read this chapter in conjunction with:

- ▶ **Book 1, Chapter 3**   Physical development
- ▶ **Book 1, Chapter 5**   Measuring and recording development

Principles of development and children's progress

principle
A basic truth which underpins an activity

A **principle** is a basic truth or law which can be applied to a certain type of activity. It is an essential factor in the progression of the activity.

The *principles of development* are a series of rules which apply to the beginning of development and its continuation throughout infancy and childhood. They are relevant to all areas of development, not just physical development.

Five principles of development

1 Development as a continual process

maturity
Complete in natural and expected development for age

From conception to **maturity**, developmental changes are gradual, continuous and flow into each other. There are periods of very rapid change in infancy, when many new skills such as walking, verbal communication and basic manipulative skills, are learned – skills which form the basis of later performance. This rapid development decreases to a slower pace in the later years of childhood.

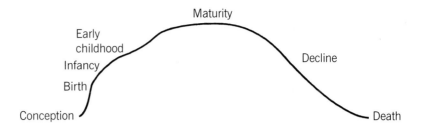

Development as a continual process, showing the steep learning curve of infancy and early childhood

2 The sequence of development

> **sequence**
> The order in which a series of milestones occur

The **sequence** (order) in which new skills are acquired is always the same, but the rate at which different children acquire them varies. For example, all children must acquire head control before they can sit unsupported, so that they can balance (see page 94). Some children with a condition such as cerebral palsy may not develop head control until they are 2 or 3 years old, and only then can they learn to sit alone.

Do this! 4.1

Give three other examples of the sequence of development (other than that of head control given on page 94).

---

3 The maturity of the nervous system

> **spinal cord**
> Nerve tissue which carries messages from the brain to the rest of the body, and vice versa

The central nervous system (CNS) is composed of the brain, the **spinal cord** and the nerves. The brain sends messages to all parts of the body down the spinal cord to the nerves which stimulate the muscles to obey the brain's command. Similarly the nerves send messages to the brain via the spinal cord; this information is constantly being transmitted and translated. The nervous system must be mature enough to be able to understand the messages it receives and to be able to send out commands.

One example of this the development of ventral suspension, shown in the diagram on page 95. Another example is toilet training. The central nervous system must be mature enough to interpret messages from the bowel or the bladder that they need emptying and to enable the child to know:

- where it is acceptable to empty them
- how to communicate this to an adult.

The brain is responsible for the way the body works; it stores information for future reference and helps children to make sense of the world around them. When a new skill has been learnt, it is essential to give a child the opportunity and incentive to practise. Praising children in their newly gained ability will encourage them to do it again, and reinforce the information in the brain.

Stage 1: about 1 month

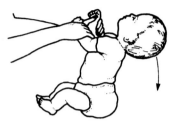

Lifts head in prone

Head lag diminishing

Stage 2: about 3 months

Supports head and
chest on forearms

Raises head with body when
pulled to sit

Stage 3: about 6 months

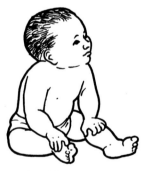

Supports head and chest on
extended forearms

Lifts head to look at feet in supine

Good head control
when sitting

Sequence of development of head control

Complete curve at birth

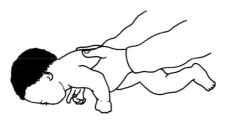

1 month: head and legs gaining more control

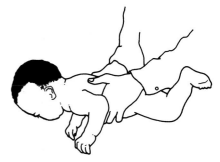

3 months: head and legs above level of the back as the nervous system matures

Ventral suspension: sequence of development

4 The replacement of reflex by voluntary actions

The primitive reflexes mostly disappear by about 3 months of age; the Moro is the last to go by 5 months (defensive and protective reflexes remain throughout life). These primitive reflexes must go so that they can be replaced by voluntary control – actions which a child chooses and wants to do. An example of this process is the fading of the palmar grasp reflex so that a baby can grasp objects with the whole hand and drop them at will, generally at about 6 months of age.

You may see some children with special needs who still have their primitive reflexes. This is a sign of damage to the central nervous system.

Do this! 4.2

Give three other examples of the replacement of reflexes by voluntary actions (other than that given above).

---

5 The directions of development: downwards and outwards

The development of gross motor (whole-body) skills begins with the control of the head and works downwards, to sitting, crawling, pulling to stand, walking.

The development of fine motor (hand–eye) skills begins in the centre of the body and works outwards to the fingers, which gradually increase in ability to perform very complicated manoeuvres.

Examples of this process are the jerky, unco-ordinated movements of the arms with fists clenched, which develop to symmetrical arm waving with the hands open; or finger-play which develops to the palmar grasp, pincer grasp, then tripod grasp, enabling the child to perform delicate movements such as using a spoon and fork, unwrapping sweets, threading beads, fastening buttons, and so on.

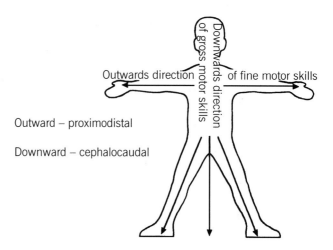

Directions of development

Progress check

1 Describe the principles of development.
2 Why is it important for children to be given the opportunity to practise new skills?
3 What is the central nervous system? (Look back at Chapter 3 if necessary.)
4 Why is it important in child development?

Do this! 4.3

1 Give examples of each principle of development to show that you understand the underlying developmental rule.

2 Observe a young child at 15–20 minute intervals for a period of at least two hours.
Evaluate the observation in terms of all-round development. Include a detailed analysis of how the principles of development relate to this particular child.

3 A friend of yours is doing a business studies course at the same college. He has recently completed an assignment on the principles of accounting and is interested to see your work on the principles of development. How could you explain this area of your studies to your friend, using examples to illustrate your meaning?

Key terms

You need to know what these words and phrases mean. Go back through the chapter to find out.

maturity
principle
sequence
spinal cord

Now try these questions

1 Describe how the principle of 'development as a continual process' can be related to the acquisition of fine motor skills from 0–7 years.

2 How can the principle of 'the sequence of development' be helpful to child-care workers in planning their play provision for a group of 1–2-year-old children?

3 Explain how the primitive reflexex are replaced by voluntary actions.

4 Apply the principle of 'the downwards and outwards directions of development' to gross motor and fine motor skills from 0–7 years.

5 Measuring and recording physical development

This chapter includes:

- The importance of measuring and recording development
- Ways of recording physical development
- Observing and recording development in a child-care establishment

Qualified child-care workers are usually competent and experienced observers of children because of their training in child development. They are in an ideal position to notice children's individual progress and to monitor any deviations from the developmental norms. However expertly a child's progress is followed, there must be a structured system of recording observations of development and formal developmental assessments. This chapter highlights the importance of recording development and offers examples of different methods of doing so.

You may find it useful to read this chapter in conjunction with:

▶ **Book 1, Chapter 1**   Physical growth
▶ **Book 1, Chapter 3**   Physical development

The importance of measuring and recording development

Every professional person who works with young children is responsible for their care and subsequent well-being. This framework of responsibility must include a sound knowledge of child development so that:

- expectations of the child are realistic, reasonable and within their capabilities
- appropriate play activities are provided to stimulate the next stage of development
- children who are not making progress are quickly identified and investigated by the health visitor and/or paediatrician.

Careful observation of children is the most effective tool for assessing developmental progress, preferably over a period of time in an environment where they feel at ease, for example at home, at playgroup, in the day nursery, at nursery or primary school.

The observation and recording must be structured and include all areas of development, not only what is interesting on that occasion. Sometimes **milestones** are used to measure development, for example that children should be walking at around 15 months. However, the use of milestones places too much emphasis on one area of development. It is vital to remember that development continues as an uninterrupted pattern of changes; the acquisition and performance of new skills must be measured against the performance of the whole child.

Many different methods have been devised to record development in a systematic manner.

milestones
Important skills which the average child should have accomplished within a specified time

 Progress check

1 Why must professionals have a thorough knowledge of child development?
2 What is the most effective way of assessing development?
3 Explain the values and pitfalls of using milestones to measure development.
4 What should a child's developmental progress be measured against?

Ways of measuring and recording development

There are various ways of recording a child's development:

narrative
A piece of factual writing

- a **narrative** description of the areas of development and the skills achieved
- making tape recordings of the child's progress
- filling in charts, such as the Denver screening checklist and development centile charts (see the examples of charts on pages 100–1, 102, 104–5).

Denver screening checklist

Age in months	Motor	Social	Hearing and speech	Eye and hand co-ordination	Signature
1	Holds head erect for a few seconds	Quieted when picked up	Startled by sounds	Follows light with eyes	
2	Head up when prone (chin clear)	Smiles	Listens to bell or rattle	Follows ring up, down and sideways	
3	Kicks well	Follows person with eyes	Searches for sound with eyes	Glances from one object to another	
4	Lifts head and chest in prone	Returns examiner's smile	Laughs	Clasps and retains cube	
5	Holds head erect with no head lag	Responds when played with	Turns head to sound	Transfers object to mouth	
6	Weight bearing and bouncing; sits with support	Turns head to person talking	Babbles or coos to voice or music	Takes cube from table	
7	Rolls from front to back	Drinks from a cup	Vocalising, makes different sounds	Looks for fallen object	
8	Tries to crawl or shuffles	Looks at mirror image	Shouts for attention	Passes toy from hand to hand	
9	Turns around on floor; stable sit	Helps to hold cup when drinking	Says *mama* or *dada*	Manipulates two objects at once	
10	Stands when held up	Smiles at mirror image	Listens to watch	Clicks two bricks together	
11	Pulls up to stand	Finger-feeds	Knows two words with meaning	Uses pincer grip	
12	Walks or side steps around pen	Claps; waves goodbye; imitates	Knows three words with meaning	Retains three small objects	
13	Stands alone	Holds cup for drinking	Looks at picture	Shows preference for one hand	
14	May walk alone	Uses spoon	Knows own name	Holds four cubes	
15	Climbs upstairs	Shows shoes	Has four or five clear words	Places one object upon another	
16	Pushes pram, toy horse, etc.	Tries to turn door knob	Has six or seven clear words	Scribbles freely	

continued

Denver screening checklist *continued*

Age in months	Motor	Social	Hearing and speech	Eye and hand co-ordination	Signature
17	Climbs on to chair	Manages cup well	Babbled conversation	Pulls (table) cloth to get toy	
18	May walk backwards; walks confidently	Takes off shoes and socks	Enjoys pictures in book	Constructive play with toys	
19	Climbs stairs up and down	Knows one part of body	Has nine words	Builds tower of three bricks	
20	Jumps	May indicate bowel awareness	Has 12 words	Builds tower of four bricks	
21	Runs	Has bladder control by day	Two-word sentences	Does circular scribble	
22	Walks upstairs	Tries to tell experiences	Listens to stories	Builds tower of five or more bricks	
23	Seats himself at table	Knows two parts of body	Has 20 words or more	Copies perpendicular stroke	
24	Walks up and down stairs; runs, walks upstairs, throws ball; cannot kick ball	Knows four parts of body; cup/spoon feeds; toilet by day; copies domestic tasks; tantrums	Names four toys; increased vocabulary; two-word phrases; constant chatter; knows parts of body	Copies horizontal stroke; picks up crumbs; unwraps sweet; circular scribble; Stycar vision toy test; six-cube tower	
30	Runs well straight forward and climbs easy nursery apparatus; pushes and pulls large toys skilfully but has difficulty in steering them round obstacles; jumps with two feet together; kicks large ball	Pulls down pants or knickers at toilet but seldom able to replace; very active, restless and rebellious; prolonged domestic make-believe	Continually asking questions beginning *What?*, *Where?*; uses pronouns *I*, *me* and *you*	Picks up pins, threads, etc., with each eye covered separately; recognises minute details in picture books; imitates horizontal line and circle (also usually T and I); recognises self in photographs when once shown	
36	Dresses, gait stands on one foot. Note hyperactivity	Feels self; toilet-trained; gives name; helps	Names parts of body and paints pictures. Talks to self	Stycar vision test. Nine-cube tower; builds block bridge; draws circle	
48	Stands on one foot; hops, runs, climbs; rides tricycle	Alertness; friendliness; aware of surroundings; co-operation; self-willed. Eats skilfully; washes self	Gardiner-Sheridan hearing test. Note speech intelligible. Sentences. Responds to questioning.	Stycar vision, near and far. Draws circle and square; grasps pencil; builds bridge; note ataxia tremor; finger and thumb opposition	

CHILD DEVELOPMENT

Name:
Address:
Date of birth:
Sex:
Clinic/Hospital (No):

Column headings (age of attainment), each subdivided into **M | V | S | B**:

6 WEEKS	6 MONTHS	8 MONTHS	1 YEAR	18 MONTHS	2–2½ YEARS	3 YEARS	4 YEARS	5 YEARS

SOCIAL BEHAVIOUR AND PLAY (B)

- Turns to regard speaker's face — HE (6 weeks)
- Smiles — HE (6 weeks)
- Plays "peek-a-boo" — H
- Hand and foot regard — H
- Puts objects into mouth — H
- Plays "pat-a-cake" — EH (1 year)
- Indicates wants (not cry) — H
- Drinks from cup — H
- Waves "bye-bye" — H
- Indicates toilet needs — H (18 months)
- Takes off shoes and socks — H
- Explores environment — H
- Holds spoon – gets food to mouth — H
- Dry through day — H (2–2½ years)
- Puts on clothing — H
- Eats with spoon and fork — H
- Plays alone — H
- Dresses with supervision — H (3 years)
- Goes to toilet alone — H
- Eats with fork and knife — H
- Dresses without supervision — H (4 years)
- Washes and dries hands — HE
- Brushes teeth — H
- Shares toys — H
- Dramatic group play — H (5 years)
- Chooses own friends — H
- Comforts friends in distress — H

HEARING AND SPEECH (S)

- Startled by noise — E (6 weeks)
- Rattle 15cm at ear level — E
- Vocalizes — E
- Distraction hearing test — E (8 months)
- Responds to own name — H
- Polysyllabic babbles — EH
- Understands several words — H (1 year)
- Uses "Mama" and "Dada" — H
- Turns to name — HE
- Obeys simple instruction "close the door" — HE (18 months)
- Points to eyes, nose and mouth — HE
- Words: 3 or more — H
- Jabbers continually — EH
- Hearing test / Speech discrimination test — HE (2–2½ years)
- Gives name — HE
- Uses plurals — H
- Recognises colours — EH (4 years)
- Sentences of 4 words — HE (3 years)
- Gives full name, sex and age — EH
- Uses prepositions — H
- Counts up to 10 — EH
- Hearing test – Audiometry — E (5 years)
- Language test — E
- Fluent and clear speech — H

FINE MOTOR AND VISION (V)

- Follows horizontally to 90° — E (6 weeks)
- Stares — EH
- Follows fallen toys — E (6 months)
- Fixes on small objects — E
- Transfers and mouths — EH
- Reaches out to grasp (palmer grasp) — HE
- Holds 2 bricks and bangs — H (1 year)
- Pincer grip — E
- Casts — HE
- Points with index finger — EH
- Builds tower of 3 or 4 bricks — H (18 months)
- Turns pages — H
- Scribbles — HE
- Delicate pincer grasp — E
- Builds tower 8 bricks — E (2–2½ years)
- Imitates vertical line — E
- Picks up "Hundreds & Thousands" — E
- Matches two colours — E (3 years)
- Threads beads — E
- Copies circle — E
- Draws man with 3 parts — E (4 years)
- Copies bridges of 3 bricks — E
- Copies cross and square — E
- Copies 3 steps from 6 bricks, 4 steps from 10 bricks — E (5 years)
- Threads beads well — E
- Draws man with all features — E
- Copies triangle — E

GROSS MOTOR (M)

- Prone — E (6 weeks)
- Ventral suspension — E
- Moro response — E
- Head control — E
- Pull to sit — E (6 months)
- Sits with support — HE
- Downward parachute — E
- Weight bears — E
- Forward parachute — E (8 months)
- Sits without support — HE
- Rolls over from back to prone — E
- Crawls — E
- Walks alone — E (1 year)
- Walks holding on to furniture — EH
- Pulls to stand — EH
- Gets to sitting — EH
- Climbs upstairs one hand held — H (18 months)
- Carries toys while walking — HE
- Walks backwards — HE
- Kicks ball — EH (2–2½ years)
- Jumps in place — E
- Climbs and descends stairs — H
- Runs fast — H (3 years)
- Stands on one foot 1 second — E
- Pedals tricycle — E
- Climbs stairs in adult manner — E
- Hops 2 metres forward — E (4 years)
- Stands on one foot 5 seconds — E
- Hops on one foot — E
- Walks heel to toe — E
- Walks backwards heel to toe — E (5 years)
- Bounces and catches ball — HE
- Walks downstairs 1 foot per step — H

Markers: *Testicles* (6 weeks, 8 months); *Hips* (6 months, 8 months, 1 year)

Bottom rows: USUAL AGE OF ATTAINMENT | DATE AND AGE | PRESENT ATTAINMENT

Legend:

** = Sheridan—Gardiner Near Vision Test, Sheridan—Gardiner Distant Vision Test
*** = Hirschberg Corneal Light Reflection Test; Cover Test

E = Pass by examination
H = Pass by history

Hips = Check for dislocation
Testicles = Check for presence and descent

by S. LINGAM, Feb. 1984

A further example of a child development chart

Development centile charts

development centile charts
A way of recording development so that the child's performance can be seen visually

Development centile charts have been devised after studying and recording the progress of thousands of children. They present the information in a highly visual way and are easy to read.

Look at the examples on pages 104–5. The figures on the bottom line (the horizontal axis) represent the age of the child, in weeks until 1 year of age and thereafter in years. The developmental items are listed down the side (the vertical axis) and are given an approximate age range. The blocks on the chart are filled in when a skill has been witnessed, in the space that relates to the child's age. Blocks which appear above the centile line indicate good developmental progress. Blocks which appear below the line may be indications of developmental difficulties; again the advantage of the chart is that it presents this information in a clear way which can quickly be interpreted.

Charts should always be completed regularly, so that any areas of difficulty are detected quickly and any necessary action taken. Look at the examples on pages 106–7 of completed charts which indicate a child's initial good progress, followed by some areas of difficulty.

The value of development centile charts

There are several benefits to child-care workers in using development centile charts.

- The information enables the reader to compare a child with itself: it is easy to compare the previous recording and note individual progress.
- A child can also be with compared with others: it is easy to note average, typical development.
- The charts can record all areas of development, making it possible to see the pattern of progress: an area of advanced development can be compared with an area of less than average progress.
- Development centile charts can identify children who are not making satisfactory progress, or are deviating from the norm; so the cause can be sought.
- The information recorded in this way allows for early intervention.
- The data is simple to read and to complete, and effective in measuring progress.

Development centile charts are used by whoever is doing the assessment, wherever the assessment is done. They are used by health visitors, nursery nurses, doctors, general practitioners, paediatricians and school nurses. They are used in the home, in baby clinics, day nurseries, family centres, hospitals, GP clinics and at medical examinations and check-ups in schools. Because of their visual nature they an ideal format to share with parents as the basis of an explanation about their child's development.

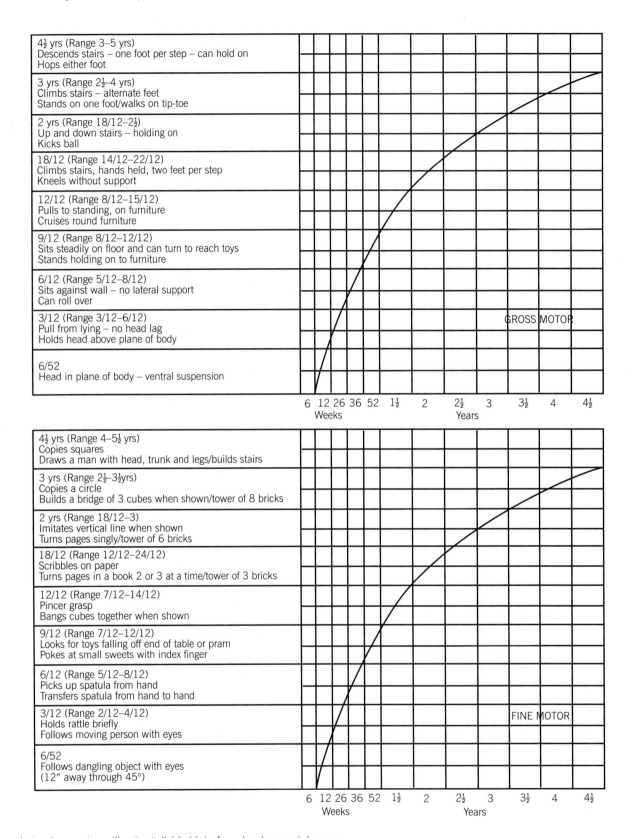

	6 12 26 36 52 1½ 2 2½ 3 3½ 4 4½

4½ yrs (Range 3–5 yrs)
Descends stairs – one foot per step – can hold on
Hops either foot

3 yrs (Range 2½–4 yrs)
Climbs stairs – alternate feet
Stands on one foot/walks on tip-toe

2 yrs (Range 18/12–2½)
Up and down stairs – holding on
Kicks ball

18/12 (Range 14/12–22/12)
Climbs stairs, hands held, two feet per step
Kneels without support

12/12 (Range 8/12–15/12)
Pulls to standing, on furniture
Cruises round furniture

9/12 (Range 8/12–12/12)
Sits steadily on floor and can turn to reach toys
Stands holding on to furniture

6/12 (Range 5/12–8/12)
Sits against wall – no lateral support
Can roll over

3/12 (Range 3/12–6/12)
Pull from lying – no head lag
Holds head above plane of body

6/52
Head in plane of body – ventral suspension

GROSS MOTOR

6 12 26 36 52 1½ 2 2½ 3 3½ 4 4½
Weeks   Years

4½ yrs (Range 4–5½ yrs)
Copies squares
Draws a man with head, trunk and legs/builds stairs

3 yrs (Range 2½–3½yrs)
Copies a circle
Builds a bridge of 3 cubes when shown/tower of 8 bricks

2 yrs (Range 18/12–3)
Imitates vertical line when shown
Turns pages singly/tower of 6 bricks

18/12 (Range 12/12–24/12)
Scribbles on paper
Turns pages in a book 2 or 3 at a time/tower of 3 bricks

12/12 (Range 7/12–14/12)
Pincer grasp
Bangs cubes together when shown

9/12 (Range 7/12–12/12)
Looks for toys falling off end of table or pram
Pokes at small sweets with index finger

6/12 (Range 5/12–8/12)
Picks up spatula from hand
Transfers spatula from hand to hand

3/12 (Range 2/12–4/12)
Holds rattle briefly
Follows moving person with eyes

6/52
Follows dangling object with eyes
(12″ away through 45°)

FINE MOTOR

6 12 26 36 52 1½ 2 2½ 3 3½ 4 4½
Weeks   Years

A development centile chart divided into four developmental areas

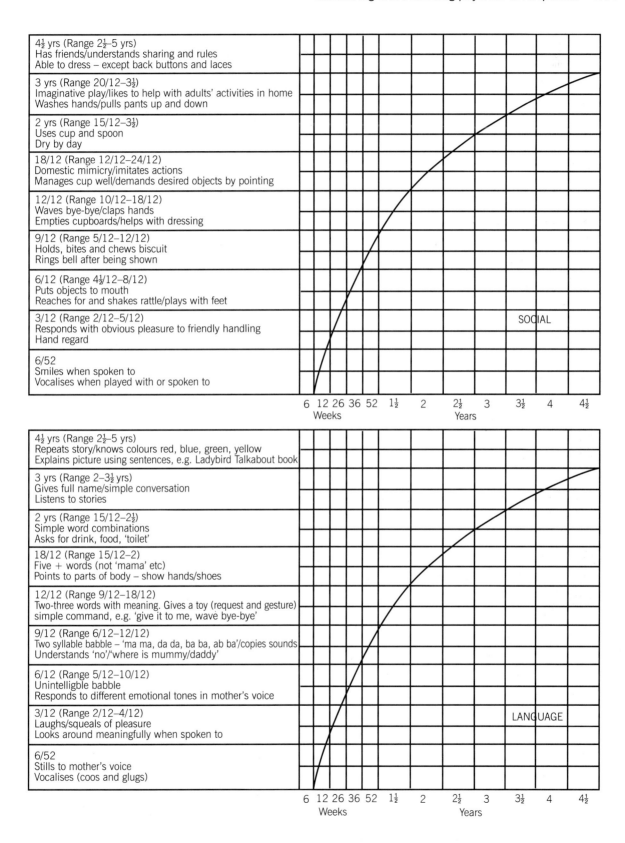

4½ yrs (Range 2½–5 yrs) Has friends/understands sharing and rules Able to dress – except back buttons and laces														
3 yrs (Range 20/12–3½) Imaginative play/likes to help with adults' activities in home Washes hands/pulls pants up and down														
2 yrs (Range 15/12–3½) Uses cup and spoon Dry by day														
18/12 (Range 12/12–24/12) Domestic mimicry/imitates actions Manages cup well/demands desired objects by pointing														
12/12 (Range 10/12–18/12) Waves bye-bye/claps hands Empties cupboards/helps with dressing														
9/12 (Range 5/12–12/12) Holds, bites and chews biscuit Rings bell after being shown														
6/12 (Range 4½/12–8/12) Puts objects to mouth Reaches for and shakes rattle/plays with feet														
3/12 (Range 2/12–5/12) Responds with obvious pleasure to friendly handling Hand regard												SOCIAL		
6/52 Smiles when spoken to Vocalises when played with or spoken to														

6 12 26 36 52   1½   2   2½   3   3½   4   4½
Weeks   Years

4½ yrs (Range 2½–5 yrs) Repeats story/knows colours red, blue, green, yellow Explains picture using sentences, e.g. Ladybird Talkabout book														
3 yrs (Range 2–3½ yrs) Gives full name/simple conversation Listens to stories														
2 yrs (Range 15/12–2½) Simple word combinations Asks for drink, food, 'toilet'														
18/12 (Range 15/12–2) Five + words (not 'mama' etc) Points to parts of body – show hands/shoes														
12/12 (Range 9/12–18/12) Two-three words with meaning. Gives a toy (request and gesture) simple command, e.g. 'give it to me, wave bye-bye'														
9/12 (Range 6/12–12/12) Two syllable babble – 'ma ma, da da, ba ba, ab ba'/copies sounds Understands 'no'/'where is mummy/daddy'														
6/12 (Range 5/12–10/12) Unintelligble babble Responds to different emotional tones in mother's voice														
3/12 (Range 2/12–4/12) Laughs/squeals of pleasure Looks around meaningfully when spoken to												LANGUAGE		
6/52 Stills to mother's voice Vocalises (coos and glugs)														

6 12 26 36 52   1½   2   2½   3   3½   4   4½
Weeks   Years

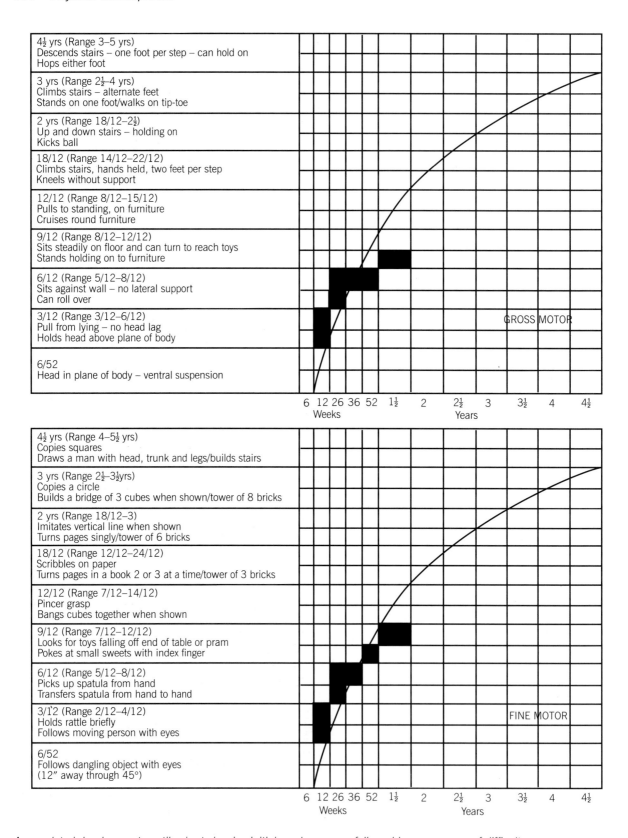

| | 6 12 26 36 52 | 1½ | 2 | 2½ | 3 | 3½ | 4 | 4½ |

4½ yrs (Range 3–5 yrs)
Descends stairs – one foot per step – can hold on
Hops either foot

3 yrs (Range 2½–4 yrs)
Climbs stairs – alternate feet
Stands on one foot/walks on tip-toe

2 yrs (Range 18/12–2½)
Up and down stairs – holding on
Kicks ball

18/12 (Range 14/12–22/12)
Climbs stairs, hands held, two feet per step
Kneels without support

12/12 (Range 8/12–15/12)
Pulls to standing, on furniture
Cruises round furniture

9/12 (Range 8/12–12/12)
Sits steadily on floor and can turn to reach toys
Stands holding on to furniture

6/12 (Range 5/12–8/12)
Sits against wall – no lateral support
Can roll over

3/12 (Range 3/12–6/12)
Pull from lying – no head lag
Holds head above plane of body

GROSS MOTOR

6/52
Head in plane of body – ventral suspension

6 12 26 36 52   1½   2   2½   3   3½   4   4½
Weeks   Years

4½ yrs (Range 4–5½ yrs)
Copies squares
Draws a man with head, trunk and legs/builds stairs

3 yrs (Range 2½–3½yrs)
Copies a circle
Builds a bridge of 3 cubes when shown/tower of 8 bricks

2 yrs (Range 18/12–3)
Imitates vertical line when shown
Turns pages singly/tower of 6 bricks

18/12 (Range 12/12–24/12)
Scribbles on paper
Turns pages in a book 2 or 3 at a time/tower of 3 bricks

12/12 (Range 7/12–14/12)
Pincer grasp
Bangs cubes together when shown

9/12 (Range 7/12–12/12)
Looks for toys falling off end of table or pram
Pokes at small sweets with index finger

6/12 (Range 5/12–8/12)
Picks up spatula from hand
Transfers spatula from hand to hand

3/12 (Range 2/12–4/12)
Holds rattle briefly
Follows moving person with eyes

FINE MOTOR

6/52
Follows dangling object with eyes
(12" away through 45°)

6 12 26 36 52   1½   2   2½   3   3½   4   4½
Weeks   Years

A completed development centile chart showing initial good progress, followed by some areas of difficulty

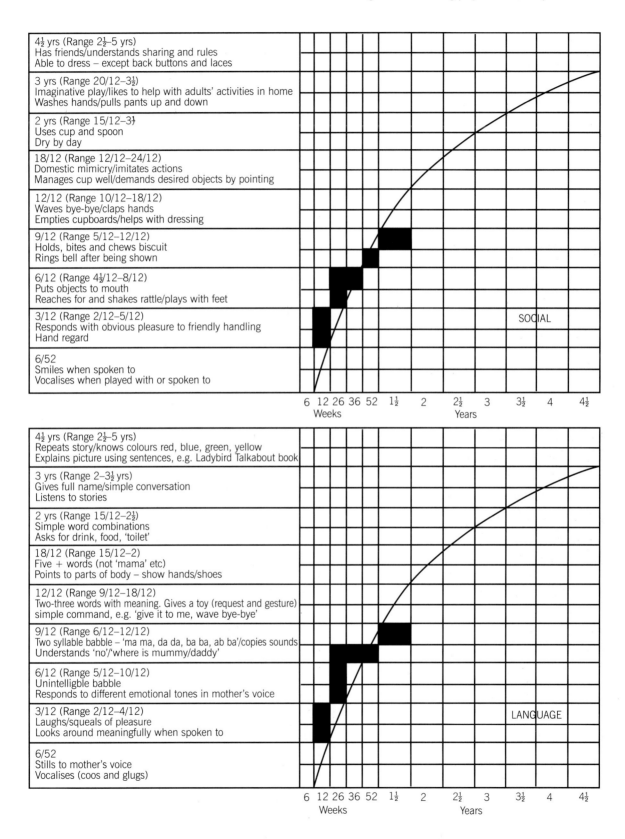

	6	12	26	36	52	1½	2	2½	3	3½	4	4½
4½ yrs (Range 2½–5 yrs) Has friends/understands sharing and rules Able to dress – except back buttons and laces												
3 yrs (Range 20/12–3½) Imaginative play/likes to help with adults' activities in home Washes hands/pulls pants up and down												
2 yrs (Range 15/12–3½) Uses cup and spoon Dry by day												
18/12 (Range 12/12–24/12) Domestic mimicry/imitates actions Manages cup well/demands desired objects by pointing												
12/12 (Range 10/12–18/12) Waves bye-bye/claps hands Empties cupboards/helps with dressing												
9/12 (Range 5/12–12/12) Holds, bites and chews biscuit Rings bell after being shown												
6/12 (Range 4½/12–8/12) Puts objects to mouth Reaches for and shakes rattle/plays with feet												
3/12 (Range 2/12–5/12) Responds with obvious pleasure to friendly handling Hand regard												SOCIAL
6/52 Smiles when spoken to Vocalises when played with or spoken to												

Weeks / Years

	6	12	26	36	52	1½	2	2½	3	3½	4	4½
4½ yrs (Range 2½–5 yrs) Repeats story/knows colours red, blue, green, yellow Explains picture using sentences, e.g. Ladybird Talkabout book												
3 yrs (Range 2–3½ yrs) Gives full name/simple conversation Listens to stories												
2 yrs (Range 15/12–2½) Simple word combinations Asks for drink, food, 'toilet'												
18/12 (Range 15/12–2) Five + words (not 'mama' etc) Points to parts of body – show hands/shoes												
12/12 (Range 9/12–18/12) Two-three words with meaning. Gives a toy (request and gesture) simple command, e.g. 'give it to me, wave bye-bye'												
9/12 (Range 6/12–12/12) Two syllable babble – 'ma ma, da da, ba ba, ab ba'/copies sounds Understands 'no'/'where is mummy/daddy'												
6/12 (Range 5/12–10/12) Unintelligble babble Responds to different emotional tones in mother's voice												
3/12 (Range 2/12–4/12) Laughs/squeals of pleasure Looks around meaningfully when spoken to												LANGUAGE
6/52 Stills to mother's voice Vocalises (coos and glugs)												

Weeks / Years

Progress check

1 Where should developmental assessments take place?
2 List four ways of recording development.
3 What are the benefits of using development centile charts?
4 Which professionals may use development centile charts?

Do this!   5.1

a) Read through the following health visitor's notes recording the development of three children.

Tahira, aged 6 months
Rolls both ways, sits for long periods with support. She adopts the crawling position but is not yet mobile. Grasps objects with a palmar grasp, transfers from hand to hand and puts to mouth. Attempts to grab objects out of reach. Plays with her feet. She is a happy baby who shouts and vocalises, laughing and enjoying sociable company.

Jack, aged 12 months
Sits unsupported for long periods of time. He bottom-shuffles at great speed. Palmar and pincer grasp seen. Helps with dressing. Waves goodbye. Bangs cubes together and gives toy when requested. Unintelligible babble constantly, no recognisable words.

Adil, aged 18 months
Walks confidently, runs and squats to collect toys from the floor. Walks upstairs with one hand held, crawls down backwards. Kneels. Kicks a ball. Builds a six-cube tower. Uses a cup and spoon and helps with household tasks, e.g. dusting and putting rubbish in the bin. Joining words to make simple sentences, asks for required objects.

b) Plot these children's development on the centile charts on pages 104–5.

c) What does the development centile chart show you about each child?

d) Are the children developing within the average range?

Think about it

Make a list of ways to stimulate each of these children to help them to continue their developmental progress.

Observing and recording development in a child-care establishment

Watching children play and observing their behaviour and social relationships reveals a great deal about their all-round development. A structured assessment in a child health clinic, or at home with the health visitor, does not usually provide such detailed insight into children's progress and achievements.

It is possible to observe without making judgements about children. Observations are factual and objective accounts of a particular child or group of children, written without making any value judgements.

Assessment of development is only possible after thorough training which includes observations of many children. To assess development, a knowledge of the particular child is required so that a child-care worker can:

- measure the child's current achievements against their previous skills
- observe the similarities with other children of a similar age/stage
- compare their progress with theory, including textbook statements about typical accomplishments at a particular age.

Methods of recording development in a busy workplace

All records should be as simple as possible and kept in a place where all staff can easily access them. There are a variety of methods of recording, but whichever one is used they should all be accurate and written down as soon as possible after the observation:

- *a skills checklist* – a list of average/typical accomplishments of children within the age-range of the group
- *information sheets about each individual child* – may be pinned to a wall or noticeboard so that all staff can quickly jot down anything of importance related to a specific child
- *the Individual Key Worker System* – involves making staff responsible for observing and assessing the development of a group of children in the establishment. Each key worker may have their own notebook or method of recording information about specific children.

All of these methods require transferral of the information to each child's individual records. Samples of their work and/or photographs of their play and achievements may also be included.

Referral procedures

To other establishments

Children will inevitably move to other establishments or different areas of the same school site for their education to progress. When they do, it is essential for child-care workers to inform their colleagues about the child's achievements in all areas of development to date. Written records can be sent directly to the new establishment, sent with parents or handed to the new carer/teacher during a visit to the new nursery, school or playgroup.

To relevant professionals

If a child's development is causing concern, or if there are any health problems with a particular child, this should be discussed sensitively with the parent or carer in the first instance. It may subsequently be necessary to discuss an individual child with the health visitor, school nurse or community paediatrician. This should always be with the parent's knowledge.

Involving parents

Parents and carers can be invited to complete a simple checklist about their child's development before they come into day care or start nursery or infant school. This will provide valuable information about the child's range of ability in all areas of development before they start in the establishment. Parents or carers may also welcome the opportunity to complete a home–establishment diary. This enables them to share their child's experiences and achievements at home with the child-care workers, whilst benefiting from receiving information about the care and education offered at nursery/school.

Giving parents information about reasonable expectations of their child and their child's peer group will also help them to be realistic about their child's progress. The experiences of home should ideally complement the experiences of a child-care establishment.

 Progress check

1 How can child-care workers assess development?
2 List three methods of recording development.
3 To whom should child-care workers give information about developmental observations and assessments?
4 Why is it important to involve parents in their child's progress at a child-care establishment?

Case study: Preparing for interview

Heather is a newly qualified nursery nurse. During her training she had been given time in her placements to observe children and to make notes during the observations. She compiled a portfolio of observations of children at varying stages of all the areas of development.

She has just received a letter to confirm her appointment as a nursery assistant with children aged 2–4 years at Larklands Day Nursery, a private establishment nearby. At her interview, the officer-in-charge had explained the nursery assistant's role in observing and recording development and the key worker system employed by the nursery. Heather will be responsible for monitoring the progress of eight children.

She is now feeling anxious because she knows that in a busy nursery where she is a member of staff, she will not be able to stand back and observe as she did as a student.

1 If you were in the same position as Heather, what would you do to prepare yourself for this new role?
2 How can Heather make sure that she records all the necessary developmental information about her group of children?

Key terms

You need to know what these words and phrases mean. Go back through the chapter to find out.

development centile chart
milestone
narrative

Now try these questions

1 Why should child-care workers be cautious about placing too much emphasis on the achievement of milestones?

2 Explain how and where development centile charts may be used.

3 Explain the role of the child-care worker in observing development.

6 Factors affecting physical development

This chapter includes:

- **Antenatal factors**
- **Perinatal factors**
- **Postnatal factors**

The development of physical skills is dependent upon good health and the absence of disease within an environment which provides the opportunity to learn and achieve. There are many factors which can have a positive or negative effect on a child's physical development and these influences begin at the time of conception, continue throughout pregnancy and birth and are also evident in childhood.

Child-care workers must have an awareness of the internal (inside the body) and external (outside the body) influences on health and development. With this information they are well-placed to provide an environment which promotes health and stimulates all areas of development.

The factors explained in this chapter are grouped according to the time that they occur: antenatal (occurring before birth), perinatal (occurring during birth) or postnatal (occurring after birth).

You may find it useful to read this chapter in conjunction with:

▶ **Book 1, Chapter 10**   An introduction to social and emotional development

Antenatal factors

Antenatal (before birth) influences on health include the general health of the parents before conception takes place, as well as the internal and external conditions during the pregnancy.

Heredity

Heredity means the transmission of characteristics from one generation to the next. Everybody is the product of their parents and bears physical resemblance to them. All children inherit most of their parents' physical features and the way their bodies function. This is because the genetic

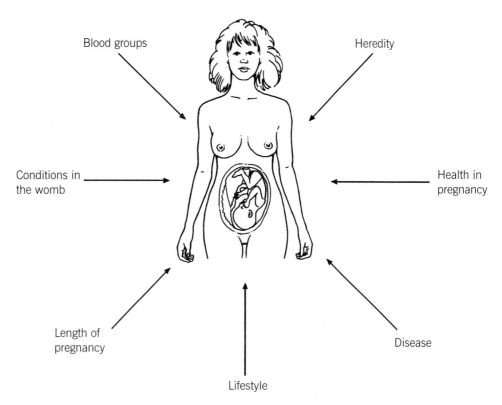

Blood groups

Heredity

Conditions in the womb

Health in pregnancy

Length of pregnancy

Disease

Lifestyle

Antenatal influences on pregnancy

chromosome
Long threads of DNA carrying hundreds of genes present in every human cell

DNA (deoxyribonucleic acid)
A chemical messenger containing genetic information found in the nucleus of every cell

gene
Detailed unit of inheritance carrying genetic information which is responsible for passing characteristics from generation to generation

sex chromosomes
The X and Y chromosomes which determine the sex of the child

information carried by the ovum (egg) and spermatazoon (sperm) influences a person's appearance and the way their body works.

In the centre of every cell in the body is a nucleus containing **chromosomes**, made up of **DNA (deoxyribonucleic acid)**.

A specific piece of genetic information is called a **gene**, and each chromosome carries many hundreds of genes. Except for identical twins, no two people have the same genetic information.

The nucleus of each ovum and sperm contains 23 separate chromosomes, the instructions for inheritance. When fertilisation occurs these chromosomes unite to make 23 pairs. One pair of chromosomes is called the **sex chromosomes** – they determine whether the baby will be a boy or a girl. They are called the X and Y chromosomes. Women only pass on the female X chromosome, but men pass on either the female X or the male Y chromosome. The XX combination results in a girl, the XY combination in a boy.

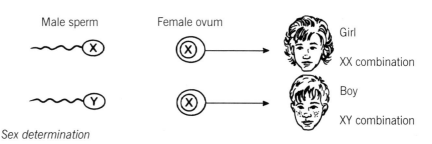

Male sperm Female ovum Girl
XX combination

Boy
XY combination

Sex determination

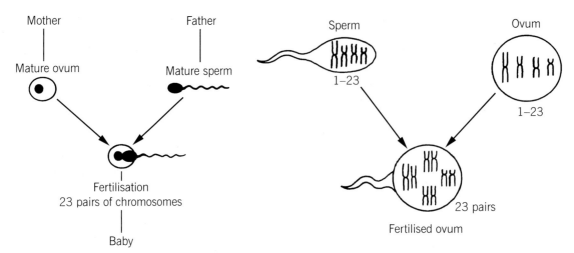

Genetic inheritance

So it is always the sperm which decides the sex of the baby. (Henry VIII's wives might have survived longer if he had been aware of this!)

The genes carry the information for characteristics which children will inherit from their parents. Just as the chromosomes pair up, so do the genes, each matching with a gene carrying similar information. The genes will influence characteristics such as height, eye colour, hair colour, skin texture and colour, as well as the physical development of such organs as the brain and muscles.

Of course, when they pair not all genes will necessarily carry the same information. If they do, then that message will be passed to the child; for example two genes for blue eyes will inevitably produce a child with blue eyes. If the parents have different coloured eyes, and pass on genes for different colours, then the **dominant gene** will determine the eye colour. The child will, however, still carry the information contained in the other

dominant gene
A powerful gene which dominates other genes at fertilisation

XX XX XX   XX XX
1   2   3   4   5

XX XX XX XX XX XX XX
6 7 8 9 10 11 12

XX XX XX   XX XX XX
13 14 15   16 17 18

XX XX   XX XX XX
19 20   21 22 X Y   Boy ☐ ♂

or

XX
X X   Girl ○ ♀
23

Note that the male Y chromosome is much smaller than the female chromosome

Normal human chromosomes

recessive gene
The weaker gene of a pair at fertilisation

gene and may pass this on to their own children: this is the influence of the **recessive gene**. This is the reason why two brown-eyed parents can produce a child with blue eyes, or how dark-haired parents can produce a child with red hair. It also explains how some characteristics may miss generations, and children can inherit the features of their ancestors.

People who have a recessive gene are called carriers, but this term usually describes people who carry a gene for a particular disease but are not affected by it themselves.

It will be useful here to examine exactly what happens when genes pair, and to see how the chances of passing on either dominant or recessive characteristics are worked out.

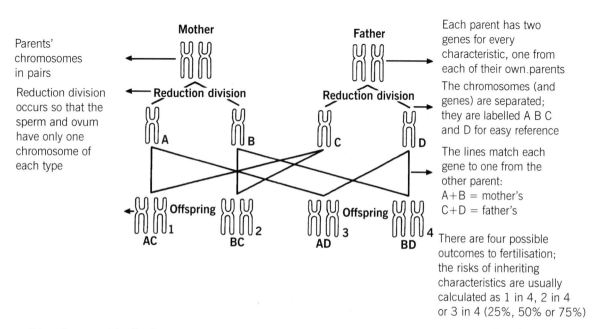

Parents' chromosomes in pairs

Reduction division occurs so that the sperm and ovum have only one chromosome of each type

Each parent has two genes for every characteristic, one from each of their own parents

The chromosomes (and genes) are separated; they are labelled A B C and D for easy reference

The lines match each gene to one from the other parent:
A+B = mother's
C+D = father's

There are four possible outcomes to fertilisation; the risks of inheriting characteristics are usually calculated as 1 in 4, 2 in 4 or 3 in 4 (25%, 50% or 75%)

The possible outcomes at fertilisation

Remember that each parent has two genes for each characteristic, but only one is present in the ovum or sperm. The pairings are entirely random.

Dominant inheritance

By matching up each gene with the genes of the other parent, it is possible to calculate the chances of dominant inheritance occurring with each pregnancy. In the example shown at the top of page 116, there is a 2:4 or 50 per cent chance. Remember that this can be applied to diseases passed on by dominant inheritance.

Recessive inheritance

If two brown-eyed parents both carry the recessive gene for blue eyes, there is a 1:4 chance of recessive inheritance with each pregnancy. There is a 2:4 chance of recessive genes being carried by the children. With each

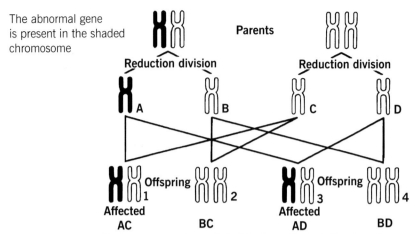

The abnormal gene is present in the shaded chromosome

Parents

Reduction division

Reduction division

A   B   C   D

Offspring 1   Offspring 2   Offspring 3   Offspring 4

Affected   BC   Affected   BD
AC   AD

Each pregnancy has a 1:2 risk of an affected offspring of either sex; thus AC and AD are affected (2:4)

Dominant inheritance

pregnancy the risk is the same, so it is possible for a couple to have four affected children or four unaffected children.

Using this combination, it is possible to see how a recessively inherited characteristic or disease could appear 'out of the blue', with no recent family history. Cystic fibrosis (CF) often appears this way. One in 20 of the white British population carries the recessive gene for CF; if two people carrying the same abnormal gene reproduce, they have a 1:4 chance of having a child with cystic fibrosis.

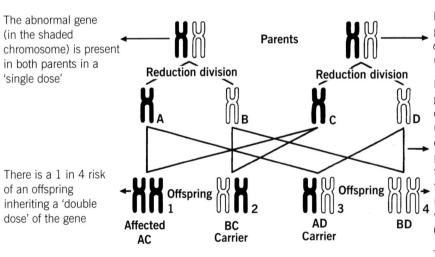

The abnormal gene (in the shaded chromosome) is present in both parents in a 'single dose'

The mother and father both carry a recessive gene. They are called *carriers* but may be unaware of its presence

Parents

Reduction division

Reduction division

A   B   C   D

Each chromosome (and gene) is labelled A, B, C or D. Each chromosome (and gene) is paired with one from the other partner; if you follow the lines you can see that each gene from the mother (A+B) is paired with one from the father (C+D).

There is a 1 in 4 risk of an offspring inheriting a 'double dose' of the gene

Offspring 1   Offspring 2   Offspring 3   Offspring 4

Affected   BC   AD   BD
AC   Carrier   Carrier

These are the possible combinations in the offspring:
• 1:4 Affected
• 2:4 Carrier
• 1:4 Unaffected

Recessive inheritance

> ## Think about it
>
> 1 Think of all the characteristics you have inherited from your parents.
> 2 Investigate a family in detail: your family or the family of a friend. Try to explain how the pattern of genetic inheritance has affected all the family members.

Sex-linked inheritance

sex-linked disorders
Characteristics and diseases inherited via the X (female) chromosome

Some diseases are carried by the genes on the female X chromosome. These are called **sex-linked disorders** or X-linked disorders. Because they are carried on the X chromosome, they almost always pass from mother to son. A healthy female X chromosome from the father will counteract any abnormality on the X chromosome from the mother, and daughters will be unaffected carriers. But the male Y chromosome is much smaller than the X chromosome (see the diagram *Normal human chromosomes* on page 114), and carries virtually no genetic information. This enables the genes on the affected X chromosome to be dominant and sons will be born with the particular condition.

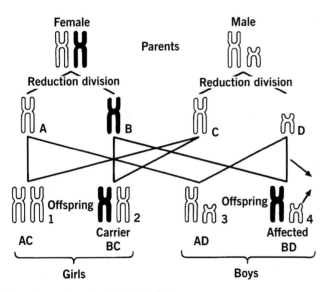

On one of her X chromosomes the mother carries an abnormal recessive gene. The father has normal X and Y chromosomes

If the baby is a boy, there is a 1:2 chance of him being affected
If the baby is a girl, there is a 1:2 chance of her being a carrier

Sex-linked inheritance: female parent carrier

You can see from the diagram above that with each pregnancy there is a 1:2 chance of:

■ each girl being a carrier or unaffected
■ each boy having the disease or being unaffected.

Haemophilia and Duchenne muscular dystrophy are passed on in this way, as is colour blindness. It is interesting to note that affected fathers cannot pass the disorder on to their sons. They can only pass the affected X on to their daughters, meaning that they will be carriers.

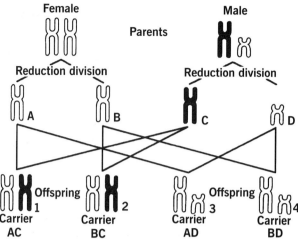

Sex-linked inheritance: male parent affected

The affected male's daughters are always carriers since he must pass on his X chromosomes with the abnormal gene (C) to female offspring AC and BC

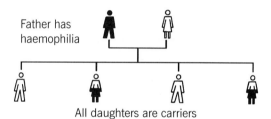

Haemophilia: the genetic inheritance pattern

Queen Victoria was a carrier of haemophilia and her daughters passed this on to the royal families of Russia and Spain, as the diagram below shows.

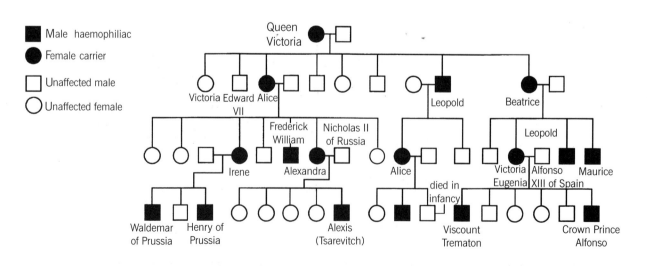

Queen Victoria's family tree, showing the incidence of haemophilia in the royal families of Europe

Case study: *Duchenne muscular dystrophy*

John Kingston, aged 3 years, has recently been diagnosed with Duchenne muscular dystrophy. His parents, James and Leila, are absolutely devastated. They feel responsible for his condition which is an inherited degenerative disease of the muscles. This sex-linked disorder only affects boys and the condition gets progressively worse as the muscles get weaker and weaker. They know that as John's walking becomes difficult he will need a wheelchair, and that the respiratory muscles and heart muscle will also weaken. Affected boys do not usually survive beyond their early twenties. James and Leila had always planned to have more children and Leila has just discovered that she is pregnant again.

1 Explain what sex-linked inheritance means.
2 What are the risks of future pregnancies resulting in boys who are affected with the disease or girls who are carriers?

Chromosomal abnormalities

Occasionally there is an error in the chromosomes. When they unite in the fertilised ovum, some may break. There may be too many chromosomes or not enough. Down's syndrome is a well-known chromosomal abnormality. It is also known as Trisomy 21 because there are three number 21 chromosomes instead of the usual two. Because of the large amount of genetic information carried on the chromosomes, any chromosomal malfunction will result in a general pattern of abnormality, affecting many of the systems of the body. Each chromosomal abnormality will produce a characteristic pattern of disabilities.

The chromosome pattern of a male infant with Down's syndrome

The chromosome pattern of a male infant with Down's syndrome. Note the presence of the extra number 21 chromosome, Trisomy 21.

Progress check

1 How are characteristics passed from parent to child?
2 What are the units of inheritance called?
3 What does XX and XY mean?
4 What is dominant inheritance?
5 What is the chance of recessive genes affecting a fetus?
6 How many pairs of chromosomes are there in a fertilised egg?

Do this!   **6.1**

1 Use a computer to make a family tree to show how the members of your household have inherited their hair and eye colour.

2 Find out about chromosomal abnormalities. Choose one and write about all the effects this may have on a child's development.

Health in pregnancy

Because the embryo develops rapidly in the first 12 weeks after conception, it is vital that parents give serious consideration to their health before pregnancy begins. The influence of many factors which could potentially affect the health of the child are operating before a pregnancy begins and in its very early stages. Doctors, midwives and health visitors provide preconceptual advice and may run clinics offering specific health-care advice before pregnancy.

Infections

placental barrier
The placenta's function in allowing the exchange of materials between mother and fetus

Some pathogenic (disease-causing) organisms are so small that they can cross the **placental barrier** from the mother's bloodstream to the baby's, causing developmental problems and sometimes death. These infections must be prevented if possible, to avoid the often disastrous effects on the postnatal development of the child.

Rubella, toxoplasmosis and listeriosis are pathogenic organisms that can have a catastrophic effect on the health of the child.

Rubella

rubella
A mild viral infection which damages the fetus in the first 12 weeks of pregnancy

Rubella (German measles) has been accepted and tolerated as a fairly mild and unavoidable childhood illness. It is fairly harmless to children, but it is very dangerous to pregnant women as it can damage the developing fetus during the first three to four months of pregnancy. It can result in deafness, blindness, heart disease or it may kill the fetus.

All pregnant women are screened for rubella antibodies. Babies are immunised at 12–15 months with the MMR (measles, mumps and rubella) vaccine, with a booster at $4\frac{1}{2}$–5 years, and schoolgirls may be immunised against rubella between the ages of 11 and 13 years if they have not had the pre-school immunisations. By preventing the illness in this way, it is less likely that women will contract the disease in pregnancy.

HIV and AIDS

AIDS (Acquired Immune Deficiency Syndrome) is caused by the Human Immunodeficiency Virus (HIV). A mother infected with HIV may pass this virus to her child through the placenta. The incidence of infected mothers having HIV infected babies is about 14 per cent. There is no evidence to suggest that the virus affects the embryo/fetus in the developmental stages. The child may be born with AIDS or develop it at any time. It may be weeks or years later. There is high risk associated with breast feeding and mothers who are known to be HIV positive or who have AIDS are advised to bottle-feed their infants. Because AIDS reduces the body's natural immunity, the child will easily become infected with many types of pathogenic organisms. They may even develop a specific type of cancer. There is no known cure for AIDS at present.

AIDS
Acquired Immune Deficiency Syndrome resulting from infection with Human Immunodeficiency Virus (HIV) which damages the immune system

Sexually-transmitted diseases

Sexually-transmitted diseases (such as gonorrhoea, syphilis or herpes) may affect the fetus, or the baby may become infected during the birth. All these diseases have effects on development.

Toxoplasmosis

Toxoplasmosis is caused by a parasite which infects cats who then shed infectious organisms in their faeces. Humans can catch it by changing cat litter trays and gardening without gloves on, by eating unwashed vegetables or raw, undercooked meat.

In pregnancy, the virus can attack the fetus, causing blindness, and it can damage the brain resulting in epilepsy and/or delayed intellectual development. In some European countries (though not in England), pregnant women are routinely screened for the disease.

toxoplasmosis
A disease caught from infected cat or dog faeces which can cross the placenta and affect the fetus

Listeriosis

Listeria is an organism which is often found in paté and soft cheeses like Brie and Camembert. It can cause the disease **listeriosis** which can damage the developing fetus.

listeriosis
A disease resulting from infection with the listeria virus which may damage the fetus

Cytomegalovirus

This infection may cause flu-like symptoms and cross the placenta to infect the fetus. The baby may develop hepatitis, inflammation of the brain and blindness. The developing child will usually have delayed motor skills and severe learning difficulties. Infected babies will excrete the virus in the urine for months and years and may infect pregnant women.

Other infections such as virulent strains of the influenza virus may cross the placental barrier.

Progress check

1 How can rubella be prevented in pregnancy?
2 Which organs might the rubella virus damage?
3 What is the name of the organism which causes AIDS?
4 How can a pregnant woman avoid getting toxoplasmosis?
5 Which sexually-transmitted diseases can affect the fetus?
6 From which sources might a person contract listeriosis?

Diseases

Diabetes

diabetes
A condition in which the body cannot metabolise carbohydrates

Diabetes is a condition in which the body does not produce enough **insulin** to enable it to use the carbohydrate (starch and sugars) eaten in the diet. The usual treatment is to inject the correct amount of insulin to enable the body to use the carbohydrate effectively. This requires a balance between insulin and carbohydrate which may be affected by pregnancy. During pregnancy this needs very careful control to monitor the mother and meet the needs of the fetus.

insulin
A hormone produced in the pancreas to metabolise carbohydrate in the bloodstream

Babies born to diabetic mothers can be much larger than average and be immature in their development. There is also a higher risk of **congenital** abnormality. (*See also* Chapter 18, page 327.)

Heart disease

congenital
A disease or disorder which occurs during pregnancy and is present from birth

A mother with heart disease may give birth to a baby prematurely or in poor condition. Both mother and baby need very special care in the antenatal period.

Toxaemia of pregnancy

toxaemia
A serious condition which only occurs in pregnancy and may damage the health of the fetus and the mother, also known as pre-eclampsia or, in its severe form, as eclampsia

Toxaemia only occurs in pregnancy. The word toxaemia means 'poisoned blood' and its diagnosis indicates the presence of toxins (poisons) in the blood which may affect the baby. The signs of toxaemia are:

- high blood pressure
- protein in the urine
- oedema (swelling of tissues) especially in the hands and feet
- rapid weight gain.

Mild toxaemia (pre-eclampsia) is common and is treated with rest and careful monitoring by the midwife and doctor. Severe toxaemia (eclampsia) can kill the mother and baby – the only cure is to deliver the baby quickly. This may be a very early delivery and the baby will have the associated problems of prematurity and will probably be **light-for-dates** as well (see *Length of pregnancy*, page 124).

light-for-dates
A baby who is smaller than expected for the length of pregnancy (gestation)

Lifestyle

The way the mother lives her life, the care she takes of her general health and the consideration she gives in pregnancy to the well-being of her baby will have an undoubted effect on the future development of her child.

Smoking

It is generally accepted that babies born to mothers who smoke during pregnancy will be smaller at birth than if the mother had not smoked. There is also a higher incidence of **premature** birth and intellectual delay.

premature
A baby born before 36 completed weeks of pregnancy

Smoking is associated with a large number of problems for children both before and after birth. Tobacco releases nicotine into the body which affects the growth and development of the baby. During pregnancy it can affect the developing embryo and fetus, causing the baby to weigh less at birth than it would have done if the mother had not smoked. There is also evidence to suggest that babies of smokers have reduced intellectual ability and are at a higher risk of Sudden Infant Death Syndrome (SIDS) or cot death, ear disease and admissions to hospital for respiratory illness.

Drugs

A drug is any substance taken into the body to produce a specific physical or psychological effect which is used for its effects on the way the body works. The word 'drug' includes nicotine in tobacco, alcohol, prescription medicines, over-the counter medicine, glue and solvents, as well as illegal drugs, such as heroin, cocaine and ecstasy.

Drugs cross the placental barrier and affect the baby. It is preferable to discontinue their use before pregnancy begins. Staff in a preconceptual clinic can advise future parents about services which are available to treat addictions and offer support and guidance. Some drugs which can be taken safely when not pregnant can cause deafness, cleft lip and palate or masculine features in female babies, if taken during pregnancy.

Doctors must be careful when prescribing drugs to pregnant women, and should avoid any that are known to have an adverse effect on the fetus. Thalidomide is a notorious drug which caused a lot of fetal damage during the 1950s and 1960s. This was prescribed by doctors to prevent morning sickness in pregnancy. It is better not to take any tablets or medicines during pregnancy unless absolutely necessary.

Mothers addicted to drugs like heroin, cocaine, barbiturates and valium will produce babies who are also addicted. They will need to be weaned off these drugs and may be delayed in their all-round development. Some babies suffer from epilepsy as a result of this condition.

Alcohol can also cross the placenta and heavy drinking can result in fetal alcohol syndrome, which is similar to alcoholism in adults with catastrophic results for the baby. Here, too, the baby would need to be weaned off the alcohol after birth. This condition affects fetal growth and causes delayed development, learning difficulties and congenital abnormalities. Even moderate drinking is thought to increase the incidence of miscarriage, minor malformations and slower development in childhood. Moderate drinking in pregnancy can result in an increased risk of miscarriage, minor malformations and slower development in childhood.

Caffeine is a substance found mainly in coffee, but it is also present in tea. It can be addictive and excessive amounts in pregnancy are thought to affect future development of the child.

Diet

Women are advised to take folic acid tablets (the recommended dose is 0.4 mg daily) for three months before pregnancy begins and for three months into the pregnancy. This vitamin is important in the formation of the brain and spinal cord and it is believed to prevent spina bifida and neural tube defects which occur in the early weeks of pregnancy.

The fetus is a parasite which means that it feeds from the mother and is totally dependent on her. The baby will always take the nutrients it needs, and if the diet is inadequate it is often the mother who suffers. She must eat a well-balanced diet to meet the needs of the fetus and to maintain her own health.

Work

Some occupations may be hazardous during pregnancy, especially those which involve contact with dangerous chemicals, radiation or radioactive materials, lead products or other dangerous substances. There is a higher risk of abnormality in the baby if the mother operates a VDU or is a computer programmer.

Exercise

Regular exercise is good for the mother and baby. High-risk sports should be avoided at the end of the pregnancy to avoid injury either to the mother or the baby.

 Progress check

1 What commonly used substances are also drugs?
2 What effect can these drugs have on a fetus?
3 Why is the mother's lifestyle important during pregnancy?

Length of pregnancy

The length of pregnancy in a human is 40 weeks. A baby born after 36–42 completed weeks of pregnancy is born *at term*. It is much better for the baby to be born at term, because then it will have completed all its fetal development and will be prepared for life outside the womb. A baby is viable when it is capable of sustaining life outside the womb. A baby born after 34 weeks will have a better chance of survival than a baby born at 26 weeks.

Sometimes babies are small or light-for-dates. This means that they do not weigh as much as expected for the length of time that they have been in the womb. A baby born at 36 weeks or before is *pre-term* or born early. Sometimes babies are both pre-term and light-for-dates. All these babies may have problems soon after birth which may affect their future development. Possible areas of difficulty may be:

hypothermia
A body temperature of less than 35° C

- breathing problems
- **hypothermia**
- bleeding in the brain
- low levels of sugar in the blood
- jaundice
- anaemia
- infection.

There may be many other complications which affect babies born too soon. It is usually true that the longer they have had to develop in the womb, the better their chance of a future healthy life. Neonatal intensive care is improving all the time and babies born at a very early gestational age are now surviving, but they may be affected by developmental delay.

 Progress check

1 What is the normal length of pregnancy?
2 When is a baby born at term?
3 Describe what is meant by pre-term and light-for-dates.
4 List five specific complications may affect a pre-term or light-for-dates baby.
5 What does viable mean?

Conditions in the uterus

The uterus (womb) is a muscular bag which should grow to accommodate the growing fetus, the placenta, the membranes and the amniotic fluid. There should be enough space for the baby to grow. There may, however, be more than one baby! Two, three or more babies may restrict movement and growth. Occasionally there is a fibroid, a fatty growth in the uterus, which may take up some of the baby's room. Another possible complication is that a contraceptive coil (IUCD) could remain in the uterus and might induce premature labour.

Blood groups

Everyone has a blood group inherited from their parents. The four main groups are A, B, O and AB. In addition, there is a substance found in the blood of some humans called the **Rhesus factor**. About 85 per cent of the population are Rhesus positive and about 15 per cent are Rhesus negative. The baby inherits two Rhesus genes, one from each parent. The Rhesus positive gene D is dominant. The Rhesus negative gene d is recessive.

During pregnancy fetal and maternal blood should not mix, but at delivery, or if a miscarriage has occurred, the baby's blood can enter the mother's system. The first pregnancy is usually straightforward, but second and subsequent babies may be affected if antibodies are allowed to

Rhesus factor
A specific factor in the blood of about 85 per cent of humans

anaemia
A condition in which the blood lacks adequate amounts of haemoglobin

jaundice
Yellowing of the skin and whites of the eyes as a result of too much bilirubin in the blood

form. If the mother is Rhesus negative and the baby Rhesus positive, the mother may react to the Rhesus factor in her baby's blood and make antibodies to attack the foreign cells (the Rhesus factor in the baby's blood).

The amount of damage can vary from mild **anaemia** and **jaundice** to haemolytic disease of the newborn, which is very serious and may require an exchange blood transfusion. Fortunately this situation is now very rare because regular blood tests during pregnancy can detect antibodies in the mother's blood. An injection of Anti-D (anti-Rhesus factor) can prevent the further formation of antibodies and protect the baby.

During birth some of the baby's Rh positive blood may pass into the mother's Rh negative blood. This may produce antibodies which can affect subsequent Rh positive babies

Rh antibody given after the birth of the baby destroys Rh positive red cells and protects any future Rh positive babies. This injection is called Anti-D

Severely affected Rhesus babies have an exchange transfusion to replace their Rh positive blood with Rh negative

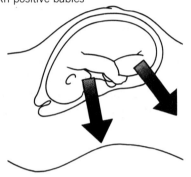
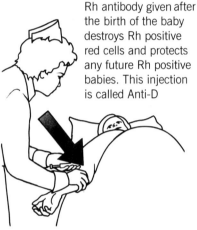
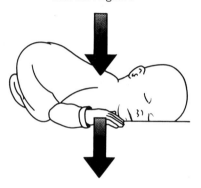

A Rhesus negative mother carrying a Rhesus positive baby

Do this! 6.2

Using your knowledge of dominant and recessive inheritance, work out the following patterns of transmission of the Rhesus factor and present your findings. Remember that the Rhesus negative gene is recessive.
a) Mother dd; Father DD
b) Mother dd; Father Dd
c) Mother dd; Father dd

✓ Progress check

1 What effects can diabetes have on the baby?
2 What does pre-eclampsia mean? Describe the signs of this disease.
3 What conditions in the womb could affect fetal growth and development?
4 What is the Rhesus factor?
5 What problems might the Rhesus factor cause in pregnancy?
6 What special care are Rhesus negative mothers given during pregnancy?

> ### Think about it
> 1 Think of routine tests and observations which may be carried out at antenatal clinics to detect the early signs of pre-eclampsia in pregnancy.
> 2 Think of jobs which may be unsuitable for a woman to undertake before or during pregnancy.

Perinatal factors

The birth process is much safer now than it was 100 or even 50 years ago. Improvements in antenatal care by trained midwives and doctors can prevent, detect and treat any abnormalities very effectively. The **infant mortality rate** and the **maternal mortality rate** (the number of mothers who die within a year of childbirth as a direct result of the pregnancy, labour or delivery) have declined, due partly to improved social conditions, but they remain higher than average in areas of deprivation (see *Mortality rates* on page 128).

It is, however, impossible to remove all the hazards at delivery: the unexpected can always happen and the delivery of a baby can only be called 'safe' when it is all over! Adverse events at delivery can be **fetal distress**, effects on the baby of anaesthetics or analgesics or an abnormal presentation.

> **infant mortality rate**
> The number of deaths in the first year of life calculated per number of live births

> **maternal mortality rate**
> The number of women who die as a result of pregnancy within a year of the birth

> **fetal distress**
> A condition of the fetus resulting from lack of oxygen, usually occurring during labour

> **anoxia**
> A deficiency of oxygen

Fetal distress

The baby may become distressed due to **anoxia**, lack of oxygen. If this persists it can cause damage to the brain. (Some cases of cerebral palsy are thought to be caused by anoxia.) This situation may require a quick delivery, using one of the following methods:

- forceps: spoon shaped cups put around the baby's head to lift it out
- ventouse extraction: a suction cap to pull the baby out
- Caesarian section: an incision into the uterus to remove the baby.

Anaesthetics and analgesics

A general anaesthetic, or painkillers, used too close to the birth may result in a baby who is slow to breathe and may require resuscitation.

Abnormal presentation

The most straightforward way for a baby to be born is head first, but sometimes babies present as bottom, legs and feet, face, shoulder or other part of the body coming first. This will prolong labour and may result in a tired mother and a shocked baby. Anoxia may occur during the birth.

The passage down the birth canal continues to be the shortest yet most hazardous journey humans ever make.

Mortality rates

Statistics are gathered yearly to assess the death rates for a range of conditions, i.e. the numbers of people dying from various causes. These figures are collated by the Office of Population, Censuses and Surveys (OPCS) and provide important information about the health of the nation. The rates which apply to children are:

- *stillbirth rate* – the number of babies born after two completed weeks of pregnancy with no signs of life. The number is calculated per 1,000 total births
- *perinatal mortality rate* – the number of babies dying in the first week of life. The number is calculated per 1,000 total births (and includes the number of stillborn babies)
- *neonatal mortality rate* – the number of babies dying in the first 28 days of life. The number is calculated per 1,000 live births
- *infant mortality rate* – the number of babies dying in the first year of life. The number is calculated per 1,000 total births. The infant mortality rate is an indicator of the health of the population. There are many countries which have lower mortality rates than the UK, so it seems that there are many improvements which could be made.

One hundred years ago, only six babies out of ten survived to adulthood. Today, the death of a child is usually unexpected and constitutes a great tragedy.

 Progress check

1 Why are pregnancy and birth safer now than they were 100 years ago?
2 What does the infant mortality rate mean?
3 What complications might arise at delivery?
4 What does anoxia mean ?
5 How may anoxia affect development?
6 What are mortality rates, and why are they collected?

Postnatal factors

Postnatal factors are those which affect a child from birth onwards. Everything that happens to a child throughout childhood can affect the progress they make.

This section describes some factors which are important to enable a child to maintain healthy growth and development.

Environment

A person's environment means their total surroundings: the family, the community and the country they live in, and must include their culture, religion and education. Children should always be seen in the context of their family and total environment, because of the many physical and social factors which have the potential to affect their health and development.

The amount of potential given to a child is decided by heredity (nature); the environment determines the extent to which that potential develops (nurture). If a child has the genetic information to grow to 150 cm, the outcome will not be affected by however much food, care and stimulation is provided; but these contributory factors will determine whether or not a child achieves their maximum, i.e. the best they can. By offering children the opportunity to fulfil their potential in all areas of growth and development, they are given a good basis for life (see Chapter 10 *An introduction to social and emotional development*).

Trigger factors

Environmental factors can sometimes act as a 'trigger' for a genetic predisposition to a certain condition. For example, a child may be born with a tendency to develop asthma because their parent(s) have the condition, but they do not become asthmatic until they come into contact with an irritant such as pollen. In this case the genetic predisposition is triggered by an environmental factor – pollen.

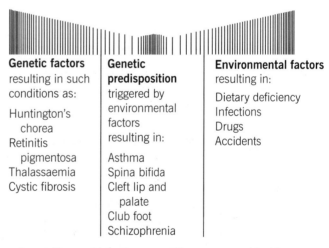

Genetic factors resulting in such conditions as:	**Genetic predisposition** triggered by environmental factors resulting in:	**Environmental factors** resulting in:
Huntington's chorea	Asthma	Dietary deficiency
Retinitis pigmentosa	Spina bifida	Infections
Thalassaemia	Cleft lip and palate	Drugs
Cystic fibrosis	Club foot	Accidents
	Schizophrenia	

Causes of disease

Inadequate nutrition and infections are still common world-wide

---

✓ *Progress check*

1 What decides the amount of potential given to a child?
2 What does the child's environment include?
3 Explain what a trigger factor is.
4 Explain the difference between nature and nurture.

Poverty

Since the beginning of the twentieth century, links have been made between poverty and negative influences on child health. Damp, inadequate and dangerous housing leads to poor health and illness by increasing the risk of accidents and encouraging the spread of infection. It is difficult to maintain adequate hygiene. The disadvantages associated with poverty, such as poor housing and overcrowding, have not been eradicated and social conditions continue to have negative effects on health and development today.

Poverty is not only about having no money – poor people experience deprivation and disadvantage in most areas of their lives. Poverty is more common in inner-city areas and children may be affected by 'multiple deprivation'.

Social disadvantage

People are described as disadvantaged if they do not have the equal opportunity to achieve what other people in society regard as normal. About two and a half million children live in poverty in the UK today. There is a well-established link between ill-health and social deprivation which can lead to low achievement at nursery and mainstream school. Children may lack a home environment which stimulates development. Children born into disadvantaged families are less likely to attend for screening services and their mothers are less likely to have received adequate antenatal care during pregnancy. National studies of child development have found that the children from disadvantaged families are on average 4 cm shorter than other children of the same age.

Pollution

Environmental pollution can seriously affect children's health and development. The most serious pollution occurs where there are large cities and many factories, so children who live in inner-city areas are more at risk from the pollution from car exhausts, industrial processes and dangerous discarded items. Children's bodies absorb toxic substances more quickly than adult's, and are slower to get rid of them. This, combined with the fact that children breath in twice as much air per pound of body weight than adults, makes them very vulnerable to the following types of pollution:

- chemical pollution
- air pollution
- radioactivity.

Unintentional (accidental) injury

Unintentional injuries are the commonest cause of death and injury to children. More children aged 1–4 years are killed or injured in road accidents – either as passengers in motor vehicles or as pedestrians – than in any other type of accident. This is closely followed by fire and flame injuries, drowning, inhalation and ingestion, falls, suffocation and poisoning. Social class can affect the chances of an accident occurring – some injuries are up to six times more common in the poorest areas compared to the most affluent.

Case study: Social deprivation

John and Frances Cooper and their three children had been rehoused in a high-rise block of flats after their house had been repossessed. John used to be a coal miner but had been unemployed for six years since the pit was closed. His local council could not provide the necessary accommodation, so the family had moved to a large town several miles away from their extended family.

The children were aged 10, 6 and 2 years. The youngest was born while the family lived in the flats and she had never been well, suffering from recurrent ear and chest infections. Money was tight and there never seemed to be enough for everything. Food was expensive from the local shops and the supermarket was 2 miles away. John and Frances sometimes went without meals so that the children could eat.

Frances was depressed about having no money, and John seemed to have given up looking for work. The family did not go out together any more and the stress of their situation lead to friction and arguments. Lack of space to play meant that when the two eldest children went out, Frances was glad to have some peace and quiet.

1 What problems associated with deprivation are this family experiencing?
2 Why are the two eldest children at risk when they go out?
3 What factors are affecting the health of this family?

Personal and community hygiene

hygiene
The study of the principles of health

Hygiene means more than keeping clean. It is the study of the principles of health. The World Health Organisation defines health as 'a complete state of mental, physical and social well-being'. This is a very difficult goal to reach, but children must be given the chance to have total health. This means that their health needs must be met so that they are given the opportunity to develop physically. Meeting a child's health needs means providing the opportunity for:

- a well-balanced diet
- rest and sleep
- exercise
- fresh air
- exposure to sunlight
- a safe environment to prevent injury
- protection from infection

- personal and communal cleanliness
- positive mental health and self-esteem
- constructive use of leisure.

These needs and the means of providing for them are explained elsewhere in this book.

Progress check

1 Why does poverty have a negative effect on children's health?
2 Explain what is meant by social disadvantage.
3 What does hygiene mean?
4 List six health needs.
5 What types of pollution are common in inner-city areas?

Think about it

Think about the reasons why social class may affect the risk of an accident occurring to a young child. Think of five different situations where a child may be unintentionally placed in a dangerous situation as a direct result of their environment.

Hormones

A hormone is a chemical substance which is made in one part of the body and carried in the bloodstream to act on tissues or organs in another part. It is a chemical messenger. Hormones are usually produced in **endocrine** (ductless) **glands**; these glands pass their secretions directly into the bloodstream, for distribution around the body to their 'target' organ.

Hormones have a direct and long-term effect on growth and development because they co-ordinate the body's response to the environment.

endocrine gland
A ductless gland which produces and stores hormones, releasing them directly into the bloodstream

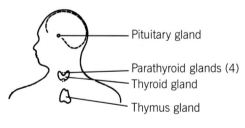

Pituitary gland

Parathyroid glands (4)
Thyroid gland

Thymus gland

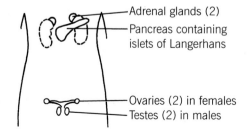

Adrenal glands (2)
Pancreas containing islets of Langerhans

Ovaries (2) in females
Testes (2) in males

Hormonal influences on development

Pituitary gland

The pituitary gland is the size of a pea and is situated at the base of the brain. It is called the 'master of the orchestra' of endocrine glands because it regulates, or controls, their hormone production. The hormones it produces affect:

■ the rate of growth (it can cause giantism or dwarfism if it produces too much or too little)
■ the development of the reproductive organs and secondary sexual characteristics
■ blood pressure
■ urine production.

Thyroid gland

The thyroid gland produces the hormone thyroxine. The function of thyroxine is to regulate:

■ general growth rate
■ bone development
■ the nervous system
■ muscle development
■ circulation
■ the function of the reproductive organs.

Insufficient thyroxine before birth causes cretinism with the following effects:

■ poor growth
■ slow movements and clumsiness
■ intellectual delay
■ a large and protruding tongue.

If the condition is recognised and treated early the child should progress to develop normally. The Guthrie test detects the amount of thyroxine in the blood so that treatment can be provided.

Parathyroid glands

The parathyroid glands produce the parathyroid hormone. Its function is to control the use of calcium and phosphorous. These are vital for healthy bones and teeth, for efficient muscle action and for blood clotting. Too much parathyroid hormone causes softening of the bones and weak muscles. Too little parathyroid hormone causes painful muscle cramps.

The pancreas

The pancreas produces the hormone insulin. Its function is to control the amount of sugar in the bloodstream. Too little insulin causes diabetes mellitus (see page 122). (*See also* Chapter 18, page 327.)

Adrenal glands

The adrenal glands produce the hormones adrenalin and cortisone. Their function is to control certain body minerals affecting growth and assist sexual maturation.

Adrenalin is the 'fight or flight' hormone which is active at times of stress. It provides the strength to fight or the energy to run away!

The testes and ovaries

The testes in the male produce the hormone testosterone, and the ovaries in the female produce oestrogen and progesterone. The function of these hormones is to control the development and functioning of the reproductive organs.

Infections and immunity

Several childhood illnesses can affect growth and development. Some of them are controlled by an immunisation programme:

- diphtheria
- tetanus
- whooping cough (pertussis)
- polio
- Hib meningitis
- measles
- mumps.

immunity
The presence of antibodies which protect the body against infectious disease

Before birth a baby is protected by the mother's **immunity**: her antibodies to infections pass through the placenta into the baby's bloodstream. After birth, babies need to develop their own immunity which depends upon their own immune system.

- The thymus gland produces thymic hormone which helps children to make antibodies. This gland is large in childhood but shrinks away during adult life.
- Tonsils and adenoids are areas of lymphatic tissue which protect the child from infection. They are the first line in defence in the respiratory tract, as they are situated in the throat and at the back of the nose. They can become enlarged and cause discomfort for some children, but doctors now prefer not to remove them because they have such an important function in fighting infection. They too shrink in size in adulthood.
- Leucocytes (white blood cells) fight infection throughout life.

Case study: The effects of pollution

Jason lives near the centre of a large industrial city, with commuter and commercial traffic filling the air with smoke and fumes. He is an asthmatic child who was diagnosed when he was 2 years old, after a year of repeated chest infections. At times his mother says she can smell and taste the pollution. This area has one of the highest rates of asthma in the region and 17 children per 1,000 are admitted to hospital each year with severe respiratory problems associated with asthma. Only 10 children per 1,000 from a nearby leafy suburb are similarly affected. In the heat of the summer the air is heavy, the heat of the sunshine acts on polluting gases to form a summertime smog.

1 Why do you think this area has such a high rate of childhood asthma?
2 How do you think the air quality in inner-city areas could be improved?

Progress check

1 What is a hormone?
2 What type of gland produces hormones?
3 Why is the pituitary gland important?
4 Which gland produces thyroxine?
5 What are the functions of thyroxine?
6 Which hormone is produced in the pancreas?
7 What is the function of adrenalin?
8 Which hormones do the testes and ovaries produce?
9 Which diseases are controlled by immunisation programmes?
10 How can children develop their own immunity?

Think about it

1   Think of as many ways as you can of meeting the health needs of children.
2   What might be the results of the failure to provide for a child's health needs?

Do this!   6.3

Using the information gained from this chapter, write a letter to a friend who is planning to have a baby, informing her of how she can achieve the best of health before becoming pregnant and how she can maintain this good health during pregnancy.

Include explanations of how she can avoid health problems before the baby is born and prevent illness in the baby after birth.

Key terms

You need to know what these words and phrases mean. Go back through the chapter to find out.

AIDS	chromosome	(DNA)
anaemia	congenital	diabetes
anoxia	deoxyribonucleic acid	dominant gene

endocrine gland	insulin	recessive gene
fetal distress	jaundice	Rhesus factor
gene	light-for-dates	rubella
hygiene	listeriosis	sex chromosomes
hypothermia	maternal mortality rate	sex-linked disorder
immunity	placental barrier	toxaemia
infant mortality rate	premature	toxoplasmosis

Now try these questions

1 Explain the importance of attention to health during pregnancy.

2 Which infections are potentially dangerous to the fetus during pregnancy and why?

3 How can knowledge about environmental influences on health help the child-care worker to meet children's needs?

4 Choose one factor from each of the groups (antenatal, perinatal and postnatal) which affect development. Describe the possible positive or negative influence these factors can have on a child's developmental progress.

Part 2: Language and Cognitive Development

This part of Book 1 looks in detail at the way in which children acquire skills of communication (language development) and at the growth of their thinking and understanding skills (cognitive development) and at how these language and cognitive skills are interlinked and interdependent in the pattern of development. The work and influence of theorists who have contributed to our understanding of this area are examined alongside their relevance to current child-care practice.

Adults have a critical part to play in assisting the acquisition of language and cognitive skills through their interactions with children and through the provision of experiences and activities to promote development in these areas. It is because of this key role in influencing and assisting development that it is important for the child-care worker to have an understanding of all aspects of language and cognitive development.

7 An introduction to language and cognitive development

This chapter includes:

- **What are language and cognitive development?**
- **Influential theorists**
- **Nature versus nurture**

This chapter looks at the work of theorists who have made significant contributions to our understanding of children's language and cognitive development. It also examines the way in which the development of cognitive and language abilities are interlinked and considers how both nature and nurture might influence children's development in these areas.

You may find it helpful to read this chapter in conjunction with:

▶ **Book 1, Chapter 8** Language development
▶ **Book 1, Chapter 9** Cognitive development

What are language and cognitive development?

language development
The development of communication skills, which includes non-verbal communication as well as spoken language

cognitive development
The development of thinking and understanding, which includes problem-solving, reasoning, concentration, memory, imagination and creativity

Examining the work of theorists, particularly psychologists, who have used scientific methods to study children's **language development** and **cognitive development** helps us to understand the sequence and pattern of growth in these areas. The conclusions made from such studies are far-reaching: the way that we organise and provide for the care and development of young children is directly influenced by the findings of research.

It is very difficult to examine and understand children's cognitive development without looking at the way that language develops alongside it. The link between the development of language and the child's ability to think and understand in an ever more complex way is very clear. As children grow up and become aware of the variety of experiences that surround them, they need to organise their thoughts, to make connections and to pose questions about what they experience. Language is the tool that human beings use to understand and interact with these experiences: as their powers of language increase, so do their abilities to make some sense and order of the world. Language is necessary for us to move away from the limitations of thinking and understanding in simple concrete images: it offers us the possibilities of complex abstract and symbolic thought.

Think about it

What does the word 'movement' mean to you when you hear (or read or write) it? Ask others in your group to share their thoughts.

Did you all have the same response? Did some of you respond with a concrete image; for example a wheel turning, a child running? Were some responses more abstract, for example, a dizzy feeling after a roundabout ride, the Green Movement?

None of these responses is right or wrong. The range of answers shows how language enables us to link common threads in apparently unconnected examples to form an idea of 'movement'.

concept
The way in which a range of knowledge and experiences can be organised, understood and referred to. Concepts can be simple, for example *wet*, *long*, *red*, or complex and abstract, such as *love*, *freedom*, *justice*

Language enables us to conceptualise, that is to organise our knowledge and experience into the **concept** of, for example, 'movement'. Without the ability to use language to order and define our experience, our understanding and thinking would be very limited indeed.

The development of children's language and thinking go hand in hand and must be considered alongside each other.

 Progress check

1 What do you understand by the term cognitive development?
2 Why are cognitive and language development linked?
3 Explain why language is necessary to enable us to think in complex ways.
4 What do you understand by the term concept? Give an example of a concept.

developmentalists
Psychologists whose work demonstrates that learning is linked to clearly defined stages of development and that children proceed through these at varying speeds

behaviourists
Psychologists whose work demonstrates that learning takes place because actions are reinforced positively, through reward, or negatively, by punishment

Influential theorists

The following pages give brief outlines of some of the major figures whose work has been very influential in the field of child care. Further reference to some of these figures is made in the subsequent chapters of this section.

The first group of psychologists discussed below are known as the **developmentalists** – their theories have at least one thing in common, that learning is linked to clearly defined stages of development and that children proceed through these at varying speeds. There are other perspectives on how and why children learn. One of these approaches is that of the **behaviourists**, who hold that learning takes place through a process called *conditioning*, that is where a particular response or behaviour is established through the experience of the outcome that is associated with it.

The developmentalists

Sigmund Freud

Sigmund Freud lived and worked in Vienna. He began his work at the end of the nineteenth century and continued until his death in 1939. He was a physician who was interested in examining the minds of his patients whilst trying to identify the cause of their physical symptoms. He used the techniques of hypnosis, dream analysis and free association. This same approach is used in psychoanalysis today and Freud is often referred to as 'the father of psychoanalysis'. Freud's methods and findings were very controversial at the time. He is most famous for recognising the influence of the unconscious or subconscious mind on human behaviour. One of the methods he used to prove the existence of the unconscious mind was to examine 'slips of the tongue', arguing that the unconscious mind was responsible for making these remarks, often against the wishes and interests of the conscious mind. Nowadays we refer to such remarks as 'Freudian slips'.

Freud is also influential in the field of child care because of the links he made between the the development of the personality in later life with early childhood experiences, and the significance and influence of the child's relationships with parents and carers. Much of Freud's work has been criticised, even ridiculed, but our recognition of the importance of impressions and experiences gained during the early years to the child's subsequent development is as a direct result of Freud's work.

Susan Isaacs

Susan Isaacs was much influenced by Freud's work. Her research, based on the observations she made of the children she worked with at the Malting House School in the 1920s and 1930s, analysed the contribution that play experiences could make to children's intellectual development, providing a theoretical foundation for nursery education. Through her observations she recognised the wide range of differences in children's needs and abilities and identified the important role that stimulating play, involving first-hand experiences, had in promoting all aspects of development.

Jean Piaget

Jean Piaget (1896–1980) was Swiss and a biologist by training. He observed his own children at play and then a wider sample of other children. He used these observations as the basis for his theory of cognitive development which identified that children pass through distinct stages in the development of their understanding and that certain kinds of experiences are appropriate and within the child's grasp at each stage. He also stressed the importance of the child's interaction with the environment as a crucial factor in learning.

Piaget's work has been criticised and many of his findings challenged. In spite of this, the child-centred environment provided by most early years settings is a result of the influence of his work on children's intellectual development. Piaget's theory of intellectual development is examined in detail in Chapter 9, pages 180–9.

Lev Semyonovich Vygotsky

Vygotsky was a Russian psychologist whose studies of children's learning were carried out in the 1920s and 1930s. Vygotsky's work looked at the importance of the social world in children's learning and emphasised that learning can be promoted through social interaction and communication. He also examined the way that children's early writing develops as they move from drawing objects to drawing speech. (*See also* Chapter 8, page 160 and Chapter 9, page 189.)

Jerome Bruner

Jerome Bruner concluded from his studies that adults can support or 'scaffold' children's learning and that this support enables the children to succeed with tasks that they are incapable of achieving alone. Scaffolding is put up around a building to support it whilst it is being built. Once the building is secure, the scaffolding can be removed and the building stands alone. Similarly, the adult 'scaffolds' the child in a new or unfamiliar task. Having achieved with support, the child may then attempt and succeed at the task without adult support.

Noam Chomsky

Chomsky's research into theories of linguistic development was published in the 1960s and 1970s. His findings conclude that human beings are born with all the complex physical and intellectual requirements needed for language and that these are triggered as the child matures.

The behaviourists

Ivan Pavlov

Pavlov's work is based on his experiments with dogs. The dogs became so familiar with the bell that was rung before their food was set down that they would salivate at the sound of the bell before the food appeared, in anticipation of this food. The dogs were conditioned to associate the bell with food so that their reflex response to the food (salivation) was triggered by its ringing. This type of response is called *classical conditioning*. Only behaviour which is mainly automatic, like reflexes, can be conditioned in this way, so this theory does not have any significant bearing on how children learn.

B. F. Skinner

The basis of Skinner's theories is his work with rats who had to learn to press levers to obtain food. He found that the rats learned how to press the levers and that this behaviour was reinforced by receiving the reward of the food pellets. The rats soon learned that to obtain another reward (food) they would have to perform the task again. These kinds of experiments resulted in the theory of *operant conditioning* which holds that if the subject performs a desired behaviour which is then reinforced with a reward for a sufficient number of times, then the behaviour will become established and no longer dependent on reward. Just about any kind of behaviour can be conditioned in this way and the technique has an obvious application in behaviour modification programmes. Positive **reinforcement**, where behaviour that is desired is rewarded, has been shown to be more effective than negative reinforcement which punishes undesirable behaviour. This is because punishment may limit an unwanted behaviour but it will not reinforce a positive behaviour to replace it.

reinforcement
Responding to an action or behaviour so that a particular consequence – a reward or punishment – is associated with the action and it is repeated (positive reinforcement) or not (negative reinforcement)

Case study: Rewarding behaviour

The Year 1 class had a tiny cloakroom and the pegs were very close together so that children found it difficult to hang coats up securely. Coats were often thrown on the floor in the scramble to get out to the playground or in the rush to get back into the classroom after lunch. The cloakroom was untidy and coats were getting wet and dirty.

Loraine, the nursery nurse student, decided to take some action and made a 'smiley face' chart and introduced this on the next Monday morning. The children were told that their helpfulness in keeping the cloakroom tidy would be monitored and that those who were judged to be helpful would have a smiley face sticker with their name underneath entered on the chart. That week Loraine spent a lot of time in the cloakroom encouraging tidiness and reminding children about the chart. All the class joined in, keen to report their own and other children's helpfulness. At the end of each day stickers were awarded and entered on the chart. By the end of the week there was a marked improvement and Loraine and the class teacher thought that they had solved the problem.

Loraine went back to college the next week. The class teacher had less time to spend in the cloakroom and on the project as she was on her own with the children and very busy. When Loraine came back for her next placement week she was disappointed to find the same old chaos in the cloakroom.

1 What principles was Loraine using to try to change the children's behaviour?
2 What did the adults do to encourage the desired behaviour?
3 Why do you think the children slipped back into their old ways when Loraine went back to college? What should she do now?

Extending knowledge and influencing practice

Taken on their own, none of the psychological studies examined briefly here can explain all of the complexities surrounding how and why children learn. By considering some of these findings we can see the influence of these thinkers on the way that we approach children's learning. Our knowledge about the way in which children learn does not stand still: studies are continually examined and re-evaluated so that those who work with children can make informed decisions about what they do and why they do it.

 Progress check

1 Why are Freud's findings important to those who work with children?
2 What is Piaget's theory of cognitive development?
3 What is the difference between the developmental approach to children's learning and that of the behaviourists?
4 Why does the research of theorists have a bearing on the way that we care for children?

Nature versus nurture

Are children born with a genetically determined intellectual capacity or does the environment they are born into encourage the development of these abilities? This is the essence of the **nature–nurture debate** that can be relied upon to provoke much discussion amongst those who have the responsibility for promoting children's learning.

Those who are persuaded by the nature side of the argument say that intelligence is innate and that the child's genetic inheritance determines intellectual achievement and, to some extent, personality.

The supporters of the nurture case hold that it is the quality of the child's environment in the crucial early years that has much to do with the growth of intelligence.

The case study and questions which follow may make the debate appear more simple than it really is: it is likely that it is the interaction of nature and nurture together that plays a significant part in children's subsequent achievement. Scientists are continually finding out more about the factors that make us who and what we are, and there are almost daily discoveries which link ever more aspects of our lives to our genetic inheritance. As child-care workers we have no influence on the child's 'nature', but it is our role and responsibility to provide a rich and stimulating environment that will 'nurture' all children and enable them to fulfil their potential.

nature–nurture debate
Discussion as to whether genetic factors (nature) or environmental factors (nurture) are the more important in influencing behaviour and achievement

Case study: A musical family

Rachel's parents have always been interested in music. Her mother is a music teacher at the local school and teaches the piano to pupils at home. Rachel's father has a large collection of records and CDs of all kinds of music and conducts a local choir in his spare time. There is always music playing in the house, coming from the CD-player or from the piano. Rachel, at 6, is already showing a real interest in music. When listening to music, she can repeat the rhythm and comments on changes in tone and pitch. She can already play a few simple tunes on the piano and is interested in the way that tunes can be written down on sheet music.

1 Do you think Rachel's musical ability is genetically determined?
2 What factors in Rachel's 'nurture' do you think contributed to her enjoyment of music?
3 Which factor do you believe is more important?

Do this!   7.1

1 Discuss the case study above with another student.

2 Think of two more case studies and write down factors that you might put for both the nature and the nurture sides of the argument.

3 Re-read the section and, in your own words, write down why you think the nature–nurture debate is relevant to those who care for children.

✔ Progress check

1 What is the nature–nurture debate?
2 Which factors are part of a child's 'nature'?
3 What contributes to the child's 'nurture'?
4 What can child-care workers influence, the child's nature or their nurture?

Key terms

You need to know what these words and phrases mean. Go back through the chapter to find out.

behaviourist
cognitive development
concept
developmentalist
language development
nature–nurture debate
reinforcement

Now try these questions

1 Explain why there is close link between the development of children's language and cognitive abilities.

2 Why is the work of theorists who have studied the way that children learn important to those who work with children?

3 Outline the main differences between the developmentalist and the behaviourist approach to understanding how children learn.

4 Summarise the nature–nurture debate. In the light of this, what is the role of the child-care worker in ensuring that children achieve their potential?

8 Language development

This chapter includes:

- **What is language?**
- **Bilingualism**
- **Psychology and language development**
- **Sequence of language development**
- **Talking with children**
- **Planning for children's language development**

Language is the way in which human beings communicate. We live in a very complex world and, therefore, we need a complex method of communication. With language, we communicate information, feelings, needs, thoughts and ideas. Unlike animals, we are born with an ability to acquire language, but children's experiences after birth are vital in their language development.

From birth, children experience language all around them, and in the first few years of life they develop and refine their skills. A rich language environment, and effective interaction between adults and children, are important for a child successfully to develop language skills. By the age of 8, the majority of children can use language to think and store information, to speak, to listen, to read and to write.

You may find it helpful to read this chapter in conjunction with:

▶ **Book 1, Chapter 7**   An introduction of language and cognitive development
▶ **Book 1, Chapter 9**   Cognitive development

What is language?

Language is the main way in which human beings communicate. We are the only species which has the ability to use language. Other species do communicate, but in ways specific to their needs, for example by making their fur stand on end to communicate danger, by spraying their territory to mark it out or by growling to deter attackers.

Humans live in a very complex world and need a complex system of communication. Language is this complex system. Language is also needed to satisfy the human need to communicate feelings, complex needs, thoughts and ideas.

Spoken language is a structured set of sounds; written language is a structured set of symbols. These symbols are shared and understood by everyone who speaks the same language. For example, consider the word *pain*. In English, this means suffering or distress. In French (and pronounced *pan*), it means bread. Therefore, what the symbols *pain* mean to an individual, and how the word is pronounced, depends upon which language the individual has been brought up to speak.

Language is learned, and the ability to operate well within society is affected by the ability to use language effectively.

There are different forms of language (see the diagram below) which are used at different times for different situations. The ability to use all these expressions of language requires a high level of skill. Young children need the opportunity to acquire these skills.

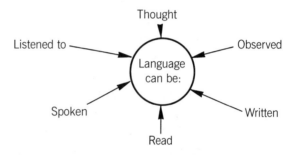

The forms of language

Think about it

1 Which of the skills shown in the diagram above would you expect a nursery-aged child to have?
2 Which of these skills would you expect an infant-aged child to be developing?
3 Why do you think there is a difference in these answers?

Spoken language

The raw materials of spoken language are sounds. These sounds come together to form words. Combinations of words are brought together in special and complex ways to form sentences. The meaning in a sentence is communicated by the way in which words are combined. Look at these sentences:

The dog bites the man.

The man bites the dog.

The same words are used each time, but because the order of the words is altered in the second sentence, so the meaning is altered.

To ensure that there is a shared understanding of what is being said, there are some rules that everyone needs to learn and use. These include pronunciation and grammar.

Pronunciation and grammar

Pronunciation
This is the way that words are said. It may vary depending on which part of the country a person comes from. These accents add interest and diversity to language, and the variations are not usually so different that people cannot be understood.

Grammar
To be able to communiate exactly what is meant, the speaker must normally use the correct grammar.

For most children, the ability to pronounce words correctly and to use appropriate grammar are acquired in the same way as other language skills. Children need good role models, the opportunity to use their language skills and positive feedback to adjust and refine these skills. Occasionally, however, some children have difficulties with pronunciation which may require help from a speech therapist. It is important to be aware of these children's needs and to seek help for the child.

Think about it

1 How many accents can you recall? Can you identify which part of the country they come from?
2 Are some accents thought to be 'better' than others? How might people be stereotyped because of their accent? What do you think about this stereotyping?
3 Consider the following sentences.
   a) 'The table is in the classroom.' How would you say that there is more than one table?
   b) 'I am playing my guitar.' How would you say this if you did this yesterday? Think of two ways of saying this.
   c) 'I run across the road.' How would you say this if it happened an hour ago?
4 Think carefully about how you changed the sentences above. What did you change? How did you know what to change?
   Once you have learned these rules you rarely get them wrong when you are speaking, even if you cannot identify the grammatical rules.

Non-verbal communication

When people are speaking and listening, there are many clues besides the actual spoken words which are picked up to help us interpret the interaction:
- tone of voice
- body posture (how and where we stand or sit)
- gesture, body movements (such as a shrug)
- facial expression
- eye contact.

This non-verbal communication may have several functions. It may:

- replace speech, for example a finger on the lips
- signal an attitude, for example yawning when someone is talking to you
- aid verbal communication, for example pointing when saying 'that one'
- express emotion, often evident in facial expression.

As with other aspects of language, there is a general shared understanding of non-verbal signals. However, they are often sent out, received and understood without us being consciously aware of them.

Case study: Non-verbal communication

As nursery began, Ruby burst into the room. 'I'm 4,' she shouted. The nursery nurse went over to Ruby and knelt down beside her. He spent a few minutes talking to her about her birthday, her presents and the party she was going to have later that day.

1 Why was it important that the nursery nurse knelt down to talk to Ruby?
2 How else, non-verbally, might he have communicated his interest in what Ruby had to say?

It is important to realise that there are some cultural differences in non-verbal communication which could result in misunderstanding. In some cultures, for example, children are expected to avoid eye contact when being addressed by an adult, whereas other cultures might interpret such behaviour as insolence on the part of the child.

Listening

Although most people are born with the ability to listen and take it for granted, it is in fact quite a complex skill. Listening involves sifting out and selecting relevant information from all the sound around us.

Like all other skills, children need to practise listening carefully. This demands good powers of concentration. This skill is often called *active listening*.

Case study: Developing listening skills

Amarjit planned a story session based on 'Goldilocks and the Three Bears'. She planned to read the story to the children and then retell it using a storyboard.

First, she read the story all the way through. Then, she showed the children the storyboard pictures and characters: Goldilocks, three bears, three bowls, three spoons, three chairs and three beds.

Then she read the story again and asked the children to look out for the bears, bowls, chairs, etc. As the children identified them, Amarjit put them on the storyboard, sequencing the story.

Lastly, Amarjit asked the children to tell her the story using the storyboard.

1 How did Amarjit encourage the children to listen carefully?
2 How did she check that the children were listening carefully and selecting the relevant information?

Do this!   8.1

1 List other activities in a nursery which involve active listening.

2 What is your role in these activities?

3 How would you make sure that the children have been listening carefully? This needs to be achieved in a positive way, for example through an activity or discussion that enables a child to demonstrate their understanding.

Thinking

Language is the main tool that human beings use for thinking. Thinking can be done without language, but at a very simple level: we can recall pictures, images and tactile sensations. However, these ways of thinking and recalling information are not complex enough for all that is demanded of human beings. A more flexible and efficient way of using and manipulating information in many different ways is needed: language is this flexible and efficient way of thinking.

Language development and cognitive development are therefore very closely linked.

Think about it

Many concepts are stored in the memory and recalled as a word. A whole range of meanings are recalled by one word.
a) What do these words mean to you:
   ■ movement?
   ■ shape?
   ■ sound?
b) Did you recall a range of meanings for each word?
These words mean many things and would, therefore, be impossible to store as one picture or image.

Do this!   8.2

a) Ask other people what meanings the words 'movement', 'shape' and 'sound' have for them.

b) Prepare, process and present this information in the form of a chart or graph.

Written language

Letters, words and sentences are symbols used to represent the spoken word. The understanding of these symbols has to be shared with people who speak and write in the same language. For example, in English this combination of symbols:

APPLE

is used to represent this object:

In Punjabi, this combination of symbols: ਸੇਬ is used to represent this object.

So that there is a shared understanding of how to write, there are rules which everyone needs to learn. In English, there are the following rules.

- You write on each line from left to right.
- You start at the top left-hand corner.
- The spacing between the letters in words and between the words in sentences is standardised.
- Words are spelled in the same way each time they are written down.
- Appropriate punctuation and grammar are usually necessary.

Some of these rules will be different in other languages.

Before a child can begin to learn to write, they need to develop a wide range of concepts and skills. These include:

- fine motor control – good hand–eye co-ordination and manipulative skills
- visual discrimination – the ability to see similarities and differences
- auditory discrimination – the ability to hear similarities and differences, especially between alphabet sounds
- sequencing – sorting, matching, patterning and sequencing items and pictures will eventually enable a child to do the same with letters and words
- an awareness of the need for writing and reading
- an ability to symbolise – this is the ability to use one thing to represent another. Children develop this skill in their play – they may use a doll to represent a baby, cuddling and feeding it, or a box to represent a car or a spaceship. Eventually, this skill can be transferred to writing, which is using squiggles (symbols) on a page to represent the spoken word.

Play activities in the nursery enable children to develop these skills and concepts. Children need plenty of opportunities, practice and encouragement to achieve this, before beginning to write.

As children's understanding about writing develops, many will begin to make writing-type marks on a page and will often tell you what it says. This is sometimes called *emergent* or *early writing*. This is an important stage of development and provides evidence that children have acquired many of the skills and concepts outlined above.

Case study: Developing writing skills

As part of the nursery's topic on 'Our Town', the role-play area was a hairdressers. As well as all the equipment that a hairdresser needs, the staff had provided an appointments book and cards.

Naomi, a trainee in the nursery, became involved in the children's play by going to the hairdressers to book an appointment. She asked for an appointment and encouraged Tim, a child playing in the area, to look in the appointments book, identify a time and write down her name. She then asked for an appointment card so that she did not forget the time that she should come. Again, Naomi encouraged Tim to write this down.

1 When did Tim use his early reading and writing skills?
2 How did Naomi encourage Tim to use these skills?
3 What was Tim learning about the needs and uses of reading and writing?

Reading

Once language is written down, it can be read by making sense of the symbols. As with writing, there is a range of skills and concepts that children need to acquire before learning to read. Many early skills and concepts are common to both reading and writing:

- visual discrimination
- auditory discrimination
- an ability to sequence
- an awareness of the needs and uses of reading and writing
- an ability to symbolise.

In addition, a child who is learning to read needs to be able to listen to, share and enjoy stories and to understand how books are organised. For example, young children need to understand that:

- the reader progresses from left to right
- the top left-hand corner is the starting point

and later that:

- there are patterns in words that reflect sound (phonics) and shape (look and say)
- punctuation ensures that the text makes sense.

These rules are learned over a period of time and children need plenty of practice at them.

bilingual
Speaking two languages

multilingual
Speaking many languages

It is important to note that these rules do not apply to all languages, and that **bilingual** and **multilingual** children may be learning to read and write languages with different conventions.

Do this!   *8.3*

1 Investigate how these rules are different in other languages.

2 How may this affect a child's acquisition of written English?

3 Go for a walk in your local area. Make a note of all the different ways that you can see or hear language being used. (Do not forget thinking!)

✓ *Progress check*

1 Identify the different aspects of language development.
2 How do children learn appropriate grammar and pronunciation in their spoken language?
3 What is non-verbal communication and why is it important?
4 How can children be encouraged to listen carefully?
5 Why do we need language to think and to store information?
6 a) Identify the skills and concepts that children need before they begin to read and to write.
   b) List some play activities that could be provided to develop and refine these skills.
7 a) What are the standardised rules in reading and written English?
   b) Why is it important that children learn and understand these rules?

Bilingualism

Many children in the UK today come from families that are bilingual or multilingual, where English is not the first or the only language used. A child may grow up in an environment where English is never spoken, where English is sometimes spoken or where English is used between some members of the family, while others converse in one or more other languages.

In order to participate fully in any experiences offered, the child will need to develop confidence and fluency in th language used in the child-care setting. This can only be achieved if child-care workers have an awareness and understanding of the child's linguistic (language) background. With this sensitivity, appropriate provision can be made for the development of language skills in English, while recognising those that the child has already achieved in their first or home language.

Language is an integral part of the cultural heritage of any group. In some situations, a family may use English for all their daily needs and not use the language of their cultural heritage on a regular basis. However, to ensure that the next generations understand and appreciate the breadth and depth of their culture, some minority groups encourage their young people to learn the language.

Children who are deaf, or who have members of their family who are deaf, may have **British Sign Language (BSL)** as their first or preferred language. This is a distinct, visual, gestural language which has a structure and grammar that are quite different from those of spoken English. As BSL does not have a written form – although line drawings of individual signs can be found in some children's books – BSL speakers use English in its literate forms, i.e. for reading and writing. BSL should not be confused with **Makaton**. BSL is a sophisticated language form which allows discussion of complex and abstract issues; Makaton is a system of simple signs used for communication with people with learning disabilities linked to very limited language skills.

British Sign Language (BSL)
The visual, gestural language of the British deaf community

Makaton
A system of simple signs used with people who have limited language skills

Do this!   8.4

Investigate the linguistic background of a group of people by asking which languages they can use. This can include languages that they are not necessarily fluent in, for example a language studied at school or an initial sign language course attended. The group could be your group at college, your staff team or any other group.

Collect the information and record the number of people in the group who are bilingual, multilingual and monolingual (who only use one language). Present your findings as a pie chart, using appropriate computer software, if available.

Consider your findings. What conclusions do you arrive at?

Identifying the needs of bilingual children

It is neither helpful nor accurate to categorise all bilingual children as having the same needs or experiences. What they do have in common is the experience of using and needing to use more than one language, but there will be other factors that may be quite different.

Case study: Bilingual situations

■ Seven-year-old Shahnaz's grandparents settled in the UK from Pakistan in the 1960s. She has grown up in an extended family where her parents speak to her in English, and where she converses with her grandparents in Punjabi. At school, she talks in English with teachers and sometimes in Punjabi to her classmates. After school, she also learns to read and write in Arabic, the language of the Qur'an.

■ Dieter is the 4-year-old son of a German student on a two-year study programme. He attends a suburban playgroup where the playgroup workers are encouraging him to use his few words of English. His mother usually speaks to him in German, but is also introducing more English at home.

■ Anna, a 6-year-old from Manchester, has moved to rural mid-Wales where her parents have opened a restaurant. All of the children in her class speak Welsh as their first language and, although there are some lessons in English, Welsh is the main language of the school and of the playground.

■ Dinh is 3 years old. His family are refugees from South-East Asia, housed in temporary bed-and-breakfast accommodation. Dinh attends a local authority day nursery and is very withdrawn. His parents communicate with the staff through an interpreter, but this service is not often available.

■ Maria's parents are profoundly deaf. She is hearing, but she uses BSL with her parents at home and with their friends at the Deaf Club. At nursery and with her brother, she communicates in spoken English.

■ Raheel is a 5-year-old from a Bangladeshi family. He has recently moved to a small village school from a large city school where many languages were spoken and valued. His last teacher felt that he was progressing well. In his new school, he is the only child for whom English is a second language. There is no ESL (English as a Second Language) support for him and he is slipping behind in his school work.

1 Read the case studies again.
2 What similarities are there in these experiences?
3 What differences are there?
4 Consider each individual child. What are the needs of each one?

Meeting the needs of bilingual children

It is important that the needs of children whose first language is not English are understood and met in the child-care setting. All children will experience some feelings of anxiety on the first days in an unfamiliar setting, such as school or playgroup. These anxieties are bound to be increased if the child is surrounded by an unfamiliar linguistic environment as well. If such children are to benefit from their experiences in nursery, school or day care, staff need to make sure that they understand, build on and value the children's first language (home language or mother tongue) capabilities.

You need to remember the following points.

■ Many children who do not speak English fluently are very capable in their first language.

■ Do not label children who speak little or no English as having language problems or language delay. Their lack of competence is in English, not language.

■ A child may be able to use language to conceptualise in their first language, but not in their second language.

■ The non-verbal language of English (the intonation, rhythm, use of gesture and eye contact) may be quite different from that of the child's first language.

■ A bilingual or multilingual child will thrive in an atmosphere where language diversity is valued.

■ Speaking more than one language is a positive attribute and should be regarded as such.

■ Fluency in a spoken language does not necessarily imply literacy in that language. Many people may not be able to read and write in an language that they can, nevertheless, speak fluently.

Any child unable to communicate in the language of the child-care setting (English, in most of the case studies above) will be disadvantaged. Specialist help needs to be available to ensure that the child learns and practises English. Given the right kind of support and an attitude of understanding from the staff, the child will soon acquire the necessary skills in English that are needed to take full advantage of all that is going on.

In our enthusiasm to get children competent in their second language, we should ensure that the development of the first language is fostered too. Studies show that children who are given an opportunity to develop their first language to an advanced level can transfer reading and writing skills to their second language quite readily. However, children who are required to tackle the complex skills of reading and writing in a language that they do not understand will often have difficulty in making similar progress.

Support for bilingual children

The kind of support available for bilingual children varies a great deal from one area to another. Funding is available from the Home Office via the local authority to support the needs of children from the New Commonwealth, defined as those whose families come from the Indian sub-continent or from the Caribbean. This means that there are many bilingual children who are excluded from this source of support: those from EU countries, for example, who rely on local initiatives to provide services to support their acquisition of English.

Here are some examples of the kinds of support that might be available.

■ *English as a Second Language (ESL) staff* These are teachers and classsroom assistants – often nursery nurses – who work alongside members of staff in schools and nurseries where there are children who would benefit from a one-to-one relationship and small group work to develop English skills. Where there are substantial numbers of children whose first language is not English, a member of an ESL team may be assigned to a particular establishment. In other cases, where there are fewer such children, a number of sessions per week might be allocated.

■ *Mother tongue (or home language) teachers or assistants or language instructors* Some local authorities employ staff whose job is to support and encourage the acquisition of the child's first (or home) language. This builds on the process that has already begun at home and allows for the growth of confidence and skills in language and in thinking.

- *Bilingual assistant (often a nursery nurse)* These assistants are usually employed in an establishment where many of the children have a common first language. The assistant works alongside the other staff, translating instructions and information for the children and also sharing stories, nursery rhymes or games, allowing the child access to the whole curriculum. The bilingual assistant can provide reassurance for the child and can be helpful in supporting a flow of information to and from parents, particularly when settling children into new situations.

- *Saturday or community schools* These are usually run by members of a local community, including parents, who are anxious that the cultural identity of the community is maintained by keeping the language alive. This is particularly true for children who are the second generation of their family to have been born in the UK. These schools sometimes have a role in religious instruction too.

Case study: Valuing language diversity

The playgroup reflected the cultural diversity of the local community in its intake of children, and within the group there was a substantial number of children whose first language was Gujerati, alongside an English-speaking majority. The playgroup made links with a local Asian Women's Project and were offered the services of Nialah, a trained Gujerati-speaking worker, for some weekly sessions.

Initially, Nialah concentrated on those children who spoke Gujerati, presenting activities and sharing stories with them in their own language. As their confidence grew, she worked alongside them in activities that were presented in English, developing and supporting their understanding in their second language. At carpet time, Nialah sometimes told a story or taught a rhyme in Gujerati for all the children to hear. Nialah's presence was very helpful to Gujerati-speaking parents, particularly when their children first started at the group and they wanted to ask questions or pass on information. After only a few weeks, the playgroup staff noted the difference that Nialah's sessions had made both in terms of the children's confidence and learning and in the involvement of the Gujerati-speaking parents involvement with the playgroup.

1 How did Nialah's involvement help the Gujerati-speaking children in the playgroup?
2 What benefits did the children's parents gain from Nialah's work in the playgroup?
3 What did all the children gain from being introduced to stories and rhymes in Gujerati?

> ### *Do this!*   8.5
>
> Find out how support is provided locally for children for whom English is a second language by asking staff in your own placement (or workplace) and finding information from other kinds of settings.

Language diversity

We are part of a world where there are many different languages, accents, dialects and other ways of communication, both written and spoken. It would be limiting for children only to be aware of their own language and ignorant of the existence of others. By promoting a positive atmosphere that celebrates language diversity, we can enhance the language experience of all children while at the same time valuing that of the bilingual child. This is an enriching experience for all children and is of as much benefit to the child in the monolingual environment as it is to the child who is already surrounded by many languages.

The following ideas are suggested for promoting language diversity in a child-care setting. It is important to value language diversity everywhere, not just in establishments where a variety of languages are spoken.

- Present welcome signs and greetings in a variety of languages.
- Choose dual-language books for your book corner (include sign language too). Draw children's attention to the differences in text and script.
- Teach songs and nursery rhymes in a number of languages. Get help from parents and friends if you need it.
- Make books for children in their own language.
- Listen to tapes of songs and poems and stories in many languages.

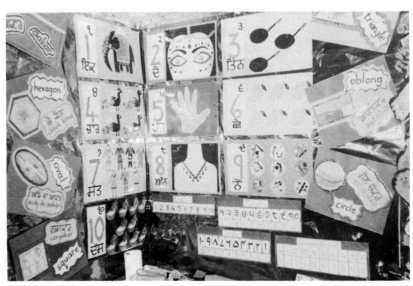

Promoting language diversity in the child-care setting

- Make a display of printed materials containing as many different languages and scripts as you can find. Get children to help by bringing in things from home.
- Choose stories from all around the world. Find someone who can tell the story in another language; tell the English version alongside this.
- Encourage children to learn simple greetings in languages other than their own.

Try to think of some more ideas to add to this list.

Do this! 8.6

1 Think of a setting that you are familiar with – a nursery, playgroup or infant school classroom – and suggest some ways of providing an environment there that would promote language diversity.

2 Draw a diagram and include on it any ideas that you have which would increase the children's experience of language diversity. Identify children and adults on the diagram and suggest what they might be doing.

✓ Progress check

1 What do you understand by the terms bilingual, multilingual and monolingual?
2 What is the role of language in maintaining the cultural identity of a community?
3 How can the child-care worker help to meet the needs of children whose first language is not that of the setting?
4 What kind of support is available to young children who speak English as a second language?
5 Why is it important for child-care workers to value and promote language diversity as part of their work with children?

Psychology and language development

Many psychologists have studied and researched how human beings acquire language. Some have concluded that language is predominantly a genetically inherited skill. Others believe that language is learned after a child is born. This is part of the nature–nurture debate (see page 144).

Vygotsky observed that children progress from drawing things to drawing speech

The nature–nurture debate on language

Nature		Nurture
Our ability for language is genetically determined.	Language is learned after we are born through a process of reinforcement.	Social interaction is important in the acquisition of language skills.
Noam Chomsky Chomsky believes that we are born with all the appropriate physical and intellectual capabilities for the acquisition of language: ■ speech-producing mechanisms: tongue, lips, palette, breath control ■ the intellectual ability to understand complex grammar ■ parts of the brain that enable understanding of language. He calls this a **Language Acquisition Device (LAD)**.	B.F. Skinner When children utter sounds and words which are part of the language that they will eventually speak, they are greeted with a positive response. This positive response is the reinforcement. It encourages the child to repeat the sound or word. Sounds and words that are not part of the language that the child will eventually speak are not reinforced and are therefore extinguished. This is called operant conditioning.	L.S. Vygotsky Vygotsky stressed the importance of the relationship between speech and writing. He saw children's early attempts at writing as significant. Children progress from drawing things to drawing speech (see the illustration page 159). This will not initially be recognisable as writing, but conceptually children have understood what writing is: the setting down or drawing of speech. This development occurs through interaction and communication with other people.

> **Language Acquisition Device (LAD)**
> The name Chomsky gives to our innate physical and intellectual abilities that enable us to acquire and use language

The nature–nurture debate on language is inconclusive. It seems likely that learning language has elements of both nature and nurture: there is some genetic sensitivity to language, but that children's experiences after birth are very important in their development of language.

 Progress check

1 What is the *nature* argument for language acquisition?
2 What is Chomsky's LAD?
3 What is the *nurture* argument for language acquisition?
4 How does operant conditioning relate to language acquisition?
5 Why is children's drawing important in the development of language skills?
6 Read about the nature–nurture debate on language acquisition again. What are the problems associated with each argument?
7 Decide for yourself what you think is the combination of nature and nurture in children's language acquisition. Give reasons for your answer.

Sequence of language development

Children's language develops through a series of identifiable stages. These stages are sequential, as outlined in the table on pages 161–3. The level of children's development depends partly on their chronological age, but their experience of language from an early age is, however, just as important a factor. If children are exposed to a rich language environment, this will be reflected in their language development. Children who have not had this opportunity will not have had the same chances for development. It is important to take this into account when assessing a child's stage of language development.

Children who are bilingual may develop their languages at a slightly slower rate than children who are monolingual. This is to be expected as they have much more to learn. Given an environment that promotes language development, bilingual children will become proficient in both languages.

The sequence of language development: Birth to 5 years

Approximate age	Developmental level
Birth	Involuntary cry
2–3 weeks	Signs of intentional communication: eye contact
4 weeks onwards	Cries are becoming voluntary, indicating, for example, unhappiness, tiredness, loneliness Children may respond by moving their eyes or head towards the speaker, kicking or stopping crying
6 weeks onwards	Children may smile when spoken to Cooing and gurgling begin in response to parent or carer's presence and voice, also to show contentment
1–2 months	Children may move their eyes or head towards the direction of the sound
3 months	Children will raise their head when sounds attract their attention
4–5 months	Playful sounds appear: cooing, gurgling, laughing, chuckling, squealing; these are in response to the human voice and to show contentment Children respond to familiar sounds by turning their head, kicking or stopping crying Shout to attract attention
6 months	The beginning of babbling: regular, repeated sounds, e.g. *gegegegeg*, *mamamam*, *dadada*; children play around with these sounds. This is important for practising sound producing mechanisms necessary for later speech Cooing laughing and gurgling become stronger Children begin to understand emotion in the parent or carer's voice Children begin to enjoy music and rhymes, particularly if accompanied by actions
9 months	Babbling continues and the repertoire increases Children begin to recognise their own name May understand simple, single words, e.g. *No*, *Bye-bye* Children continue to enjoy music and rhymes and will now attempt to join in with the actions, e.g. playing pat-a-cake
9–12 months	Babbling begins to reflect the intonation of speech Children may imitate simple words. This is usually an extension of babbling, e.g. *dada* Pointing begins. This is often accompanied by a sound or the beginnings of a word. This demonstrates an increasing awareness that words are associated with people and objects
12 months	Children's vocabulary starts to develop. First word(s) appear, usually names of people and objects that the child is familiar with. They are built around the child's babbling sound repertoire Children understand far more than they can say. This is called a *passive* vocabulary. Spoken words are referred to as an active vocabulary They begin be able to respond to simple instructions, e.g. 'Give me the ball', 'Come here', 'Clap your hands'

continued

The sequence of language development: Birth to 5 years *continued*

Approximate age	Developmental level
15 months	Active vocabulary development remains quite limited as children concentrate on achieving mobility Passive vocabulary increases rapidly Pointing accompanied by a single word is the basis of communication
18 months	Children's active vocabulary increases; this tends to be names of familiar things and people Children use their language to name belongings and point out named objects Generalisation of words is difficult, e.g. cat can only be their cat, not the one next door One word and intonation is used to indicate meaning, e.g. cup may mean, 'I want a drink', 'I have lost my cup', 'Where is my cup?'. The intonation (and possibly the situation) would indicate the meaning to people who are familiar with the child Children will repeat words and sentences
21 months	Both passive and active vocabularies rapidly increase; the passive vocabulary, however, remains larger than the active Children begin to name objects and people that are not there: this shows an awareness of what language is for Sentences begin. Initially as two word phrases, e.g. *Mummy gone*, *Coat on* Gesture is still a fundamental part of communication Children begin asking questions, usually *What?*, *Who?* and *Where?*
2 years	Both active and passive vocabularies continue to increase Children can generalise words but this sometimes means that they over-generalise, e.g. all men are daddy, all furry animals with four legs are dog Personal pronouns (words used instead of actual names) are used, e.g. *I, she, he, you, they*. They are not always used correctly Sentences become longer although they tend to be in telegraphic speech, i.e. only the main sense-conveying words are used, e.g. *Mummy gone work*, *Me go bike* Questions are asked frequently, *What?* and *Why?*
2 years 6 months	Vocabulary increases rapidly; there is less imbalance between passive and active vocabularies Word use is more specific so there are fewer over- and under-generalisations Sentences get longer and more precise, although they are still usually abbreviated versions of adult sentences Word order in sentences is sometimes incorrect Children can use language to protect their own rights and interests and to maintain their own comfort and pleasure, e.g. *It's mine, Get off, I'm playing with that* Children can listen to stories and are interested in them
3 years	Vocabulary develops rapidly; new words are picked up quickly Sentences continue to become longer and more like adult speech Children talk to themselves during play: this is to plan and order their play, which is evidence of children using language to think Language can now be used to report on what is happening, to direct their own and others' actions, to express ideas and to initiate and maintain friendships Pronouns are usually used correctly Questions such as *Why?*, *Who?* and *What for?* are used frequently Rhymes and melody are attractive
3 years 6 months	Children have a wide vocabulary and word usage is usually correct; this continues to increase They are now able to use complete sentences although word order is sometimes incorrect Language can now be used to report on past experiences Incorrect word endings are sometimes used, e.g. *swimmed, runned, seed*

continued

The sequence of language development: Birth to 5 years *continued*

Approximate age	Developmental level
4 years	Children's vocabulary is now extensive; new words are added regularly Longer and more complex sentences are used; sentences may be joined with *because*, which demonstrates an awareness of causes and relationships Children are able to narrate long stories including the sequence of events Play involves running commentaries The boundaries between fact and fiction are blurred and this is reflected in children's speech Speech is fully intelligible with few, minor incorrect uses Questioning is at its peak. *When?* is used alongside other questions. By this stage children can usually use language to share, take turns, collaborate, argue, predict what may happen, compare possible alternatives, anticipate, give explanations, justify behaviour, create situations in imaginative play, reflect upon their own feelings and begin to describe how other people feel
5 years	Children have a wide vocabulary and can use it appropriately Vocabulary can include colours, shapes, numbers and common opposites, e.g. big/small, hard/soft Sentences are usually correctly structured although incorrect grammar may still be used Pronunciation may still be childish Language continues to be used and developed as described in the section on 4-year-olds; this may now include phrases heard on the television and associated with children's toys Questions and discussions are for enquiry and information; questions become more precise as children's cognitive skills develop Children will offer opinions in discussion

Language development: 5–8 years

Between the ages of 5 and 8 years children use, practise, adapt and refine their language skills. Language is used for a wide range of purposes. Joan Tough in her book, *Listening to Children Talking* (Ward Lock Educational, 1976), identifies seven main uses of language. They provide a useful tool for observation and analysis of children's development. The uses are hierarchical, that is, that children progress through the seven stages in this order. The early stages will be observed in most children before the age of 5.

Joan Tough's seven uses of language

Use	Using language to
1 Self-maintaining	1.1 Protect oneself: *Stop it.* *Go away.* *You're hurting me.* 1.2 Meet physical and psychological needs: *I'm thirsty.* *You're hurting me.*

continued

Joan Tough's seven uses of language continued

Use	Using language to
2 Directing	Direct the actions of self and others: *You push the lorry round the track.* *I just need to put this brick here, then I've finished.*
3 Reporting	3.1 Label the component parts of a scene: *There is a car, a lorry and a bus.* 3.2 Refer to detail, the colour, shape, size or position of an object 3.3 Talk about an incident: *I fell out of bed last night.* 3.4 Refer to a sequence of events: *We walked to the bus stop and then caught the bus to school.* 3.5 Reflect on the meanings of experiences, including feelings: *I like playing in the shop, especially with Sarah.*
4 Towards logical reasoning	4.1 Explain a process: *I made some tea. First I put the teabag in the pot, then I poured boiling water onto it.* 4.2. Recognise causal and dependent relationships: *You have put sugar in this tea so it doesn't taste very nice.* 4.3 Recognise problems and their causes: *This box isn't big enough to put all these cars in. We need a bigger box.* 4.4 Justify judgments and actions: *I didn't want to go out because I hadn't finished my drawing.*
5 Predicting	5.1 Anticipate or forecast: *We're going to have a hamster and it will have to have a cage with a wheel.* 5.2 Predict the consequences of actions or events: *That propeller will fall off if you don't stick it on properly.*
6 Projecting	6.1 Project into the experiences, feelings and reactions of others: *He was stuck in there and didn't know how to get out and he was frightened.* 6.2 Project into a situation never experienced: *I wouldn't like to be a rabbit and live in a cage, would you?*
7 Imagining	In an imagined context: *Hello, this is Hot Scissors hairdressers. Would you like to make an appointment?*

 Progress check

1 What are the important factors in children's language development?
2 What is a rich language environment?
3 Why is it impossible to give an exact age for each stage of development?

Talking with children

The most important factor in children's language development is interaction with other people. It is important that people who work with young children adopt practices that contribute positively to children's language development. There is a recognised link between the quality of adult input and the quality of children's language. Listed opposite are some important points to remember when talking with children. However, these are only practical points. A sensitivity towards children's needs and knowledge of them as individuals are the basis of positive interaction.

When talking to children, remember:

The tone of your voice	Does it convey warmth and interest in the child?
How quickly you speak	Do you speak at a pace that is appropriate for the child or children you are talking with?
Listening	How do you show the child that you are listening? Eye contact and getting down to the child's level show that you are listening. Becoming involved in the conversation also indicates that you are listening and interested.
Waiting	Do you leave enough time for the child to respond? Young children may need time to formulate their response. It is important to remember that pauses and silences are part of conversation.
Questions	Do you ask too many questions? This may make the conversation feel like a question-and-answer session, especially if your response is 'That's right'. What type of questions do you ask? Closed questions require a one-word answer and do not give the child the opportunity to practise and develop their language skills. Open questions have a range of possible answers. and do give the child the opportunity to practise and develop their language skills.
Your personal contribution	Do you contribute your own experience and/or opinions to the conversation? Conversation is a two-way process. It involves both people sharing information. This should be the same with children. It is important that the choice of what to talk about is shared.
What do you talk about?	How much of what you say is management talk? How much is conversation and chatting? How much is explaining? How much is playful talk? Children need to be involved in a wide range of language experiences to enable them to practise and develop their own language.
Developing thought	Do you ask for and give reasons and explanations when talking with children? Do you encourage the child to make predictions in real and imaginary situations? Do you encourage the children to give accounts of what they are doing or have done? Children's language and cognitive skills can be developed in this way.
Who do you talk to?	You must talk to all children within the group. All children need the opportunity to practise their language. There will be a range of developmental levels within every group of children and it is important that each child's needs are met.

Do this!   8.7

1 a) Read the following three conversations between adults and children.
       The dots indicate a pause.

   Conversation 1
   (Three children are playing at a clay activity.)
   Adult   What are you playing with?
   Child   Clay.
   Adult   What are you making?
   Child   Dinner.
   Adult   What does the clay feel like?
   Child   ...Cold...wet.
   Adult   Is it smooth?
   Child   Yes...

Conversation 2

(A child arrives at nursery.)

Adult Hello, James...What have you brought with you?

Child ...my Fluffy...

(The adult sits down on a chair near to the child.)

Adult Have you brought it to show to us?

Child Yes..

Adult Let me have a look...He's lovely...I've got a teddy that looks just like Fluffy...Little brown eyes *(The adult points to them)*...A big nose...I take mine to bed with me...What do you do with Fluffy?

Child ...Go to bed with him...Bring him to nursery...Take him to Nan's...My Nan makes toys...

Adult Does she...What does she make?

Conversation 3

(A child comes in from playing outside.)

Child I don't like it outside.

Adult Why not? *(She is tidying the room)*

Child It's cold.

Adult No it's not...Fasten your coat up...*(She continues to tidy up)*...What have you been playing with?

Child ...The bike and on the grass...with Simon...

Adult What did you do with Simon?

Child ....Played...*(The child wanders off)*

b) Make a list of the positive and negative aspects of communication for each conversation.

c) Which of the conversations demonstrates the best adult communication skills? Give reasons for your choice.

2 a) Tape yourself talking with a child who is under 7 years of age.

b) Listen to the tape and assess your communication skills: refer to the section on talking with children.

c) What is the child's stage of language development? Give reasons for your answer backed up with examples from the tape.

d) Suggest ways in which you can improve your communication skills.

e) Suggest ways for enhancing the child's communication skills.

Progress check

1 Why is it important that people who work with young children know how to interact effectively with children?
2 What is the basis for positive interaction with children?
3 Identify some of the ways in which adults can interact with children effectively.

Planning for and monitoring children's language development

Children learn and develop their language skills through interaction with other people. Adults therefore have a vital role to play in children's language development through talking and listening to them. Careful consideration also needs to be given to the activities and experiences provided for children. Appropriately planned activities or experiences provide the opportunity for children to use their existing skills and develop others.

Before planning it is necessary to assess each child's level of development. This can be done through careful observation of the child. Once the level is established, relevant experiences and activities can be planned to meet the child's needs. During the experience or activity the adult needs to adopt a variety of strategies to promote each child's language development.

The child/children
■ What language is being used?
■ Are the children's needs being met?
■ Are all children able to participate in a group situation?
■ Was there anything significant about what was observed?
■ Does anything need recording?
The activity or experience
■ Are the activities or experiences provided appropriate for child/children?
■ Were the adults involved clear about the focus?
■ Was the timing appropriate?
■ Was there anything significant about what was observed?
■ Does any information need recording?

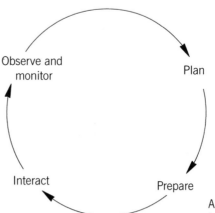

Observe and monitor

Plan

Interact

Prepare

What are the child/children's language needs?
What are the child/children's development levels?
What is the range of development levels?
What time is available?
What are the staffing levels and responsibilities?

Are the staff aware of the focus of the activity or experience?
Are all the necessary equipment and materials available?

Strategies for interaction with the child/children include:
■ discussing events with the child/children
■ providing a commentary on what is happening
■ describing events
■ asking open-ended questions
■ introducing new vocabulary
■ suggest ideas for extending the experience or activity.

Planning and monitoring children's language development

The monitoring, planning, preparation and interaction with children is a continual process. As children develop their language skills the adult needs to respond to their changing needs.

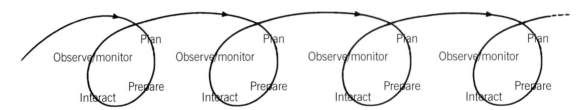

The ongoing process

Monitoring children's language development

A key aspect of effective planning and interaction with children is monitoring their developmental level. In this way the activities and experiences can be made relevant to the children's needs. Monitoring development, in all areas, is an ongoing process. It can be done in many ways. However children's development is monitored, ways need to be found to incorporate this information into the planning process, so that provision is relevant to the children in the group.

Effective child-care workers informally monitor children's development through their daily interaction with the children. Their intimate knowledge of individual children enables them to identify when progress has been made, and when a child may need support. This can be particularly effective where there is a key worker system in place. This information should inform the planning process, and interaction should be adjusted accordingly.

Some establishments also monitor children's language development formally. They may use a checklist, developmental chart or diary. In this way, a written record of each child's development is available to inform planning and interaction.

It is important to be aware, when assessing children's language developmental level, that there is sometimes a difference between a child's actual language ability and their ability to use expressive (spoken) language. What you may actually be observing are a child's social skills. For example, some children whose grasp of language is excellent may be quiet in a group of children. This is not a reflection of their language ability, but of the way in which they operate socially. Similarly, bilingual children may be very competent in their first language and passively understand most things in their second language. Their apparent lack of expressive skills is not necessarily an indication of their language developmental level.

Do this!   **8.8**

1 a) Chose an appropriate experience that promotes language development of a child or children within a specified age group.

   b) Refer to the section on interaction on page 164. List specific examples of how you would interact with the child to promote their language development.

2 Consider the monitoring techniques outlined above. What are the strengths and weaknesses of those described?

3 Identify ways in which information about children's language development level can be incorporated into the planning process.

Progress check

1 Why is it important for an adult to be aware of each child's level of language development?
2 What is involved in monitoring children's language use and developmental level?
3 What is involved in planning experiences or activities to promote language development?
4 Why is it important that all the adults involved with the child are aware of the focus of the language work?
5 List the ways in which an adult can interact with a child to promote their language development.

Factors affecting language development

To develop language successfully children need a rich, stimulating environment that provides the opportunity for experiences appropriate to their level of development. There are a number of factors that influence the quality of the language environment:

■ the presence of positive role models
■ the opportunity for the children to practise their language skills
■ positive feedback to enable the children to pick up language and to adjust and refine their language skills.

Do this!   **8.9**

Consider the situations of the following children:

■ Rachel, a 2½-year-old who is at a day nursery for the whole day

■ Three-year-old Brendan, who attends a nursery unit attached to a school for half the day; spending the other half of the day at home

■ Two-year-old Shamila who is cared for by a bilingual childminder. The childminder also cares for three other children, two 2-year-olds and a 4-year-old. All the children are being brought up bilingually

■ George who is 3 and an only child, at home all day with his mother

Answer the following questions for each child. Your answer should refer to the factors that affect development (see the beginning of this section) and to the child's needs relative to their stage in the sequence of language development (see pages 160–3). Present your findings in written form, with a section for each child.

a) Who provides the child with positive role models for language?

b) What opportunities might the child have to practise language skills?

c) How could the child's language development be encouraged through interaction and feedback?

The effects of television

Television, video and computer games are enjoyed by many young children. They have a useful role to play in broadening children's experience, bringing the wider world within their reach, and they provide very good entertainment. However, there are some concerns that long spells in front of the television, video or computer can have a detrimental affect on children's language development. For children's language to develop successfully, they need to practise their skills with someone who knows them and is aware of their capabilities and needs. They rely on feedback which is individual and immediate to encourage them to respond and develop their skills. The point is not that television in itself is harmful to children's language development, but rather that it is no substitute for the carer who is 'tuned in' to the child and can plan for and meet the child's language needs. There are also concerns that too many hours in front of the computer screen can interfere with children's abilities to use language socially in face to face situations.

Supporting children with language delay

All children come to a care setting with different experiences. This includes their experience of language. Because the experiences that a child has had are so influential in their development, the pace at which children develop language is not uniform. Within any group of children there will be a wide range of proficiency in language. This could include children who have delayed language development in relation to the expected range of norms; it could also include children who are beyond the expected range of norms. It is important that each child is treated as an individual and that their needs are assessed and met.

When a child's language development is delayed there are a number of agencies who may be involved in meeting the child's needs. The extent of provision for children with language delay will vary from area to area. Some of the agencies who may be involved are:

- health visitor
- speech therapist
- Portage worker
- language unit
- nursery staff
- individual classroom support
- support from charitable organisations, for example Barnardos, NCH Action for Children
- local initiatives, including self-help groups.

Do this! 8.10

Prepare an information sheet for parents that outlines the support that is available locally for children with language delay. Include details about how children gain access to these services. If it is available, use computer software to present your information in a readable and accessible format.

 Progress check

1 List the factors that contribute positively to children's language development.
2 Why might television and videos have a detrimental effect on children's language development?
3 What do you understand by the term 'language delay'?
4 Name four agencies that might be involved in supporting children with language delay.

Key terms

You need to know what these words and phrases mean. Go back through the chapter to find out.
bilingual
British Sign Language (BSL)
Language Acquisition Device (LAD)
Makaton
multilingual

Now try these questions

1 What is meant by the term language development?
2 How can the carer support the language development of:
   a) a 1-year-old?
   b) a 4-year-old?
3 How can the child-care setting meet the needs of bilingual children?
4 Describe the adult's role in planning and monitoring children's language development.
5 How can the child-care worker contribute positively to children's language development?

9 Cognitive development

This chapter includes:

- **What is cognitive development?**
- **Piaget's theory of cognitive development**
- **The role of the adult in promoting cognitive development**

This chapter examines imagination, creativity, problem-solving, concept formation, reasoning, memory and concentration as aspects of cognitive development. It looks at Piaget's theory of cognitive development in some detail, assessing its influence alongside criticisms of his findings and conclusions from other studies in this area. The chapter concludes by examining how carers can support and encourage children's cognitive development.

You may find it helpful to read this chapter in conjunction with:

▶ **Book 1, Chapter 7**   An introduction of language and cognitive development
▶ **Book 1, Chapter 8**   Language development

What is cognitive development?

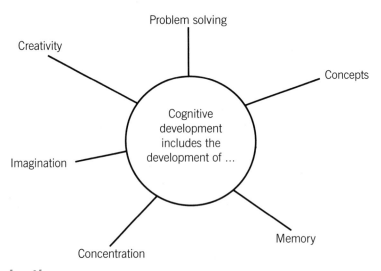

imagination
The ability to form mental images, or concepts of objects not present or that do not exist

Imagination

Imagination is the ability to form mental images, or concepts of objects not present, or that do not exist. It is fairly easy to conjure up images of, for example, a beach, outer space, grandparents, school or chocolate.

The imagination is the basis for many of the activities we regard as enjoyable:

- books
- films and television
- dance
- art
- music
- design.

These are part of the culture of a society. They are often the basis for activities which people choose to be involved in, in their own time. They provide relaxation and add to the quality of life.

Imagination is also part of the following activities:

- **problem-solving**
- innovative and original thought.

problem-solving
The ability to draw together and assess information about a situation in order to find a solution

Change comes about through new and innovative ideas and by finding solutions to problems. Imagination is an important aspect of ideas. The idea might be an invention, for example the telephone, television, the car, the aeroplane. All these started as ideas in someone's imagination. The idea might also be a solution to an existing problem which might be an everyday or individual problem, scientific or medical problem, society or world problem. The process is the same: solving problems in new or unusual ways requires imagination.

Imaginative play in young children also contributes to the development of other important skills. Through using their imagination to play, children develop the ability to use one object to represent another, for example, using a doll to represent a baby, using a pan to represent a hat, using sand and toy cars to represent a race track. This is called *symbolic play*: one object is being used as a symbol for another.

This skill is transferable. If a child can use symbols in a play situation, they can transfer this skill to learning to read and to write, as reading and writing involve use of the same skill of using symbols, in this case letters and words to represent the spoken word (see Chapter 8, *Language development*).

Children and imagination

Children do not need to be taught to be imaginative. Their play is full of examples where they are using their imagination. Here are some examples; there are many more:

- during creative activities such as painting or collage
- being someone, or something, else in **role-play**
- creating an object or design
- thinking up a story or poem
- creating objects from large empty boxes
- moving to music or dancing
- making music
- listening to stories.

role-play
Involves acting out being somebody, or something, else

It is important that these imaginative skills are nurtured, which means giving children the opportunity to express and develop their ideas. Your role is to provide the time, space, materials and encouragement to enable the children to do this.

Do this!   9.1

a) List three different activities where children use their imagination.

b) List the time, space and materials needed for each activity.

c) Discuss in a group what your role would be in these activities. How would you encourage the children to develop their own imaginative ideas?

Role-play

Role-play involves the child becoming somebody, or something else. Imagination is an important part of this play. The child may be imitating someone, or something, that they have seen, for example a shop assistant, a doctor, a waiter or a television character. Children also create new, sometimes unique, characters or situations in their play. They create these new characters and situations in their imagination.

Role-play of all types is important as it enables the child to try on different roles, for example:

- create imaginary characters and try out new and different roles
- imitate people that they have seen
- act out situations that they have been involved in
- create new characters and situations.

Role-play enables children to discover, enquire, organise and make sense of their environment. They can practise and develop their communication skills; feelings can be explored. All this can be done in a safe environment because they can opt out of the play at any time. This is an important part of their all-round development.

Do this!   9.2

a) Observe a child involved in role-play and look carefully at the following aspects:
    - the child's language
    - what the child may be feeling
    - how the child fits into the group involved in the play.

b) Observe the same child in a situation when they are not involved in role-play.

c) Compare what you have observed in the two situations. How do you think the child benefited from role-play?

✓ **Progress check**

1 a) What is imagination?
   b) Name some things that imagination is needed for.
   c) Explain why imagination is important.
2 a) What is symbolic play?
   b) Why is symbolic play important?
   c) How does the ability to symbolise help children to read and write?
3 a) What is role-play?
   b) Name two ways in which children are involved in role-play.
   c) What are the benefits of role-play?

Creativity

creativity
The expression of ideas in a personal and unique way

Creativity is the expression of imaginative ideas in a personal and unique way. When people write books, make films, play or write music, act, dance, paint, create beautiful buildings or gardens or find innovative solutions to problems, we say that they have been creative.

There is a lot of debate about what creativity is and whether it is taught or innate. It is hard, therefore, to say precisely what is and what is not creative, but for something to be described as creative it should have a number of the following features:

- use of the imagination
- begin with an open-ended outcome
- be a personal expression of ideas
- be unique in its process and product
- have the process as equally important as the product.

Think about it

1 What do you do now that could be described as creative?
2 Why do you get involved in this activity?
3 What are the benefits of this activity to you?
4 Are there any creative activities that you used to be involved in when you were younger?
5 If so, why are you not still involved in them?

Do this!   **9.3**

a) Collect information about creative activities people in your group are involved in now, and creative activities they were involved in when they were children.

b) Prepare, process and present this information on a graph or chart.

c) Write up your findings and suggest reasons for them.

Children and creativity

Creative activities for children provide the opportunity for them to think beyond what is obvious and to develop their own ideas. This is an important skill for later learning. Children do not need to be taught to be creative. They need the time, space, materials and encouragement to develop their own ideas. This is important: being creative is the expression of personal ideas, not copying or imitating someone else's ideas.

Sometimes it is enough to provide children with the opportunity to be creative and allow them to play without any intervention, for example putting out a range of different sizes and shapes of boxes and letting the children develop their own play themes and ideas.

At other times, adults may have more influence in the activity by providing a framework for it. It is important that the framework still allows the child the opportunity to develop their own ideas. Frameworks can be provided in many different ways:

- by the type of materials provided
- by the introduction of a theme for the activity
- by suggestion while the child is engaged in an activity
- by the siting of the activity
- through group work: the child works within the framework agreed by the group.

Case study: Children and creativity

Catherine, aged 4, was fascinated by woods and forests. She had seen a spectacular bluebell display in a wood whilst out with her parents. The following day she came into playgroup eager to get to the painting easels. As she painted she provided a running commentary to a member of staff about the trees, squirrels and flowers. She took great care with the details and choice of colour. When she was satisfied that she had everything that she wanted in the scene, she covered the whole of her picture with a thick layer of black paint. She explained that it was so dark in the wood, as the trees were very close together, that the sunshine couldn't get through. Catherine was very pleased with her painting.

1 Why did the member of staff stand back and watch when Catherine covered her picture with black paint?
2 Why do you think that Catherine was pleased with her painting?
3 In what ways is this a creative activity?

Progress check

1 What is creativity?
2 List some activities that require a person to be creative.
3 What features should a creative activity have?
4 Do children need to be taught to be creative?
5 How can you provide a framework for a creative activity?
6 Why is copying not creative?

Concentration

> **concentration**
> The skill of focusing all your attention on one task

Concentration is the skill of focusing all your attention on one task. It is necessary for successful learning to take place. Children need to be encouraged to focus their attention and therefore develop their skills of concentration and perseverance. Children will be encouraged to concentrate at activities when:

- the activities are at an appropriate level
- they are attractively presented
- an adult joins the activity to offer praise and make suggestions.

Young children are likely to have relatively short concentration spans. This needs to be taken into account when planning activities. However, it is also important to be aware that children need to develop their skill of concentration and to plan and organise activities that stretch their ability. This can be achieved in many ways, by:

- encouraging children to listen to a story all the way through without interruption
- encouraging children to complete an activity, for example a jigsaw
- playing board games through to the end
- providing group activities where children co-operate to complete a task, for example, building the train track
- joining in an activity to encourage and develop the play sequence, for example, being a customer in the cafe
- providing a focus for an activity, for example, asking children to listen carefully to a story so that they can retell it using puppets.

 Progress check

1 What is the ability to concentrate?
2 Why is it important?
3 How can an adult help a child to concentrate?

Memory

> **memory**
> The part of the brain where information is stored and retrieved from

There are three basic stages in learning:

1 Taking in information – we do this through our five senses
2 Storing the information – this takes place in our **memory**

3 Recalling the information – information is retrieved from our memory, we call this remembering.

Learning requires all three stages to be completed. For us to successfully store information in our memory and remember it when appropriate, activities and experiences have to meet certain criteria:

- the concept or skill to be learned should be at an appropriate level for the learner
- the information should be presented in a relevant way for the learner
- the learner should have some previous learning that the information can be linked to
- the information usually needs to be repeated, and/or used in context, for it to be stored and recalled successfully.

The following case study shows this process for a young child.

Case study: Learning and memory

Hannah, a nursery nurse, planned a series of activities to enable the children in the nursery to recognise written numbers to 10.

She knew that the children knew many number rhymes and songs, so that they could say numbers to 10. Over a period of weeks activities were introduced to the children to develop their understanding of written numbers:

- As the children sang number rhymes and songs, for example, 'Five little ducks went swimming one day', she held up the relevant number for the children to see.
- As the children began to recognise the numbers they held up the relevant numbers as they sang the song.
- Daily activities using numbers were provided, for example, number jigsaws, lotto, writing numbers in the sand and making them out of dough. Staff drew children's attention to the numbers during the activities.
- Gradually, the activities were extended during group time, for example, the children lined themselves up according to the number card that they held and the other children checked to see if it was correct, the children put the correct number against a collection of items.
- Hannah also created a number table where children sorted items into numbered boxes.
- The children went on a walk in the local environment to see where numbers were written, on their return they painted pictures of what they had seen and made a display.

This series of activities meets the criteria for learning, that is, storing the information in the memory and recalling it when appropriate. They are at an appropriate level for the children and they are presented in a relevant way. The children have previous knowledge of numbers to draw on and the staff provide opportunities for the children to repeat and use the information in different ways.

Progress check

1 What are the three stages in learning?
2 Why is memory an important part of learning?
3 What are the criteria for successful learning?
4 Give an example of this process for young children.

Problem-solving

The ability to solve problems is another aspect of cognitive development. Problem-solving does not just mean complex problems; it also includes everyday problems that all people come across, for example which route to take on a journey or how to put objects into a bag so that they all fit. Experience of the world and of how things work means that most problems are quickly solved.

When older children and adults are faced with a problem, they draw together all that they know about a situation to enable them to solve it. Logic is used to assess possible solutions: for example, to fit things into a bag you need to know about, sizes, shapes, capacity, tessellation (how items fit together) and rotation. You will very quickly be able to assess the problem and come up with a range of ideas to solve it. Children need to develop these skills. Their knowledge and experience of the world is more limited than older children and adults, so they have less information to draw on to enable then to solve a problem that they face.

There is a developmental sequence in children's ability to solve problems. **Trial-and-error learning** is the earliest stage in development. The child is trying out solutions to a problem in a random way and will try and fail, try and fail, until they arrive at a solution. This will probably involve returning to the problem many times. At this stage the child is not able to identify clearly the problem that they are attempting to solve. Trial-and-error learning can be very frustrating for a child and in this case careful adult intervention is needed to suggest ways forward for the child.

The next stage in development is a growing ability to identify the problem facing them and work out a possible solution before they try anything out. Children begin to be able to predict what might happen. This **hypothesis** is based on their increasing knowledge and experience of the world. The greater their knowledge and experience the more accurate the hypothesis becomes.

trial-and-error learning
The earliest stage in problem-solving. Young children randomly try out solutions to a problem, often making errors, until finding a solution or giving up

hypothesis
The provisional explanation or solution to a problem reached by assessment of the observed facts

Do this! 9.4

a) Observe a child under 2 years old attempting to do a jigsaw puzzle.
b) Observe an older child doing a jigsaw puzzle.
c) What are the differences in their approach to the problems of fitting each piece?
d) Make a list of the things that the child must know to be able to solve the problems of fitting each piece.

Progress check

1 What is problem-solving?
2 What is trial-and-error learning?
3 What is an hypothesis?
4 What is the developmental sequence in problem-solving skills?
5 Suggest reasons for the difference in how young and older children solve problems.

Piaget's theory of cognitive development

Piaget's work on the development of children's thinking is the basis for the way that we provide care and education for young children. His theory looked at the way that children process their everyday experiences and build up an understanding of the world. He demonstrated that the child passes through particular and distinct stages on the way to an ever more complete and complex understanding of their surroundings. Using information gathered from observation of children, he identified the kind of learning that the child is capable of at each of these stages, emphasising that children's thinking is fundamentally different to that of adults.

Some of Piaget's findings have been challenged by more recent psychological studies but, nevertheless, there is still much in his work that enables us to understand the development of children's thinking. It is his work that has been so significant in influencing the child-centred, 'learning by doing' approach that characterises much early years provision.

Piaget's stages

Piaget identified four distinct stages of cognitive development, each with its own characteristics. It is important to remember that the ages given are approximate and are intended only as a guide.

1 Sensory-motor (birth to 2 years)

At the sensory-motor stage the child:

- learns principally through the senses of sight and touch and through movement
- is **egocentric**, that is, can only see the world from their own viewpoint
- processes information visually, as images
- becomes aware that objects continue to exist when not in view (**object permanence**). This awareness occurs at around 8 to 12 months
- uses abilities intelligently and begins to learn through trial-and-error methods.

egocentric
Seeing everything only from your own viewpoint

object permanence
An understanding that objects continue to exist when not in view

2 Pre-operations (2 to 7 years)

This encompasses the pre-conceptual stage and the intuitive stage. It is during this period that children's language abilities develop rapidly enabling them to represent and process information and to think in more complex ways.

Pre-conceptual (2 to 4 years)

Now the child:

- still processes information visually, as images, but as language develops, it makes possible representation of information in other ways
- gathers information through the senses of sight and touch, although hearing becomes increasingly important
- uses symbols in play, for example a doll for a baby, a lump of playdough for a cake
- has a tendency to see everything from their own point of view
- believes that everything that exists has a consciousness (**animism**). At this stage, the child may blame the table that they have bumped into.

> **animism**
> The belief that everything that exists has a consciousness

Intuitive (4 to 7 years)

By now, the child:

- is involved in more complex symbolic play
- is still likely to see things only from their own point of view
- increasingly uses language to process and order information
- uses hearing to gather information
- will find abstract thought difficult and be dependent on immediate perceptions
- understands right and wrong in a simplistic way, often in terms of the most obvious factors. (See the case study below.)

3 Concrete operations (7 to 11 years)

By this stage, the child:

- can see things from another's point of view, that is, can **decentre**
- is capable of more complex reasoning but needs concrete objects to assist this process, for example, uses apparatus to solve mathematical problems
- knows that things are not always as they look, understands **conservation**
- knows the difference between real and pretend
- can understand and participate in play with rules.

> **decentre**
> Being able to see things from another's point of view

> **conservation**
> An understanding that the quantity of a substance remains the same if nothing is added or taken away, even though it may appear different

4 Formal operations (12 years to adult)

Characteristics of this stage include:

- the ability to think logically
- abstract thought with no need for props.

The stage of formal operations represents the most complex level of thinking and understanding that Piaget identified. However, research has

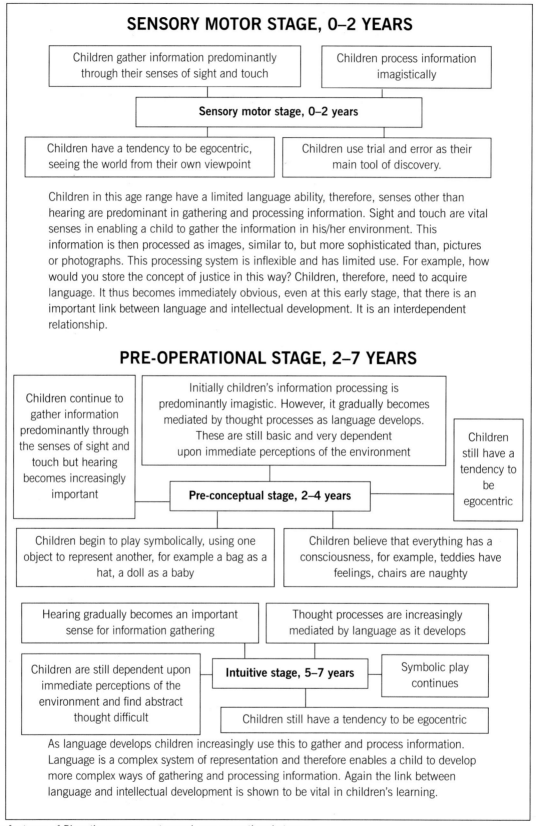

The main features of Piaget's sensory motor and pre-operational stages

shown that progression to this stage is not universal and that many adults function capably in the world without ever reaching this level of thinking.

Case study: Understanding right and wrong

The following situation was presented to Laurie, aged 4:

'Mummy asked Peter and Patsy to help by putting some plates away into the cupboard. Patsy said that she was too busy and didn't want to help, but Peter started moving the plates. Mummy went out of the room but Peter carried on. He picked up too many at once and dropped them, smashing all six plates. Patsy liked the noise of the plates breaking and, picking up one for herself, she threw it onto the floor and smashed it.'

Laurie was asked if she thought that either of the children had been naughty. She replied yes, that Peter had been naughty.

1 Why do you think Laurie decided that Peter had been naughty?
2 What aspects of Piaget's theory does this example illustrate?
3 What can this tell about how children of this age understand notions of right and wrong?

Piaget's stages and play

Recognition of Piaget's stages can help us plan and provide for the kinds of play experiences that are most appropriate for each stage of development.

At the sensory-motor stage, play involves:

- using the senses
- being self-absorbed
- movement
- lots of practice, often of the same skill. Piaget used the term 'mastery' to describe the child's need to persevere and achieve.

Play for children at the pre-operational stage involves:

- using symbols, for example a cardboard box for a house
- using language to communicate, with oneself, with others, with objects
- make-believe and fantasy
- beginning to play games with simple, straightforward rules
- being alone sometimes, more often with others.

By the concrete operations stage, play involves:

- more complicated rules
- taking responsibility and roles
- an awareness of the difference between fantasy and reality
- an ability to consider the needs and feelings of other people
- working with others, sharing decisions.

> ### Do this! 9.5
>
> Plan three different activities, one to encourage the development of cognitive skills for children in each of the following age groups: 0 to 2 years; 2 to 4 years and 5 to 7 years. Describe each activity, indicating resources required and identifying which cognitive skills are to be developed. Outline how the adult will interact with the children to introduce and reinforce the skills to be developed. If you have an opportunity, carry out one of your planned activities and evaluate its effect. Present your plans in an appropriate format.

Piaget and the development of concepts

schema
Piaget's term for all the ideas, memories and information that a child might have about a concept or experience

Piaget uses the term **schema** to describe the skills and concepts that children acquire through the following processes as they interact with their environment:

- *accommodation* – the way in which children take in information from their experiences
- *assimilation* – the process of fitting what the child has learnt from new experiences into their existing concepts or schemas.
- *adaptation* – occurs as a result of the interaction between accommodation and assimilation: the child now knows more about certain aspects of the world and can act upon this knowledge.

Piaget used the term *equilibrium* to describe the stage at which the child has successfully incorporated new understanding into an existing schema. Similarly, *disequilibrium* occurs when something unfamiliar is presented, requiring the schema to be modified. Piaget considered that the experience of disequilibrium was a crucial motivation to learning whereby the child needs to make sense of their environment by incorporating new experiences into existing knowledge. These processes are not confined to children's learning. As adults, we are constantly adapting existing concepts as we accommodate and assimilate new information.

A schema for bricks

The following is a simplified example of these terms in context, showing how a child's schema or concept about the physical characteristics of bricks might develop. The same schema is presented in diagrammatic form on page 185.

Anna is used to playing with bricks. Her present schema for bricks tells her that they can be different sizes and different colours but that they are all the same shape – cuboid – and that they are wooden (equilibrium). One day some arch-shaped bricks appear in the brick box (disequilibrium). She investigates these new additions, playing with them alongside the more familiar bricks (accommodation). She soon discovers that she can use these new toys in much the same way as the bricks she

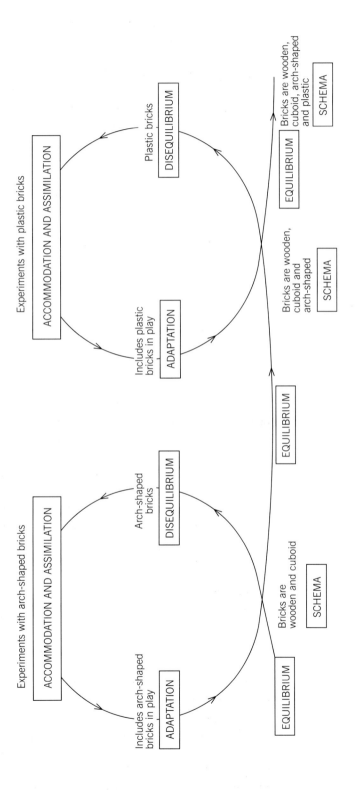

An example of a child developing a schema for bricks

already has (assimilation), but that the different shapes present her with new possibilities and problems in her building (adaptation). Her schema for bricks is once again in a state of equilibrium. The next time that she gets out the box some plastic bricks have been added (disequilibrium) and as she incorporates these into her play, she moves through the process again. As a result of these additions, the child's original schema for bricks has developed considerably.

Do this! 9.6

Go through the previous example again and discuss it with another student. Make sure that you understand the terms used. Devise another example that explains assimilation, accommodation and adaptation and present in a similar diagram.

Experiments in thinking

Piaget derived his theory of cognitive development from his observations of children who were asked to solve particular problems. If we pose similar problems to children their responses will identify their stage of cognitive development. The tests most often used are the test for conservation and Piaget's test for decentring, the mountain test.

Conservation

Piaget argued that a child at the pre-operational stage does not understand that a quantity of a substance can be presented in a variety of different ways and provided that nothing is added or taken away, the amount remains the same. Children at this stage are likely to be tricked by the visual appearance of the substance and say that the amount has changed. They are unable to *conserve*. There are a number of ways of testing for conservation. Here are some examples.

Conservation of mass
Playdough is used to make two balls of the same size. The child is asked if there is the same amount of playdough in each ball. If the child agrees that the amounts are the same, the adult rolls one of the balls of dough into a sausage shape, making sure that the child can see what is happening. The child is then asked again whether one of the dough shapes has more in it than the other, or if they are both the same. The child who has not yet learned to conserve will be misled by the appearance of the dough and say that there is more in one than the other.

Conservation of number
Two equal rows of counters (or buttons or sweets) are set out in front of the child. She agrees that each row contains the same number of counters. When the adult, again in full view, moves the counters so that one line is

longer than the other, the child who is unable to conserve number is likely to say that the longer line contains more counters.

Conservation of capacity
Conservation of capacity can be demonstrated in a similar way, by using the same amounts of liquid in a tall thin beaker and a short squat one.

Case study: Which has more in it?

Paul, aged 3, observed his father filling two identical bottles of water. They talked about the bottles and Paul agreed that they were both the same size and had the same amount of water in them. Paul watched while his father emptied each bottle, in turn, into a different container. One container was tall and thin; the other was wide and shallow. Paul agreed that no water had been spilt during pouring. His father then asked whether one container had more in it than the other or if they both contained the same. Paul answered straightaway that the tall thin container had more in it. When his father asked him why he'd come to that conclusion, he replied that the tall one was bigger.

1 Why did Paul's father ask questions about the size of the bottles and whether any had been spilt?
2 Why do you think Paul chose the tall, thin container?
3 Where, in Piaget's stages of cognitive development, would you place Paul?

Decentring

Piaget's test to show whether a child was able to take another's point of view – the ability to decentre – was his famous mountain experiment. A model comprising three mountains with different features was placed before a 5-year-old child. The child was asked to describe the model from their point of view saying which mountain was furthest away, closest, and so on. A doll was then placed alongside the model, with a different perspective from that of the child. The child was then asked to describe the mountain scene from the point of view of the doll (see the diagram below). Piaget believed that the inability of the child to describe the

Piaget's mountain test for decentring

mountain scene from the doll's perspective showed that they could not yet decentre.

More recent research has re-evaluated Piaget's findings from this test and criticised some of his methods.

Piaget evaluated

Piaget's work remains important and his influence on early years provision is significant. However, research by the Edinburgh group in the 1970s, led by Margaret Donaldson has questioned some of his assumptions. In particular, there has been some criticism of his questioning techniques and of the design of some of his experiments. Donaldson's group held that pre-school aged children respond better to questions that are posed as they arise naturally in a meaningful context, rather than in the artificial environment of the laboratory. They devised a number of tests, used a more child-friendly questioning format and came to different conclusions. The most significant of these was Martin Hughes' reworking of Piaget's mountain test for decentring.

Martin Hughes' model (see the diagram below) contained two dolls, a policeman (in a fixed position) and a boy (who could be moved). The child was asked to move the boy doll to a position where the policeman could not see it, thus looking at the model from the policeman's point of view. Children who were unable to see Piaget's mountain from the doll's point of view had much more success in hiding the boy doll from the policeman. It is thought that Piaget's task seemed irrelevant to the children and that they did not understand what they were being asked to do. Hiding the doll from the policeman seemed much more straightforward and showed that, if there was enough reason to do so, children could decentre and see the world from another's perspective.

Piaget's theory of cognitive development has been constantly re-examined and modified. Piaget stressed the importance of the environment in children's learning, seeing children as instinctively and

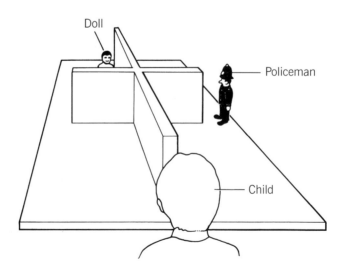

Hughes' policeman doll

actively curious about their surroundings. His belief that children learn most effectively through first-hand experiences has provided the rationale for the discovery learning, or 'learning by doing', child-centred approach to education. The child is seen as an individual who, through interaction with an environment that provides the right kind of learning experiences, progresses according to his stage of development.

Vygotsky's studies on the ways that children learn emphasised not just the individual child but the social context of learning. His findings showed that children had a great deal to learn from each other through interaction and communication. Unlike Piaget, Vygotsky felt that the child's level of ability should not be judged merely on what they could do alone but on what they were capable of with help. He used the term **zone of proximal development** to explain those tasks that might be beyond the child's capability alone but that were possible with assistance. The child would then be provided with a more challenging and stimulating environment than if left to discover and learn alone.

The work of Jerome Bruner pays particular attention to the role of the adult in children's learning. He sees the adult's role as not merely to provide a rich environment for children to discover, but to have an active part to play alongside them through scaffolding, that is, providing a structure that supports this learning. There are links here with Vygotsky's work, but the emphasis in Bruner's work is on the skilled adult, tuned in to the child's capabilities who can offer support that enables the child to break out of a repetitive activity, consolidate what has been learned and move on to the next step.

Recent studies have found that there are aspects of children's learning that Piaget did not give significant consideration to in his initial work on cognitive development. The effects of social interaction with other children and the involvement of skilled and sensitive adults have been shown to have a significant bearing on the way that children learn.

zone of proximal development
Vygotsky's term for the range of learning that the child is incapable of achieving alone but that is possible with assistance

---

✓ *Progress check*

1 Identify the stages in Piaget's theory of cognitive development.
2 According to Piaget, what kind of play is developmentally appropriate for:
   a) 2-year-olds?
   b) 5-year-olds?
3 Describe the process through which children develop schema.
4 Why do young children understand most effectively through a 'learning through experience' approach?
5 Why have some of Piaget's initial findings been criticised?
6 What influence does Piaget's work have on the provision of services for young children?

The role of the adult in promoting cognitive development

Conclusions from research and an examination of the nature–nurture debate indicate that children's learning is significantly influenced by the quality of their environment. Included in any consideration of the environment are the adults who care for children. It is important, therefore, when providing for children's cognitive development, that we are aware of how to plan, prepare and monitor children's activities and also how to interact with children during the activities so that their learning is optimised. Careful consideration of the environment provided for children can contribute to their achieving their potential. The principles outlined in the diagram below are similar to those outlined in Chapter 8, page 167.

This is an ongoing process; the areas are interdependent, as illustrated by the diagram opposite.

■ *Planning* is based on observation and monitoring of the children's needs and development. It is also based on observation of practical considerations concerning the use of space, time, equipment and staff.

What are the children's needs?
What are the children's developmental levels?
What is the range of developmental levels within the group?
What space is available?
How much time is available?
What are the staffing levels and responsibilities?
Is there a current theme/topic?

What learning is taking place?
Is the activity at the appropriate level for the children?
Were the children's needs met?
Were all the children able to participate in an activity?
Was an appropriate space used for each activity?
Did the children have enough time?
Was staff time used appropriately?
What is significant about what was observed?
Does anything that was observed need to be recorded?

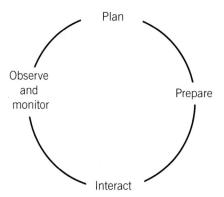

Are all the necessary equipment and materials accessible?
Is the activity attractively presented and inviting for the children?
Is the available space used appropriately?

Ways of interacting with children include:
■ talking with the children
■ asking questions
■ offering encouragement
■ playing alongside the children
■ offering suggestions and guidance to extend the children's learning. This may include suggesting the use of other equipment where appropriate.

The role of the adult in promoting cognitive development

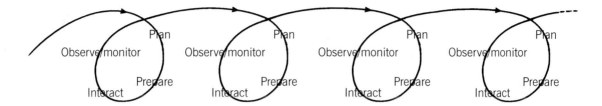

The planning cycle

- *Preparation* is based on careful planning so that the environment provided meets the needs of the children across the developmental range. Again, practical considerations are important when preparing an area.
- *Interaction* with the children takes account of their individual developmental needs. Some of this information is gathered through observation and must be incorporated into the planning. Practical considerations of staff time are an important issue here.
- *Observation and monitoring* provide valuable information on the children. This forms the basis of planning and preparing the area and also for interaction with the children.

Research has shown that the quality of adult–child interaction is a crucial factor in promoting children's cognitive development and that play experiences that are accompanied by a high level of adult-to-child involvement optimise learning. An adult will encourage children to persevere at a task and will extend understanding on an individual basis by presenting a new task or exploring another aspect of the original one. Skilful questioning and the posing of problems by an adult can enable a child to move from one level of understanding to the next. This is not to say that children do not benefit from the opportunity to play alone and uninterrupted, but without the active involvement of sensitive adults who know the children and are aware of their developmental needs, play activities can become circular, repetitive and lack intellectual challenge.

Case study: Planning and interacting in play

For some time the nursery staff had been concerned about the way that the home corner was being used by the children. Staff observed that children moved rapidly in and out of the area and rarely became involved in any play that lasted for more than a couple of minutes. They also noticed that a significant number of the children never went into the home corner, ignoring the activity completely. Adults only went into the home corner to find some equipment or to sort out a disagreement.

At the planning meeting, the staff decided that they needed to take positive action to improve the quality of the play in this area. The term's topic was planned around the story of 'The Three Bears' and the home corner was quickly transformed into the bears' cottage in the woods. For some of every session, a member of staff was to be based in the cottage and a number of different, focused activities were planned, all of which linked to the Three Bears theme.

After a week the staff reflected on the changes. All children had visited the bears' cottage and most had participated in a range of planned activities, successfully matching bears to the right sized bed, laying the table for breakfast, making porridge and so on. They devised their own play too and seemed to be approaching this with more concentration and involvement. Staff agreed that the children were initially attracted by the new focus of the cottage but felt that as they became used to this it was the presence of an adult in the area that enabled children to develop their play and become immersed in what was happening.

1 Why do you think the home corner was neglected by the children?
2 Why were the staff concerned?
3 What was the role of the adult here?
4 How might the nursery develop this kind of play in future?

 Progress check

1 Name the four elements of the planning cycle.
2 Why should we see the planning cycle as a continuous process?
3 Why is the quality of adult–child interaction important in promoting children's cognitive development?
4 What do you understand by the term 'circular play'?
5 Why is it important that adults know the capabilities of the children that they work with?
6 How can adults present children with intellectual challenge?

Key terms

You need to know what these words and phrases mean. Go back through the chapter to find out.

animism
concentration
conservation
creativity
decentre
egocentric
hypothesis
imagination
memory
object permanence
problem-solving
role-play
schema
trial-and-error learning
zone of proximal
    development

Now try these questions

1 Describe what is meant by the term cognitive development by including reference to all its aspects.

2 Why is creativity an important aspect of children's cognitive development?

3 How has Piaget's work influenced our understanding of children's cognitive development?

4 What are the features of Piaget's stages of cognitive development?

5 How can the adult make a positive contribution to children's cognitive development?

Part 3: Social and Emotional Development

Adults have a crucial role to play in promoting children's social and emotional development. Without social contact with others, children fail to develop emotionally and socially. Children have the need for positive caring relationships to ensure their healthy development.

   Although the family is the primary provider of care, all young children spend time with substitute carers, whether at school, in nurseries, or with nannies or childminders. The role of child-care workers in providing substitute care means that it is essential that they have a knowledge and understanding of children's feelings and behaviour at different stages of their development. Child-care workers have an important role in promoting healthy development. Positive handling of children is vital to ensuring the growth of self-esteem.

Workers also need to understand the possible reactions of children when they are separated from their primary carers and spend time with substitute carers in either a domestic environment, a nursery or school. It is important that workers develop appropriate ways to support and nurture the children for whom they care, and to ease children's transitions between them.

10 An introduction to social and emotional development

This chapter includes:

- **What is social and emotional development?**
- **The connection between ages and stages of development**
- **Average ages of development**
- **Theories of development**
- **Social and emotional needs**

Most people believe that children's social and emotional development begins from birth. These two areas of development are closely linked and strongly affect one another. There are a number of theories about how and why emotional and social development happens, and ideas about children's emotional and social needs, and the best way to meet them to promote healthy development. Both areas involve the growth of children's feelings, their awareness of themselves and their relationships with others.

You may find it helpful to read this chapter in conjunction with:

- ▶ **Book 1, Chapter 3**   Physical development
- ▶ **Book 1, Chapter 4**   The principles of physical development
- ▶ **Book 1, Chapter 7**   An introduction to language and cognitive development
- ▶ **Book 1, Chapter 12** Socialisation and social development
- ▶ **Book 1, Chapter 14** The development of self-image and self-concept
- ▶ **Book 1, Chapter 15** Bonding and attachment

---

social development
The growth of the ability to relate to others appropriately and become independent, within a social framework

socialisation
The process by which children learn the culture (or way of life) of the society into which they are born

What is social and emotional development?

Social development

Social development is the growth of a child's ability to relate to others appropriately, and become independent, within a social framework. It includes:

- the growth of the child's relationships with others
- **socialisation**, the process by which children learn the culture (or way of life) of the society into which they are born
- the development of social skills.

Emotional development

> **emotional development**
> The growth of the ability to feel and express an increasing range of emotions appropriately, including those about oneself

Emotional development is the growth of a child's ability to feel and express an increasing range of emotions appropriately. It includes:

- the growth of the child's feelings and awareness of themselves
- the development of feelings towards other people
- the development of self-image and self-identity.

The path of social and emotional development

> **maturity**
> Being fully developed and capable of self-control

> **independence**
> The development of skills that lead to less reliance on other people for help or support

Children's development in both areas follows a path towards **maturity** and **independence**. Maturity means being fully developed and capable of control. Achieving independence involves the development of skills that gradually lead to less reliance on other people for help or support.

The links between different areas of development

In this book the different areas of development are often separated, but in fact all areas of development are linked. They affect and are affected by each other. Some examples of the close links that exist between different areas of development are:

- *walking* – this milestone of physical development gives greater mobility and therefore independence, which then increases possible social contacts and therefore promotes social development
- *talking* – language development enables children to move from non-verbal communication with close carers to being able to communicate with other people in more complex ways and therefore also promotes social development

There are close links between the different areas of development

■ *adjusting to separation from main carer(s)* – a stage of emotional development that presents a wider range of experiences and relationships. This increases children's opportunities for play and learning and therefore their intellectual development.

The connection between ages and stages of development

chronological age
The age of a child in years and months

There is wide variation in the **chronological age** at which children reach different developmental stages. Some of the most important things to remember when considering ages and stages of development are that:

■ there are recognisable stages of social and emotional development that children reach
■ children pass through them at different ages – one child will be able to do things at an earlier age than another. The fact that one child is younger than another when they reach an observable stage need be of no significance at all; it does not necessarily mean that there are any developmental problems
■ the development of any skill depends both on the maturation of the nervous system and the opportunity to practise that skill.

Do this!	**10.1**

Carry out some research of your own by doing the following:
a) Make a list of some recognised developmental stages that you are aware of, for example smiling at carer, sitting unsupported, starting to talk, playing happily without a main carer present. Try to include some social and emotional milestones.
b) Ask the parents of a small number of children at what age their children reached these stages.
c) Make a chart to show the variation in their ages of development.
d) Using your results, write a conclusion about ages and stages of development.

Average ages of development

From observations of children, it is clear that they vary in their rates of development and the age at which they reach different stages of development. It is nevertheless useful to describe an **average** age at which children might be expected to reach a specific developmental stage.

average
A medium, a standard or a 'norm'

It is appropriate to describe children whose development is what we would expect at that age as 'age appropriate', and children whose development is not what we would expect at that age or behind the average as 'not having reached the stage of development expected at their age'. It is *not* helpful to use the word 'normal' to describe development, even though the word 'normal' is linked to that of a norm or average, because anything that does not fit this pattern might then be described as 'abnormal' and this is not an appropriate or acceptable term to use to describe developmental delay.

Case study: Playing together

Aisha and Jenny are 4 years old. They live next door to each other and frequently play in each other's houses and gardens. One of their favourite games is making a tent from old covers and having a picnic. Sometimes they argue and a parent intervenes to help them to solve their problems. Recently they have been joined in their play by Aisha's little brother Jamil, who is 2 years old. Jamil keeps taking their picnic things and filling them with sand, he screams if they try to stop him and throws himself on the ground when his mother comes to see what the noise is. Aisha says he can play with them but only if he does as they say.

1 List all the examples in this story of children's behaviour that is age appropriate.
2 Are there any examples of developmental delay?

Normative measurements

In order to establish average ages for development, the observations of many people in different professional fields have been put together. These have been used to describe an average or norm against which any individual child's development can be measured. These measurements are called **normative measurements**. For example, the many observations of children's first social smile have led to the understanding that the average age for this to happen is around 6 weeks. There are advantages and disadvantages of using normative measurements, as outlined below.

normative measurements
An average or norm against which any individual child's development can be measured

Advantages of using normative measurements

Using averages or norms of development is useful because:
■ it satisfies the curiosity of carers about what a child should be doing at a given age, and it helps them to know what to expect
■ it gives background information and a framework within which to assess developmental delay
■ it helps people to assess a child's progress after an injury or illness, and can be used to decide whether the child needs additional help and stimulation.

Disadvantages of using normative measurements

The disadvantages of using norms of development are:
■ carers may be tempted to think that children are 'good' when they are level with the norm and 'bad' if they fall behind it
■ carers and other people may wrongly think a child has an impairment, when in fact they are simply slow to develop in some way.

Progress check

1 What in your own words is social and emotional development?
2 Why is it not helpful to talk about 'normal' development?
3 What is a normative measure of development?
4 What are the advantages and disadvantages of using average measurements of development?

Theories of development

Why does social and emotional development occur?

It is very useful for anyone involved in the care of children to stand back and ask why social and emotional development occurs. This increases our understanding of both how and why development occurs and clarifies how the adult carer can encourage healthy development.

The two basic **theories of development** are:

- development happens because human beings are genetically programmed to develop in a certain way. These are called **biological theories** (the nature or heredity idea)
- people learn their responses and skills. These are called **learning theories** (the nurture or environment idea).

People tend to use a combination of these ideas, or theories, to guide their practice with children. Below is an outline of some of the theories of social and emotional development.

Biological theories

A biological or genetic explanation of how social behaviour and personality develop includes the following points.

- We are born with a definite personality and this determines how we respond and behave.
- Our temperament, sociability, emotional responses and intelligence are determined by what we inherit from our biological parents.
- The way we behave and the pattern our development takes is programmed in our genes, and is sometimes affected by chemical changes in our bodies.
- The way we mature and change follows a pre-set programmed pattern.

Support for this theory can be illustrated by the observation of parents who have more than one child. They comment that their children develop very different personalities and social skills even though they have grown up in the same environment.

It is interesting, however, to look at what happens to children who have little or no contact with other people as they grow up. There are two main ways that this separation occurs:

---

theories of development
Ideas about how and why development occurs

biological theories
Our temperament, sociability, emotional responses and intelligence are determined by what we inherit genetically from our biological parents

learning theories
Children develop as they do because they have contact with other people and learn from them

- a child may be abandoned or lost in a deserted place and cared for by animals
- a child may be locked away and given enough nourishment to stay alive, but little or no human contact.

Such children have occasionally been discovered. The story of Tarzan illustrates this. When found, these children are hardly recognisable as human. They do not walk or run, or have many human physical skills. They also have no recognisable language. They do not eat with their hands or use a toilet. When found, they do not respond or relate to the people who then care for them. These children demonstrate that very few skills, even physical ones, develop automatically. They show clearly that in the absence of other people, children do not develop social skills or recognisable human emotional responses.

Although it is commonly believed that some aspects of children's personalities are inherited, much evidence points to the fact that children *learn* most of their social skills and emotional responses. Physical development, on the other hand, is more strongly influenced by genetic inheritance.

Do this! 10.2

Find any references you can to children such as those described above (sometimes referred to as *feral* children) from books, magazines and by using information technology. For example, you might find information about Kaspar Hauser, Amala and Kamala or Jeannie (the subject of a TV documentary). Make notes on where they were found, what their condition was, and what happened to them.

Learning theories

Learning theories hold that children develop as they do because they have contact with other people and learn from them. With regard to social and emotional development, learning theories hold that:

- children develop by learning from their experiences
- the only things babies are born with are some primitive reflexes; they do not have any social behaviour that is instinctive, or occurs automatically
- the environment, rather than inherited characteristics, is of the greatest importance in determining how children develop emotionally.

How children learn social behaviour is covered in detail in Chapter 12, *Socialisation and social developemnt*, which includes how children learn by:

- being rewarded or punished
- copying or pretending they are other people
- experiencing pressure from their **peer group**.

There is much evidence which points to nurture, or learning, being a very important factor in determining how children develop socially and emotionally.

Psychoanalytical theories

Sigmund Freud, working at the beginning of the twentieth century, was the founder of modern **psychoanalytical theory**. Many others have since used his ideas.

Psychoanalytical theories are in some respects a mixture of biological and learning theories. They hold that:

■ children are born with a set of needs, for example the need for love, affection and security and dependency
■ these needs appear at different ages and stages through childhood
■ children develop healthily only if these needs are met
■ a child's future development can be badly affected if at any stage the appropriate needs are not met.

A good example is the need of the infant to be near a familiar carer. Children need this for many reasons. Through it they remain safe and develop a sense of security and trust. If this need is not met, and infants have a large number of carers when very young, they may find it difficult to learn to trust people. This in turn may have a profound effect on the way they relate to people later both as children and adults.

It is useful to look at children in terms of their basic needs. Understanding these needs enables adults to know how to care for them appropriately and increases awareness of how they can encourage healthy development.

> **psychoanalytical theory**
> A mixture of biological and learning theories, involving the idea that a child's development can be badly affected if at any stage their needs are not met appropriately

Case study: The nanny

A child-care and education worker is employed as a nanny to work in a family home. She has full day-time care of three children – Megan aged 6, William aged 3 and Bronwen aged 1. Megan attends a local school, William attends a nursery class each morning, and Bronwen is at home all day. The children's parents have their own business and are sometimes away from home overnight.

1 What are some of the particular emotional needs of the three children?
2 How can the worker best meet these needs during the day?

Conclusions about theories of development

There are several conclusions to be drawn about theories of development.

■ There are a number of different theories about how and why children learn behaviour.
■ It is not necessary to believe one theory entirely and reject the others: they can all be useful in different circumstances to help to explain behaviour and development.
■ Learning and the environment (nurture) play a relatively greater part in emotional and social development than heredity and biological factors (see the diagram on page 202).

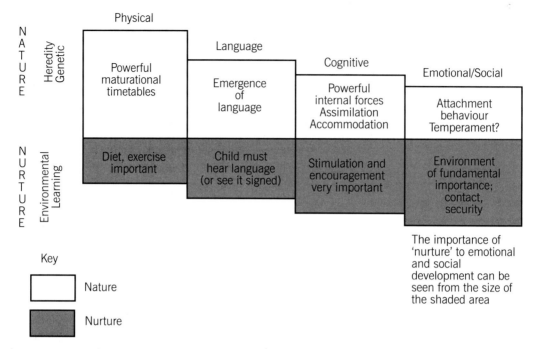

The relative influence of nature and nurture on the different developmental areas

■ An awareness of these theories can help carers to find the most appropriate way to respond to and care for children.

 Progress check

1 What is a theory?
2 What are the two contrasting ideas about why development occurs in the way that it does?
3 Describe the three main theories that explain how and why children develop emotionally and socially?
4 How does the development of children who have grown up without frequent human contact seem to be affected?

Social and emotional needs

bond of attachment
An affectionate two-way relationship that develops between an infant and an adult

From the beginning of life, through to maturity, children have social and emotional needs which may be met, to some extent, by all the people they have contact with. However, their primary carers, those with whom they have a close **bond of attachment**, are the most significant and influential. This is especially true in the early, formative years. These social and emotional needs are discussed below.

Children need love and affection

Children need unconditional love, affection and acceptance. They need to know that, no matter what they do, they will always be loved. This need is met by children experiencing, from birth onwards, a stable, continuous, dependable and loving relationship with a small group of carers. In the early years, close physical contact is protective as well as affectionate. For example, when babies are in their carer's arms, a loud noise will startle them far less, and a mild digestive upset will be endured more easily. Love and affection are essential to all aspects of children's development, not just social and emotional.

Early relationships which are consistent, unconditional, affectionate and loving encourage children to:

self-image and self-concept
The picture we have of ourselves and the way we think other people see us

moral conscience
An understanding of right and wrong

- value themselves and therefore develop a positive **self-image and self-concept**
- develop trust, and as a result become emotionally involved with other people
- receive and give affection
- care for others, including in time, their own children
- adjust their behaviour to please a loved person
- develop a **moral conscience** as they feel shame and guilt when they do something they know their carer would disapprove of
- respond increasingly to adult expectations and become a socially acceptable member of society.

Love and affection provide protection and security

Think about it

In what circumstances may it be difficult for a carer to meet a child's need for love and affection, and how may the lack of love and affection influence a child's intellectual development?

Children need security

A child needs to feel secure in order to cope with all that is new and changing in their world. This need can be met in the early years by:

personal continuity
A sense of having a past, a present and a future

coherent self-image and self-concept
A view of oneself that fits together and makes a complete whole

- the experience of a stable family life and family relationships; this gives a child **personal continuity**. It encourages children to develop a **coherent self-image and self-concept**
- the security of a familiar place and familiar routines; these provide a predictable and dependable framework from which a child can venture out. Notice the contrast between a young child's usual behaviour at home, and their behaviour in an unfamiliar place
- having access to familiar objects, which can be a teddy bear, comfort blanket or other favourite toy; these objects can give reassurance and a sense of security. Children show a strong desire to retain them or return to them during a stressful experience.

Think about it

In what circumstances may it be difficult for children to develop a positive and coherent self-image?

Familiar objects give reassurance and a sense of security

Do this!   10.3

Plan and record a daily routine for a mother of a 2-year-old child to ensure the child's sense of security.

Children need consistent care and reasonable guidelines

Children need to be able to rely on consistent care by their primary caregivers. They need to be given reasonable guidelines for appropriate behaviour in a variety of situations. This need is met by carers when they:

- *demonstrate consistent attitudes and behaviour* Children do not learn underlying values if similar behaviour causes different reactions in their carers at different times. For example, if children are consistently forbidden to touch the TV controls, they learn not to. If, however, they are allowed to touch them sometimes but not others, they receive inconsistent messages. They are then both more likely to constantly test the adult's response and less likely to learn the underlying principle, that some things must not be touched
- *give consistent discipline* that is appropriate for what the child has done, and allow the child to make up for what they have done
- *seek to develop their child's self-control and self-discipline* These are more likely to develop if carers reason with their child and discuss expectations with them. Children are less likely to develop self-discipline if they have to obey an adult unquestioningly out of fear of punishment, withholding of affection, or emotional threats
- *have reasonable expectations of their child* based on knowledge of their age and stage of development
- *give reasonable guidelines for acceptable behaviour* and explain these freely.

Imagine being in a room where the walls move outwards when you push them. Although this may bring an initial sense of power, even an adult would ultimately feel insecure. If each time a child pushes for what they want, the adult gives in, the child will have less and less idea of what is reliable and firm. They may feel an initial sense of extreme power, but eventually they will feel insecure and uncertain.

Children need praise, encouragement and recognition

To grow from a helpless infant into a self-reliant, self-accepting adult requires an immense amount of emotional, social and intellectual learning. Children need the motivation of praise and encouragement to achieve this. They need to feel valued and recognised for themselves as well as for their accomplishments and achievements. This need is met if carers respond to their children by:

- praising them for effort more than for achievement
- showing pleasure at their successes
- seeking to develop a good relationship with them, which will result in their children wanting to behave in a way that will please them
- actively encouraging them in all aspects of their development
- demonstrating that they recognise their individuality, for example by not comparing them to other children
- having a reasonable level of expectations of them, based on their age and stage of development; too little expectation can lead children to adopt too low a standard of effort and achievement. Too high a level of expectation can make them feel they cannot live up to what is expected. This can lead to children feeling discouraged and making less effort
- allowing them to make mistakes and fail without expressing disapproval
- demonstrating a positive, optimistic attitude towards them.

> **Think about it**
>
> 1 How do you feel when you receive praise or encouragement?
> 2 Why is it important for children, especially those with learning difficulties, to be recognised and accepted for who they are? Why do they need to be given praise for effort rather than achievement?

> ### Do this! 10.4
>
> Choose one day when you are working with a child as part of a team. Record the number of times the child receives praise and encouragement, how this is given and for what. Interpret and present the results. Draw conclusions about the effects of praise and encouragement on the child.

Children need appropriate responsibility

> **Think about it**
>
> Why do carers of disabled children often experience difficulty in providing them with appropriate responsibility? What may be the result for disabled children?

For children to learn how to act in a responsible way, they need to be given appropriate responsibility. This need is met by carers encouraging and enabling children to:

- gain personal independence; children can do this initially through learning to feed, dress, wash and toilet themselves
- become increasingly independent by doing more and more for themselves
- have their own possessions over which they are allowed to have absolute ownership
- exercise choice appropriate to their age and stage of development, for example in food, play, clothes, choice of friends, study and hobbies
- understand the results of their own decisions and choices
- meet and interact with peers.

Children who are given appropriate responsibility and encouraged to be independent are more likely to become confident and accept responsibility as they mature.

> ### Do this! 10.5
>
> Observe a child with their parent/carer over a period of time. Aim to observe the parent/carer managing their child's challenging or unacceptable behaviour. Use the information from this section to inform your evaluation.

> ### ✅ Progress check
>
> 1 Describe five characteristics of children who had their need for love and affection met in their early years.

2 How can a child's need to feel secure be met in their early years?

3 How can parent/carers meet their child's need for consistent care and reasonable guidelines?

4 How can parent/carers ensure their child feels valued?

5 How do children learn to act responsibly?

Key terms

You need to know what these words and phrases mean. Go back through the chapter to find out.

average

biological theories

bond of attachment

chronological age

coherent self-image
    and self-concept

emotional
    development

independence

learning theories

maturity

moral conscience

normative
    measurement

peer group

personal continuity

psychoanalytical
    theories

self-image and self-
    concept

social development

socialisation

theories of
    development

Now try these questions

1 Why does the chronological age at which children reach certain developmental stages often differ?

2 Why is it important for children to mix with their peers?

3 Why do controls, reasonable guidelines and expectations help children to feel secure?

4 What are the social and emotional needs of children?

5 Explain how carers and parents could meet the emotional and social needs of an average 4-year-old child during a single day.

11 The stages of social and emotional development

This chapter includes:

- The principles and path of emotional and social development
- Ages and stages of social and emotional development (1): 0–1 year
- Ages and stages of social and emotional development (2): 1–4 years
- Ages and stages of social and emotional development (3): 4–7 years 11 months

Emotional development is the growth of a child's ability to feel and express an increasing range of emotions appropriately. Social development is the growth of a child's ability to relate to others appropriately, and become independent, within a social framework. Development is a whole process, usually made up of a period of rapid growth followed by a period of relative calm. The path moves from complete immaturity and dependence towards social and emotional maturity, and the development of social skills and independence.

In this chapter the stages of social and emotional development are outlined separately from physical, language and cognitive development. This is because it is simpler and easier to understand children's developmental progress by examining one area of development at a time.

You may find it helpful to read this chapter in conjunction with:

- **Book 1, Chapter 3**   Physical development
- **Book 1, Chapter 8**   Language development
- **Book 1, Chapter 9**   Cognitive development
- **All the chapters in Book 1, Part 3**

The principles and path of social and emotional development

Principles of social and emotional development

There are important things to remember when studying social and emotional development.

- Development is a whole process; all areas of development are integrated and interact with each other; they mix together and are affected by each other.
- The interaction of different areas results in an individual pattern of development that varies from one child to another.
- Development is usually made up of a period of rapid growth followed by a period of relative calm. During this period of calm, the previous growth is consolidated. This means that it becomes a definite and practised part of the child's being. One developmental area may be relatively calm whilst there is more rapid growth in another.
- Children do not develop in isolation; they develop within family systems. Families have individual characteristics that influence each child differently.
- A child's family exists within a larger cultural system. The experience of this cultural environment has a profound effect on both the family and a child's behaviour.
- Family and cultural environments interact with and affect children's developing skills, their awareness of themselves and their relationships with others.

Path of social and emotional development

Think about it

What do you think are the most important factors that determine a child's personality?

The following sections of this chapter describe the path of emotional and social development of a newborn baby until the age of 8. (The growth of self-image and self-esteem are described in Chapter 14.) The path moves from complete immaturity and dependence towards social and emotional maturity and includes the development of social skills and independence. The main aspects of development covered are:

- *emotional* – the development of children's feelings about and for other people, and their ability to express them appropriately and with self-control
- *social* – children's relationships with other people
- *social skills* – the development of skills that lead to independence.
- *self-image and identity* – children's view and awareness of themselves.

Progress check

1 Why is it usual to study the different areas of development separately?
2 Suggest why children have individual patterns of development.
3 What usually follows a period of rapid developmental growth?
4 What happens during the period when growth is consolidated?
5 What external influences affect a child's development?
6 What path does development take?

Ages and stages of social and emotional development (1): 0–1 year

Birth

At birth and for the first month or so of life, a baby's behaviour is largely governed by in-built reflexes and reactions. These reflexes govern the way the infant listens, looks around, explores and relates to others. However, even at this stage carers become aware of characteristics that they see as individual to the child and that seem to be the product of nature. Newborn infants begin to learn as soon as they are born, but at this stage their behaviour and communication with adults is limited. In general newborn babies cry to make their needs known and are peaceful when those needs are met.

Development

At this stage babies:
- are utterly dependent on others
- have rooting, sucking and swallowing reflexes
- sleep most of the time
- prefer to be left undisturbed
- startle to noise, and turn to the light, providing it is not too bright
- cry when hungry, in pain or unattended to
- are usually content in close contact with carer.

The newborn is usually content in close contact with the carer

1 month

Babies are observed to smile spontaneously from birth; but when they are 4–8 weeks old they begin to smile in response to happenings outside themselves. The baby learns to smile at a voice and a face; they are also attracted to the movement of faces.

Development

Around this age babies:

- sleep most of the time when not being handled or fed
- cry for their needs to be attended to (different cries are evident for hunger, pain, panic and discomfort)
- will turn to the breast
- look briefly at a human face
- will quieten in response to a human voice and smile in response to the main carer's voice
- develop a social smile and respond with vocalisations to the sight and sound of a person (at around 6 weeks)
- grasp a finger if the hand is opened and the palm is touched.

2 months

From 2 months babies have less primitive reactions and gradually learn a range of responses and behaviour. These are the result both of physical maturation and of the baby beginning to explore the environment. At 2 months the baby is capable of having 'conversations' with the carer. These are a mixture of gestures and noises, but follow the pattern of a conversation in that one person is quiet while the other speaks.

Development

Around this age babies:
- stop crying when they are picked up
- sleep less during the day and more during the night
- differentiate between objects, and begin to tell one face from another
- follow a human face when it moves
- smile and become more responsive to others
- explore using their five senses.

3 months

Babies take a lot of interest in their environment at this stage. Physical maturation continues rapidly. Babies turn their heads in response to different sounds and to see what people are doing. They are rapidly beginning to learn a range of social skills from the people around them. Even during this early period, it is essential for babies that someone takes the time to communicate and be with them. Babies appear to have a natural capacity to communicate, but this does not develop without contact and interaction with other people. They need to be handled and talked to. By 3 months babies have learned to respond with pleasure to friendly handling. An infant and carer gradually build up a complex pattern of responses.

Development

Around this age infants:
- respond to friendly handling and smile at most people
- use sounds to interact socially and reach out to the human face
- become more oriented to their mother and other main carers, look at their carer's face when feeding

At 3 months babies respond to friendly handling and smile at most people

- begin to connect what they hear with what they see
- are able to show an increasingly wide range of feelings and responses including pleasure, fear, excitement, contentment, unhappiness
- have some awareness of the feelings and emotions of others.

6 months

Development during the first 6 months is very rapid. Infants are awake for much longer periods by 6 months of age. If they have been stimulated by the presence of other people during this period, they will show great interest in their environment and respond happily to positive attention. Babies of 6 months laugh, show excitement and delight and will also show likes and dislikes strongly.

Development

Around this age infants:
- show a marked preference for their main carer(s)
- reach out for familiar people and show a desire to be picked up and held
- begin to be more reserved with, or afraid of, strangers
- smile at their own image in a mirror
- may like to play peek-a-boo
- show eagerness, anger and pleasure by body movements, facial expression and vocally
- play alone with contentment
- stop crying when communicated with
- become more aware of themselves in relation to other people and things.

They may have the following skills:
- look at their hands and feet with interest
- increasing use of their hands to hold things
- drink from a cup that is held for them.

Bonding and attachment

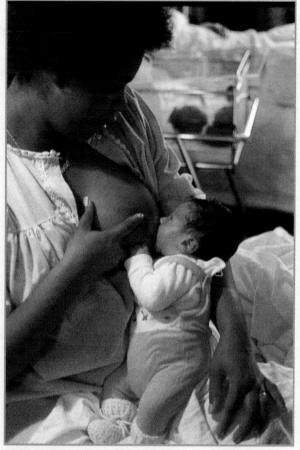

Close contact...

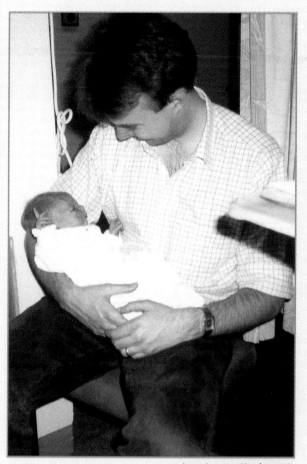

...promotes strong attachments

Siblings bond too

The baby is welcomed into the wider family

Development: birth–12 months

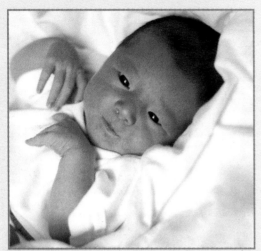

New born

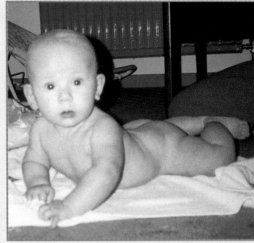

3 months: head held high, propped on forearms

6 months: sitting with support

9 months: sitting without support

11 months: standing with support

12 months: walking alone (with encouragement)

Developing control

Holding a large ball

Handling with care

Fine motor skills: using pegs

Tripod grasp developing

The mature pincer grasp

Stretching, grasping and balancing

Expressing feelings and learning to care

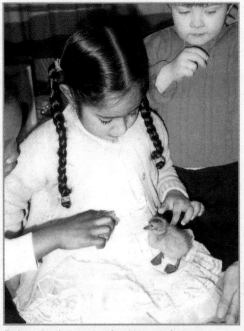

Being gentle: expressing care and concern

Showing apprehension

Mixed feelings

Total absorption and concentration

At 6 months babies show a preference for a main carer and begin to be more reserved with strangers

9 months

By this age, given the right opportunities, infants will have formed strong attachments with their main carer(s). They will also usually have begun to move around independently. These developments require new adaptations to be made by both infants and carers. Infants take great pleasure in playing with their carers and learn a great deal from this interaction. They can be a delight to be with. The development of infants who do not experience this positive interaction will probably be adversely affected.

Development

Around this age infants:

- clearly distinguish familiar people and show a marked preference for them
- show a fear of strangers and need reassurance when in their company, often clinging to the known adult and hiding their face in them
- play peek-a-boo, copy hand clapping and pat a mirror image
- still cry for attention to their needs, but also their use their voice to attract people to themselves

Think about it

If a baby is given hardly any attention by adults, what will happen to that baby's development?

At 9 months babies show a fear of strangers, need reassurance, cling to known adult and hide their face in them

- show some signs of willingness to wait for attention
- show pleasure and interest at familiar words
- understand 'No'
- begin to respond to their own name
- try to copy sounds
- offer objects to others but do not release them.

They may have the following skills:
- put their hands around a cup or bottle when feeding.

12 months

By this age, many children have started to stand independently and possibly walk. They therefore gain a very different view of the world around them. Their physical skills enable them to pick up small objects, and to explore the environment. In a secure environment children can experience rich and varied interaction with adults. Their development will be adversely affected if they are not spoken to or played with at this age.

Development

Around this age infants:
- like to be within sight and hearing of a familiar adult
- can distinguish between different members of the family and act socially with them
- will wave goodbye
- may be shy with strangers
- are capable of a variety of emotional responses including fear, anger, happiness and humour
- show rage when thwarted
- become increasingly aware of the emotions of others
- actively seek attention by vocalising rather than by crying
- copy actions and sounds of adults or children
- will obey simple instructions
- know their own name.

At 12 months infants like to be within sight and hearing of a familiar adult and will wave goodbye

They may have the following skills:

- assist with feeding themselves by holding a spoon and may drink from a cup by themselves
- help with dressing by holding out their arms or legs.

 Progress check

1 What is a newborn baby's behaviour largely determined by?
2 At about what age do babies develop a social smile?
3 In order to develop communication skills what is it essential for babies to experience in their early life?
4 By what age do babies show a preference to be with their main carers?
5 How do 9-month-olds often respond to strangers?
6 What range of emotional responses are babies capable of at 1 year?

Ages and stages of social and emotional development (2): 1–4 years

15 months

By this age toddlers use their main carer as a safe base from which to explore the world. They are anxious and apprehensive about being physically separated from them, and tend to be very much 'under the feet' of their carers. They are very curious about their environment and their exploration of it can lead to conflicts with their carers.

Development

Around this age children:

- have a sense of 'me' and 'mine' and begin to express themselves defiantly
- begin to distinguish between 'you' and 'me', but do not understand that others are individuals just like themselves
- can point to members of the family in answer to questions like 'Where's granny?'
- tend to show off
- are not dissuaded from undesirable behaviour by verbal reasoning, react poorly to the sound of sharp discipline (the most useful disciplinary technique in this period is to distract a child and change the environment)
- have an interest in strangers, but can be fearful or wary of them
- show interest in other children
- show jealousy of the attention given by adults to other children
- throw toys when angry
- are emotionally changeable and unstable

- resist changes in routine or sudden transitions
- swing from dependence to wanting to be independent.

They may have the following skills:

- hold a cup and drink without assistance
- hold a spoon and bring it to the mouth, spilling some food in the process
- help with dressing and undressing.

At 15 months toddlers will hold a spoon and bring it to the mouth, probably spilling some food in the process

18 months

At this age children are very **egocentric**. They are also often defiant and resistant in this period. They have only recently discovered themselves as separate individuals. Their defiant behaviour can be seen as an attempt to protect themselves and their individuality.

Development

At this age children:

- are trying to establish themselves as members of the social group
- begin to **internalise** the values of the people around them
- respond by stopping doing something when the word 'No' is used, but this usually needs **reinforcement**
- are still very dependent on a familiar carer and also often return to a fear of strangers
- tend to follow their carer around, be sociable and imitate them by helping with small household tasks
- are conscious of their family group
- imitate and mimic others during their play; engage in solitary or parallel play but like to do this near a familiar adult or sibling
- show intense curiosity
- show some social emotions, for example sympathy for someone who is hurt
- cannot tolerate frustration
- have intense mood swings, from dependence to independence, eagerness to irritation, co-operation to resistance.

---

egocentric
Self-centred, from the words *ego* meaning self and *centric* meaning centred on; seeing things only from one's own viewpoint

internalise
To understand the things that adults think are important and begin to believe and behave similarly

reinforcement
Responding to an action or behaviour so that a particular consequence – a reward or punishment – is associated with the action and it is repeated (positive reinforcement) or not (negative reinforcement)

They may have the following skills:

- use a cup and spoon well, and successfully get food into their mouth
- take off a piece of clothing and help with dressing themselves
- although still in nappies, they can make their carers aware of their toileting needs through words or by restless behaviour.

Around 18 months children imitate others during solitary play

2 years

At this age children do not fully accept that their parent is a separate individual. Sometimes a child can be very self-contained; at other times they will be very dependent. Children by this stage are capable of a wide range of feelings and able to empathise with the feelings of those close to them. For example if their carer is upset, they are capable of trying to comfort them. By this stage, children are able to use symbols in language and these newly acquired linguistic skills enable the children to achieve new levels of social development.

Development

Around this age children:

- demand their carer's attention and want their needs to be met immediately they make demands
- can however respond to a reasonable demand to wait for attention or for the satisfaction of their needs
- will ask for food
- sometimes have tantrums if crossed or frustrated, or if they have to share the attention of their carer with another person
- are capable of being loving and responsive
- will try to be independent

At 2 years children can lift up a mug and put it down again

- are possessive of their own toys and objects, and have little idea of sharing
- tend to play parallel to other children, engage in role play, but are beginning to play interactive games
- tend to be easily distracted by an adult if they are frustrated or angry
- join in when an adult sings or tells a simple story
- can point to parts of the body and other features when asked.

They may have the following skills:
- feed themselves without spilling
- lift a cup up and put it down
- put some clothes on with supervision
- say when they need the toilet; become dry in the daytime.

2 years 6 months

Children between the ages of 2 and 3 are still emotionally and socially very dependent on familiar adult carers; they are also capable of being very independent in some of their behaviour. During this period extremes of moods and behaviour are common. Children can change between aggressive and withdrawn behaviour, awkwardness and helpfulness very rapidly. They are also beginning to develop an understanding of those around them which enables them to make friends with other children to the extent of playing games based on shared interests.

Development

Around this age children:
- develop their sense of self-identity: they know their name, their position in the family, and their **gender**
- play with other children, among other things this tends to reinforce their developing concept of gender roles. They also learn that different toys are intended for girls and boys
- may engage in pretend play including role or make-believe play
- behave impulsively, wanting to have anything they see, and do anything that occurs to them
- throw tantrums when thwarted and are not so easy to distract
- are often in conflict with their carers. Carers have to limit their children's behaviour and impulses at this stage, both for their future social development and the child's own survival.

They may have the following skills:
- awareness of and ability to avoid certain hazards (like stairs and hot stoves)
- the ability to use a spoon well, and possibly a fork or chop sticks
- the ability to pour from one container to another and therefore to get themselves a drink
- dress with supervision, unzip zips, unbuckle and buckle, and unbutton and button clothing
- are toilet-trained during the day, and can be dry at night, especially if lifted.

> **gender**
> Being either male or female

At 2 years 6 months children can dress with supervision

3 years

By this age children are usually happier and more contented than during their previous year. They have gained a certain amount of physical and emotional control. This can lead to more settled feelings and more balance in the way they express them. They are generally friendly and helpful in their manner to others.

Development

Around this age children:

- can feel secure when in a strange place away from their main carers, as long as they are with people with whom they became familiar when they were with their carer
- can wait for their needs to be met
- are less rebellious and use language rather than physical outbursts to express themselves
- still respond to distraction as a method of controlling their behaviour; they are, however, also ready to respond to reasoning and bargaining
- are beginning to learn the appropriate behaviour for a range of different social settings; for example they can understand when it is necessary to be quiet or when they can be noisy
- adopt the attitudes and moods of adults
- want the approval of loved adults
- can show affection for younger siblings
- have an ability to share things and to take turns
- enjoy make-believe play both alone and with other children
- project their own experiences onto dolls and toys
- may have imaginary fears and anxieties
- towards the end of this year show some insecurity, expressed as shyness, irritability and self-consciousness.

At 3 years children can toilet themselves and wash their hands

They may have the following skills:

■ ability to use a fork and spoon to eat (in some cultures it will be more appropriate to use hands to eat some food) and can be proficient with chop sticks
■ toilet themselves during the day, and may be dry through the night; will wash their hands but may have difficulty drying them
■ learning to dress without supervision.

Case study: Separation

Tom is 3 years and 6 months. His parents recently moved to another part of the country, but they had to stay in temporary accommodation for some weeks before their house was ready. Tom is the eldest of two boys born 16 months apart. Tom happily attended a playgroup for several months before they moved, and often went to play with friends at their houses.

Shortly after the family eventually moved into their new home, Tom was invited to a 4-year-old's birthday party at a neighbour's house. His mother left him, as she had to take his brother to the doctor. When she returned she was upset to find Tom asleep. Apparently he had cried so much when she left that he had exhausted himself. Following this Tom would not be left anywhere for several months and then only if his younger brother remained with him.

1 Would you have expected Tom to have been staying on his own quite happily at playgroup at his age and why?
2 Why do you think Tom was so upset when his mother left him at the party?
3 Why was Tom not happy to be left for a few months after this, and what difference did his brother staying make?
4 How would you assess Tom's behaviour?

---

4 years

At this age children are constantly trying to understand and make sense of their experiences and of the world around them. Although they can be very sociable at this age, they often return to a more stubborn phase. This may involve at times them using some physically and/or verbally aggressive behaviour.

Development

By this age children:

■ are capable of being very sociable with, and talkative to, both adults and children, and enjoy 'silly' talk
■ may have one particular friend
■ can be confident and self-assured
■ may be afraid of the dark and have other fears
■ have adopted the standards of behaviour of the adults to whom they are closest
■ turn to adults for comfort when overtired, ill or hurt

- play with groups of children; groups tend to centre around an activity, then disperse and re-form
- can take turns but are not consistent about this
- are often very dramatic in their play; engage in elaborate and prolonged imaginative play
- are developing a strong sense of past and future
- are able to cope with delay in having their needs met
- show purpose and persistence and some control over their emotions
- can be dogmatic and argumentative; may blame others when they misbehave, and may even behave badly in order to arouse a reaction
- may swear and use bad language.

They may have the following skills:
- feed themselves proficiently
- dress and undress, but may have difficulty with back buttons, ties and laces
- wash and dry hands and face and clean teeth.

Between 3 and 4 years children can feel secure away from their main carers, are learning appropriate behaviour, are able to take turns and play in a group of children

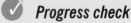 **Progress check**

1 Name some of the emotions can children express at 1 year?
2 At what age is a child most likely to begin to say 'it's mine'?
3 Children begin to 'internalise' the values of the people around them at around 18 months old, what does this mean that they do?
4 At what age do children tend to begin to have tantrums if they are cross?
5 When are children able to feel secure even if taken and left in a strange place? And what does this depend on?
6 Use six words to describe a typical 4-year-old child.

Ages and stages of social and emotional development (3): 4–7 years 11 months

4–5 years

Between 4 and 5 years children achieve a level of balance, self-containment and independence. They are usually friendly, willing to talk to anyone, and are able to be polite.

Development

By this age children:

- enjoy brief separations from home and carers
- show good overall control of emotions
- are increasingly aware of a range of differences between themselves and other people, including gender and status differences
- want the approval of adults
- are developing a sense of shame (an important development which affects the adult's ability to discipline and control the child)
- argue with parents when they request something
- still respond to discipline based on bargaining
- are not so easily distracted from their own anger as when they were younger
- often show the stress of conflict by being overactive; may regain their balance by having 'time-out'
- prefer games of rivalry to team games
- enjoy co-operative group play, but often need an adult to arbitrate
- boast, show off and threaten
- show a desire to excel, and can be purposeful and persistent.

They may have the following skills:

- use a knife and fork well
- are able to dress and undress
- may be able to lace shoes and tie ties
- wash and dry face and hands, but need supervision to complete other washing.

At 5 years children can undress and dress themselves

Case study: A typical 5-year-old

Christopher is 5 years old. He responds well to his parents and smiles and enjoys it when they praise his efforts. He enjoys going to school. He especially likes playing in the playground with his two friends, Joel and James. Although he has a happy disposition, his parents are sometimes frustrated when he argues about going to bed, and other domestic routines. However, he usually responds well once his parents point out that they will be doing something enjoyable the next day or at the weekend, providing he gets enough sleep. He sometimes plays outside his home, as he lives on a safe cul-de-sac. He likes having races with his friends on their bikes. Sometimes they play imaginative games involving space travel and monsters, but they also argue and a parent sometimes has to come out and sort things out before they will continue playing. On occasions Christopher has to come indoors to calm down a little.

1 How does Christopher relate to his peers?
2 How does he respond to his parents?
3 How does he like to play?
4 In what ways is Christopher's behaviour typical of a 5-year-old?
5 Do you think he is at an appropriate developmental stage emotionally and socially?

6–7 years

Throughout these years children grow steadily more independent and truly sociable. They are generally self-confident and friendly; they are able to co-operate in quite sophisticated ways with adults and children. Their peer group becomes increasingly significant to them. Children's all-round development is increasingly sophisticated. This sophistication, coupled with skills of perseverance, opens up opportunities for success in many varied activities of increasing complexity, for example sewing, painting, playing a musical instrument and so on.

By 6 years of age:
- children have progressed a long way along the path to independence and maturity
- they have developed a wide range of appropriate emotional responses
- they are able to behave appropriately in a variety of social situations
- they have learned all the basic skills needed for independence in eating, hygiene and toileting routines.

Development

At 6 years children:
- are often irritable and possessive about their own things
- may have spells of being rebellious and aggressive.

At 7 years children:
- become very self-critical about their work
- may be miserable and sulky, and give up trying for short periods
- may be so enthusiastic for life that carers have to guard against them becoming overtired
- are more aware of gender characteristics; friendship groups are often separated by gender
- are influenced by the peer group, which becomes increasingly important to children over these years; peer group opinion is increasingly influential and will be used and quoted by children to carers as either their own ideas or to justify what they want to do. 'Hero' figures become influential and are used as role models by children at this stage.

7 years–7 years 11 months

The saying 'Give me a child until he is seven and I will give you the man' sums up the fact that much of the child's personality is established by the end of this period. By the time they are 8 years old, children's experiences in their families and in their social and cultural environments will have led to the establishment of their:

- personal identity
- social and cultural identity
- gender role
- attitudes to life.

Disabled children

It is often at this stage that the differences of disabled children become more apparent. The development of sophisticated skills is the norm for children at this age; because of this the carers of a child who has a disability may be faced more starkly with their child's difference. They may struggle between:

- a concern to see their child treated as 'normal'
- acceptance of their child's disability and a recognition of the need for special support.

Do this!   **11.1**

Go back through this chapter and make a chart that gives an outline of the main stages of:
a) emotional development
b) social development
c) the growth of social skills
between the ages of 0 and 7 years 11 months.

 Progress check

1 What aspect of development can make it easier for an adult to control a child of 5 years?
2 What are some of the more positive aspects of a typical 5-year-old child?
3 What difficulties can 5-year-olds experience?
4 Describe the basic personal skills that most 6-year-olds have developed.
5 What is the significance of the peer group to 7-year-olds?
6 What is established by the time a child is 8 years old?

Key terms

You need to know what these words and phrases mean. Go back through the chapter to find out.

egocentric

gender

internalise

reinforcement

Now try these questions

1 What are the main aspects of emotional and social development?

2 What relationship do all the different areas of development have to each other?

3 Describe the emotional and social development of a typical 6-month-old.

4 Describe the emotional and social development of a typical 3-year-old.

5 Why do the differences of some children with disabilities become more apparent by the time children are 7 years old?

12 Socialisation and social development

This chapter includes:

- **The process of socialisation**
- **The family and primary and secondary socialisation**
- **Culture and social development**
- **Social development and the learning of social roles**
- **The social status of the family**

Socialisation is the process through which children learn the way of life, the acceptable and appropriate behaviour and the language of the society of which they are a part. It starts at birth, continues through childhood and throughout life. This process is fundamental to the social development of all children. The family forms the most significant environment within which this social development takes place. All families exist within a social and cultural framework, and differences between cultures lead to some differences in the socialisation process and its outcomes.

You may find it helpful to read this chapter in conjunction with:

▶ **Book 1, Chapter 13** Bonding and attachment
▶ **Book 1, Chapter 14** The development of self-image and self-concept

process
A continuous series of events which leads to an outcome

culture
The way of life, the language and the behaviour that is acceptable and appropriate to the society in which a person lives

social role
A position in society that is associated with particular group of expected behaviours

The process of socialisation

Socialisation is the **process** through which children learn the way of life, the language and the behaviour that is acceptable and appropriate to the society in which they live. This is their **culture**. The process of socialisation involves children learning from the experiences and relationships they have during childhood.

The socialisation process enables children to learn how to behave in ways that are expected and appropriate to their society. Through it they learn to become adult members of society. Throughout the process, children learn how to behave appropriately in a large number of **social roles** – positions in society that are associated with a particular set of expected behaviour.

How behaviour is learned during the process of socialisation

There are several different ways in which children learn the behaviour that is expected of them.

Rewards and punishments

Adults encourage acceptable behaviour in children by rewarding it. A reward can be a very simple thing like a smile, saying thank you, giving praise or a hug; it also includes giving children things such as toys, food or a treat. Children can also feel rewarded by the good feeling they get when they please an adult. Children want rewards to be repeated, and this encourages them to repeat the behaviour that brought the reward.

Adults discourage behaviour by punishing or ignoring it. Punishments, like rewards, can take a variety of forms: they include telling children they are wrong, physically or emotionally hurting them, depriving them of something they want, ignoring or isolating them. Children usually enjoy adults' attention and do not like to be ignored.

There are many different views about the relative effectiveness of rewards and punishments in changing behaviour.

Copying and imitation of adults

> **role model**
> A person whose behaviour is used as an example by someone else as the right way to behave

Children learn how to behave by copying people in different roles. They use people as **role models**. For example, children copy what their mothers or fathers do and learn a lot about the roles of men and women. The idea that children develop partly by copying behaviour has implications for child-care workers as they will also be used as role models by children.

Role-play

> **role-play**
> Acting out a role as someone else

Children enjoy pretending to be someone else. In their play they sometimes act as if they are another person; this is called **role-play**. They often copy the adults who are close to them, or the ones they see on the television. When they do this, they may not be able to tell whether or not the adult's behaviour is socially acceptable. This may happen, for example, when children copy violent parents in their play or general behaviour.

Peer group pressure

> **Think about it**
> What can adults do to prevent bullying?

There can be very strong pressure on children from their peers to behave in certain ways. Children change their behaviour when they are with their peer group, and may sometimes behave in ways that they know are unacceptable to adults. A peer group can punish a child who does not conform to their expectations by excluding the child from the group or by making the child feel different. The fear of exclusion from the group can be stronger to some children than fear of adult punishment. This peer group pressure can become a form of bullying. There is an increasing awareness of the different forms that bullying can take, and a greater commitment by many schools to introduce policies to try to prevent it.

Case study: Using praise

Jo attends a nursery school. She is a lively and responsive 4-year-old child who uses the nursery resources enthusiastically. One morning Jo is sitting in the book area looking at different books, she asks a child-care and education worker who is standing near the area if she can read a book to the worker. The worker knows that Jo can read very few words, but willingly agrees, knowing that the policy of the school is to encourage free reading in this way. Jo turns the pages of the book and mainly uses the pictures to tell the story; she also reads a few words correctly and the worker helps her with a few others. The worker says 'I think you are very clever, well done! Would you like to read another book to me?'

1 Why would this response encourage Jo to want to go on reading books?
2 If the worker had said to Jo 'That wasn't very good, you didn't know many words', what effect could this have on the child's behaviour in future?
3 What knowledge about children's behaviour is the worker basing her responses on?
4 List some other rewards that can be used in a school to encourage acceptable behaviour.

Do this! 12.1

1 Take part in a discussion with your colleagues about how you can be a good role model to the children in your care. List the things that you commonly do, and ways that you behave when you are with children, that make you a good role model.

2 Discuss any things that you might do that are inappropriate for a child to copy?

3 Produce a staff behaviour policy that aims to ensure you are good role models.

Progress check

1 What are the main things that children learn during the socialisation process?
2 What are the main things that influence children's behaviour?
3 What rewards can encourage behaviour?
4 What is role-play?
5 What do children fear their peer group might do?
6 What is a role model?

The family and primary and secondary socialisation

It is useful to look at two periods in the process of socialisation:
- *primary socialisation* that occurs in the early years of life
- *secondary socialisation* that takes place as children grow older.

These two periods overlap in a child's life. A child does not leave one and go into the other; the first merges into the second. Anyone working with children may be involved in either or both of these processes.

Primary socialisation and the family

Primary socialisation is the name given to the first part of the socialisation process that takes place in the early years of a child's life, predominantly within the child's close family, but also in the day-care setting, if the child attends. It is a very important period, because during this time the child is learning the basic patterns of behaviour, skills and responses that are appropriate and acceptable both within the family and also in society. This lays the foundation for the social development of the child.

Primary socialisation takes place in the early years of life mainly within the child's close family

The role of adults during primary socialisation

The main influences during this early period are the people closest to the child. These people are usually the child's close family, together with any substitute carers, for example a child minder, a nanny or a day-nursery officer. The diagram on page 230 shows the people who may be involved in the primary socialisation process.

Research shows that it is better for children to have close contact with a small number of main carers during this early period. This enables them

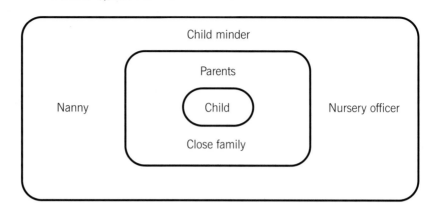

The main influences in primary socialisation

to experience continuity and consistency in the way they are handled. It also helps them to build up a pattern of acceptable behaviour: they learn what is right and wrong from the adults around them. If children receive conflicting messages about appropriate behaviour during this early period, they may not establish a consistent pattern of behaviour. Healthy emotional development is promoted by having a limited number of carers.

This knowledge has been reflected in recent legislation and child-care practice. The Children Act (1989) has clear guidelines about the ratios of staff to children required in day-care settings; the younger the children the higher the ratio of staff required. The Children Act also gives guidelines about a suitable environment and accommodation for children. It is partly for this reason that many child-care settings have introduced a key worker system to enable a worker to form a special relationship with a child and gain a thorough knowledge and understanding of them. This enables them to meet the individual needs of the child and also to work more effectively in partnership with parents.

Secondary socialisation, the family and other influences

Secondary socialisation begins when children are exposed to influences outside the family and their close environment. They develop friendships, mix with their peers, go to school, watch the television, read books and magazines, join clubs and begin to learn the rules for behaviour in the wider society. These activities lay the foundation for children becoming adult members of that society. The diagram opposite shows the main influences during the secondary socialisation process.

The role of adults during secondary socialisation

Growing children need to be encouraged and enabled to develop a range of relationships and interests. This can be done by extending the child's experiences beyond the immediate family and close social group. Through this children develop the ability to adapt to a variety of situations. They therefore become increasingly independent and socially mature. Children develop differences in values and ways of behaving that

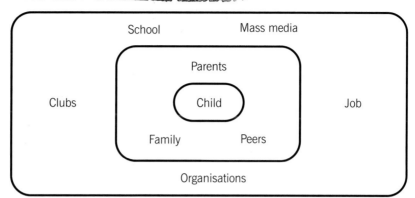

The main influences in secondary socialisation

customs
Special guidelines for behaviour which are followed by particular groups of people

in part reflect differences in their environment. Adults need to encourage children to be sensitive to other people who may have different **customs**.

Do this!   12.2

1 Imagine that you are caring for an infant during a typical day in a nursery. Make a list of any basic social skills that you will be helping the child to develop.

2 Build up and store a source of information of ways that the staff in an establishment, for example nursery or infant school, could help children to develop wider social awareness. Your ideas could include the following:
   ■ places the children could visit
   ■ visitors the staff could invite to the school
   ■ topics the children could investigate
   ■ ways in which displays could be used.

3 Discuss other ways that children can be stimulated to take an interest in their social environment.

 Progress check

1 What is primary socialisation and where does it mainly take place?
2 What is secondary socialisation and what are the main influences during this period?
3 List some advantages of a key worker system in a day-care setting.

Culture and social development

Culture

An important aspect of the socialisation process involves children learning the culture of their society.

Culture is the learned, shared behaviour of people in a society. It

values
Beliefs that certain things
are important and to be
valued, for example a
person's right to their own
belongings

norms
The rules and guidelines
that turn values into
action

includes a shared language, **values**, **norms** and customs. Values are beliefs that certain things are important and to be valued, for example a person's right to personal freedom or to own their belongings. Norms are the rules and guidelines that turn values into action. A custom is another word used to describe particular norms. Customs are special guidelines for behaviour which are followed by particular groups of people.

Values and norms guide people and inform them about how to behave or do something. The value that children are precious and should be protected from harm leads to the norm that children should learn how to cross the road. The origins of customs often go back a long way into the past. An example of a custom is the celebration of birthdays.

The learning of culture and the role of adults

In the early stages of the socialisation process, children learn acceptable behaviour from the people who are very close to them. This is usually their close family, but also includes any substitute carers (see diagram on page 230, *The main influences in primary socialisation*). Part of the carer's role is to teach children appropriate behaviour. Such teaching has to be repeated until children behave automatically in certain situations, for example remaining on the pavement and not running into the road, or how to greet familiar people. Sometimes it is sufficient to reinforce rules and customs by rewarding children. It may also help to explain to them the reasons that certain behaviour is expected. In this way carers are also helping children to understand the underlying values.

Schools, playgroups and nurseries also have values, norms and customs. It is important in any group that rules are kept by everyone, that the norms for behaviour are shared. Social contact would be very unpredictable without this, as we would have no way of knowing how people are likely to behave.

Do this! 12.3

1 Discuss with colleagues and list the norms for behaviour that you will be involved in teaching young children. Write beside them some of the values or beliefs that they are based on.

2 Produce a behaviour policy for a particular setting based on the information above.

Social development and child care in a multicultural society

multicultural society
A society whose members
have a variety of cultural
backgrounds

A **multicultural society** is one whose members have a variety of cultural backgrounds. In order to promote equality of opportunity for all, it is essential that anyone caring for children examines the particular rules and customs of their establishment. They need to distinguish between rules that are essential for everyone to follow (for example, rules concerning safety and mutual respect) and those that can be varied (for example, those connected to dress, food and religious customs). Establishments sometimes have rules that are both unessential and culturally biased. The Children Act requires establishments to have a multicultural approach to caring, and most establishments encourage understanding and respect for the customs of all children and their families. Many have examined their rules to ensure that they promote equal opportunities and avoid discriminatory practices.

Many establishments now encourage understanding and respect for the customs of all children and their families

The role of the adult in promoting children's positive self-image in a multicultural society

Children build up pictures of themselves and images of how others see them through the process of socialisation. All children need to develop a positive identity. One of the things that helps them to do this is if they see **positive images** of themselves in everyday life and in special roles. A positive image in this context is the representation of a cross-section of people in objects, pictures, and books in a wide variety of roles and everyday situations.

For example, it is important that classroom displays show a representative range of people of different races so that black people are not invisible and therefore unimportant. Doctors, for example, are valued in society so showing a black doctor in a book or on television will help a black child's positive self-identity, as the child can identify with a black person in a valued role. The positive visual portrayal of black people also enables white children and adults to build up positive images of black people in society. Similarly it is important that people with disabilities are shown participating fully in all areas of life.

> **positive image**
> The representation of a cross-section of in a whole variety of roles and everyday situations

When children are not of the dominant ethnic group in a society, they may find it more difficult to see positive visual images of themselves. Their teachers, people on the television, children and adults in books are more likely to be of the majority ethnic group, which in the case of the UK is white. The need for a positive identity has been recognised in the Children Act 1989. This legislation recognises for the first time every child's right to be part of a community that is free from racial discrimination and a society that values different backgrounds and encourages a sense of identity. The importance of this principle, and its relevance to every aspect of children's care, is emphasised throughout the guidance to the Children Act. When people provide day-care for children they are required to:

- take account of their religious persuasion, racial origin and cultural background
- have a commitment to treat all children as individuals and with equal concern
- enable children to develop positive attitudes to differences of race, culture and language.

Do this! 12.4

Draw up an action plan for a school or nursery outlining what can be done to help both staff and children to learn about the customs of people who come from a variety of social and cultural backgrounds. Remember to include activities, resources, visits, visitors and displays.

 Progress check

1 What is culture?
2 What is a multicultural society?
3 What is a value?
4 What is a norm?
5 What does the Children Act 1989 recognise about culture?

Social development and the learning of social roles

The learning of social roles

During the process of socialisation, children learn an increasing number of social roles. This means that they learn the appropriate behaviour associated with different social positions. This learning may include the behaviour appropriate to being a daughter or a son, a sibling, a grandchild, a school pupil, a friend or a member of a club.

The learning of social roles helps children to:
- know how to behave in a wide range of social situations
- know how to expect other people to behave
- understand that people will respond differently to them according to that person's role; for example, they will understand that a teacher will behave differently to them from a grandparent, and also learn to cope with this difference
- perceive their social world as structured and predictable, and therefore have a feeling of security
- be aware that they have a place and belong in a social system.

The role of the adult in helping children to learn social roles

Adult carers can help children to learn about social roles by:
- giving them opportunities for imaginative play where they can explore their social world in a safe manner
- providing a good role model themselves
- making clear to the child the behaviour that is appropriate and expected
- supporting them at times of potential stress as they learn social roles.

The table below shows the potential stress associated with the learning of social roles.

Potential stress associated with the learning of social roles

Cause of stress	Definition	Example	Adult role
Role transition	Children move from one role to another	Change from pre-school to school child	Provide preparation and support
Role loss	Lose one role completely	From an only child to having a sibling	Give special attention, understanding, make allowances
Role conflict	Meeting the demands of one role clashes with meeting another's demands	Peer group encourages behaviour not approved by carer	Show understanding, provide firm boundaries

---

Do this!   12.5

1 List some further examples to those shown in the table of when children may experience role transition, role loss and role conflict.

2 Produce a leaflet for parents that will help them to recognise the possible behaviour of a young child who is experiencing difficulty accepting the birth of a sibling, and gives them suggested ways of managing this.

The learning of gender roles

stereotyping
When people think that all the members of a group have the same characteristics as each other

Sex-role **stereotyping** is still present in society. Stereotyping occurs when people think that all the members of a group have the same characteristics as each other, for example boys are tough and active, girls are soft and passive.

Sex stereotypes develop in children's minds when they learn what behaviour is expected of them as a boy or a girl. Although the process may be less pronounced than in the past, by the time children are 5 or 6, they appear to have a clear awareness of gender differences and the behaviour that goes with them. These ideas are firmly held by the time they are 7 or 8.

Children learn rules about how boys and girls behave from a variety of sources. They learn from their adult carers, other children, and from television and the mass media in general.

Children are disadvantaged by sex-role stereotyping if it limits the opportunities available to them. This happens when children believe they cannot do something because of their gender, or when those around them believe this. Developing an awareness of stereotyping and how to avoid it is vital for those who care for children.

Avoiding sex-role stereotyping

No one can argue with the fact that there are physical differences between girls and boys. However, when you aim to provide an environment for children that avoids gender bias, it is preferable to ignore the differences and to concentrate on the many similarities between girls and boys. It is also preferable to avoid dividing children into groups according to their gender as this unnecessarily draws attention to gender.

It is preferable to concentrate on the many similarities between girls and boys

Dividing children into gender groups increases the likelihood of differences being emphasised. When this happens, children are seen in terms of their gender first and as individuals second. One of the problems created by stereotyping is that children (and adults) begin to believe the picture others have of them and start to behave in ways that are expected of them. If a girl repeatedly hears a teacher asking for 'a nice strong boy' to carry something and 'a nice tidy girl' to clear up, she may begin to believe she is not strong and that her role is to clear up after others.

Children sometimes see differences between gender emphasised in books and other visual images. Girls have traditionally been portrayed as passive and domesticated, boys as active and dominant. Schools and nurseries are increasingly aware of this bias and avoid using such books. Good practice is to present positive images of both genders through the staff, range of activities, books, displays, visitors, and any other means that can be used.

Workers who avoid making any divisions between children on the basis of their gender will be more likely to provide an environment in which all children reach their full potential.

Do this!   12.6

1 a) Read the following list of possible characteristics that can be found in children. Make two columns headed 'Boys' and 'Girls' and then place the characteristics in the columns according to those which you think have traditionally been thought to apply to one gender more than the other.

aggressive	tactful	robust
ambitious	dominant	skilful
competent	illogical	active
caring	gentle	sensitive
warm	expressive	assertive
noisy	quiet	sentimental

   b) Think of occupations, tasks or activities that have been traditionally been given to girls/women and to boys/men and add these to the columns.

   c) Make a note of the conclusions you can draw about sex-role stereo-typing from this exercise.

2 Discuss any ways in which boys and girls have traditionally been or still are divided unnecessarily on the basis of gender. For example it used to be common in schools for girls and boys to have separate entrances, to line up separately, to have different columns in a register, etc.

3 Carry out some research by looking at a range of children's books and recording whether they present people in stereotypical ways or not. Remember many authors are now very aware of the need to avoid bias.

Progress check

1 What is a social role?
2 What does stereotyping mean?
3 What practices reinforce gender stereotyping?
4 What good practices can prevent gender stereotyping?

The social status of the family

The influence of social status on social development

social status
The value that a society puts on people in particular roles in society

Child-care and education workers need to have some awareness of the extent to which a family's **social status** affects the socialisation process and how far this influences the child's potential to be successful in their society. Social status is the value that a society puts on people in particular roles in society.

In all societies there are some people who are more successful than others. Success is usually measured in terms of the power that a person has. In most societies, people who have power and influence also have higher social status. What constitutes or makes up high social status varies between societies: in some societies, religious leaders have the most power and highest status, in others it may be military leaders, business people, politicians, or people with inherited wealth and status.

Power includes:

■ having easy access to things that are valued (for example, wealth, education and health)
■ the potential to influence directly what happens to other people (for example, religious, military or political power).

The possibility of any child being successful within their society depends firstly on the openness of that society. Some societies, such as the UK, are considered to be 'open societies'. The structures of the society (for example, the education system, job opportunities) enable a child to change their position within their lifetime. We have seen in recent years how the children of a grocer and a circus performer can become prime ministers in the UK. A closed society is one in which it is impossible for a child to move beyond the social status of their birth family, as for example in the Hindu caste system in India.

Through education, people in the UK and other European countries can achieve high social and economic status. Since the introduction of comprehensive education, educational success for all children has been made progressively more possible.

Despite this, however, a large body of research shows that success in education and in society in the UK are not directly linked to children's ability alone and that others factors must be significant. League tables and other research shows that children from families of lower social status are less likely to achieve success in the education system. Whatever the intentions, children do not appear to experience equality of opportunity.

The differing influences of the family on social development and educational success

A child whose family has low social status is *statistically less likely* to do well at school. While wanting to avoid the possibility of generalising and stereotyping a whole group of people, it is important to recognise and understand this fact when we aim to promote equality of opportunity for all children. Only by finding out the causes of inequality can we begin to support and compensate children who are less successful.

Children who are successful at school are more likely to be:

- brought up in a secure and loving environment
- have parents or carers see the value of educational achievement
- experiencing a language-rich environment with opportunities for play.

The experience of a secure and loving environment

Families from all social backgrounds can provide security and love for their children. Children brought up in a secure and loving environment are more likely to be responsive, confident, and to behave in a socially acceptable way, to have high self-esteem, to be more willing to learn and therefore more successful.

The experience of life of some families, however, disturbs their ability to put the needs of their children first and to provide security during the crucial period of primary socialisation. This inability may be because of the experience of difficult relationships within the family and these can exist within any social group. However, relationship difficulties may also be linked to the stress caused by living in long-term poverty, poor housing or a run-down environment, and these are more commonly experienced by people in lower social groups. Many people, however, continue to achieve a happy secure home for their children in these difficult circumstances.

Supportive parents or carers

Parents and carers who recognise the value of educational achievement are more likely to encourage their children's intellectual and social development. They recognise the value of encouraging socially acceptable behaviour, and realise that this is more likely to lead to success at school. Such parents visit the school and show interest in their children's progress. Any family, regardless of social status, can to do this.

However, carers who have themselves achieved success through the education system inevitably have a greater understanding and knowledge of how to succeed. They are more likely to feel at ease with teachers because they are similar to them. There is less to prevent them, both practically and psychologically (in their mind), from going into school to see how their child is progressing or from helping in the classroom.

Children who experience a language-rich environment with opportunities for play establish early speech and thought patterns which are essential to the development of literacy skills (reading and writing) when they go to school. A good experience of play is essential to their future intellectual development.

An environment rich in language

Carers who have a close and loving relationship with their children are more likely to spend time with them, establish language-rich communication patterns and encourage play. Children from any social background can be deprived of this if their parents' attention is directed elsewhere. Parents may be distracted from close contact with their children by the demands of their jobs and careers, by their own physical or mental health or by their personal, social or economic circumstances.

Parents who have money, power and higher social status are more likely to pay for care and education for their children to complement the time they spend with their children. This care may be by a nanny or in a nursery. The disadvantages experienced by some children from families with low social status, whose carers cannot pay for substitute care, has been recognised by some local authorities who provide nursery education primarily in areas of high social deprivation; it is a central feature of the Labour government's policy (in 1998) to provide subsidised child care. The aim is to enable children to have play experiences and language stimulation which will enable them to benefit fully from statutory education at 5 years.

Children have very different experiences during socialisation. Some of these directly affect their social development and their potential to be socially successful. Some of these differences are common to all social groups; others, notably those that are affected by economic status, are more likely to occur within a high or lower social and economic group.

Carers who have a close and loving relationship with their children are more likely to spend time with them and establish language-rich communication patterns

Case study: Success at school

Winston is an only child and lives with his mother in a small house on a private housing estate. His parents are separated. He sees his father occasionally and his extended family regularly. He and his mother have a warm, close relationship. His mother visits his school for regular parents evenings and knows that he is a bright child. If she ever feels that Winston is experiencing any particular difficulties, she makes an appointment to see his teacher. His mother and he eat together each evening and they discuss what they have done that day and often laugh and joke about things that have happened. Each day his mother listens to him read and they look at books together.

1 How would you describe Winston and his mother's relationship?
2 Why do you think it is likely that Winston will do well at school?
3 Write a description of child, and their family, who might be less likely to succeed at school.

Conclusion

The following points review this discussion of socialisation.

- Infants and young children become truly human through contact with other people. This is one of the reasons that working with and caring for young children is important and responsible work.
- Children need close contact with carers during primary socialisation.
- The learning process is continuous.
- Caring adults help children to develop social skills, relationships, rules for behaviour, maturity and independence.
- It is essential that a carer integrates into their practice a knowledge of the social and cultural backgrounds of children in their care.
- Families provide differing social environments for children and these affect outcomes of the socialisation process and social development.

✓ Progress check

1 What does the term social status refer to?
2 What are the advantages of having high social status?
3 What should the introduction of comprehensive schools have ensured?
4 What remains the main influence on children's educational success?

Key terms

You need to know what these words and phrases mean. Go back through the chapter to find out.

culture
customs
multicultural society
norms
positive image
process
role model
role-play
social role
social status
socialisation
stereotyping
values

Now try these questions

1 How do children learn social behaviour from others?

2 Describe the socialisation process.

3 What positive steps can a school or nursery take to promote equality of opportunity?

4 What features of a family environment are more likely to lead to children achieving success within the education system?

5 Describe ways in which a child-care and education worker can be a good role model for children.

13 Children's behaviour

This chapter includes:

- **What is behaviour?**
- **How is behaviour learned?**
- **Young children's behaviour**
- **Managing children's behaviour**

Behaviour is acting or reacting in a particular way. It includes everything that we exhibit to other people, both acceptable and unacceptable. Behaviour is learned. Young children acquire their patterns of behaviour from the people around them. If children's behaviour is managed well, they are likely to develop acceptable patterns of behaviour. Child-care workers need to know how to help children establish positive patterns of behaviour.

However, some children learn and exhibit unacceptable patterns of behaviour. There is often a reason why this behaviour occurs. The reason may be obvious, or it may be hidden, unconscious, or in the past. It is likely to be linked to how a child is feeling. When unacceptable behaviour occurs, it needs to be managed in an planned and effective way.

You may find it helpful to read this chapter in conjunction with:

▶ **Book 1, Chapter 9**   Cognitive development

What is behaviour?

> **behaviour**
> Acting or reacting in a specific way, both unacceptably and acceptably

Behaviour is acting or reacting in a specific way. It is what we exhibit to others. It includes all that we do and say, both acceptable and unacceptable.

Patterns of behaviour are learned from the people with whom we have contact, both direct and indirect. This includes such influences as television, books and magazines. However, our earliest and most powerful influences are parents or carers and other influential adults in the immediate community.

Behaviour is therefore socially and culturally defined. We learn our behaviour from the social and cultural groups in which we grow up. There are, of course, many similarities between societies and cultures. There are also many differences in expectations and what is regarded as acceptable behaviour. This is important – do not assume that because someone's behaviour is unusual to you it is necessarily unacceptable.

Ideas of what are acceptable patterns of behaviour are acquired from a number of sources:

- history, culture and/or national heritage
- immediate and extended family
- local community
- peer group
- national government.

At different times in an individual's life, different influences will predominate. For young children, the family is the most powerful influence. As children get older, peers and the wider community become increasingly important.

Think about it

1 What is meant by 'behaviour is socially and culturally defined'?
2 Why do you think that different influences predominate at different times in life?

 Progress check

1 Who and what are patterns of behaviour learned from?
2 Who are the most powerful influences in a young child's learning?
3 From what other sources are patterns of acceptable behaviour learned?

How is behaviour learned?

Behaviour is learned through a complex process of imitation of role models, expectation expressed verbally and non-verbally, and rewards and **sanctions** that mould behaviour. Much of this process is **subconscious**: we are not aware that it is happening. It is a constant, life-long process. Both acceptable and unacceptable behaviour is learned in this way.

The patterns of behaviour that are established in childhood influence behaviour throughout our lives. It is essential therefore that young children are given the opportunity to develop acceptable patterns of behaviour from an early age. To enable them to achieve this, children need:

- positive role models
- loving adults who have realistic expectations of young children's behaviour
- clear and consistent expectations expressed verbally and non-verbally
- fair and consistent boundaries of acceptable behaviour, rewarded when appropriate.

Where these conditions exist most children will develop acceptable patterns of behaviour with a minimum of conflict.

sanction
A negative outcome attached to a specific behaviour

subconscious
Thoughts and feelings that a person is not fully aware of

Behaviours that children learn are more complex merely than what is either acceptable or unacceptable. They also learn different roles. Children pick up the different expectations that society has of different groups of people. For example, how does society expect a female to behave? How is a male expected to behave?

Many people feel that the expectations of society are unfair to some groups of people, for example, the expectation that females should be responsible for all the domestic work in a home, or the expectation that males do not cry when upset. These roles are perceived to be restrictive because they do not reflect what individual people are really like. The learning processes described above, however, are so powerful that many people conform to the expectations.

Children also learn the value placed upon each role by society. They learn that the behaviour of some groups is more highly valued than others. This leads to **prejudice** and **discrimination** against some groups of people. Prejudice and discrimination are not acceptable. People who have contact with young children have a unique opportunity to work towards changing this through the powerful influence they have on children's expectations of what is acceptable and what is unacceptable behaviour.

prejudice
An opinion, usually unfavourable, about someone or something, based on incomplete facts

discrimination
Behaviour based on prejudice which results in someone being treated unfairly

Think about it

Identify some different groups within society.
a) What behaviour or roles are traditionally expected of these groups?
b) What are your views on these roles? Give reasons for your answers.
c) If you think that change is necessary, how can this be achieved in your contact with young children?

Do this!   13.1

Observe a group of children during imaginative play.
a) What roles do they adopt?
b) Where do you think the children get their ideas of the role they have adopted?
c) What are the implications for the children's perception of these roles within society?

✓ Progress check

1 How do young children acquire patterns of behaviour?
2 How long does this process last?
3 What conditions are necessary for children to develop acceptable patterns of behaviour?
4 What is likely to happen if these conditions are met?

Young children's behaviour

It is important to have realistic expectations of young children's behaviour. If expectations are unrealistic, the possibility for conflict and **labelling** arises. Acceptable behaviour causes little concern. Unacceptable behaviour needs more careful consideration and is therefore the focus of this chapter. The following points are important in the discussion.

- The vast majority of children want to be approved by adults and others and therefore wish to behave in an appropriate way. With positive role models, loving adults who are fair and consistent in their expectations and who set clear boundaries, most children will develop acceptable patterns of behaviour.
- Behaviour is not 'naughty' just because it does not conform to adult standards of behaviour. Children need to learn which behaviour is acceptable and which is unacceptable.
- There is often a reason why a behaviour occurs. This reason may be hidden, unconscious or in the past.
- Behaviour can often be attributed to how a child is feeling. The feelings that a child has exist and cannot be changed. It is the behaviour that results from the feeling that is either acceptable or not acceptable. You must never reject a child's feelings, only their behaviour.
- Similar feelings in children can lead to very different behaviours. For example, the feeling of anger may result in one child being physically or verbally aggressive, but another child may well become withdrawn.
- Some behaviours are well established and it is difficult to understand why they occur.

Most young children will consistently exhibit acceptable behaviours as they grow and learn what is expected of them. However, while they are still in the process of learning, it is important that adults have appropriate expectations of what is common behaviour for young children. This will reduce the possibility of conflict and labelling. If the child is in an environment that promotes positive behaviour unacceptable behaviours will diminish with time as the child learns and grows.

Some common behaviours in young children

Some common behaviours include:
- physical aggression
- use of aggressive language
- temper tantrums
- defiance
- withdrawing
- jealousy.

Why do these behaviours occur?

There are many reasons for a behaviour occurring. Listed below are some suggested answers to this question. However, the reasons are not always

labelling
Giving a reputation (or label) to someone based upon a small part of their behaviour. For example, a child who is very noisy may be labelled as disruptive. This creates a prejudiced view of the child

straightforward; simple solutions are not easy to find, and the feelings and reasons that influence the behaviours are not always obvious.

Curiosity

curiosity
An inquisitive interest

A child learns by being active and interacting with their environment, and by being curious about their environment. There may be a clash between the child's **curiosity** and need to be active and the adult's wish for the child to be safe and/or to establish boundaries of what is acceptable.

There may be a clash between the child's need to be active and the adult's wish for the child to be safe

Imitation

imitate
To copy closely, take as a model

Children will **imitate** what they see others doing. This may at times be acceptable behaviour for an adult or older child, but not for a young child. Who or what are the child's role models?

Egocentricism

egocentric
Seeing things only from one's own viewpoint

Being **egocentric** means seeing things only from one's own viewpoint. It is not the same as being selfish, when both sides can be seen and the selfish one is chosen. Some psychologists believe that young children are incapable of seeing things from another person's viewpoint. It is a skill that children need to acquire over a period of time.

Developing independence

Children need to find ways of exhibiting their growing independence, and this may result in them trying to influence others in unacceptable ways.

Attention-seeking

Human beings need and want attention from other people. Children's behaviour can be a way of attention-seeking, that is attracting the attention of other people. For some children negative attention is better than none at all.

Anger and/or frustration

A lack of experience of the world sometimes means that children have unrealistic expectations of what is and what is not possible. This may result in anger or frustration, which is shown in their behaviour. For example, a child may have a tantrum when told that mummy cannot stop it raining so they can go to the park.

Anxiety or fear

A lack of experience and understanding of the world may lead to an unrealistic interpretation of events. For example, a child who experiences anxiety at being left in child care may be aggressive towards a parent who picks them up at the end of the session. This is often an expression of relief that the parent has returned.

Children may also become anxious and/or fearful when changes in familiar patterns and/or routines occur. This is likely to be reflected in their behaviour. Examples might be a new baby in the home, moving house, change in child care, starting school, changes in friendships, lack of sleep. The feelings associated with these changes and the resulting behaviour is often short-term and behaviour usually settles down once new or different routines are established.

Emotional needs

Children have many emotional needs, for:

- **affection** – the feeling of being loved by parents, carers, family, friends and the wider social community
- **belonging** – the feeling of being wanted by a group
- **consistency** – the feeling that things are predictable
- **independence** – the feeling of managing and directing your own life
- **achievement** – the feeling of satisfaction gained from success
- **social approval** – the feeling that others approve of your conduct and efforts
- **self-esteem** – the feeling liking and valuing oneself.

The absence of any of the above may lead to unacceptable behaviour as children struggle to get what they need. These can be long-term problems which require long-term strategies to mould behaviour so that it becomes acceptable.

Remember that all children are individuals and that the same feelings or events can result in different behaviours in different children.

---

affection
The emotional need to feel loved by parents, carers, family, friends and the wider social community

belonging
The emotional need to feel wanted by a group

consistency
The emotional need to feel that things are predictable

independence
The emotional need to feel you are managing and directing your own life

achievement
The emotional need for the satisfaction gained from success

social approval
When a person's conduct and efforts are approved of by others

self-esteem
Liking and valuing oneself

Think about it

1 Why may unrealistic expectations of children's behaviour lead to conflict and labelling?
2 Why may changes in familiar patterns and/or routines in a child's life affect a child's behaviour?
3 How can an adult who is caring for children meet their emotional needs?
4 Why may the same feeling result in different behaviour in different children?

Do this!   *13.2*

a) Prepare, process and present a chart, similar to the table below, to show feelings linked to possible behaviours.

b) Think of different behaviours that may result from each feeling, and note them on the chart.

Feeling	Possible behaviour
Anger	Physical aggression, verbal aggression, withdrawn

 Progress check

1 Why is it important to have realistic expectations of young children's behaviour?
2 List some common behaviours for young children.
3 Suggest some reasons why these behaviours occur.

Managing children's behaviour

Behaviour is learned. People who work with children need therefore to be aware of effective ways of managing and moulding children's behaviour. The same techniques can be applied during the child's initial learning and when it is necessary to alter existing unacceptable behaviour.

The ABC of behaviour

ABC of behaviour
The pattern of all behaviour: *Antecedent* – what happens before the behaviour occurs; *Behaviour* – the resulting behaviour, acceptable or unacceptable; *Consequence* – the result of the behaviour, positive or negative

All behaviours that occur, both acceptable and unacceptable, follow a similar pattern, known as the **ABC of behaviour**:

■ the *Antecedent* – what happens before the behaviour occurs
■ the *Behaviour* – the resulting behaviour, either acceptable or unacceptable
■ the *Consequence* – the results that occur because of the behaviour, either positive or negative.

The most effective way of managing young children's behaviour is by controlling the antecedent. By being aware of what leads up to a particular behaviour, it is possible to have some influence on the behaviour that follows. Careful observation of situations is required for the antecedent to be identified before changes can be made. By anticipating the antecedents to behaviour, carers can encourage children to behave in an acceptable way and the possibility for conflict is minimised. This can be done, for example, by:

- reminding children to put their coats on before going outside to play; it is very likely that most children will do as asked
- welcoming children by name to the establishment; this is likely to produce a feeling of being part of the group, and can exert a powerful influence on behaviour
- being careful about grouping children where there are some within the group who do not work well together
- providing enough space and equipment to reduce the likelihood of problems occurring.
- praising effort; this likely to encourage a child to continue trying this and other activities.

Changing the antecedent of unacceptable behaviour is one way of beginning to manage children's behaviour effectively so that it becomes more acceptable. Again, careful observation of situations is necessary to establish the antecedent. For example:

- temper tantrums: When do they occur? What leads up to them? Can this be altered?
- physical aggression: Who is involved? When does it occur? What leads up to it? Who or what are the child's role models?
- verbal aggression: Who is involved? Who or what are their role models? When does it occur? What leads up to the behaviour?

Children's behaviour can also be managed by altering the consequence of a behaviour. This may mean rewarding acceptable behaviour, or attaching a negative outcome to a behaviour. For this to be effective, it is important that the child is aware of the consequence of the behaviour, both positive and negative. It is also important that the resulting outcome is applied consistently. Where possible all the adults who have close contact with the child need to be applying the same consequences to behaviours.

Case study: Managing behaviour effectively

Tom, aged 3, who was normally quite a placid child, often become upset and difficult when activity time ended and the children came together for a story. He wouldn't put his toys away and shouted at the staff that he didn't want to have a story. This was clearly upsetting to Tom and disruptive to the group.

The staff decided to observe Tom over a period of a week to try and establish the pattern of events that led up to this behaviour. The staff noted many things:

- that Tom often became engrossed in the activities, especially construction activities
- that he produced quite complex structures with the equipment
- that when the children were asked to clear up, he became agitated, he quickly tried to finish his construction and became anxious that the other children were going to break it up

- this behaviour only occurred when he was part-way through an activity at story time.

The staff implemented the following plan:

- Tom was told, ten minutes before story time, that the session was ending soon to give him time to complete what he was doing.
- Completed models were kept until the following day.
- If Tom didn't finish what he was doing, his partly finished model would be saved until the following day when he could chose either to finish it or to break it up himself.

1 What were the antecedents to Tom's behaviour?
2 What unacceptable behaviour was evident?
3 What consequences did this behaviour have?
4 How did the staff establish what was causing this behaviour?
5 How did they plan to manage Tom's behaviour?

Think about it

1 Why is altering the antecedent to a behaviour an effective way of managing children's behaviour?
2 List some examples of where this could be effective in an identified establishment.
3 Think of some ways that an antecedent to a behaviour could be established.
4 Why is it important that the children are aware of the consequences of a behaviour?
5 Why is it important for all the adults who have close contact with a child to apply the same consequences to a behaviour?

Do this!   13.3

a) Observe a child. Make a note of the antecedents, behaviours and their consequences.

b) From your observations, identify any situations where you could alter either the antecedent or the consequence of behaviour to manage it more effectively. Give reasons for the changes.

✓ Progress check

1 What is the ABC of behaviour? Explain each element.
2 What is the most effective way of managing children's behaviour?
3 Give some examples of changing the antecedent.
4 How else can children's behaviour be managed?
5 What are the important features of managing behaviour by altering the consequence?

Behaviour modification

Behaviour modification is the term used for techniques which bring about changes in children's behaviour so that it becomes acceptable. It is based on the work of B.F. Skinner and his theory of operant conditioning. It works on the basis that:

- children will repeat behaviour that receives a positive response
- children will not repeat behaviour that receives no response or a negative response.

Behaviour is therefore moulded by manipulating the outcomes of a behaviour. This may be done by attaching a positive outcome to a behaviour so that the child is encouraged to repeat it. It may be done by ignoring a behaviour. It may also be done by attaching a negative outcome to a behaviour, so that the child is discouraged from repeating it. (This is the same as altering the consequence of a behaviour in the ABC of behaviour outlined above.)

This way of modifying children's behaviour is a long-term strategy. The rewards and/or sanctions need to be applied over a substantial period of time for them to be effective, especially if the unacceptable behaviour has been evident for some time.

For behaviour modification to be successful an assessment of how a child behaves is essential. This can be done using the ABC of behaviour. Patterns within a child's behaviour can be established through observation. Their needs can then be assessed and decisions made about a suitable behaviour-modification programme.

Attaching positive outcomes to children's behaviour

The following outcomes may be attached to behaviours to encourage repetition:

- adult attention: this can be verbal or non-verbal (nods, smiles, winks)
- adult praise directed solely at the child
- peer group attention: the group's attention is drawn to the child and the behaviour
- attention from other groups within the establishment
- responsibilities within the group
- extended privileges
- choice of activity
- tokens to exchange for privileges/activities/extended time at an activity
- positive reports to the parent or carer.

Attaching negative outcomes to children's behaviour

The following outcomes may be attached to behaviours to discourage children from copying or repeating them:

- ignoring the behaviour
- adult attention directed towards a child who is behaving acceptably
- removal from a positive situation to a neutral or negative situation, for example 'time out'

- adult disapproval, verbal or non-verbal, directed solely at the child
- peer group disapproval: this must come from the other children, not as a result of humiliating comments from the adult
- loss of responsibility or privileges.

Where a sanction is applied, it should wherever possible follow a pattern of natural justice, which means putting things right; for example picking up litter for dropping it.

For behaviour modification to work effectively, it must meet the following criteria.

- Rules must be established and the children must be aware of them.
- The children must be aware of the outcomes attached to behaviours, whether they are positive or negative.
- The outcomes must be appropriate to the children's age and/or stage of development and understanding.
- The outcomes must be applied each time the behaviour occurs.
- The outcomes must be applied immediately.
- Outcomes must take individual likes and dislikes into account. What an adult sees as a negative outcome may be positive for a child. For example, removing a child from a group for being disruptive: the child may not want to remain in the group and by removing them the adult has actually rewarded the unacceptable behaviour.
- Behaviour modification needs to involve all adults who have close contact with the child or children. This means that the rules are consistently reinforced within an establishment and at home.

Think about it

1 Why do you think children will repeat behaviour that has a positive outcome linked with it?
2 Why is it important to establish patterns within a child's behaviour?
3 List the ways that you could do this.
4 Why is it important that the child or children involved in behaviour modification are aware of the rules and the possible rewards or sanctions?
5 Why must the reward be something that is of value to the child?
6 Why must the reward or the sanction be applied immediately following the behaviour?
7 Why is consistency important?

Do this! 13.4

a) Write a profile of a child who is known to you and who behaves in an unacceptable way.
b) Decide which aspect of this behaviour is most unacceptable.
c) Compile a behaviour-modification programme for the child. Think about:
   - the rule(s), expressed positively where possible
   - the reward for keeping to the rules
   - the sanction that could be applied if using 'Reward and Ignore' does not work.

Making contracts

> **contract**
> An agreement between an adult and child – the child agrees to behave in a particular way and the adult agrees to reward that behaviour when it occurs

To encourage a child to behave in an acceptable way over a period of time, a **contract** may be drawn up between the child and an adult. The child agrees to behave in a particular way over the period of time and the adult agrees to reward the acceptable behaviour.

For young children this can be done by filling in a chart. Each time a child behaves in an appropriate way a section of the chart is filled in. When the chart is completed an agreed reward is received. Examples of such charts are shown opposite.

The benefit of this is to encourage the child to be behave consistently in an acceptable way, as the reward is not received until the child has maintained the behaviour over a period of time.

Key terms

You need to know what these words and phrases mean. Go back through the chapter and find out.
ABC of behaviour
achievement
affection
attention-seeking
behaviour modification
belonging
consistency
contract
curiosity
discrimination
egocentric
imitate
independence
labelling
prejudice
sanction
self-esteem
social approval
subconscious

 Progress check

1 What is behaviour modification?
2 What are the underlying principles?
3 What is meant by 'attaching a positive outcome to behaviour'?
4 Give some examples of positive outcomes.
5 What is meant by 'attaching a negative outcome to behaviour'?
6 What are the benefits of making behaviour contracts with children?

Now try these questions

1 What is behaviour?

2 How do humans learn their patterns of behaviour?

3 What does a child need to develop positive patterns of behaviour?

4 Describe some common behaviours in young children and outline why they may occur.

5 Describe the ways in which unacceptable patterns of behaviour can be effectively managed.

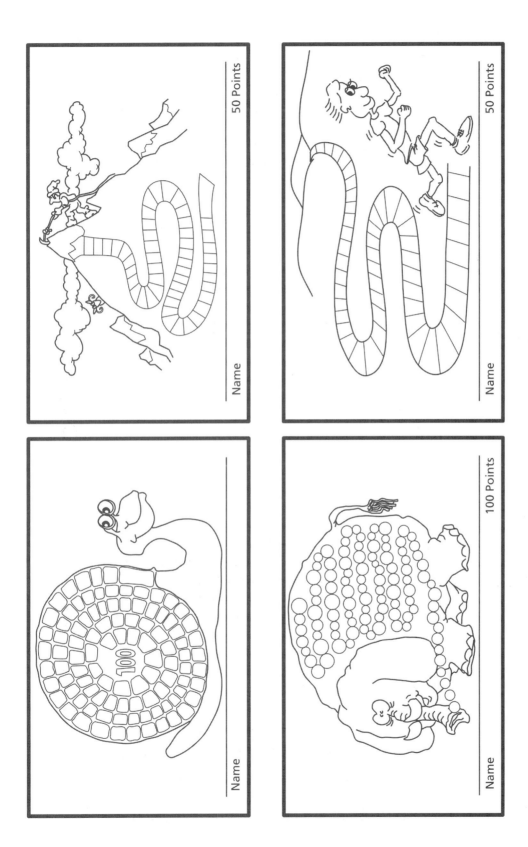

Examples of behaviour charts to be filled in by the child

14 The development of self-image and self-concept

This chapter includes:

- Stages in the development of self-image and self-concept (1): Birth to 2 years
- Stages in the development of self-image and self-concept (2): 2 to 8 years
- Encouraging the development of a positive self-image and self-concept

An important strand in social and emotional development is the development of self-concept and self-image. This is the picture we have of ourselves and the way we think other people see us. Self-identity includes the characteristics that make us separate and different from others. It could also be referred to as our personality. If child-care workers understand the importance of having a positive self-image and the need to value themselves, they are more likely to develop self-esteem in children.

A child's self-concept and self-image is established gradually over the first few years of their life. By recognising and understanding the stages in this development, child-care workers can encourage the process and also enable children to feel worthwhile and valued. This is vital to their emotional well-being. Children's self-image and self-concept will influence their relationships through to adulthood.

You may find it helpful to read this chapter in conjunction with:

- **Book 1, Chapter 10**   An introduction to social and emotional development
- **Book 1, Chapter 11**   The stages of social and emotional development
- **Book 1, Chapter 12**   Socialisation and social development
- **Book 1, Chapter 13**   Children's behaviour
- **Book 1, Chapter 15**   Bonding and attachment
- **Book 1, Chapter 16**   Separation and loss

Stages in the development of self-concept and self-image (1): Birth to 2 years

Birth to 1 month

New babies are not aware of themselves as separate beings. They do not realise that people and things exist apart and separate from them. It is thought that carers are perceived only as 'relievers of their distress', whether this is hunger, pain or loneliness. Gradually children learn to recognise themselves as separate individuals, through interaction with their carers.

Children also learn to **differentiate** between themselves and other people or things by exploration, using their five senses. Through these early relationships and exploratory experiences, children gradually come to a realisation of who they are – their **personal identity** – and what they think and feel about themselves – their self-image and self-concept.

1 to 3 months

During this stage, children start to recognise their carer's face, hands and voice. They may stop crying if they sense (i.e. hear, see or feel) their carer. This implies that they are beginning to be aware of their separateness, of the carer existing independently of themselves.

This period will probably see the first 'social smile', the baby's response to a person separate from themselves.

Early recognition of a child's **sensory impairment** will enable carers to adapt their approach to meet the child's needs, for example by using sign language with a deaf child. Carers who themselves have a sensory

---

differentiate
To distinguish and classify as different

personal identity (or self-identity)
One's own individuality, the characteristics that make us separate and different from others, our personality

sensory impairment
Hearing or sight loss

Think about it

How can parent/carers enable a baby to explore using their five senses?

The baby smiles in response

impairment are often skilled in adapting to accommodate the needs of their children.

During this stage, babies learn that touching a toy feels completely different to touching their own hand. In feeling the difference, they learn that the moving thing they see is their own hand, a part of them.

When they are held during feeding, changing and cuddling, babies learn that there are two kinds of feeling: one that comes from outside themselves, and the other, for example when they touch their own hand or chew on their own toes, that does not. These exploratory experiences start the process of differentiation between themselves and other people or things.

Is this part of me?

Do this!   14.2

Plan an activity for a baby aged 1–3 months that would encourage them to discover where they begin and end, and to develop their awareness of other people, separate from themselves.

---

3 to 6 months

Self-image

Once children have distinguished themselves as separate, they will start to build a picture or image of themselves. Gradually they discover what kind of person they are and what they can do. This picture of themselves can be either:

- a **positive self-image** – the child feels they are valuable and worthwhile
- a **negative self-image** – the child feels worthless and useless.

Children measure their own worth by the responses of adults and children who are significant to them. They need to experience the approval and acceptance of these people to develop feelings of **self-approval** and **self-acceptance**.

At this stage, infants still react to the world as if they alone make things exist or disappear. If they are looking at something, it exists; if they don't see it, it doesn't exist. If something or someone disappears from their view, babies will keep looking at the place where they were before they disappeared, as if waiting for them to come back. If they do not return, the baby will probably forget about them. If it is a person who is important to them, they will probably cry.

positive self-image
A view of oneself as worthwhile and valuable

negative self-image
A view of oneself as not worthwhile or valuable

self-approval
Being pleased with oneself

self-acceptance
Approving of oneself, not constantly striving to change oneself

stranger anxiety
Fear of strangers

separation distress
Infants becoming upset when separated from the person to whom they are attached

Think about it

How can adults enable children aged 3–6 months to feel accepted and approved of, at this stage in their development?

The end of this period may see the beginning of **stranger anxiety** and **separation distress**. This implies that babies recognise their separateness, and feel vulnerable without the support of the attachment relationship. If carers meet babies' needs at this stage, they will help to reinforce the babies' view of themselves as separate, but worthwhile.

6 to 12 months

Learning by experience

Children of 6 to 12 months are more able to join in play activities because of their developing physical skills. Infants will develop a positive self-image as they are encouraged and enabled to learn by experience.

The adult role

Play, at this stage, can be enhanced by the involvement of an interested adult. Their responses to the child, both positive and negative, will influence the child's self-image. Infants are aware of the feelings and emotions of other people. They experience all these emotions as reactions to themselves. They do not have the knowledge that would help them to see that anger and disappointment are not always caused by them. Infants start to feel towards themselves what they sense in others around them.

Object permanence

During this stage, children are learning that people and things have a permanent existence. Even if they cannot see them, people and things still exist. This awareness is reinforced through games such as peek-a-boo: the infants are discovering that people and things that disappear temporarily are still there, but have to be looked for.

Awareness of self as separate

By the end of this stage, babies are aware of themselves as persons in relation to other people. They start to realise that they are separate beings and that people and things exist apart from them. They show this development in many ways, for example, they:

- enjoy looking at themselves and things around them in a mirror
- usually know their name and respond to it
- appreciate an audience and will repeat something that produced a laugh before
- begin to imitate actions they have seen others do
- respond affectionately to certain people
- recognise other people's emotions and moods and express their own
- learn to show love to others, if they have been shown love themselves.

These behaviours indicate that infants have become aware of themselves as separate from others, and have formed a definite image of other people who are significant to them.

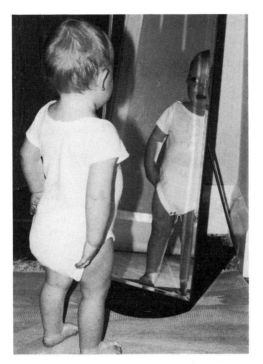 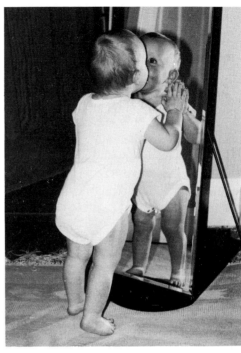

Is that me?

Do this! 14.3

Observe a baby of 6–12 months from time to time, over a few weeks. Note down the behaviours that demonstrate their growing understanding of their separateness and that of others.

Evaluate your observation and make some suggestions about how to develop the child's understanding in these areas over the next few months.

---

1 to 2 years

Children are aware of themselves as people in their own right and begin to exert their will, sometimes in defiant and negative ways.

The influence of cognitive development

Children's memory skills for objects and people are improving. By the end of their second year, they can remember whole situations and ideas as well as concrete things. They could, for example, demonstrate their memory of a trip to the park with grandma. They could demonstrate that they remember the things in the park (the slide, swings, etc.), the fact that they went with grandma and that they enjoyed coming down the slide.

This growing intellectual ability enables them to know people by what they do, for example the person who dresses them, the one who smokes a pipe and so on, and it also enables them to define people outside themselves and remember them.

Children's developing language skills

Children's developing language skills enable them to express their needs more specifically and to express their will. Their growing understanding of language can have a positive or negative effect on their emerging self-image and self-concept. What is expressed to a child and how it is expressed are both significant. Between 18 months and 2 years children begin to call themselves by their name and talk about things as 'mine'. They recognise that some things belong to them and they can distinguish between 'mine' and 'yours'. They think of themselves as separate individuals and are learning to understand themselves in relation to others.

Adult acceptance and approval

Infants learn to feel toward themselves what they sense in the responses of others. This applies both to them and their activities and efforts. Children begin to feel unworthy, incompetent, afraid and useless if:

- others are impatient with their attempts to do things for themselves
- they are not allowed to explore and make new discoveries for themselves
- they always sense fear when they attempt new physical skills.

Infants' self-image is fragile at this stage. Even if others are generally encouraging and approving, their feelings about themselves can swing dramatically. One moment a child may feel very powerful and successful, having learnt a new skill. The next moment they may feel small and weak when they find they cannot do what they have tried or seen another person do.

The importance of praise and encouragement

Appropriate encouragement and praise for the effort children make at this stage is vital. Encouragement and praise for effort is more likely to develop a positive self-image than praise for achievement. This is especially true for children with learning difficulties, who may not be able to achieve in certain areas.

Children need to be encouraged to feel proud of any new accomplishments or independence skills, in effect to feel proud of themselves. Their feelings about themselves will have a significant effect on their relationships with other people.

Do this!   *14.4*

Read the following phrases which may be said to a child of 1–2 years:

'You've done it wrong again.'
'Silly boy!'
'I don't think you can do that.'
'It's OK, but you spoilt it at the end.'
'You should have thought about that before.'
'How could you be so stupid?'

'That won't work!'
'It's too hard for you; I'll do it.'
a) Why would each of these phrases have a negative affect on a child's self-esteem?
b) Write a list of phrases that would have a positive affect on a child's self-esteem.

Parallel play

Towards the end of this period a child may be involved in playing alongside other children. They may form strong attachments to other children of the same age or older, although peers have not yet become very significant to their developing self-image.

Social emotions

social emotions
Empathy with the feelings of others; the ability to understand how others feel

empathy
An understanding of how other people feel

self-awareness
A knowledge and understanding of oneself

By the age of 2, some children have become sensitive to the feelings of others and display **social emotions**, such as sympathy if a person is hurt. This implies that children understand how such experiences make them feel (**empathy**), and is an indication of their growing **self-awareness**.

Do this! 14.5

Prepare a story with a story aid for children aged 2–3 years to encourage the development of empathy

Think about it

1 Why does praising a child for effort encourage a positive self-image more than praising them for achievement? Why is this particularly important to children with learning difficulties?
2 Why is it important for children to develop social emotions?

✓ Progress check

1 How do babies learn to recognise themselves as separate individuals and differentiate between themselves and other people?
2 At what stage will babies first:
   a) demonstrate a 'social smile'?
   b) exhibit stranger anxiety and separation distress?
   c) understand object permanence?
   d) usually know their name and respond to it?
   e) imitate something they have seen others do?
   f) call themselves by their name?
   g) engage in parallel play?
   h) demonstrate social emotions?

Stages in the development of self-concept and self-image (2): 2 to 8 years

2 to 3 years

Role-play

Between 2 and 3 years, children continue to develop their understanding of who they are and what they are like. They do this largely by observing and imitating the behaviour of people around them, particularly those that are significant to them.

This is shown in role-play and imitation of actions and behaviours they have observed in others, such as feeding a doll or talking on the telephone.

Is anyone there?

Pretending they are someone else helps children to take the point of view of others, to observe others and to generalise about the important aspects of other people's behaviour.

Such behaviour implies that children have developed a self-image and a view of other people separate from themselves. It may demonstrate something of what children think and feel about themselves in relation to other people.

Do this!	*14.6*
Observe children aged 2–3 years engaged in role-play. Record the roles they adopt. What do they convey about their understanding of other people's behaviour, thoughts and feelings? Do they reveal anything about their perception of themselves?	

Role models

Role models with whom a child can identify are important. Disabled children and those from minority groups need to be able to model themselves on adults who are like them, rather than always seeing themselves as different from the significant adults in their world.

The development of independence

Children at this stage are becoming significantly more independent. They will respond well to having certain things set apart as theirs, for example their own coat hook with their name and picture on it. These things confirm children's separateness, individuality and value.

With improved motor development, children learn self-help skills such as feeding themselves competently. They learn to use the implements of their cultural group: this may involve using chapatis and their hands, chop sticks or spoons and forks.

They learn to take care of their own toiletting, wash their own hands and begin to undress themselves. These are important steps toward **self-reliance**, socialisation and, consequently, towards competence and **self-worth**.

self-reliance
The ability to depend on oneself to manage

self-worth
Thinking of oneself as having value and worth

I can do this myself

> ### Do this!   14.7
>
> In a small group discuss how you can encourage children of 2–3 years to see themselves as separate individuals with value and worth:
> a) in the home situation
> b) in a day-care setting.

The child's developing language skills

Growing self-awareness depends on the development of a child's memory, the experiences they encounter and also on the development of language. Children who are encouraged to use language will develop more confidence in their own ability. This is because language enables children to:

■ explain how they feel, and to express more complex emotions than they could by non-verbal communication
■ receive reassurance and explanations
■ handle problem situations.

Do this!   **14.8**

1 Plan an activity for children aged 2–3 years to encourage them to express their thoughts and feelings using language.

2 In a small group, discuss the reasons why a child's language skills are important if they are in a new environment, for example if they are hospitalised.

Managing negative behaviour

Children's behaviour in the middle of this stage may seem rigid and inflexible. They do not like change, cannot wait and will not give in, often doing the opposite of what they are told. In fact, there may be good reason for these behaviours. Children are just beginning to understand themselves and the world they live in. They are discovering that they have a will of their own and may practise exerting it!

The responses and reactions of adults at this time are vital to the child's emerging self-concept. Children need to be given clear guidelines for acceptable behaviour, but should not be 'put down' in a way that has a negative effect on their self-image.

Manageable challenges

Being exposed to too many things they cannot do can also have a negative effect. Tasks that present children with a manageable challenge will give the opportunity for success and consequent enhancement of self-esteem. Too much frustration and consequent failure may produce a negative self-image and low self-esteem. This is one reason why disabled children, or those with learning difficulties, are more likely to have low self-esteem and a negative self-image.

3 to 4 years

Self-concept

Between the ages of 3 and 5, the foundation of a child's self-concept is established. By 3 years, children call themselves 'I' and have a set of feelings about themselves. Their self-concept at this stage will influence how they respond to relationships and experiences now and in the future. It is still affected by the attitudes and behaviour of those around them. They see themselves as they think others see them.

Peer group influences

At 3 to 4 years, children are more conscious of and concerned about others. They usually enjoy being with other children, and they begin to make strong attachments to individual children.

During this period, children test themselves out in different roles, for example as leader or as follower. Through this process they learn more about who they are and what they are like.

At this stage the reactions and responses of peers are very important and a child's self-concept will be affected by them. Comments like 'Here comes that dummy' and 'Oh no, it's that stupid boy again' will have a negative effect on a child's self-esteem and confidence. An insight into children's views of themselves may be gained from observing if, and how, they join in group activities.

Those who work with children are likely to find that a child with a positive self-image is easier to manage in a group situation.

Do this! 14.9

Discuss the reasons why children with a positive self-image are easier to manage in group situations.

Social emotions

They are beginning to understand that other people have feelings, just as they do. They learn to sympathise with other children, and can be encouraged to think about their own and other people's feelings.

Think about it

How can children be encouraged to think about other people's feelings?

Role-play

Children continue to test out their self-image and explore that of others through role-play. They also use role-play to express their understanding of themselves and others' roles, behaviour and attitudes. Children can be involved in simple drama and take on characters and feelings. Role-play can be used to help children understand other people's thoughts and feelings.

Do this! 14.10

Observe a group of children aged 3–4 years over a period of time. Identify individual children adopting a role, for example as leader, follower or comic. Do individual children adopt a variety of roles?

Cultural background

In this period, children are beginning to learn the way of life of the culture into which they are born. An important part of learning self-worth and self-confidence involves learning to value and be proud of their own cultural background. Children should never be made to feel that what they learn in their own cultural setting is less valuable than what they learn in other cultural settings.

Role models

All children will model themselves on the adults around them. Disabled children need to identify with disabled role models to construct their self-concept. It is not unknown for disabled children to think that they would grow out of their disability!

Avoiding gender stereotypes

From 3 years most children know their own gender (that they are male or female) and start to learn society's ideas about appropriate attitudes and activities for each gender. To construct their self-concept, a child needs to identify with an adult role model of the same gender, but models of either gender should present children with choices of behaviours, activities and goals, not with **stereotyped roles**, such as men going out to work and women taking care of the home. Seeing men and women adopting non-stereotypical roles allows children of either gender to see that they can do and be anything they want. They do not have to be restricted by their gender.

stereotyped roles
Pre-determined, fixed ideas that individuals are expected to conform to

---

Do this!   14.11

Discuss the reasons why children need male and female role models in child-care settings? Why is this difficult to provide?

Giving permission to fail

Children's feelings of confidence and self-worth will be strengthened by encouraging them to develop independence skills and also by letting them try to do things by and for themselves. Children need support to learn to accept their mistakes and not let them affect their feelings of self-worth. They need to be given permission to fail, with the message that it is perfectly acceptable to make mistakes.

Managing negative behaviour

By this stage, fear of punishment should be less important to children than their own internal set of standards – the standards by which they judge themselves, and that guide their behaviour. Rules should be explained, so that children can understand and apply the appropriate rule to themselves. Praise for trying to do what they feel is right is more effective than punishment for doing wrong. If children misbehave, they should be given a chance to explain why they did so. This shows respect for the development of their inner **conscience**.

conscience
The faculty by which we know right from wrong

Children need to feel cared for, worthy and acceptable to their carers. This is especially important when they are being controlled or corrected. They need to feel that while some actions are unacceptable, their participation in such activities does not make them bad people.

Think about it

Why is praise for effort toward positive behaviour more effective than punishment for negative behaviour?

Case study: Self-concept and behaviour

Elisha, aged 3 years 5 months, is of mixed parentage. Her adoptive parents are white and Elisha has no contact with her birth parents. The family live in a predominantly white, suburban area. Elisha was referred to a family centre, run by the social services department. Her rigid and inflexible behaviour had become difficult for her adoptive parents to manage. Elisha refuses to co-operate in day-to-day tasks such as washing, dressing toileting, etc. She has severe temper tantrums and is deemed to be beyond her parents' control. Her adoptive mother explained that in the past she always did everything for Elisha, her 'little pet', but since becoming pregnant, she needs Elisha to 'grow up'.

The family centre is in the city centre and includes children from a variety of cultural backgrounds.

1 Why may Elisha's behaviour pattern have developed?
2 How will the staff in the family centre need to manage Elisha's difficult behaviour?
3 Devise an outline plan to include a range of activities to develop Elisha's self-esteem.
4 How can staff in the family centre work with Elisha's adoptive parents to prepare for and support them through the arrival of a new baby?

4 to 5 years plus

By 4 to 5 years, most children have developed a stable self-concept (i.e. a view of themselves that remains constant and fixed). This is likely to be based on their own inner understanding and knowledge about who they are. If it is based only on other people's views, it will not be stable, but will change according to other people's ideas of them. Children at this stage who see themselves as likeable will not change this view of themselves when, from time to time, other children say that they do not like them.

Internalising social rules

At this stage, social rules (for example not taking other people's things without their agreement) have been internalised by children. They do not have to be told what is right and wrong all the time. This does not mean, however, that they will always obey these internalised rules.

Children start to rely on their own judgement of their behaviour. They are beginning to understand the words 'good' and 'bad' in terms of consequences. They learn best if things are explained in terms of themselves as well as others, for example 'If you share your toys with Zaida, she will share hers with you'. Although children may not be able fully to put themselves into someone else's situation they can understand if the explanation is given in terms of themselves.

Think about it

How do children acquire their own set of internal rules for behaviour? How can this process be encouraged?

Summary

Between the ages of 4 and 5, children are likely to have developed:

- a stable self-concept
- internalised social rules
- awareness of others, particularly other children
- the desire to see a task through to completion for their own self-satisfaction
- willingness to do things to increase their own feelings of competence and self-worth
- willingness to model themselves on someone similar to themselves who is competent in some area that appeals the child
- an inner conscience by which they judge their own behaviour (although this is still fragile at this stage)
- an ability to do things for themselves without support
- sensitivity to the needs of others
- responsibility for other people and things
- a desire for acceptance by other children.

Do this! 14.12

Word-process and illustrate a list of statements to be displayed in a primary school to encourage all staff and pupils to value each other's cultural backgrounds.

 Progress check

1 Why is role-play important for children at this stage of development?
2 Why is it important that the tasks given to children are a manageable challenge?
3 Explain the importance of a child's involvement with their peer group at this stage?
4 Why is it important for a child to feel cared for, worthy and acceptable to their carers?
5 How do children develop an inner conscience?

Encouraging the development of a positive self-image and self-concept

It is obvious that in this area of development children are fundamentally affected by the thoughts and actions of others. The following guidelines summarise, in a practical way, some of the principles involved in encouraging the development of a positive self-image and self-concept.

Twenty golden rules

1 From the earliest age, demonstrate love and give children affection, as well as meeting their all-round developmental needs.

2 Provide babies with opportunities to explore using their five senses.
3 Encourage children to be self-dependent and responsible.
4 Explain why rules exist and why children should do what you are asking. Use 'do' rather than 'don't' and emphasise what you want the child to do rather than what is not acceptable. When children misbehave, explain to them why it is wrong.
5 Encourage children to value their own cultural background.
6 Encourage children to do as much for themselves as they can, to be responsible and to follow through activities to completion.
7 Do not use put-downs or sarcasm.
8 Give children activities that are a manageable challenge. If a child is doing nothing, ask questions to find out why. Remember that they may need time alone to work things out.
9 Give appropriate praise for effort, more than achievement.
10 Demonstrate that you value children's work.
11 Provide opportunities for children to develop their memory skills
12 Encourage children to use language to express their own feelings and thoughts and how they think others feel.
13 Provide children with their own things, labelled with their name.
14 Provide opportunities for role-play.
15 Give children the opportunity to experiment with different roles, for example leader, follower.
16 Provide good flexible role models with regard to gender ethnicity and disability.
17 Stay on the child's side! Assume they mean to do right rather than wrong. Do not presume on your authority with instructions such as 'You must do this because I'm the teacher and I tell you to', unless the child is in danger.
18 Be interested in what children say; be an active listener. Give complete attention when you can and do not laugh at a child's response, unless it is really funny.
19 Avoid having favourites and victims.
20 Stimulate children with interesting questions that make them think.

Think about it

Taking each of the 20 golden rules in turn, explain why it is important to do what it says.

Key terms

You need to know what these words and phrases mean. Go back through the chapter to find out.
conscience
differentiate
empathy
negative self-image
personal identity (or self-identity)
positive self-image

Now try these questions

1 List the needs of babies at 3–6 months? How can these needs be met in a way that confirms an infant's view of themselves as separate, but worthwhile?

2 How can child-care workers encourage children to be independent and self-reliant when they are developing self-help skills?

3 How do children's feelings about themselves affect their relationships with other people?

4 How does cognitive and language development affect the development of self-concept and self-image?

5 Why is a disabled child more likely to develop a negative self-image? How can carers encourage the development of a positive self-image?

self-acceptance
self-approval
self-awareness
self-reliance
self-worth
sensory impairment
separation distress
social emotions
stereotyped roles
stranger anxiety

6 Why is it important for a child to value their own cultural background?

7 How can child-care workers encourage the development of a positive self-image in the children they work with?

15 Bonding and attachment

This chapter includes:

- **What is a bond of attachment?**
- **Theories about why bonds of attachment occur**
- **Our present understanding about why bonds of attachment occur**
- **How a bond of attachment forms, develops and is established**
- **The importance of bonds of attachment**

Children's social and emotional development is significantly influenced by their early relationships. In this chapter we will look, in detail, at the nature of these early relationships and how they affect children's social and emotional development. We will consider the special bond that develops between infants and the person or people who care for them.

You may find it helpful to read this chapter in conjunction with:

▶ **Book 1, Chapter 10** An introduction to social and emotional development
▶ **Book 1, Chapter 11** The stages of social and emotional development
▶ **Book 1, Chapter 12** Socialisation and social development
▶ **Book 1, Chapter 13** Children's behaviour
▶ **Book 1, Chapter 14** The development of self-image and self-concept
▶ **Book 1, Chapter 16** Separation and loss

What is a bond of attachment?

bond of attachment
An affectionate two-way relationship that develops between an infant and an adult

The term **bond of attachment** is used to describe an affectionate two-way relationship that develops between an infant and an adult. When the bond is established, the infant will try to stay close to that adult, and will appear to want to be cared for by them. By the end of their first year, the infant will show a marked preference for that person and may show stranger anxiety. Infants may well become distressed and show separation distress if they are separated from those adults to whom they are attached.

Experiencing a bond of attachment is crucial to children's healthy social and emotional development. Child-care workers need to understand why and how these bonds develop and why they are so important.

Theories about why bonds of attachment occur

Biological or instinctive explanations

Biological or instinctive explanations suggest that the bond of attachment occurs naturally as a result of **innate** (inborn) urges or **instincts** on the part of the baby and their carer.

| **innate** |
| Existing from birth |

| **instincts** |
| Patterns of behaviour that are not learned |

Instincts

Instincts are patterns of behaviour that are not learned. They exist in all members of a particular species. Different instincts and reflexes exist in different species; some birds have a homing instinct that enables them to find their way back from distant places to their home or base. Humans and animals are born with certain instincts and reflexes that automatically make them behave in certain ways; for example if you tripped and fell, your hand would automatically reach out to cushion your fall.

Maternal instincts

The notion that all women have 'maternal instincts' used to be widely accepted. These instincts are said to be innate and to motivate a mother to love and care for her child. They are thought to be connected to a woman having the physical attributes needed to carry and deliver a child.

Think about it

1 Is the idea of 'love at first sight' always true for a mother with her newborn infant?
2 Do all women have maternal instincts?

Do this!   15.1

Discuss the implications of the widely accepted view that all women have maternal instincts for the following groups:
a) prospective mothers
b) mothers who do not feel affection for their baby
c) women who do not choose motherhood.

John Bowlby

Our understanding of why babies form bonds of attachment has developed in part from the work of John Bowlby, an influential British child-psychiatrist. Although some of Bowlby's ideas have been modified over the years, they remain fundamental to an understanding of bonding and attachment.

John Bowlby conducted a major investigation of attachment bonds during the 1940s and 1950s. He studied why and how babies make attachments and concluded that babies have a biological need, or instinct, to form an attachment to the person who feeds and cares for them. Bowlby maintained that this was a survival instinct. Without it the helpless infant would be exposed to danger and might die.

Imprinting

imprinting
An attachment that forms rapidly

critical or sensitive period
A period of time vital for the achievement of a particular skill

ethologist
A person who studies human nature, intellect and character systematically

Imprinting is a rapid form of attachment. It is said to occur only during a **critical or sensitive period** in an animal's life, for example immediately after hatching.

Konrad Lorenz

Konrad Lorenz was an **ethologist**, who studied the biological reasons for animal behaviour. His work appeared to confirm Bowlby's idea that we are born with an instinct to attach to our mothers. It also suggested that there is a critical or sensitive period during which an instinctive bond will be formed. During the 1930s he observed that newly hatched greylag geese followed the first thing they saw after hatching. It appeared to be an instinctive reaction.

Lorenz also noticed a group of newly-hatched goslings following him. Lorenz called this specific behaviour imprinting. This would suggest that, in the case of human infants, there is a critical or sensitive period, during which the bond of attachment will occur.

Do humans have a similar need to imprint?

Affection or contact comfort

John Bowlby concluded that contact comfort, or affection, is very important to the formation of a bond of attachment. The adult's demonstration of physical affection is crucial. From the experiments of Margaret and Harry Harlow with rhesus monkeys it would seem to be more important to the emotional development of a baby than nourishment.

Margaret and Harry Harlow

A number of experiments on rhesus monkeys were conducted during the 1960s and 1970s by Margaret and Harry Harlow.

The infants seemed to need the comfort they received from contact with the towelling covered surrogate

In one experiment, they isolated eight monkeys in two different cages each containing a substitute or surrogate mother. Four monkeys were put into a cage where the surrogate was a doll made of wire mesh; the other four into a cage where the surrogate was a doll made of wood and covered in towelling. Both surrogates had a feeding bottle attached. All the monkeys clung onto the towelling model for around 15 hours a day, whether or not the bottle was being used by another monkey. No animal spent more than an hour or two in any 24 on the wire model.

The Harlows concluded that contact comfort was more important than feeding. This was especially true when the animals were afraid. If frightening objects, such as a mechanical teddy bear or a wooden spider, were put in their cages, the monkeys would cling onto their substitute mother.

When put into a test room containing various toys, the monkeys would explore and play so long as the cloth mother was present. If it was not there, or if the wire model was there, the monkeys would rush across the test room and throw themselves face downwards, clutching their heads and bodies. They clearly received no comfort from the wire surrogate.

 Progress check

1 Explain Konrad Lorenz's theory of imprinting.
2 Describe the two substitute mothers in the Harlows' experiment.
3 How much time did the infant monkeys spend:
   a) clinging to the towelling model?
   b) on the wire model?
4 What conclusions can be drawn about the infant monkeys?
5 What does this experiment imply about the importance of physical affection to human infants?

Do this!   *15.2*

Look through various parenting magazines and books.
a) What image of motherhood is portrayed?
b) What do the pictures illustrate about parenting?
c) What advice is offered to mothers who may not feel warmth and affection for their baby?

Our present understanding about why bonds of attachment occur

Sensitive responsiveness theory

The idea that there is a simple instinctive urge that binds mothers and carers and their babies is not now widely accepted. We may be born with an instinctive predisposition or preference for forming relationships with our care givers, but these urges are far more flexible than simple imprinting.

Humans rely much less on instincts than animals do. Babies are more able to learn and change their behaviour in response to what they have learned.

Many psychologists now believe that human infants are born with some skills that allow them to attract and keep someone's attention. They appear to be programmed to become aware of, and to respond to, people around them. They seem to prefer things that are human, like voices and faces. From an early age, babies give out strong signals that draw adults to them, and make them respond, for example crying, smiling, gazing, grasping.

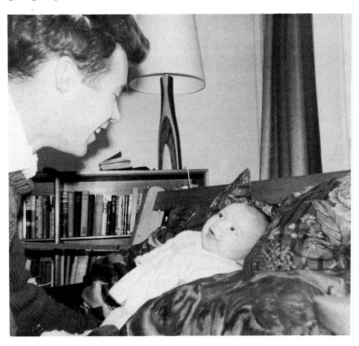

Infants seem to prefer things that are human

The carer's role in forming attachments

An adult must want both to become emotionally involved and to spend time with a child. A bond of attachment is not formed in five minutes. Carers who are sensitive to the signals given by the infant encourage the bond to occur and develop.

Making multiple attachments

John Bowlby maintained that babies need to attach to their mothers or at least a permanent mother substitute. He claimed that there would be a 'hierarchy of attachments with mother at the top'; in other words, mother is best. However, it is now recognised that a child is capable of multiple attachments, for example with father and other family and carers. Babies who attach to several adults can be just as deeply attached to each.

In 1964, a study of 60 Glasgow children, from birth to 18 months, was undertaken by Rudi Schaffer and Peggy Emerson. They concluded that when several adults took an interest in a baby, the baby could attach to them all. Schaffer and Emerson found that each attachment was much the same in quality. The infants responded in the same way to each attached adult. They seemed to use different adults for different things: if they were frightened they usually preferred their mother; if they wanted to play they usually preferred their father.

Schaffer and Emerson concluded that attachments are more likely to be formed with those people who are most sensitive to the baby's needs. They do not necessarily attach to those people who spend most time with them.

Do this! 15.3

Discuss the implications of Schaffer and Emerson's research for those who care for children in the absence of their primary carer, for example nannies. How can they develop a bond of attachment with the child? Why is this important?

 Progress check

1 Explain, according to our present understanding, what causes bonds of attachment to develop.
2 What do babies do to attract and keep an adult's attention?
3 What response is necessary from the adult?

How a bond of attachment forms, develops and is established

Conditions necessary to the formation of a bond of attachment

Certain conditions are thought necessary to the formation of a bond of attachment.

■ Interaction needs to occur between the baby and carers who want to spend time and get involved with them.
■ Relationships need to develop with a few people who will stay with the baby most of the time, not deserting them.
■ Communication needs to develop with carers who respond sensitively to the baby.
■ Loving physical affection is needed from carers.

In order to develop a bond of attachment, babies need to experience a warm, continuous, loving relationship with a small and relatively permanent group of carers who respond sensitively to them.

Stages in the development of a bond of attachment

A bond of attachment is established over a period of time. This period can be divided up into four main stages:

- during pregnancy
- at delivery
- immediately after delivery
- during the first six months.

Factors that encourage the development of a bond of attachment

Factors that may encourage the development of a bond of attachment include the responses of both infant and carers, and external or environmental factors, such as financial security. You will notice that some factors apply to more than one stage in the process. These are not necessarily repeated in the list.

During pregnancy

A positive bond is encouraged by:

- a planned, confirmed, wanted pregnancy, welcomed by partners and the wider family
- partners having a stable and mutually supportive relationship
- a normal healthy pregnancy; feeling fetal movements
- making full use of antenatal health care, which includes an understanding of the process of pregnancy and preparation for delivery
- security in material things such as finances and housing
- making physical preparations for the baby's arrival
- parents being emotionally stable and mature.

During delivery

A positive bond is encouraged by:

- a planned and expected delivery
- a natural delivery with little medical intervention, fulfilling parents' expectations, over which they felt they had control
- having health-care staff in attendance who are known and caring, in a friendly, non-medical setting
- being supported by a partner or relative or friend
- having a healthy 'normal' baby of the desired gender whose appearance fulfils parents' expectations
- the baby being given immediately to parents and placed in contact with their skin or put to the breast
- the baby remaining undisturbed with the parents in the first few hours of life.

The period shortly after birth

This can be a very sensitive period. Research has shown that bonding is encouraged by:

- the baby staying physically close to the parents, not separated for long periods of time
- the parents feeling well and emotionally stable, being emotionally mature, having experienced a strong bond of attachment with their own parent or carer
- the mother sharing the parenting role with a chosen adult
- health-care staff being supportive but not intrusive
- the baby remaining healthy and thriving, feeding, sleeping well
- the baby being welcomed by siblings and the wider family.

The first six months of life

By the end of this stage, infants will usually have established a bond of attachment. Their experiences during this period are crucial. Many of the factors already listed will continue to influence the development of the bond of attachment. However, the interaction between carers and baby becomes more significant. This interaction often focuses on carers meeting the child's needs, but positive feedback from baby to carer will also strengthen the bond. For example, the baby expresses needs by crying, smiling, babbling, clinging or raising her arms. The carer meets the baby's needs by feeding her, talking to her, cuddling her. Gradually the infant learns to trust that the carer will meet her needs and the bond is established.

The carer, for their part, may initiate positive interaction, for example talking to the baby. The baby responds positively by perhaps cooing or smiling. The carer is then motivated to initiate further positive interaction and the cycle begins again. This leads to feelings of self-esteem and self-worth on the part of the carer and strengthens the bond of attachment.

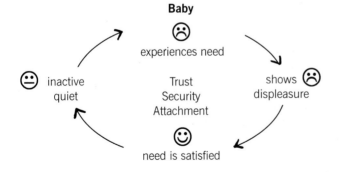

The baby expresses needs:
crying
smiling
babbling
scanning
sucking
clinging
raising arms

Both share:
skin contact
eye contact
general interaction

Carers in turn:
talk to the baby
smile at her
feed her
change the nappies
cuddle
lift
make the baby comfortable

Developing a bond of attachment: the first six months

Quality of care

We can see that meeting children's needs encourages a bond of attachment to develop. The success and the intensity of the attachment does not, however, depend on the amount of time the carer spends with the infant, but rather on the quality of that involvement. Infants can develop bonds of attachment with people who spend relatively short periods of time with them, for example an hour a day. This will happen if that time is spent in certain ways: these include the carer playing with the baby, cuddling them, providing them with individual attention, entering into 'conversations' with them, and generally creating a situation in which both of them are enjoying each other's company. The baby forms a stronger attachment with this person than with someone who cares for them physically for a longer period of time, but does not play with them.

This aspect of bonding has implications for those providing substitute care for a child, in the absence of their primary carers, either in residential or day-care settings.

Do this! 15.4

1 Discuss the implications, for those providing substitute care, of our present understanding of how an attachment develops.

2 Observe a baby interacting with the person with whom they have a bond of attachment. Aim to note the behaviours of the adult that encourage the development of the bond of attachment. Ask the carer about the baby's reaction to other people.

Child care in a kibbutz

In Israel about 4 per cent of the population live in large agricultural communes called kibbutzim. There are farms, some light industry, and some shops and offices in each *kibbutz*. The people try to be self-sufficient, growing and making enough to keep everyone fully employed. Everything is shared equally between all those who live in the kibbutz. Everyone works and receives the same wage and a share in the profits. The aim is for everyone to be regarded as equal in all respects, and there is no discrimination.

This way of life has important implications for child care. In order to return to work and start contributing again, the mothers of newborn babies only stay with them for a few weeks. During this time, intense bonding behaviour usually occurs, with cuddling, talking, playing and handling. The mother starts to go back to work, just for an hour or two a day. A trained nurse called a *metapelet* looks after the baby. Gradually the mother increases the number of hours she works and the metapelet increases her time with the baby.

By the end of the first year, the mother has returned to full-time work and the child is living in the children's house with all the other youngsters. The children spend an hour or so in the evenings with their parents before returning to sleep in the children's house.

Children brought up in a kibbutz stay more closely attached to their parents, who spend just an hour or two each day with them, than they do with the metapelet who is with them all day. The parents have not abandoned the child; they just leave the routine of childminding to someone else.

Think about it

1 Why is the process of intense bonding, carried out by mothers in the first few weeks after birth, so important?
2 In a kibbutz, what features of the process of handing over routine care to the metapelet are important in maintaining the bond of attachment?
3 Why do the children in the kibbutz remain more closely attached to their parents than to the metapelet?

Do this!   *15.5*

Discuss what you can learn from the description of child care on a kibbutz about your role in caring for children in the absence of their primary carer.

The implications of disability

The media often portray disability in a negative way. Society tends to view disability as a a condition to be pitied rather than a difference to be celebrated. Consequently, parents of disabled children may feel a sense of disappointment and failure when they discover their child has a disability. This may lead to difficulty or delay in the formation of a bond of attachment.

Recognising the differences

The formation of a bond of attachment may be encouraged in a different way by disabled carers and/or children. While recognising that all disabled people are individuals, it is important to think about the possible implications of particular disabilities on the bonding process.

Disabled children and carers have the same needs as other people, but the methods of meeting these needs may vary according to the nature of the disability. Children and carers with sensory impairment, sight or hearing loss in particular, will need to have alternative or additional ways of responding to one another.

Responding appropriately

Blind babies or carers may not be able to join in communication games that rely on visual clues such as facial expression or body posture. They will not recognise the carers'/baby's face by sight and respond to this. If sight loss has not been diagnosed, babies may be considered unresponsive by their carers. For example, when the carer of a blind baby enters the room, the baby 'freezes' so they can listen very hard. Some carers may interpret this as the baby not welcoming them. Strategies need to be worked out to encourage alternative patterns of interaction.

Carers and/or children with hearing loss will also need to use alternative methods of responding to one another. This is vital to the development of the bond which in turn affects all-round development.

The importance of language

Many of the difficulties disabled children and adults face are related to the responses of other people to them, rather than to the disability itself.

For example, children with hearing loss often experience difficulty in developing an understanding of language. The development of language relies on communication between children and others. This communication must be accessible and meaningful to children. Recent research indicates that early use of sign language develops deaf children's understanding and does not delay the acquisition of spoken language.

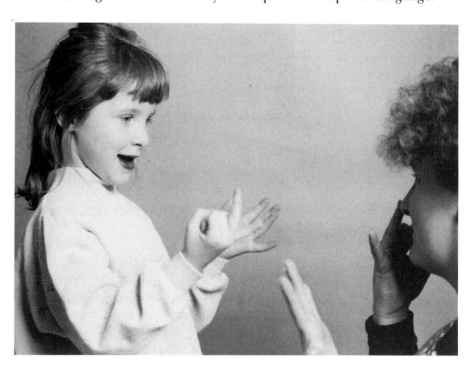

Early use of sign language develops deaf children's understanding and does not delay the acquisition of spoken language

Relatively few deaf children are exposed to sign language early enough. The exception to this are deaf children with deaf carers. Research by Susan Gregory and Susan Barlow (1989) highlighted the skills deaf parents show in interaction with their deaf children. This research confirmed subjective observations that deaf children with deaf carers tend to be more advanced in all-round development than other deaf children.

Think about it

1 How could carers encourage interaction between themselves and their blind baby?
2 How could you learn about the needs of children with a sight loss?
3 Why do deaf carers often develop a strong bond of attachment with deaf children?
4 What can child-care workers learn from deaf carers?

Do this!   **15.6**

Write a letter to a voluntary organisation for children with a sensory impairment, requesting information. Produce an information leaflet for parent/carers about the possible implications of this impairment.

Attachment behaviour patterns

By around 6–8 months, if the conditions have been fulfilled, most babies will be firmly attached to their primary caregivers. Evidence for this can be observed in two ways. Firstly, a baby with a firm attachment bond at this age or stage will show stranger anxiety (fear of strangers); secondly, they will show separation distress, that is, they become upset when they are separated from the person to whom they are attached.

Up to 3–4 months

Except for breast-fed hungry babies, babies generally do not mind who is with them; they will often smile at strangers.

3–5 months

Babies start to decide who they feel safe with. They may 'freeze' if approached by a stranger.

6–7 months

Babies express their preference clearly. Stranger anxiety begins. This will be more severe if the baby is not being held by the person they have an attachment to and is in a strange place. The way the stranger approaches the baby is also significant. If the stranger approaches slowly, does not get too close, does not try to pick up the baby, and does not talk too loudly, the baby will show less fear.

8–18 months

Babies start to make additional attachments if other adults are willing, and fulfil the conditions necessary.

2 years onwards

Stranger anxiety and separation distress slowly disappear in well-attached children, so long as the separation is not for too long. Well-attached children will be increasingly independent and willing to explore new situations. Less well-attached children are less adventurous and less independent.

3–5 years

Children are becoming steadily less clingy to primary carers. Peer group relationships become important.

Think about it

What are the implications of the behaviour patterns outlined above for substitute carers?

Do this!   *15.7*

1 Develop an outline plan, to include routines and detailed plans to encourage the development of a bond of attachment between a baby and their substitute carer.

2 Talk to some parents of a young child about the number of people their child is attached to. Discuss how much time each adult spends with the child. Is there any difference in the way each of the adults interacts with the child?

 Progress check

1 What conditions are necessary to the formation of a bond of attachment?
2 What factors are important to the development of a bond of attachment:
  a) during pregnancy?
  b) at delivery?
  c) shortly after the birth?
3 Explain how meeting a baby's needs helps to develop a bond of attachment during the first six months.
4 Describe the way in which children are brought up in a kibbutz.
5 Why may blind babies be considered unresponsive by their carers?
6 At what age may stranger anxiety occur?

The importance of bonds of attachment

Why bonds of attachment are important

Bonds of attachment are important because they affect all aspects of children's development. A poor or weak bond of attachment has far-reaching implications for the child. Its effects may extend into the next generation. ·

This section looks the importance of the bond of attachment to each aspect of children's development: physical, cognitive, language, emotional and social. This separation into different areas of development is for clarity only – a child develops as a whole person and areas of development are interrelated and interdependent.

Physical development

A strong bond of attachment helps to motivate carers to meet children's physical needs. In a young baby this can be a very demanding task. If a baby is responsive, the carers' self-esteem will be increased, and the bond of attachment will provide the motivation to put the needs of the baby before their own, for example getting up in the night, sacrificing their own sleep to meet the baby's need for food.

Failure to meet children's physical needs may lead to neglect and **failure to thrive**.

failure to thrive
Failing to grow normally for no organic reason

Think about it

1 What are the physical needs of children?
2 In what ways could they be neglected?
3 What are the effects on children of neglecting their physical needs?

Case study: *Failure to thrive*

Philippa had always assumed she would have a second child but had not planned to get pregnant. She and her partner John, both used to their way of life in the Services, were not suprised when John was posted abroad for six months during the pregnancy.

Philippa did, however, feel let down and unsupported when John was unable to return for the delivery. After a long and difficult labour, James was born by Caesarean section. Slow to start breathing, he was placed in the Special Care Baby Unit for the first few weeks of his life. A few days after delivery, Philippa, still feeling very tired, was relieved to leave hospital without James. She was anxious to return to caring for Thomas, her eldest child, who was only $2\frac{1}{2}$. Finally, James was allowed home.

Philippa was visited by the health visitor when James was 3 months old because she had not attended any of the baby clinics. The health visitor found Philippa and Thomas playing together in the lounge. James was in his cot in the bedroom. There were no baby things visible and Philippa seemed surprised at the health visitor's interest in James.

After careful monitoring, and despite adequate feeding, James was deemed to be failing to thrive and was re-admitted to hospital. Once in hospital, he gained weight. James was subsequently accommodated away from home by the local authority social services department.

1 What factors may have led to the weak bond of attachment between Philippa and James?
2 Why did James put on weight in hospital?
3 Why was James accommodated away from home by the social services department?
4 Why was his brother Thomas not accommodated away from home by the social services department?
5 How could James be re-integrated into the family?

Cognitive development

Children with a strong bond of attachment will have the confidence to explore and make discoveries. Attachment and dependency are not the same thing. The researcher Mary Ainsworth concluded that 'the anxious, insecure child may appear more strongly attached to his mother than the secure child who can explore fairly freely in a strange situation, using his mother as a safe base'.

Children who have a strong bond of attachment are more secure and confident and are more likely to learn, because they feel free to leave their carers and explore.

During the first year of life, children learn consequences and they learn cause and effect. For example, they learn that being fed stops the discomfort of hunger; they learn that crying brings adult attention. Cognitive development is built on this foundation. Studies in the USA show that children in the care system (who are therefore more likely to have had erratic parenting and a weak bond of attachment) are four or five times more likely to have learning difficulties.

> ### Do this! 15.8
> Discuss how children develop intellectually and how a weak bond of attachment may affect cognitive (intellectual) development.

Language development

Bonds of attachment develop through interaction between carers and babies, and they also encourage further interaction. Long before babies can talk or understand words, carers and babies hold 'conversations'. These conversations are a mixture of words and gestures from the carer and noises and movement from the baby, patterned like adult conversation. Early signs of pre-speech are evident even in newborn babies. It seems that babies may be born with a natural drive towards communication. A bond of attachment will motivate carer and baby to engage in early conversations that encourage the development of language.

> ### Think about it
> 1 Why are early 'conversations' important in the development of language?
> 2 Why does a bond of attachment encourage these conversations?
> 3 What are the implications for children and carers with sensory impairments?

Emotional development

Coping with frustration

If babies have their emotional needs met through the attachment relationship, they will be more able to cope with stress and frustration. This is true both in childhood and later in life.

Think about it

1 What kinds of frustration do young children experience?
2 Why is it easier for children to cope with frustration if their own needs have been met?

Developing independence

From her research, Mary Ainsworth concludes that 'an infant whose mother has responded promptly to his cries in the past should develop both trust in her responsiveness and confidence in his increased ability to control what happens to him'. Ainsworth used the term 'sensitive mother' to refer to one who is quick to respond to her baby's needs. These babies she says feel loved and secure, which helps them become more independent later on. Babies whose needs are not dealt with sensitively may tend to become more demanding and clingy.

A poem *Food for Thought* ends with the following lines:
If children live with security, they learn to have faith.
If they live with approval, they learn to like themselves.
If they live with acceptance and friendship, they learn to find love in the world.

In terms of emotional development, a child learns to be independent by experiencing dependence.

Do this!   *15.9*

1 Discuss what it means to spoil a child. Is it possible to spoil an infant by meeting their needs?
2 List the differences between attachment and dependency.

Developing a positive self-image

Another important result of a strong bond is the development of a positive self-image. Children learn to understand themselves through the responses and reactions of those close to them. They believe the messages that are repeatedly given to them. If these messages are largely positive, in other words if they reinforce the child's belief that they are worthwhile and worth attention from the adult, they will help to build self-esteem and a positive self-image.

Responding to control and discipline

Children with a positive self-image, who think they are worthwhile valuable human beings, will be able to tolerate frustration more easily; they will also be easier to manage, control or discipline. Methods of control or discipline often rely on children wanting to be close or attached to their carer. The carer disciplines the child by distancing them physically and emotionally, for example with disapproving looks or perhaps sending the child to their room. They rely on children wanting to re-establish closeness. This process will only work with children who are attached and who modify their behaviour to re-establish closeness.

Children who feel worthwhile and valued will feel that they deserve good things to happen to them. If the carer then controls through positive re-inforcement, for example 'If you (pick up the toys), something good will happen (you will have a story read)', then children are more likely to believe them. They believe that they are worthy of a reward, and they trust the carer to give it to them. They then modify their behaviour to obtain the reward.

Think about it

Why are children with a positive self-image easier to manage?

Coping with fears and worries

Children with a strong bond of attachment are better able to cope with fears and worries. Their experience of life leads them to feel safe and to trust that people will care for them and protect them from overwhelming fears and anxieties.

Social development

Making relationships

A strong bond of attachment develops children's feelings of trust in their carer and their sense of security. This makes children feel safe, but also encourages them to rely on other people. This is essential to the development of any relationship.

Later relationships will be built on the foundation of the attachment relationship. The child's experience of this will influence their desire and ability later to be part of other relationships. Through the development of the bond of attachment, children are learning how to take their part in a reciprocal (give-and-take) relationship.

Think about it

1 Why does a sense of security encourage children to rely on others?
2 Why is the ability to rely on others essential to the development of a relationship?

The development of social emotions

Around the age of 18 months, children with a good bond of attachment demonstrate social emotions. Toddlers can display some empathy or understanding of how other people feel in particular situations. They can demonstrate care for others, sympathy (feeling sorry for others), pride and embarrassment. Children whose own needs have been met by the attachment relationship are freer to care for others.

The development of conscience

Through experiencing embarrassment, children can be made to feel shame and guilt. In the right balance, these feelings are healthy; they lead on to the development of conscience, in other words, the ability to know right from wrong. A conscience is important to the development of relationships. Without conscience, children's behaviour may be entirely self-centred. Self-centred children have difficulty forming and maintaining relationships.

Think about it

1 Why do feelings of embarrassment, shame and guilt lead on to the development of conscience?
2 Why is the development of conscience important to the ability to make and maintain relationships?

✓ Progress check

1 Why is it important for a baby's physical well-being that they are responsive?
2 How does the bond of attachment encourage cognitive development?
3 According to Mary Ainsworth, what does a 'sensitive mother' do?
4 Give an example of managing children's behaviour through positive re-inforcement.
5 Why are children with a strong bond of attachment better able to cope with fears and worries?
6 What are social emotions?

Do this!   15.10

Produce an information leaflet for prospective parents on 'Developing a bond of attachment'.

Key terms

You need to know what these words and phrases mean. Go back through the chapter and find out.
bond of attachment
instincts
innate
imprinting
ethologist
failure to thrive
critical or sensitive period

Now try these questions

1 According to our present understanding, why do bonds of attachment occur?
2 Describe the factors that encourage the development of a bond of attachment during the first six months of a baby's life.
3 How do we know if attachment has occurred?
4 Why are bonds of attachment important?
5 What may be the results of a poor or weak bond of attachment?

16 Separation and loss

This chapter includes:
- **The consequences of separation**
- **Transitions**
- **Loss and grief**

The experience of a good bond of attachment is very important to children's all-round development.

Adults need to be aware not only of the possible effects on a child of a weak or poor bond, but also of the consequences of an interruption to any bond caused by the separation of the child from the parent, either temporarily or permanently.

The preparation for separation and loss, and the nature and type of substitute care provided, are significant to the long- and short-term effects on children. The child-care worker has a significant role to play in minimising the negative effects of separation and loss, and in caring for children who are experiencing grief.

You may find it helpful to read this chapter in conjunction with:

▶ **Book 1, Chapter 10**   An introduction to social and emotional development
▶ **Book 1, Chapter 11**   The stages of social and emotional development
▶ **Book 1, Chapter 12**   Socialisation and social development
▶ **Book 1, Chapter 13**   Children's behaviour
▶ **Book 1, Chapter 14**   The development of self-image and self-concept
▶ **Book 1, Chapter 15**   Bonding and attachment

The consequences of separation

Separation of child from parent/carer

Situations that involve separation for a child include:
- situations brought about by a change of full-time carers (short- and long-term)
- transitions that a child experiences when moving from one care situation to another on a daily basis
- situations experienced by children following the total loss of their carer, in particular a death.

Think about it

What circumstances may bring about a change of full-time carer for a child?

maternal deprivation
'The prolonged deprivation of young children of maternal care' (Bowlby)

distress syndrome
The pattern of behaviour shown by the children who experience loss of a familiar carer with no one to take their place

Think about it

Was it morally wrong to observe and film children in the way the Robertsons did?

Maternal deprivation

During the 1930s and 1940s, John Bowlby, whose work has been mentioned in Chapter 15, studied young people who persistently broke the law. In his book *Maternal Care and Mental Health*, he put their delinquency down to 'the prolonged deprivation of young children of maternal care'. He maintained that this 'had grave and far reaching effects on young children's character and future life'. This lack of maternal care came to be referred to as **maternal deprivation**. (This term will be referred to later, but is not now in common use.) It can be defined as the loss by children of their mother's love.

During the 1950s and 1960s, James and Joyce Robertson, colleagues of John Bowlby, undertook observations of children who went into hospital or residential nurseries. They were convinced that separating babies from their mothers was harmful. At this time the idea was contrary to medical opinion. The researchers used a cine-camera to film children during periods of separation, both in hospitals and residential nurseries. (These films or videos are still available to hire or buy.) The Robertsons noted that during periods of separation, many of the children went through a similar sequence of behaviour. This process, which appears to occur if children are separated and do not receive adequate care, is referred to as the **distress syndrome**.

The distress syndrome

The distress syndrome is the name given to the following pattern of behaviour shown by the children.

- The pattern of behaviour started with a period of *distress* or protest, shown by crying, screaming, and other expressions of anger at being left.
- This gave way to a period of *despair* when the children, apparently fearing their carer might not return, became listless, needed more rest, were dull, disinterested and refused to play.
- Finally, there was a period of *detachment:* if the children became convinced that their carer would never return, they appeared to try to separate themselves from any memory of the past. They were unable to make any deep relationships. Their behaviour lacked concentration; they flitted from one thing to another. Behaviour was also erratic; the children sometimes seemed dull and lifeless, sometimes highly active and excitable.

The Robertsons also noted the difficulty children experienced in linking up and relating to their mothers or carers when the separation ended. They followed the children up after separation and noted changes in their behaviour. They found that the separated children cried more than previously, had tantrums and did not show as much affection as before the separation. The Robertsons concluded that these separation experiences might have long-term effects.

> ### *Do this!* 16.1
>
> Describe the behaviour that you might observe in a 2-year-old child during each stage of the distress syndrome.

Implications for child-care practice

Bowlby's view that maternal deprivation can lead to delinquent behaviour and mental ill-health has now been changed and modified (added to) by others. His views, however, together with those of the Robertsons and other researchers, have resulted in far-reaching changes to child-care practice. Many professions concerned with children have changed their practices to avoid the unnecessary separation of children from their parents.

These changes include:
- new babies being kept beside their mothers on maternity wards
- parents of babies in special care baby units being encouraged to be involved in the care of their ill or tiny babies
- parents being encouraged to remain with their children in hospital, and the provision of facilities for them to stay overnight
- many social workers being taught to regard the separation of children from their primary carers as the worst possible solution to a family's problems
- the introduction of Child Benefit (previously called Family Allowance) to encourage a parent to stay at home and look after young children.

> ### Think about it
>
> Why might each of the changes to current child-care practice encourage children and their carers to develop and retain bonds of attachment?

Substitute care

substitute care
The care given to children during periods of separation from their main carers

The Robertson's observations also highlighted the importance of the type of replacement or **substitute care** given to children during periods of separation. Substitute care is poor when it is organised in a way that fails to meet the emotional needs of children. Substitute care is unlikely to meet children's needs if children are:
- cared for by constantly changing caregivers, with limited time to provide individual attention
- given little opportunity to form an attachment with any one caregiver
- poorly prepared for separation or for being reunited
- not encouraged to keep in contact with the people they were attached to.

The research of the Robertsons and others has had an effect on the provision of substitute care for children. In the past, children were often cared for in large institutions. The staff, who worked shifts, had responsibility for many children and were not encouraged to develop special relationships with individuals.

Today, children who cannot remain with their parents are cared for, if possible, by members of their extended family or by people they know. Those who are cared for by the local authority social services department are now placed in foster homes or small group homes. Residential nurseries are now rare.

The emphasis now is on substitute care that is as much like family care as possible. Substitute carers are encouraged to develop a bond with the children. Children in small children's homes will have a limited number of carers, one of whom will be their **key worker** or special carer. In addition, many children in the long-term care of the social services department may now be adopted. Disabled children, previously cared for in residential institutions, may also be placed with adopters.

Under the Children Act 1989, local authorities are encouraged to provide a range of services to enable 'children in need' to remain in their own homes and to be cared for by their own families. This avoids the emotional damage that can be caused by separation. These services include:

- day nurseries
- family centres
- family aids – people employed by the social services who go into homes to give practical help with child care and domestic tasks
- respite care, for disabled children – this provides short-term care which enables families to have a break, and hopefully prevents family breakdown
- liaison with voluntary agencies providing services to children and their families.

> **key worker**
> Works with, and is concerned with the care and assessment of, particular children

---

Do this! 16.2

Try to watch one of the early film records (available on video) by James and Joyce Robertson. The film *John* is particularly relevant. Take part in a discussion with others who have seen these films.

Case study: Hospital admission

Jill was born in 1948. She had a happy childhood and had never been apart from her parents. When she was 4, after periods prolonged illness, it was decided that she needed to have her tonsils removed, for which she would be in hospital for 10 days. The hospital was in the country many miles outside her home town and her family had no car so travel was a problem. Her parents were told that, although there was a visiting hour each afternoon, it was better not to visit because 'it might upset her'. Her parents therefore did not visit her for the whole time and she was taken and brought home in a hospital car.

When Jill first arrived at the hospital, she was cheerful and interested, but was quickly frightened when she was made to drink some medicine and change into a hospital gown. Nobody in particular looked after her, the nurses took their duties in turns. The preparation for the operation was bewildering for her and she started to cry for her mother. After the operation she was very uncomfortable and cried even more. No one was actually unkind to her, but little notice was taken. She gradually became quiet and subdued and took little notice of anyone.

When she was taken home, Jill was cold and distant from her parents. She did not respond to their attempts to cuddle her. She became a tense and nervous child, and when she started school at 5 years old she was very distressed and took a long time to settle.

1 What pattern of behaviour do Jill's responses illustrate?
2 Why do you think she responded in this way?
3 Why did her parents not visit her?
4 What long-term effects did the experience appear to have?
5 In what ways are the admission of children to hospital different today?

Think about it

1 Why is substitute care now organised to be as much like care in a family as possible?
2 What would you say to those people who advise workers not to get too close to the children they care for?

Think about it

In what ways can poorly organised care fail to meet the emotional needs of children?

Maternal deprivation reassessed

Michael Rutter, in his book *Maternal Deprivation Reassessed*, concluded that children's needs can be met satisfactorily by substitute care, if it is organised in a way that is sensitive to their needs. Researchers now seem to agree that the 'maternal deprivation' observed by both Bowlby and the Robertsons happened not simply because the children missed their carers, but also because they missed their individual caring behaviour. If a caring environment provides this type of care, children are less likely to be so profoundly affected by separation. How such care can be provided will be considered in the following section about transitions.

 Progress check

1 What is maternal deprivation?
2 Describe the distress syndrome.
3 What are the measures laid down in the Children Act to enable 'children in need' to remain in their own home?

Transitions

A **transition**, in the context of child care, refers to the movement of a child from one care situation to another. This usually involves a change of physical environment and a change of carer(s) for part or all of the day, for example when a child goes to school. Young children need stability and security in their environment, and because of this they need help to cope with any transitions they may have to make. Transitions involve change and loss, both of which are potentially threatening to children's feelings of security and trust.

When children have formed an attachment to a carer, they may experience feelings of loss if they are separated from that carer. We will now look at:

- situations involving separation
- how children can be prepared for separation
- the best ways to care for children during the separation
- how to help children when they are reunited with their carer(s).

Situations involving transition and separation

Children may experience separation from their main carers in a variety of situations. These can be divided into two main types: **residential care** and **day care**.

Residential care

Residential care is the care of children both during the day and the night. This can be in foster homes, residential accommodation such as community children's homes, or in hospitals. Such children are said either to be 'provided with accommodation' (voluntary care under the Children Act 1989) or 'received into the care of the local authority' following a compulsory Care Order from a court, or admitted to hospital.

Day care

Day care means care for children who are looked after for the whole or part of the day, but who return to their main carers at night. This may be with childminders, in day nurseries, nursery schools and primary schools. Children looked after by nannies usually remain in their own home and may or may not have their parent(s) present for the some of the time, they may still experience some loss.

How to help children cope with transitions

The Children Act 1989

The research that has been carried out into the effects of loss has had a direct effect on the way that children are both prepared for transitions and cared for in residential and day care. The conclusions reached by research underpin some of the principles of the Children Act 1989 which suggest the best ways to care for children in any setting.

Preparation for transition and change

Children's reactions to separation can be affected by the way they are prepared for change. In the past, there was little or no awareness of the value of preparation. Children were taken to school or hospital and left to cope with the experience. Good preparation is now accepted as beneficial to all children when moving to any setting. Preparation has become part of the policy of most institutions, including nurseries, schools, hospitals, childminders and long-term foster care.

Preparation is often built into the **procedures** of a day-care setting or school. A procedure is a pre-set agreed way of doing something. People dealing with children at times of change need to understand and be sensitive to children's needs.

The following guidelines for preparation can be applied to a variety of settings including schools and hospitals.

> **procedure**
> A pre-set agreed way of doing something

Preparation

Before a transition, prepare children by:

- talking to them and explaining honestly what is about to happen
- listening to and reassuring them
- reading books and watching relevant videos with them
- providing experiences for imaginative and expressive play which will help children to express their feelings
- arranging introductory visits for them and their carers, when information and experiences can be given both at their own and an adult's level
- making sure that any relevant personal details about a child, including their likes and dislikes and cultural background, are available to the substitute carer.

Reading relevant books can help to prepare a child for change

Effective ways to care for children during separation

It is essential that professional carers have a thorough knowledge and understanding of child development, so they can assess behaviour that needs attention. They also need to be aware of the particular stages of development that the children in their care have reached to see if any is a cause for concern. As shown in the table opposite, the Children Act (1989) recognises that younger children have a need for close contact with a familiar carer. It therefore provides guidance for the ratios of children to carers: the younger the child, the higher the ratio. Many day-care settings have key workers who are concerned with the care and assessment of particular children.

When caring for children the following points are relevant.

- Children under 3 years benefit from a one-to-one relationship with a specific person.
- The particular needs and background of children need to be known.
- Children's comfort objects should be readily available to them.
- Children should be provided with activities appropriate to their developmental age and stage, especially play that encourages the expression of feelings.

Suggested adult to child ratios (Children Act 1989)

Setting	Age	Children:carer ratio
Day-care	Under 2	3:1
	Over 2 but under 3	4:1
	Over 3 but under 5	8:1
	Over 5 but under 8	8:1
Childminders	Under 5	3:1
	Over 5 but under 8	6:1
	Under 8 (of whom no more than three are under 5)	6:1

- Honest reassurance should be given.
- Children's parents should have access to them if appropriate whenever possible.
- Children should have reminders of their parents or carers, such as photographs when they are apart.
- Positive images of parents should always be promoted.

Reuniting children with their main carers

Children who have been prepared for separation and cared for appropriately will find it easier to be reunited with their carers and to readjust to their home environment. This can apply as much to children starting school as to children who are returning home from full-time care. Children can be helped with being reunited if carers remember to:

- be honest about when they will be reunited
- allow them to talk and express their feelings through play
- advise the parent(s) to expect and accept some disturbance in their child's feelings and possibly some *regressive* (going back to an earlier developmental stage) behaviour.

Children's comfort objects should be readily available to them

Allow the child to talk and express feelings through play

Starting nursery or school

Most children go to school. Some may start by attending a nursery school, others start when they are the statutory school age of 5. Whatever their age children may experience anxiety and stress when they start school. Possible sources of anxiety when starting nursery or school are:

- separation from their carer
- being among a large unfamiliar group of children who may already be established in friendship groups
- the day may seem very long
- they may be unfamiliar with the predominant culture and language of the school
- the routines will be unfamiliar and they may have a fear of doing something wrong
- different activities such as PE, playtime, milk and dinner time can feel strange to them
- the scale and unfamiliarity of the buildings may be frightening
- being directed and having to concentrate for longer than they are used to.

The routines may be unfamiliar and they may have a fear of doing something wrong

---

Do this!   **16.3**

Design a school brochure that will help children and parents to cope with the transition to infant school.

Easing the transition from home to school

Possible sources of help for children when they start school are shown in the table opposite. These sources include the policies of the school, both towards admissions and to parents, the staff of the school and the child's parents or family.

Do this!   **16.4**

Write an illustrated article for a magazine about a 3-year-old's planned stay in hospital for a three-week period. Include:
- the ways that the child can be prepared for the stay, including the things that can be done at home, at school and by the hospital

Policies

School policies can include:

- an appropriate admission programme
- an admission policy that staggers the intake of children
- a helpful and informative brochure, provided in the home languages of parents and children
- appropriate classrooms and staff
- good liaison with parents
- a welcoming environment.

Sources of help when starting school

Staff

Staff (teachers, nursery nurses, classroom assistants, etc.) can provide:

- a relaxed classroom routine
- appropriate activities and expectations
- individual attention
- observation and monitoring of new children
- an awareness of cultural and language differences
- a welcome to parents to participate.

Parents

Parents and carers can help by:

- encouraging independence skills, e.g. dressing, washing, eating
- giving children some experience of separation before they start school
- being there for the child when they need reassurance
- having a positive attitude towards school
- reading books about starting school and encouraging realistic expectations
- establishing routines (e.g. bedtime) that will fit in with school
- providing the appropriate equipment (e.g. lunch box, PE kit).

Sources of help when starting school

- a description of how the child's emotional needs can best be met during the stay in hospital
- an outline of some play activities that it would be appropriate to provide for the child in hospital.

Case study: Starting school

Marcus started in the reception class at his local infants school the week after his fifth birthday. This was the school policy for all admissions. Previously, he went to a private day nursery full-time for four years while his mother and father worked. His parents were given a helpful information brochure about the school and attended a meeting held for parents of all new children. Marcus attended pre-school sessions with other new children during the term before he started. These were held in one of the school classrooms on one afternoon a week, with the reception teacher.

1 How was Marcus prepared for the reception class?
2 How could Marcus's parents use the information they were given about school?
3 How well do you think Marcus settled into school and why do you think this?
4 Why might Marcus not have settled without this preparation?

Frequent transitions

Children whose admission to school is handled sensitively, with attention to the points above, usually learn to cope with attending school each day. Children can also be helped to adjust to frequent hospital admissions if necessary. Some children also have to cope with movement between their family home and residential accommodation or foster care. This may be because of family difficulties; parents may be unable to care for them because they are experiencing problems. Sometimes, if a child has a disability, a period of **respite care** in a community children's home enables the child to receive training or assessment. It also gives their families a rest. If it is handled well, a child can adjust to periodic changes of residence of this kind.

respite care
Short-term care for a child to receive training and assessment and/or to allow their family to have a break

Multiple transitions

Some children, however, experience frequent moves. This may be because of constant and unpredictable family breakdowns. Such children become increasingly distrustful of adults. They become accustomed to change, but become increasingly unable to relate closely to any carers. Their emotional and social development is disturbed and this makes them difficult to care for. It is for this reason that frequent changes of environment for young children are to be avoided, if at all possible. Social workers try to make long-term, permanent plans for children. These may involve placing children with adopters or long-term foster parents.

Do this! 16.5

a) Make some observations of children. Record your observations in either a narrative form or as a chart, time sample or tick list. For all observations, evaluate what you record, and assess how far the social and emotional needs of the children were met.

Use the following ideas:
- If you are working in a school, observe the reactions of a new child who has just come to school.
- If you are working in a nursery, observe the reactions of a new child who has just started attending the nursery.

■ If possible, observe the reactions of a child who has just started attending a nursery where the dominant language is not the one used at home.

■ If possible, observe the reactions of a child who has attended a nursery for some months whose mother has just had a baby.

b) Plan activities that you could use with each of these children.

✅ *Progress check*

1 What is a key worker?
2 What is a transition?
3 When might children experience separation from their main carers?
4 What can significantly affect children's reactions to a transition?
5 What are the main sources of anxiety for children when starting nursery or school?

Loss and grief

We have a limited number of very close attachments in our lives. Amongst the closest relationships are those between grandparents, parents and children, between siblings, and between life partners.

We have a limited number of very close attachments in our lives. Amongst the closest relationships are those between siblings

grief
Feelings of deep sorrow at the loss, through death, of a loved person

The term **grief** is usually reserved for feelings of deep sorrow at the loss, through death, of a loved person. The term also applies to the feelings and reactions of children to the long-term loss in other circumstances of a person with whom they have formed an attachment. This long-term loss may occur when a carer:

- separates or divorces from their partner and loses contact with the child
- is in prison for a long period
- is seriously ill and unable to communicate (for example, in a coma)
- goes away, including to another country, leaving the child behind.

If any of the above happens, the child may experience feelings of grief. Research has shown that grief felt by both children and adults follows a recognisable path or pattern. It is essential to have an awareness of this pattern when working with children who are experiencing grief. This awareness will enable you to:

- understand the child's feelings and behaviour
- be sensitive to the child's needs
- be able to provide and care for the child in the most appropriate way.

The stages of grief

This section will concentrate on the child whose carer has died, however a child may feel as if a carer has died in any of the circumstances listed above.

The process of grief can be understood as a number of stages that people pass through. Each stage involves experiencing feelings and behaving in certain ways. One stage has to be worked through, at least in part, before a person can move on to the next. Although it is useful to look at stages in this way, it can make the process appear orderly and systematic. In practice the stages tend to merge into one another. Children (and adults) may return to the feelings of a previous stage at any time during the process of grieving.

The strength of feeling people have when they lose someone or something is directly linked to the strength of feeling they have for the person or to the value they place on the object. The length of time the feelings last varies with the importance of the loss. Children may work through the main stages of grief for a person within a year. Adults may take considerably longer; three years can be quite normal. It is usually necessary for the dates of special anniversaries associated with the lost person, for example their birthday, to pass at least once before both children and adults can begin fully to adjust to the loss.

The table opposite summarises the possible feelings and behaviour of a child during stages of grief. The stages of grief that a child (or an adult) goes through when they lose a person can be divided into early grief, acute grief and subsiding grief.

The stages of grief

Stage of grief	Possible feelings of the child	Possible behaviour of the child
Early grief Immediately after the death or loss	Shock, numbness, disbelief, denial, panic, alarm	Listlessness, or hyperactivity, dislike of being alone, prone to illness
Acute grief Follows the acceptance of the death	Extreme sadness, anger, guilt, shame, yearning, despair	Pining, searching, restlessness, crying, compulsive and irrational acts, lack of concentration, prone to illness
Subsiding grief When acute feelings have been worked through	Less absorbed by grief, calmer, less preoccupied, shows interest in other things, higher self-esteem	Shows interest in life, forms other attachments, involved in activities, better concentration

Case study: An experience of loss

The following description is of a woman who loses a treasured piece of jewellery. It shows the range of typical feelings and reactions that people often pass through when they lose something precious.

When Martha saw that the ring was no longer on her finger she could not believe it. Where had it gone? Perhaps she hadn't put it on after all. She looked everywhere. She even searched in places she had not been to that day. Finally she had to admit that it was lost. She sat down and wept. The ring had belonged to her grandmother. How could she have been so careless? What would her grandfather say when she told him? It was her mother's fault for not taking it to the jewellers for her to get the size adjusted. She could think of nothing else.

In the days that followed, she often burst into tears. She did not feel like eating, and she slept badly. Her mother was very understanding. She let her talk and cry and get things sorted out in her mind. Gradually, she began to forget about the loss for longer periods of time. She got on with other things. She knew, however, that there would always be a feeling of sadness and regret locked away inside her.

1 What behaviour did Martha display that is typical of the early stage of grief?
2 When did she enter the second stage and what did she do?
3 What behaviour showed that she was at the stage of subsiding grief?

Working with a grieving child

If you can understand and empathise with the feelings of Martha in the case study above, you will also be able to understand the much more powerful feelings of grief people usually experience when they lose a person with whom they have an emotional bond and therefore really care about. In any person's life, the number of people with whom they have such a bond is quite limited. Children will always experience some grief at the loss of a close carer.

Children are immature and very vulnerable at times of loss. They need special consideration and care. However, it is possible that the adults who are closest to them could also be suffering the same loss. This means that the child's needs may not always be given the highest priority. It is very common in white British culture, unlike perhaps Asian families, for children to be excluded during the period of mourning for the death of a relative for example. They may not be informed of a death until later, they may not be allowed to attend a funeral even if they want to, or they may be sent away to stay with people who are not directly involved. This exclusion is probably the result of adults believing it is better not to upset the child, and also feeling that they do not have the emotional energy to cope with the child's grief as well as their own. Whatever the reasons all available research shows that excluding a child at this time can create problems for the child later on. In the long term their unexpressed and unresolved feelings can return and complicate their adult mental health.

Adults who are not themselves involved in the grief of a child, for example child-care workers and teachers, can be of great help to a child. They can give the child uncomplicated attention and consideration. Despite this, many adults find such involvement difficult. This may be because:

- they themselves have unresolved grief. Perhaps they were denied a period of mourning when they were young. Any contact with a grieving child can therefore activate painful memories
- they do not understand the process of grief, or the time that it takes, or the appropriate way to respond.
- they have, along with many people, a fear of death, and an unconscious wish to avoid any contact with death.

It should be a part of any child-care worker's training to examine their own feelings and attitudes, and to learn as much as possible about the process of grief. Avoidance is not helpful to a child.

The role of the adult when working with a grieving child

The table on pages 305–6 sets out the possible feelings and behaviour of a child during each stage of grief and outlines some practical ways that an adult can help the child at each stage.

The effects of grief on growth and development

Grief can be such a powerful experience that the developmental growth of a child may be affected in every area. The possible effects of grief on development are summarised in the table on page 306.

Stages of grief and the role of the adult

Stage of grief	Child's feelings and behaviour	What must be done for the child and why	Role of the adult carer
Early grief	Shock	Give the child advance warning of the loss, if possible, to lessen the initial shock and disbelief	Tell the child if a parent is terminally ill (i.e. will not recover; death is the only possible end) Tell the child if carers are about to separate or divorce Explain what long-term imprisonment will mean
	Denial and disbelief	Encourage the child to accept that the loss is real Be honest with the child	Keep the child at home; do not send them away Allow the child to see and share other people's sorrow Involve the child appropriately in a funeral
	Panic and alarm	Comfort the child: physical comfort is especially important	Provide a comfortable and quiet environment Hold and cuddle the child Give soft food that can be easily swallowed, e.g. soups Give favourite foods
Acute grief	Extreme feelings of sadness, anger, guilt and shame	Accept that the child will suffer pain Allow the child to express feelings: adults usually want to protect children from suffering and distract them from sad feelings, but if a child does not express the feelings that arise from loss it can be damaging to long-term development	Give the child time and attention Include the child in the feelings of adults who may also be grieving Help the child to be patient with their feelings Reassure the child that the hurt is inevitable Tell them that grieving takes time Reassure them that the pain will gradually ease
	Yearning and pining	Accept the child's need to do this Acknowledge that these feelings will probably come back to the child throughout life Recognise the child's desire to return to and hold on to the past	Make allowances if the child regresses Recognise that the child is going back to a simpler and familiar stage of life Do not criticise or appear to be shocked Provide play therapy through which children can resolve some of their conflicting feelings
	Searching	Recognise that the child has to know that the lost person cannot be retrieved. Recognise that loss usually leads to a strong effort by the child to recover the person who is lost Understand that this may lead to the child behaving restlessly and irrationally	Allow the child to search and feel they have tried to regain the carer Be honest and clear with the child; when parents separate it is vital that children are given a clear message. The child must not think that they have the power to reunite their parents

continued

Stages of grief and the role of the adult *continued*

Stage of grief	Child's feelings and behaviour	What must be done for the child and why	Role of the adult carer
	Disorganisation and despair	Adult support needed because: ■ they may find it difficult to concentrate ■ school performance may decline ■ they may have over emotional responses to things ■ movement and speech may slow down	Make allowances for the disorganisation Not be so demanding, especially within an organised environment like a school Help the child to organise him or herself Listen to the child, give time and good attention Protect the child and share their feelings
Subsiding grief	Feelings are less acute, more normal, for longer periods of time	Help to focus on the future as they gradually begin to adjust to the loss and become able to form attachments to other people	Encourage the child to participate in a range of activities Promote the child's physical well-being and self-esteem Make sure that the child can always trust the adult carer

The possible effects of grief on areas of development

Area of development	Possible effect of grief on development
Physical	Child may not want to eat or run around
Cognitive	Child may be unable to concentrate or be too sad to play
Language	Child may be self-absorbed and unwilling to communicate
Emotional	Child may feel insecure, lose trust in adults, have low self-esteem
Social	Child may not want to be with friends or relatives

Grief and mourning in a multicultural society

People have differing cultural practices for dealing with death and mourning. The mourning period is the time when people show conventional signs of grief, such as wearing black, or wearing white, weeping together, closing curtains. A knowledge of and respect for different customs and beliefs is vital when you are working with children whose cultural and religious background is different from yours. Without this knowledge, a child-care worker might respond unsuitably, or offer words of comfort that are inappropriate and even offensive.

 Progress check

1 What are the main stages of grief?
2 How can an adult best provide for a child who is experiencing early grief?
3 How can an adult best provide for a child who is experiencing acute grief?
4 How can an adult best provide for a child who is experiencing subsiding grief?

Now try these questions

1 Describe the possible consequences of long-term separation of an infant from their parent/carer.

2 Describe the characteristics of good substitute care.

3 What are the advantages for young children of foster care, rather than care in a residential establishment?

4 How do you feel when you lose something? Record the range of feelings and behaviour that occur when you lose something valuable, for example, a bag, a purse or wallet, or a piece of jewellery.

5 Why is it that adults who work with children might find it difficult to respond appropriately to a grieving child?

Part 4: Disabled Children and Their Families

Understanding the needs of disabled children requires a thorough knowledge of child development. The earlier chapters of this book provide detailed information on each aspect of children's development: physical development, language and cognitive development, and social and emotional development. All of this is relevant to the development of disabled children and their needs should be considered alongside those of all children.

The information given here cannot cover every aspect of disability. There are many condition- or impairment-specific organisations working with particular groups of disabled people that produce useful information and offer disability-awareness training. To be authentic, such information and training should include those most closely involved: disabled people themselves.

It is now more likely that disabled children will be included in all settings, such as nursery classes, schools, day nurseries, family centres or residential establishments. For child-care practice to be truly inclusive, the needs of disabled children and their families must be recognised and met.

17 *Understanding disability*

This chapter includes:

- **The implications of history**
- **Models of disability**
- **The importance of terminology**

Disability is generally seen as an undesirable condition experienced by other people that individuals hope will never happen to them. Disability in children is often regarded as a tragedy, eliciting pity for the 'victims' and their families. These and other attitudes, together with the environment, for example physical access to buildings, often cause unnecessary disability. Ignorance and fear can lead to separation, exclusion, prejudice and discrimination against disabled people.

The information given in this chapter aims to affect readers' attitudes as much as to increase their knowledge. Working with young children provides an ideal opportunity to influence attitudes. Children do not exclude or devalue each other until they are taught to do so by the unconscious or uninformed behaviour of adults.

You may find it helpful to read this chapter in conjunction with:

▶ **Book 1, Chapter 18**   Conditions and impairments
▶ **Book 1, Chapter 19**   The needs of disabled children and their families
▶ **Book 1, Chapter 20**   The legal framework
▶ **Book 1, Chapter 21**   Providing inclusive care and education
▶ **Book 1, Chapter 22**   The role of professionals

disability
The disadvantage or restriction of activity caused by society which takes little or no account of people who have physical or mental impairments and thus excludes them from the mainstream of social activities. According to the social model, disability is defined as 'socially imposed restriction' Oliver (1981)

The implications of history

During the Industrial Revolution in Britain there was a move away from small, family-based cottage industry to employment in large factories. This served to discriminate against disabled people because they were no longer able to control their own surroundings nor their pace of work. Disabled people were forced into dependency and poverty, losing the status that comes from employment.

At about the same time, the influence of the medical profession was increasing. Doctors sought to treat people and cure their **impairments** so

impairment
Lacking part or all of a limb, or having altered or reduced function in a limb, organ or mechanism of the body. According to the social model, impairment is defined as 'individual limitation' (Oliver 1981)

that they could fit into society. If this was not possible, disabled people were hidden away in hospitals and long-stay institutions out of sight; there was little contact with the outside world.

Children with disabilities were hidden away in long-stay institutions

 Progress check

1 How is disability often seen by society?
2 What causes unnecessary disability?
3 During the Industrial Revolution, what served to discriminate against disabled people?
4 What happened to disabled people, if their impairments could not be cured?

Models of disability

The medical model

medical model
A view of disability as requiring medical intervention

The result of the past is that society has become conditioned to treat disabled people according to a **medical model** (also known as the personal tragedy model). Society separates and excludes incurably disabled people as if they are somehow not quite human. Disability is viewed predominantly as a personal tragedy needing medical intervention. This encourages a negative view, focusing on what a person cannot do, rather than what they can. Disability is seen as a problem to be solved or cured, rather than as a difference to be accepted. It is all too easy, within this medical model, to see disabled people themselves as problem individuals who should adapt themselves to fit into society.

The social model

Disabled people, however, are no longer prepared to accept the medical model of disability. Through organisations such as the Disability Movement, they are campaigning for acceptance of a **social model** of disability. They want people to see impairment (the medically-defined **condition**) as a challenge, and to change society to include disabled people whether or not they are cured. This will involve responding to their true needs.

The social model views disability as a problem within society rather than within disabled people. It maintains that many of the difficulties disabled people face could be eliminated by changes in people's attitudes and in the environment. According to the social model, a mobility problem, for example, is seen to be caused by the presence of steps rather than by an individual's inability to walk; a deaf person's difficulty with accessing information is seen to be caused by other people's lack of skill in British Sign Language rather than by an individual's hearing loss.

> **social model**
> A view of disability as a problem within society

> **condition**
> Medically-defined illness

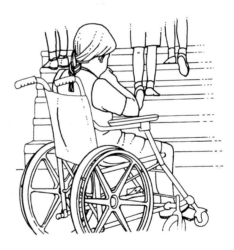

A mobility problem is seen to be caused by the presence of steps rather than by an individual's inability to walk

Disabled people have taken the social model a stage further and defined disability as a **social creation**, a problem created by the institutions, organisations and processes that make up society. This model of disability has led to disabled people coming together to campaign for their rights, for social change and to fight against **institutional oppression**.

One example of this was the Campaign for Accessible Transport: mass attempts were organised for wheelchair users to get on buses and tube trains in London. This direct action was intended to draw attention to public transport systems that serve only non-disabled people and discriminate against disabled people.

> **social creation**
> Brought about by society

> **institutional oppression**
> The power of organisations brought to bear on an individual to keep them in their place

Think about it

Think of as many examples as you can of the ways institutions and organisations create problems for disabled people.

Do this! 17.1

Discuss the implications of accepting a social model of disability:
a) for society
b) for you in your role.

 Progress check

Define the medical and social models of disability.

The importance of terminology

Why is terminology important?

Terminology reflects and influences the way disability is viewed by society, including disabled people themselves. It also influences people's perceptions and attitudes, which subsequently affect the provision of resources and services.

Over the years, disabled people have been referred to and labelled using many different terms, usually conferred on them by non-disabled professionals. These have included general classifications which dehumanise, like 'the infirm' and 'the handicapped', or even 'the disabled'.

In addition, people have been referred to in such a way that they become their impairment: 'Jane is a spastic', 'John is an epileptic', 'Our Down's syndrome child', 'Paul is a wheelchair case'. Many of these terms are patronising and contemptuous of disabled people. Some terms are used as a form of abuse amongst non-disabled people, for example 'cripples', 'dummies', 'spazzies', 'idiots', 'mongols', 'invalids', and worse.

There are many different conditions or impairments which disabled people have; when the condition or impairment is known, the correct name should be used for it. This is particularly true for disabled children, who are often denied accurate information about themselves.

Explaining terminology to young children, both non-disabled and disabled, provides an opportunity to teach basic information about such topics as bodies, health or illness. This is not a taboo topic to young children who need, and like, to know the truth. It provides an opportunity to dispel some of the myths and fears surrounding disability, and to influence attitudes at a formative stage.

Think about it

1 How do the terms listed above reflect and influence the way disabled people are viewed by others?
2 How may these terms affect a disabled person's self-image?
3 Why are some of these terms used as a form of abuse?

Children do not exclude or devalue each other until they are taught to do so by the unconscious or uninformed behaviour of adults

Definitions of terms

The definitions used in this book seek to respect the views of disabled people and promote good practice in the use of terminology. They were devised by the Union of the Physically Impaired Against Segregation in 1976. They are widely accepted by the Disability Movement and those working on disability equality issues.

Impairment may be described as lacking part or all of a limb, or having altered or reduced function in a limb, organ or mechanism of the body. Oliver (1981) defines impairment as 'individual limitation'.

Disability may be described as the disadvantage or restriction of activity caused by contemporary social organisation (society) which takes little or no account of people who have physical or mental impairments and thus excludes them from the mainstream of social activities. Oliver defines disability as 'socially imposed restriction'.

It is important to remember that disabled people are individuals with names. However, using the above definitions, it is appropriate to refer to *disabled people* or *disabled children*. These terms enable individual disabled people to identify themselves as a group with a common struggle, to end oppression by a disabling society. The adjective 'disabled' is similar to the term 'black' in that it was a negative term but now represents the pride people feel in their identity.

It follows from the above definitions that people may have physical impairments, sensory impairments, and/or learning impairments. There may, however, be preference for other terms within these groups of disabled people. For example, some adults who have lost their hearing in later life may refer to themselves as 'hard of hearing'. People born with a hearing loss may refer to themselves as 'deaf', 'partially hearing' or 'partially deaf'. Some people with learning impairments prefer to be referred to as 'having learning difficulties'.

Children with special needs

special educational needs
Learning difficulties requiring special educational provision to be made

The term special needs (in full, **special educational needs**) is now in common usage, especially in educational settings, in relation to children. The 1981 Education Act introduced the concept of special educational needs. Children with special needs include those whose learning difficulties call for special educational provision to be made. The Act states that children have learning difficulties if they have:

- significantly greater difficulty in learning than the majority of children their age, or
- a disability which prevents or hinders them from making use of educational facilities of a kind generally provided in school, for children of their age, within the local authority concerned.

In the past children with special needs may have been categorised as 'handicapped' or 'subnormal'. Individual children may have been labelled as 'physically handicapped', 'visually handicapped' or 'mentally subnormal'.

Those who advocate use of the term special needs suggest that these other labels are unsatisfactory because they:

- focus on weaknesses, not strengths
- do not indicate the practical effects of the difficulty and so the measures which may support the child
- suggest that all 'handicapped' or 'subnormal' children are the same and need the same kind of support
- encourage people to focus on the condition and view children with particular difficulties in stereotypical ways; for example, children with Down's syndrome are seen as sweet, innocent and lovable; deaf children are assumed to be slow on the uptake
- imply a clear-cut division between 'handicapped' and 'subnormal' children and other children.

Supporters of the term special needs seek to emphasise the *similarities* between children with special needs and children who are developing according to the norm. They hope that the change in terminology from 'handicap' to 'needs' will encourage the treatment of each child as a unique individual with their own personality, ideas, sense of humour and level of ability. However. the term 'special needs' still conforms to the medical model of disability.

Within the term 'special needs', children can be considered to have:

- moderate to severe learning difficulties
- sensory impairment, that is hearing and/or visual impairment
- physical or neurological (linked to the function of the brain) impairment
- speech and language difficulties
- emotional or behavioural difficulties
- **specific learning difficulties**; this term is used to describe children's difficulties learning to read, write, spell or in doing mathematics. Such children do not have difficulty learning other skills.

specific learning difficulties
Difficulties learning to read, write or spell or in doing mathematics, not related to generalised learning difficulties

✓ *Progress check*

1 Define the terms impairment and disability.
2 Where is the term special needs in common usage?

Do this!   17.2

1   Notice the terminology used by the media to refer to disabled people. Draw up a list and place them in to one of two categories, acceptable and unacceptable.

2   Find out how you can have your awareness raised about the implications of each of the above 'special needs'. Any disability awareness programme should include disabled people's views!

Key terms

You need to know what these words and phrases mean. Go back through the chapter and find out.

condition
disability
impairment
institutional
   oppression
medical model
social creation
social model
special educational
   needs
specific learning
   difficulties

Now try these questions

1   Explain the implications of history for disabled people.

2   Describe a medical and a social model of disability.

3   Why is it important to use appropriate terminology to describe disabled people?

4   What are the advantages and disadvantages of the term special needs?

5   Why is it important for child-care workers to have disability equality training. Why should this be delivered by disabled people?

18 Conditions and impairments

This chapter includes outlines of the following conditions and impairments:

- Asthma
- Autism
- Cerebral palsy
- Cleft lip and/or palate
- Coeliac condition
- Congenital dislocation of the hip
- Cystic fibrosis
- Diabetes
- Down's syndrome
- Epilepsy
- Haemophilia
- Hearing impairment
- Muscular dystrophy; Duchenne
- Phenylketonuria
- Sickle cell anaemia
- Spina bifida
- Visual impairment

This chapter provides an outline of each condition/impairment. The information is brief, containing only the main points, and is designed to give an overview. It also gives information that will help you to provide appropriate support and encourage the all-round development of children. The way a child is affected will vary, and it is important that the child-care worker responds to each child's individual needs.

Those working with children who have a specific condition/impairment will need to obtain more information. A useful source is the support agencies; they will have helpful, up-to-date information. Their addresses are included. Support agencies usually rely on money from donations to support their work, so if you request information from them, a contribution will be appreciated.

Information about each condition or impairment is given under the following headings:

- Causes
- Characteristics
- Diagnosis
- Treatment and progress
- Support agency.

You may find it helpful to read this chapter in conjunction with:

▶ Book 1, Chapter 6   Factors affecting physical development

Asthma

Causes

asthma
Difficulty in breathing when the airways in the lungs become narrowed; triggered by allergies, infections, exercise, emotional upset

Asthma (reversible airways obstruction) is a condition in which the airways in the lungs become narrowed. Allergy to certain substances, such as pollen, house dust mite or pet hair, causes the lining of the airways to swell. Children may also be allergic to certain foods, for example, peanuts. There may also be spasm of the airways causing further narrowing, restricting the supply of air. Other factors such as infection, exercise, the weather, cold air, or emotional upset may also precipitate attacks.

Characteristics

Breathing becomes difficult as the airways go into spasm and the child wheezes and is breathless. The airways may also become narrowed when the linings swell and by increased secretions of mucus. Attacks vary in severity. In a severe attack, breathing becomes very difficult and the child is anxious and afraid. Between attacks breathing is normal. Severe asthma attacks are serious and can be fatal.

Diagnosis

Diagnosis is made by observing the attacks. Skin tests may help identify the allergen.

Treatment and progress

bronchodilator
A drug that helps the airways to expand

The usual form of treatment is to give drugs called **bronchodilators** which help the airways to relax and dilate (widen or expand). These are commonly called *relievers* and are given by inhaler so that the drug is breathed in and goes straight to the affected air passages. Drugs can also be given in tablet or linctus form. It is important to try to prevent attacks by avoiding allergens and situations, which are known to be problematic. Drugs called *preventers* can also be given by inhaler on a regular basis to help to prevent attacks occurring.

Relievers are given in blue inhalers; preventers are given in brown/orange inhalers.

Management of an asthma attack

- Reassure the child.
- Stay with the child.
- Encourage relaxed breathing.
- Give the child their reliever inhaler.
- Sit the child upright in a comfortable position.
- Keep calm and continue to comfort and reassure until the attack subsides.

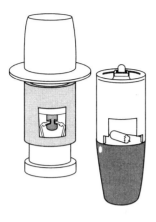 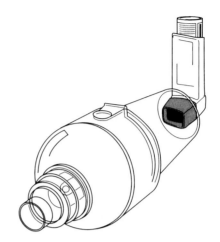

Different types of inhaler used by asthma sufferers

When to call an ambulance

- If this is the first attack.
- There is no improvement 5–10 minutes after the above steps have been taken.
- The child is becoming increasingly distressed.
- The lips mouth or face are turning blue.

Support agency

The National Asthma Campaign
Providence House, Providence Place, London N1 0NT

Case study: Asthma and allergy

Amy is a lively little 4-year-old who enjoys coming to the nursery three times each week. She celebrated her birthday just recently with a lovely party. inviting all her new friends from the nursery. She was especially happy because she had been given lots of presents, including a kitten from her granny. Amy loved the kitten and played with it all day and it came into her bedroom to sleep at night.

Several weeks after her birthday, the staff at the nursery noticed that Amy seemed to get out of breath very quickly. Her mother had also noticed that she had noisy breathing and had developed a cough at night.

1 What is Amy showing symptoms of?
2 What new circumstances in Amy's life could have caused her symptoms?
3 What treatment may help her?

Autism

Causes

autism
Difficulty in relating to other people and making sense of the social world

A child with **autism** has difficulty in relating to other people and making sense of the social world. The primary cause is unknown. Autism occurs in all parts of the world and usually begins from birth.

Characteristics

An autistic child may:
- lack awareness of other people
- pay more attention to objects than people
- have a problem in using non-verbal and/or verbal communication
- may not develop language
- lack imagination and the ability to play
- repeat activities and have unco-ordinated body movements
- have learning difficulties.

Some children may have an ability in which they excel, such as drawing.

Diagnosis

Diagnosis is made by observation of the child's progress. Parents or carers often recognise that their child is behaving differently from an early age. They are frequently frustrated that no diagnosis is made. The things they notice may include lack of eye contact, difficulty with feeding, screaming, lack of motor co-ordination, resistance to change.

Treatment and progress

Treatment is centred on modifying the child's behaviour. Consistent one-to-one care requires patience and skill on the part of all the family members. Pre-school activities are important. Respite care and long-term provision are helpful in enabling young people to gain some independence.

Support agency

The National Autistic Society
393 City Road, London EC10 1NE

Cerebral palsy

Causes

cerebral palsy
A disorder of movement and posture; part of the brain that controls movement and posture is damaged or fails to develop

Cerebral palsy is a disorder of movement and posture; the part of the brain that controls movement and posture is damaged or fails to develop.

There are many causes that may occur before, during or after birth. These include:

- the mother catching rubella during pregnancy
- lack of oxygen to the brain of the baby before or during birth
- Rhesus incompatibility (see Chapter 6)
- toxaemia of pregnancy (see Chapter 6)
- birth injury
- accidents or infections after birth.

Characteristics

The term cerebral palsy covers a wide range of impairment. There are three main types of impairment of movement:

- *spasticity*, where the movements are stiff, the muscles are tight and the limbs are held rigidly and turned in towards the body
- *athetosis*, when the limbs are floppy; movements are frequent and involuntary, especially when attempts are made to make the movements purposeful
- *ataxia*, lack of balance and poor co-ordination.

Cerebral palsy may affect and involve one or more limbs.

Diagnosis

Diagnosis is made by observing the child's progress associated with a history of possible brain damage.

Treatment and progress

No way has been found to repair the damage to the brain. Early assessment is very important. Therapy needs to be individual and works at maximising the child's potential; it may involve physiotherapy, speech therapy, occupational therapy or **conductive education**. Equipment can aid communication, mobility and independent living.

> **conductive education**
> A teaching method aimed at enabling motor-impaired children to function in society, *see* Chapter 22

Support agency

SCOPE
6–10 Market Road, London N7 9PW

 Progress check

1 What substances might affect the airways of a child who has asthma?
2 What other factors might bring on an asthma attack?
3 What is a bronchodilator?

4 What are the characteristics of a child with autism?
5 What are the three main types of impairment of movement that might occur in a child with cerebral palsy?
6 Which part of the body is damaged or impaired if a child has cerebral palsy?

Cleft lip and/or palate

Causes

> **cleft lip or palate**
> A structural impairment of the top lip, palate or both

A **cleft lip or palate** is a structural impairment of the top lip, palate or both. The development of the lip and/or the palate fails to take place in the early weeks of fetal life.

Characteristics

The failure of the development of the top lip and palate may occur in different ways:

- the lip only may be affected and will be divided into two or three sections by one or two clefts
- the palate only may be divided into two or three sections by one or two clefts
- the lip and the palate may both be divided into two or three sections by one or two clefts.

Diagnosis

Diagnosis is made by the examination of all babies at or soon after birth.

Treatment and progress

Treatment varies depending on the extent of the impairment; it can be lengthy and involve a series of operations to repair the gaps in the lip and palate. In general, the lip is repaired first, the palate later. Feeding will need careful management, and speech therapy may be required. The medical team treating the child will work closely together to produce the best results. Progress is individual and positive, with good results in many instances.

Support agency

Cleft Lip and Palate Association
134 Buckingham Palace Road, London SW1 9SA

Coeliac condition

Causes

coeliac condition
A metabolic disorder involving sensitivity to gluten; there is difficulty in digesting food

Coeliac condition is a **metabolic** disorder involving sensitivity to **gluten** (a protein found in wheat, rye, barley and oats); there is difficulty in digesting food. There is thought to be a familial tendency to the disease. The lining of the small intestine is sensitive to gluten and the resulting damage reduces the ability to absorb nutrients from the food broken down by the digestive process.

metabolic
Related to the process of digesting, absorbing and using food

Characteristics

The child exhibits the signs of malnutrition and does not gain weight and grow normally. The child may also be irritable, have pale, bulky, foul-smelling stools, and may vomit.

gluten
A protein found in wheat, rye, barley and oats

Diagnosis

Diagnosis in children is made by observation of the failure to grow and gain weight satisfactorily, particularly after weaning onto foods containing gluten. Diagnosis is also by biopsy and examination of tissue taken from the intestine.

Treatment and progress

A diet free of gluten must be followed. Gluten is found in many foods but the Coeliac Society produces food lists to help parents and carers. Foods like meat, fish, fresh fruit and vegetables are gluten-free, while anything containing flour contains gluten. The intestine usually recovers and the child will begin to grow normally.

Support agency

The Coeliac Society
PO Box 220, High Wycombe, Bucks HP11 2HY

Congenital dislocation of the hip

Causes

congenital
Present at birth

Congenital means occurring at birth. The hip joint consists of the head of the **femur** (the long bone in the thigh) and the socket in the **pelvis** (hip girdle). In **congenital dislocation of the hip**, the hip joint is unstable because of failure to develop properly before birth; this may be associated with the position of the fetus in the uterus, but there may also be a genetic link.

femur
The long bone in the thigh

pelvis
The bones that make up the hip girdle

Characteristics

When the hip is dislocated or unstable, the head of the femur may become displaced from the socket in the pelvis. One leg then appears to be shorter than the other. If left untreated the development of walking will be affected.

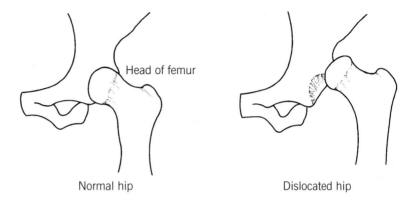

Congenital dislocation of the hip

Head of femur

Normal hip   Dislocated hip

Diagnosis

The baby's hips are tested soon after birth and then at regular intervals up to 1 year. The baby's legs are abducted (turned outwards) and the typical 'click' can be felt as the dislocated head of the femur slips back into the socket.

Treatment and progress

The treatment takes place in stages and is aimed at preventing dislocation and at making the hip joint stable. The baby's legs are held in the abducted position by the use of splints or a 'frog plaster'. Progress is usually good and normal walking can usually be achieved.

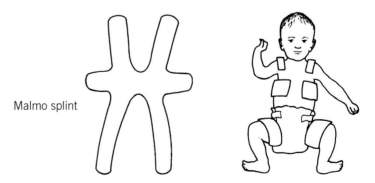

Malmo splint

Treatment for congenital dislocation of the hip

Support agency

There is no national support agency but support will be available locally from health visitors and the hospital to which the child is referred.

Progress check

1 Describe three ways in which the development of the lip and/or palate can be affected.
2 What substance in the diet is a child with coeliac disease sensitive to?
3 Which part of the digestive tract is affected by the coeliac condition?
4 Which bone and socket is affected by congenital dislocation of the hip?
5 When are a baby's hips normally tested?

Cystic fibrosis (CF)

Causes

> **cystic fibrosis**
> An hereditary, life-treatening condition affecting the lungs and digestive tract

Cystic fibrosis is a hereditary and life-threatening condition that affects the lungs and the digestive system. It is a recessively inherited condition. For the child to be affected both parents must carry the CF gene. (See Chapter 6, pages 115–16.)

Characteristics

> **pancreas**
> A gland that secretes insulin and enzymes that aid digestion

> **enzyme**
> A substance that helps to digest food

Mucus throughout the body is thick and sticky and the airways in the lungs become clogged. There are breathing difficulties, coughing and repeated chest infections. The **pancreas** fails to develop properly and mucus clogs the ducts, affecting the flow of **enzymes** into the digestive tract. Food is not digested and absorbed properly. The child fails to gain weight and grow satisfactorily.

Diagnosis

Family history and genetic counselling may mean that prenatal diagnosis is possible. A blood test is carried out on the sixth day after the birth as part of routine screening. Later, diagnosis is by observation of the baby's symptoms, followed by a sweat test and/or a blood test.

Treatment and progress

The treatment is aimed at:
- keeping the lungs free from infection, with antibiotic therapy
- respiratory education and therapy to expel mucus and keep the lungs clear
- pancreatic enzymes taken with every meal; a high-protein diet with vitamin and mineral supplements is prescribed.

Treatment is time-consuming, but children gradually become more independent and are able to manage and understand their condition.

Support agency

The Cystic Fibrosis Trust
Alexandra House, 11 London Road, Bromley, Kent BR1 1BY

Diabetes

Cause

diabetes
A condition in which the body cannot metabolise carbohydrates, resulting in high levels of sugar in the blood and urine

Diabetes occurs when the pancreas gland produces insufficient amounts of **insulin** or none at all, resulting in high levels of sugar (glucose) in the blood. Insulin controls the amount of glucose in the body; its absence results in abnormally high levels of glucose in the blood and urine.

There are two types of diabetes:

- Type 1, usually starting before 30 years of age and requiring insulin injections
- Type 2, common in older people and controlled with diet and medication.

insulin
A hormone produced in the pancreas to metabolise carbohydrate in the bloodstream and regulate glucose

Characteristics

Early symptoms of diabetes are excessive thirst, frequent passing of urine; children may lose weight. Complications include visual impairment, kidney damage and problems with circulation. Untreated diabetes will lead to the insulin levels dropping; unconsciousness and coma quickly follow.

Diagnosis

Diagnosis is by observation of the child's symptoms, and by testing the blood and/or urine for sugar.

Treatment and progress

For children, treatment is by injections of insulin together with a carefully controlled diet that restricts the amount of carbohydrate that can be eaten. Children quickly learn how to test their own blood and/or urine and keep a record of the results. They also learn how to give their own insulin. To keep healthy requires regular meals, regular insulin, regular exercise and regular medical supervision. Once the child and family have adjusted to the need for regular treatment and diet, a full and active life is possible.

One of the possible complications that may occur when a child is in your care is **hypoglycaemia** – low levels of glucose in the blood.

hypoglycaemia
Low levels of glucose in the blood

Signs of hypoglycaemia

- Irritability
- Confusion loss of co-ordination and concentration
- Rapid breathing
- Sweating
- Dizziness

Management of a hypoglycaemic attack

- Stay with the child.
- Give glucose to drink if the child is conscious and able to swallow.

■ If the child is unconscious put them in the recovery position (see Book 2, Chapter 24) and get someone to call an ambulance. Stay with the child.

Support agency

British Diabetic Association
10 Queen Anne Street, London WIM 0BD

Case study: Recognising signs and symptoms of diabetes

Ben is 5 years old and has just started at his local infant school. He had not been coming to school long before his mother became worried about him. She came into school to discuss the situation with the class teacher and the nursery nurse. Ben's mum had noticed that he was always tired these days, having previously been a really lively boy. He had lost his appetite, but seemed to need a lot more to drink. His mum wondered if this was why he had wet the bed a few times. Ben's class teacher and nursery nurse had noticed that Ben seemed to be unable to concentrate, he also seemed to be drowsy and sweaty at times. Ben's mum was taking him to the family doctor that evening.

1 List Ben's symptoms.
2 What do you think might be wrong with Ben?
3 How will a diagnosis of Ben's condition be made?
4 What is the likely treatment for Ben's condition?

Down's syndrome

Cause

Down's syndrome A condition caused by an abnormal chromosome, which affects a person's appearance and development

Down's syndrome is caused by an abnormal chromosome; usually chromosome 21 (see section on *Heredity* in Chapter 6, page 119).

Characteristics

Down's syndrome may affect the child's appearance and development. The condition may be identified soon after birth by the presence of typical characteristics. Not all the children will show all the characteristics to the same degree, but they may include some of the following:

■ almond-shaped eyes
■ short hands and feet; the hands may have a single palmar crease
■ small jaw, so that the tongue appears large
■ poor muscle tone

■ poorly developed, nose, sinuses and lungs, with increased susceptibility to infections.

There may be other impairments, such as heart disease.

Diagnosis

amniocentesis
A sample of amniotic fluid is taken via a needle inserted into the uterus through the abdominal wall; used to detect chromosomal abnormalities

Prenatal tests are available for high-risk groups. The most common is **amniocentesis**, which is carried out after the 16th week of pregnancy. **Chorionic villus sampling (CVS)** carried out at 8–11 weeks of pregnancy can also be used to detect Down's syndrome. Diagnosis can also be made by observation of the characteristics after birth.

Treatment and progress

chorionic villus sampling (CVS)
A small sample of placental tissue is removed via the vagina; used to detect chromosomal and other abnormalities

Treatment is given to respiratory tract infections and any other impairment which may affect the child. There is assessment and help with areas of development that may be affected. A stimulating environment and positive attitude help the children reach their full potential.

Support agency

Down's Syndrome Association
153 Mitcham Road, Tooting, London SW17 9PG

✅ Progress check

1 What is the cause of cystic fibrosis?
2 How is a child with cystic fibrosis affected?
3 What causes diabetes?
4 What is the treatment for type 1 diabetes?
5 What is the cause of Down's syndrome?
6 Describe one test carried out in pregnancy to detect Down's syndrome.

Epilepsy

Cause

epilepsy
Recurrent attacks of temporary disturbance of brain function

Epilepsy is a condition in which there are recurrent attacks of temporary disturbance of brain function. It may be caused by severe injury, stroke or brain tumour. It may occur spontaneously or be triggered by stimuli such as flickering lights, fever or drugs. There may be a familial tendency towards the condition.

Characteristics

Epilepsy can take many different forms. The condition is different for each child and ranges from disturbances in consciousness that are scarcely noticeable, such as mild sensations and lapses of concentration, to severe seizures with convulsions.

Diagnosis

Diagnosis is by observation and history of seizures, by EEG (electroencephalogram) which measures the electrical activity of the brain. Tests are also undertaken to exclude other causes.

Treatment and progress

anti-convulsant
A drug that is given to prevent fits

Anti-convulsant drugs are used to control the seizures. Care is important so that obvious dangers are avoided and to make sure that medication is taken regularly. Fear and misconception have always reinforced the stigma of epilepsy, so the child will need plenty of understanding and support. Most children with epilepsy go to mainstream schools.

Recognising major epilepsy

A fit progresses through the following stages:
- sudden falling into unconsciousness
- rigidity and arching of the back
- jerking movements
- breathing may cease
- froth or bubbles round the mouth
- bladder or bowel control lost
- regains consciousness within a few minutes
- feels dazed or confused
- may need to sleep.

Managing an epileptic attack

- Clear a space around the child.
- Protect the head with padding.
- Do not restrain or put anything in the mouth.
- When the convulsions have stopped check airway and breathing.
- Put in the recovery position (see Book 2, Chapter 24).
- Stay with the child at all times and reassure.
- If the child has never had a fit before, if they fit again, or remain unconscious for more than 10 minutes, call an ambulance.

Support agency

National Society for Epilepsy
Chalfont Centre, Chalfont St Peter, Gerrards Cross, Bucks SL9 0RJ

Haemophilia

Cause

Haemophilia is an inherited blood disorder where there is a defect in one of the clotting factors (see the section on *Heredity* in Chapter 6, page 118). It is inherited through the female line, but causes bleeding only in the male.

Characteristics

Bleeding will occur for much longer than normal after an injury; it may occur spontaneously into joints and elsewhere in the body; bruising is common. The child may experience severe pain when bleeding occurs into a joint.

Diagnosis

Diagnosis is made by knowing the family history, followed by prenatal tests such as chorionic villus sampling; and by observation of the symptoms after birth.

Treatment and progress

Haemophilia centres provide treatment and support. Treatment is given with injections of the appropriate clotting factor. Progress will depend on a balance being achieved between adequate protection and allowing the child to grow up into a well-adjusted healthy adult. Although the chance of bleeding is always present, it is important that child-care workers enable children with haemophilia to take part in normal activities as far as possible.

Support agency

The Haemophilia Society
123 Westminster Bridge Road, London SE1 7HR

Hearing impairment

Causes

Causes of **hearing impairment** include:
- heredity
- impairment of the cochlea nerve
- maternal rubella in pregnancy
- congenital defects
- head injury
- otitis media (infection of the middle ear)

- infections such as meningitis
- toxic action of drugs, such as streptomycin
- blockage of the ear canal by wax or other foreign bodies.

Characteristics

There is a wide range of impairment affecting a substantial proportion of people in the UK. Hearing impairment falls into two main categories:

- **conductive deafness**, an interruption to the mechanical process of conducting sound through the ear drum and across the middle ear
- **nerve deafness**, which is damage to the cochlea (part of the inner ear), the auditory nerve or the hearing centres in the brain; the range of impairment is very wide, from slight loss to profound deafness.

conductive deafness
Deafness caused by an interruption to the process of sounds passing through the ear drum and the middle ear

nerve deafness
Deafness caused by damage to the inner ear, or to the nerves, or hearing centres in the brain

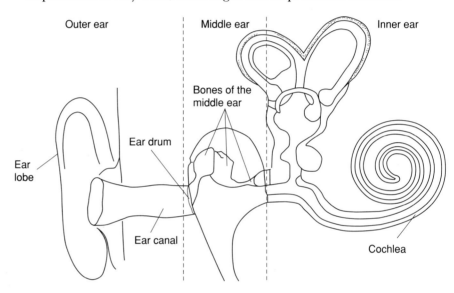

The structure of the ear

Diagnosis

Initially parents or carers often suspect a hearing difficulty. Diagnosis is by hearing tests; the first hearing test is usually at 7 months, but testing is possible at any age. (See Book 2, Chapter 21.)

Treatment and progress

Conductive deafness can often be treated by removing blockages, treating infections, and some surgical treatments. Nerve deafness is much more difficult to treat but a cochlea implant has recently become available.

Early diagnosis is very important. Child-care workers need to be aware that most children will experience hearing loss at some time, usually caused by middle ear infections related to colds. Carers need to be aware and supportive.

Support agency

The Royal National Institute for the Deaf
19–23 Featherstone Street, London EC1Y 8SL

Progress check

1 What should you do if a child in your care has a major epileptic convulsion?
2 What is the cause of haemophilia?
3 What are the two main types of deafness?
4 When is a child's hearing first normally tested?
5 What is the most common cause of a middle ear infection?

Hydrocephalus

Cause

> **hydrocephalus**
> A condition involving an increase in the fluid surrounding the brain, often associated with spina bifida

Hydrocephalus is an increase in the fluid surrounding the brain. The cause is not known but it is often associated with spina bifida (see page 336).

Characteristics

> **cerebro-spinal fluid**
> The fluid surrounding the brain and spinal cord

Cerebro-spinal fluid (surrounding the brain and spinal cord) increases because it is unable to drain in the usual way. The head becomes larger and in a small baby the fontanelles and sutures may widen. Increasing pressure on the brain causes pain and brain damage.

Treatment and progress

Early diagnosis is by measuring the head circumference. The introduction of a valve (shunt) allows the cerebro-spinal fluid to drain satisfactorily. Early detection stops damage to the brain. The child should then be able to make progress, although frequent hospital visits and susceptibility to repeated infection may be a problem.

Support agency

Association for Spina Bifida and Hydrocephalus
22 Upper Woburn Place, London WC1 0EP

Muscular dystrophy (Duchenne)

Cause

> **muscular dystrophy (Duchenne)**
> A condition involving progressive destruction of muscle tissue, which only affects boys

Duchenne muscular dystrophy is a life-threatening condition involving progressive destruction of muscle tissue. The condition only affects boys and is an abnormality of the X chromosome inherited through the female line. (See the section on *Heredity* in Chapter 6, page 117.)

Characteristics

Duchenne is the most common and most severe type of muscular dystrophy. At birth there is usually no sign of disability. Later clumsiness in walking, frequent falls and difficulty in running become evident. Muscle weakness is slowly progressive so that everyday activities become more difficult. As walking becomes impossible, a wheelchair will be needed. Eventually the muscles of the hands, face, and respiration are affected, and respiratory tract infections usually prove fatal.

Diagnosis

Diagnosis is made by knowing the family history. Prenatal tests, such as amniocentesis can be used to detect Duchenne muscular dystrophy. There will also be observation of the above characteristics after birth.

Treatment and progress

Parents or carers may often know that there is a problem early on. Treatment is aimed at maintaining mobility and independence for as long as possible. Parents or carers and families will need information and support. The child will need to be able to discuss his feelings and have long-term support to understand the progressive nature of his condition. Child-care workers will need to support and maintain mobility and independence for as long as possible.

Support agency

Muscular Dystrophy Group of Great Britain
Presscott House, 7–11 Presscott Place, London SW4 6BS

Phenylketonuria (PKU)

Cause

phenylketonuria (PKU)
A metabolic impairment that prevents the normal digestion of protein; recessively inherited

Phenylketonuria (PKU) is a metabolic impairment that prevents the normal digestion of protein. It is recessively inherited (see Chapter 6, page 115). A child will develop PKU if both parents carry and pass on one altered PKU gene. There is an inherited defect in an enzyme, called phenylalanine hydroxylase. This means that the child cannot use the amino acid phenylalanine, which is part of protein, in the usual way. This substance builds up in the body and causes progressive brain damage.

Characteristics

If left untreated, the high levels of phenylalanine which build up in the body will damage the developing brain. All areas of development may be affected.

Diagnosis

All babies born in the UK are screened for PKU by a blood test. This test is called the **Guthrie test** and is taken on the sixth day after birth and after the baby has had some milk feeds (breast or formula). The midwife takes a sample of the baby's blood, usually by pricking the heel. This blood test is also used to detect other possible problems such as hypothyroidism, which is an endocrine disorder in which the thyroid gland is not working properly.

Treatment and progress

Early diagnosis means that babies with PKU can be given a diet in which the amount of phenylalanine is carefully controlled. The treatment is complex but with support the children can learn to manage their diet and be independent.

Support agency

The National Society for Phenylketonuria and Allied Disorders
7 Southfield Close, Willen, Milton Keynes, Bucks MK15 9LL

> **Progress check**
>
> 1 Describe hydrocephalus.
> 2 What is the cause of Duchenne muscular dystrophy?
> 3 Who may be affected by Duchenne muscular dystrophy and why?
> 4 Describe the test for PKU.
> 5 If a child has PKU, which of the main food groups needs to be modified?

Sickle cell anaemia

Cause

Sickle cell anaemia (or sickle cell condition) is an inherited condition of **haemoglobin** formation. If a child inherits sickle haemoglobin from one parent, they will have *sickle cell trait*, which is symptom-free. If, however, a child inherits sickle haemoglobin from both parents, they will have sickle cell anaemia.

Characteristics

Sickle cell anaemia causes bouts of anaemia, pain, jaundice and infection, called *crises*. Painful crises are caused by the red cells in the blood changing their shape from the normal round shape to a crescent or sickle shape. The sickle cells clump together and block the smaller blood vessels causing pain and swelling. Pain is common in the arms, legs, back and stomach. There may be swelling of the hands and feet. The sickle cells are also removed more quickly from the bloodstream, causing anaemia.

Guthrie test
On the sixth day after birth, a sample of the baby's blood is taken, usually by pricking the heel, to test for phenylketonuria

sickle cell anaemia
An inherited condition of haemoglobin formation

haemoglobin
A red oxygen carrying protein containing iron present in the red blood cells

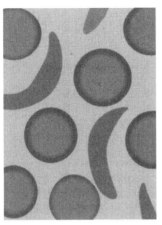

Normal and sickle red blood cells

Diagnosis

Diagnosis is made by knowing the family history, prenatal tests, and a specific blood test after birth and by observation of any symptoms.

Treatment and progress

Prompt recognition and treatment are important. Carers will aim to maintain good general health and diet and arrange for early treatment of infections, keeping the child warm and dry with plenty of rest. Blood transfusions may be needed. Support and understanding are needed particularly during crises. Co-operation between home, school and hospital will give the child the best opportunity to manage the condition and become independent.

Support agency

Sickle Cell Society
54 Station Road, Harlesden, London NW10 4UA

Spina bifida

Cause

> **spina bifida**
> A condition in which the spine fails to develop properly before birth

Spina bifida occurs when an area of the spine fails to develop properly before birth. There is a gap in the bones of the spine leaving the contents of the spinal cord exposed. The fault can occur anywhere on the spine. The precise cause is not known, but there are thought to be environmental and genetic factors that prevent the normal development of the bones of the spine.

Characteristics

There are two main forms of spina bifida:
- *spina bifida occulta*, in which the skin is intact; this rarely causes disability
- *spina bifida cystica*, which has two types:
  - *meningocele*, in which there is a fluid-filled sac on the back, where the fluid and membranes of the spinal cord protrude through the gap in the bones of the spine
  - *mylomeningocele*, in which the sac contains spinal fluid and the nerves of the spinal cord. This is the most severe form. As a result there is some degree of paralysis below the lesion.

Diagnosis

Diagnosis is by prenatal blood tests, ultrasound scan and/or amniocentesis.

Treatment and progress

Treatment is by closure of the lesion and prevention of infection. There will also be treatment of associated hydrocephalus (see page 333). Ongoing support is needed to enable the child to take part in all the usual activities for their age, such as playgroup, nursery or mainstream school.

Support agency

Association for Spina Bifida and Hydrocephalus
ASBAH House, 42 Park Road, Peterborough, Cambridgeshire PE1 2UP

Visual impairment

Causes

visual impairment
Impairment of sight ranging from blindness to partial sight

Visual impairment may be present at birth (congenital) or may occur later. The causes of congenital blindness include infections in pregnancy, such as rubella and syphilis, optic nerve atrophy or tumour. Causes after birth include cataract, glaucoma and infections such as measles and the herpes virus. There are some hereditary conditions such as retinitis pigmentosa.

Characteristics

There are three main categories of visual impairment:
- blind
- partially sighted and entitled to use the services appropriate to blind people
- partially sighted.

The experience of visual loss is very different for those who become blind and can use their experience of sight, from those who are born blind.

Diagnosis

The condition is usually detected early as parents or carers recognise the lack of response to visual stimuli and eye contact. Later, vision tests may confirm earlier problems.

Treatment and progress

Early diagnosis is followed with support, practical information and time for families to adjust. Spectacles and contact lenses are valuable aids for some partially sighted children. Carers will need to encourage exploration and independence. The Royal National Institute for the Blind has a full range of support services, including education advice services, specialist schools and a wide range of supporting aids, books in Braille, Moon and talking books. Progress towards independence will vary with individual children.

Support agency

Royal National Institute for the Blind
224 Great Portland Street, London W1N 6AA

 Progress check

1 What happens to the red blood cells if a child has sickle cell condition?
2 What causes a painful crisis?
3 Briefly describe spina bifida.
4 What are the three main types of spina bifida?
5 What are the early signs of visual impairment?

Do this!   **18.1**

1 Carry out a survey of your child-care setting. List all the things you might have to check out or do if a child with a condition, which affects their physical mobility, was joining you.

2 Choose one of the conditions or impairments explained in this chapter. Imagine that you have to explain this to the children in your infant class. How would you do this? What four strategies could you use?

Key terms

You need to know what these words and phrases mean. Go back through the chapter and find out.

all the conditions and impairments described in this chapter	conductive deafness	haemophilia
	conductive education	hypoglycaemia
	congenital	insulin
amniocentesis	enzyme	metabolic
anti-convulsant	femur	nerve deafness
bronchodilator	gluten	pancreas
cerebro-spinal fluid	Guthrie test	pelvis
chorionic villus sampling (CVS)	haemoglobin	

Now try these questions

1 A child in your care has asthma. How could you ensure that the risk of an asthma attack is reduced? Describe how you would manage an asthma attack.

2 What is the Guthrie test? When is this test done and what conditions does it detect?

3 Briefly describe sickle cell condition. What important points would you need to consider if you were caring for a child with this condition?

4 Describe the causes of hearing impairment.

5 Describe the stages of a major epileptic attack.

19 The needs of disabled children and their families

This chapter includes:

- Disabled children's needs
- The needs of disabled children's families

We will consider the needs of disabled children and their families in some detail in this chapter. Understanding the needs of disabled children requires a thorough knowledge of child development. The earlier chapters of this book provide detailed information on each aspect of children's development: physical, cognitive and language, and social and emotional. All of this is relevant to the development of disabled children and their needs should be considered alongside those of all children. Working in partnership with parents extends to the parents of disabled children, and this chapter will help the child-care worker to empathise with their needs.

You may find it helpful to read this chapter in conjunction with:

- ▶ **Book 1, Chapter 17**   Understanding disability
- ▶ **Book 1, Chapter 18**   Conditions and impairments
- ▶ **Book 1, Chapter 20**   The legal framework
- ▶ **Book 1, Chapter 21**   Providing inclusive care and education
- ▶ **Book 1, Chapter 22**   The role of professionals

Disabled children's needs

Understanding the needs of disabled children

This book emphasises the fact that development does not correlate with age. Children may reach stages, or milestones, of development at different ages. Individual children also proceed at different rates through the different stages of the developmental areas.

Disabled children are often made to feel that they are younger than they are because they have not reached so-called 'normal' milestones in all aspects of their development. If, for example, a disabled child needs to wear nappies at 5 years or ride a three-wheeler at 10 years, they may well be treated as younger than they are.

Special needs of disabled children

Another danger for disabled children is that their special needs override their ordinary needs. Following the medical model of disability, the implication is that there is something wrong, and that the child's efforts should be directed to **specific therapeutic goals**. This attitude may be encouraged through special programmes such as conductive education.

> **specific therapeutic goals**
> Identified objectives to counteract the effects of the condition or impairment

Disabled children may need physiotherapy, speech therapy or special learning programmes, but these should not always override their ordinary needs. All children need periods of self-directed play. Disabled children need adults who will facilitate, rather than always direct, play activities.

Think about it

1 Why do all children need periods of self-directed play?
2 How can adults facilitate self-directed play for young disabled children in group settings?

Do this!   **19.1**

Discuss the advantages and disadvantages of special programmes such as Portage and conductive education? (See Chapter 22 for information about these programmes.)

Meeting disabled children's needs

Each disabled child is an individual with unique gifts and needs. In order to meet their needs, some knowledge of the causes and medical implications of their specific impairment or condition may be helpful.

This knowledge will be most helpful when combined with a positive attitude and a willingness to learn how to maximise individual children's potential. You can support your knowledge by further reading or talking to professionals, but remember that the full-time carer of each child may often be the best source of information and guidance.

In order to meet the needs of disabled children, attitudes and assumptions about disability need to be examined. Disability equality training, led by an experienced DET trainer, and involving disabled people themselves, is one of the best ways of doing this.

Do this!   **19.2**

Consider any condition or impairment. List the main needs of childen with this condition/impairment.

Empowerment

empower
To enable children to take part in the world

Like all children, disabled children need to be enabled (**empowered**) to take part in the world effectively, but this needs to be on their own terms, rather than having to conform to the expectations of non-disabled people. This may be encouraged by:

- responding to disabled children's expressed needs and initiatives. Disabled children may not find self-expression or communication easy. They need adults who will listen, wait and recognise the smallest indications that a choice has been made, or a need expressed. Adults may need to make guesses, try many alternatives and keep looking to see if they have judged correctly

- praising and rewarding effort rather than achievement. Children, especially disabled children, should not be compared to one another. It is better to compare their success and achievement to their own previous attempts

innate ability
Natural ability

- responding positively to the things over which children have control, rather than to **innate ability** or attributes. Adults often praise young children for achievements over which the child has little control, for example their size, speed, or their cleverness and physical skill: 'Oh, she smiled at three days', 'He's eating solids already!', 'She never cries', 'He started reading before he went to school'. This serves to devalue children who are small, slow, inept, and so on. Comments like 'Oh, that was a kind thing to do!' and 'You have worked really hard today' help to give value to the things over which children do have control.

✓ *Progress check*

1 Why are disabled children often treated as younger than they are?
2 Name two special educational programmes for disabled children.
3 How can disabled children be empowered?
4 Who is usually the best source of information and guidance about individual disabled children?
5 What is one of the best ways of examining attitudes and assumptions about disability?

Do this!   *19.3*

Read some books, articles or leaflets about a particular condition or impairment, and talk to a disabled adult with this condition/impairment.

What do the books/articles/leaflets suggest are the main needs of children with this condition/impairment?

Ask the disabled adult about their childhood. Find out what they felt their needs were. Were these needs met? If not, why not?

Are the needs they express the same as those you thought yourself or read about?

The needs of disabled children's families

Diagnosis

When a child is born with a specific condition or impairment, or one is later diagnosed, parents or carers will react in their own individual way. Society predominantly views disability as a tragedy, and it is possible to recognise in many parents or carers a pattern of response similar to that experienced following other 'tragedies', such as bereavement

This pattern of response is divided into four stages. Individuals may progress through these stages at different rates:

- *shock and disbelief* – 'This can't be happening to us'
- *a period of mourning and isolation* – 'We were grief stricken. We felt we were being punished. We didn't want to be with anyone who did not know about our child'
- *a period of adaptation* – 'We felt it was a challenge. We wanted information, help and understanding, and not to feel alone'
- *adjustment* – 'We are learning to cope, and enjoy our child. When we could face up to telling friends and relatives things became easier'.

As with bereavement and loss in other circumstances, some people do not move through the stages of 'grief' but may remain stuck at one particular stage.

> **Think about it**
>
> Why is it important for parent/carers to be supported at this time?

The needs of parents and carers

In common with all parents or carers, those of disabled children need to find pleasure in their child, and to feel confident and pleased with themselves as parents. In order to accomplish this they are likely to need:

- information about their child's condition or impairment, the social model of disability, the services available, new ideas, etc.
- emotional support, and help in finding pleasure in their child
- practical help, for example child-sitting, respite care, environmental aids and adaptations, domestic help, financial support
- contact with other parents or carers of disabled children, and opportunities to work together to obtain the services they need
- reassurance by service providers (of education and care), that their child is wanted and can be coped with
- contact with disabled adults for advice, support, information, etc.
- training in **self-advocacy** and getting what they need for themselves and their family
- time to be themselves and meet their own needs and the needs of other family members
- recognition that usually they are the ones who know their child best.

> **self-advocacy**
> Putting forward one's own viewpoint

> ***Do this!*** *19.4*
>
> Describe the role of the various professionals who are likely to be involved with parent/carers at this time?

The needs of siblings

It is impossible to generalise about the effects on siblings of having a disabled child in the family. Much will depend on factors such as the nature of the condition or impairment, the number of children in the family, their birth order and so on.

The need of brothers and sisters may be similar to the overriding need of parents or carers, that is to find pleasure in having a disabled sibling. In addition they may have the following needs:

- encouragement to express their feelings openly and honestly
- information with meaningful terms at a level they can understand
- preparation for the possible negative attitudes and behaviour of other people
- reassurance of their own and their disabled sibling's value and worth
- individual attention
- involvement in the care of the disabled child, without overwhelming responsibility.

While it is relatively easy to outline possible disadvantages, it is possible for siblings to benefit from growing up alongside a disabled child.

Do this! 19.5

1 List the advantages and disadvantages of having a sibling with:
   a) cerebral palsy
   b) a hearing loss
   c) cystic fibrosis.

2 Plan an activity or story to explain one the following to a 5-year-old child:
   a) brain damage
   b) spinal injury
   c) cerebral palsy
   d) epilepsy.

Disabled parents and carers

Many disabled people are themselves parents or carers. Often they are not recognised by society as capable of being responsible caring adults, with much to give. Their own understanding and experience of the possible effects of specific conditions or impairments may not be used by those around them.

In professional and non-professional roles, disabled adults may be willing to support the carers of disabled children. They may also be willing to act as role models for disabled children.

It is possible for young disabled children to grow up with little or no contact with disabled adults. This has implications for the process of **identification** and the development of self-image.

identification
Making oneself the same as those who are significant to us

Many disabled people are themselves parents or carers

Disabled parents and carers are sometimes thought to disadvantage their own children. This has, on occasions, led to their children being accomodated away from home by a local authority. Often alternative measures such as help with domestic chores, environmental aids and adaptations or financial support could be used to overcome the difficulties.

Disabled adults sometimes find themselves excluded from the services provided for their children. **Inclusive** care and education will consider their needs alongside other service users. The emphasis on parents and carers as partners with professionals should include disabled carers as well.

inclusive
Organised in a way that enables all to take a full and active part; meeting the needs of all children

Case study: A baby just like me

My hearing friends were surprised when they asked me 'Claire do want a boy or a girl?' and I said 'I don't mind, so long as the baby is deaf.' You see I'm profoundly deaf and the imminent prospect of becoming a parent myself has made me think about my own childhood again.

There was no getting away from the fact that I was a disappointment to my parents. A tragedy really. How could this have happened to them? What had they done wrong? Now, I can understand their reaction; then, I could only experience it.

Their determination that I would be just like any other child was well meaning, but impossible for me to achieve. My earliest memories are of seemingly endless waits in various clinics. The look of disappointment on my parents' faces. The speech training that seemed to go on for hours and hours, and when I produced my best efforts the look of total incomprehension on hearing people's faces!

Eventually they gave up the fight and sent me to the Deaf School. What joy! Other children just like me and adults who communicated at a remarkable speed using their whole bodies.

In the end, my parents started to learn British Sign Language and even came to the Deaf Club occasionally. My sister is training to be a sign language interpreter. I guess she's got me to thank for being bilingual.

If my baby is hearing, we'll cope, but naturally we all want a baby just like us!

1 What do these thoughts tell us about Claire's childhood?
2 Why does she want a deaf baby?
3 Why did Claire's parents see sending her to a Deaf School as giving up?
4 How was Claire's sister affected by her deafness?

Think about it

1 Why is it important for disabled children to have contact with disabled adults?
2 How could this be achieved in practice?

Do this! 19.6

Draw up a checklist to ensure the inclusion of disabled adults in your workplace.

✓ *Progress check*

1 Describe the pattern or response that may be demonstrated by parents or carers when their child's disability is diagnosed.
2 What are the needs of parents or carers of disabled children following diagnosis?
3 What are the needs of the siblings of disabled children following diagnosis?
4 What can disabled parents or carers offer to disabled children?

Key terms

You need to know what these words and phrases mean. Go back through the chapter and find out.

empower
identification
inclusive
self-advocacy
specific therapeutic goals

Now try these questions

1 Why is it important to have a thorough knowledge of child development in order to understand the needs of disabled children?
2 Explain why it is important to ensure that the special needs of disabled children do overide their ordinary needs.
3 Describe the possible reactions of parents after their child is diagnosed with a particular condition or impairment.
4 What are the needs of disabled children's families?
5 Why is it important for child-care workers to have contact with disabled adults?

20 The legal framework

This chapter includes:

- The Education Act 1944
- The Warnock Report 1978
- The Education Act 1981
- The Education Reform Act 1988
- The Children Act 1989
- The Education Act 1994

Legislation concerning the care and education of disabled children is regularly changed and updated. This chapter aims to explain the underlying principles contained in current legislation. You will need, however, to refer to the legislation itself for more detail, and to update yourself regularly on recent changes.

You may find it helpful to read this chapter in conjunction with:

The Education Act 1944

legislation
Laws that have been made

This was the first piece of **legislation** to describe and define special educational needs and provision. Doctors were central to the process, and children were assessed as having one of eleven 'disorders' before being placed in a specialist school.

At this time children with severe learning difficulties were not thought to be able to benefit from education, and were looked after in junior training centres run by health authorities.

Think about it

What may have been the effect of lack of educational provision for children with severe learning difficulties?

Do this!   20.1

Find out how disabled children have been looked after in residential settings in the past. What safeguards do you think should be in place to protect disabled children?

The Warnock Report 1978

This report reviewed the provision that was available to all children with special needs. The Warnock Report was very important because it informed the 1981 Education Act.

The Education Act 1981

statutory duty
Duty required by law

The Education Act stated that local education authorities (LEAs) have a **statutory duty** to ensure that special educational provision is made for pupils who have special educational needs.

The Act aimed to shift the focus to *individual* children rather than on to their impairments. The term 'children with special needs' included those whose learning difficulties called for special educational provision to be made. The Act stated that children had learning difficulties if:

■ they had significantly greater difficulty in learning than the majority of children of their age
■ they had a disability which prevented or hindered them from making use of educational facilities of a kind generally provided in school, for children of their age, within the local authority concerned.

Think about it

In what ways did the 1981 Education Act seek to change attitudes toward disabled children? Was it successful?

Statutory assessment procedures

The 1981 Education Act also stated that LEAs have a statutory duty to identify and assess children with special educational needs in order to determine the educational provision that will meet their needs. A multi-professional assessment procedure was to be set up.

LEAs are required to:

■ respond to parents' requests for their child's assessment, as long as the request is reasonable (parents have the right of appeal to the Secretary of State for Education)
■ involve parents in the assessment process.

psychological
From the study of the mind

A subsequent circular, 1/83, *Assessments and Statements of Special Educational Needs* advised that assessments should follow the five stages laid down in the Warnock Report. The assessments should not be an end in themselves, but part of a continuous process involving regular reviews, to reflect the changing needs of the children as they get older. The assessments should include:

■ direct representations from parents (verbal or written)
■ evidence submitted either by the parent or at the request of the parent
■ written educational, medical and **psychological** advice
■ information relating to the health and welfare of the child from the district health or social services authorities.

Think about it

Which professionals may be involved in a multi-professional assessment procedure?

Statements of Special Educational Needs

Statement of Special Educational Needs
A written report setting out a disabled child's needs and the resources needed to meet these needs

As a result of the statutory assessment procedures, a **Statement of Special Educational Needs** would be drawn up, which would describe in detail a child's needs and the resources that should be made available to meet these needs.

It was noted that, where possible, provision should be made within a child's local school.

Every statement should be in five parts:

- Part 1, introductory page, including factual information such as name, address, age, etc.
- Part 2, the child's special educational needs as identified by the professionals involved in the assessment
- Part 3, the educational provision considered necessary to meet the child's special educational needs, specifying any facilities, teaching arrangements, curriculum and equipment needed for the pupil
- Part 4, the type of school or establishment (for example, hospital) thought appropriate for the child
- Part 5, any additional non-educational provision considered necessary to enable the child to benefit from the proposed educational provision, for example hearing aids from the health authority, or a family provided by social services.

*Note: An additional part now describes **how** a child will get the help described in Part 5.*

Initially, the statement should be in draft form. It should be sent to the parents, with an explanation of their right to appeal. If the parent disagrees with any of the content they have 15 days in which to put their views to the local education authority. Ultimately, the parents have right of appeal to the Secretary of State for Education, whose decision is binding on the parents and the local authority.

The confidentiality of the statements is crucial. In most circumstances, no disclosure from the statement can be made without the parents' consent. The statement is usually kept in the administrative offices of the local authority.

The progress of children who are the subject of a statement of special educational need must be reviewed at least once every 12 months. This is called the Annual Review. Children, parents, professionals and all other interested parties are given the opportunity to contribute to these reviews. The review should consider any progress made and set new aims and targets for the coming year.

Think about it

1 What is the purpose of a statement of special educational needs?
2 How are the rights of parents safeguarded in the process of drawing up a statement of special educational needs?

The Education Reform Act 1988

National Curriculum
A course of study, laid down by government, that all children in state schools in the UK must follow

The 1988 Act requires all maintained schools, including special schools, to provide the **National Curriculum**. For a child with a statement, it is not necessary to modify or exempt the child from the requirements of the National Curriculum, but it is possible if modification is in the child's best interests. The 1988 Act encourages *inclusion* rather than *exclusion* of children with special needs in the National Curriculum. Most importantly, it states that all children with special educational needs have a right to a broad and well-balanced education. This includes as much access as possible to the National Curriculum.

The Children Act 1989

The Children Act 1989 brings together most public and private laws relating to children. It includes the functions of social services departments in relation to disabled children. Disabled children are treated in the Act in the same way as all other children.

The Act defines a category of 'children in need' for whom the social services department should provide services. Disabled children are included in this category. The Children Act defines disability as follows:

> 'A child is disabled if he is blind, deaf or dumb or suffers from mental disorder of any kind or is substantially and permanently handicapped by illness, injury or **congenital deformity** or such other disability as may be prescribed.'

congenital deformity
A term used in the Children Act 1989; a disability evident at the time of birth

---

Do this! 20.2

'The Children Act appears to support an inclusive model – disabled children being treated in the Act in the same way as all other children – and yet it uses a definition of disability that supports a medical model and uses terminology that many disabled people would find offensive.' Discuss.

Think about it

Why does the Act lay emphasis on children being brought up within their own families?

Duties of local authorities

The Act places a general duty on the local authority to provide an appropriate range and level of services to safeguard and promote the welfare of 'children in need'. This is to be done in a way that promotes the upbringing of such children within their own families.

Underlying principles

The Children Act outlines the following principles for work with disabled children:

Think about it

What are the possible implications of these underlying principles to the lives of disabled children and their families?

- the welfare of the child should be safeguarded and promoted by those providing services
- a primary aim should be to promote access for all children to the same range of services
- the need to remember that disabled children are *children* first, not disabled people
- the importance in children's lives of parents and families
- partnership between parents and local authorities and other agencies
- the views of children and parents should be sought and taken into account.

domiciliary services
Services provided in the home

Portage Home Teaching scheme
A scheme to help parents/carers to teach their children with learning difficulties in their own homes, by setting short-term, achievable goals (*see* Chapter 22)

Services

In order to encourage families to care for disabled children at home, local authorities are encouraged to provide the following services, either directly or through voluntary organisations:

- **domiciliary services**, for example the **Portage Home Teaching scheme** and befriending schemes
- guidance and counselling or social work

- respite care; this would be provided in co-operation with district health care trusts, and may be in health service settings, or in settings run by voluntary organisations
- day-care services, including family centres and child minding services; wherever possible these would be in day-care settings available to all children rather than in separate or segregated settings
- services from occupational therapists, rehabilitation workers, technical officers, specialist social workers and provision of **environmental aids and adaptations**
- information on a range of services provided by other agencies
- **advocacy** and representation for children and parents
- help with transport costs to visit children living away from home
- holiday play schemes
- toy libraries
- support groups
- loans of equipment or play materials.

Other services for the disabled child and their family may include:
- identifying a need in their area and publicising services available
- working together with local education authorities and district health authorities
- compiling a register of children with disabilities in their area
- assessing, reassessing and reviewing children in need and planning for their long-term future
- planning services in partnership with parents and disabled children themselves.

> ### Do this! 20.3
>
> Find out the range of services provided by your own local authority for disabled children and their families.
>
> Where did you obtain the information? How easy was it to obtain?

> **Think about it**
>
> 1 Is access to these services guaranteed for all disabled children and their families?
> 2 On what does provision depend?

environmental aids and adaptations
For example, a flashing light doorbell for deaf people, modified utensils and eating tools, bathing aids, etc.

advocacy
Speaking on behalf of, or in favour of disabled people

accommodation away from home
A placement with a foster carer or in a residential setting arranged by the local authority social services department

Accommodation away from home

Disabled children may be **accommodated away from home** in foster care or residential settings. The Act provides new safeguards for them:
- their cases must be reviewed
- consideration must be given to their welfare
- they and their parents must be consulted before decisions are taken.

Think about it

Why is it necessary to spell out the rights of disabled children who are accomodated away from home?

The Act requires local authorities to ensure that the accommodation they provide or that provided by education or health authorities for disabled children is suitable to the child's needs.

This means, in practice, that disabled children should have access to all the accommodation and the same rights to privacy as their non-disabled counterparts. Homes that accommodate disabled children must provide the necessary equipment, facilities and adaptations. The aim should be to integrate children in every aspect of life in the home. Health and safety aspects concerning disabled children must be considered.

 Progress check

1 What does the Children Act bring together in one Act?
2 What is the LEA's responsibility toward 'children in need' according to the Children Act?
3 What services are local authorities encouraged to provide for disabled children and their families?

The Education Act 1993

The 1993 Education Act builds upon and largely replaces the 1981 Education Act. It includes a code of practice giving practical guidance on how to identify and assess special educational needs.

The Special Educational Needs Code of Practice

The 1993 Code of Practice for children with special educational needs revised the 1981 Education Act. Some terms from the old legislation, such as Statements of Special Educational Need, were retained.

The Code of Practice is a guide for schools and LEAs about the practical help they can give to children with special educational needs. Since 1 September 1994, all state schools should identify children's needs and take action to meet those needs as early as possible, working with parents.

Most importantly, under the Code of Practice, schools are given clearer guidance on how to identify and manage the needs of all children. Assessment of all children is now seen as a staged process, and within this, only some will reach a level where the local education authority will assess and issue a statement.

Think about it

1 Why was the Code of Practice introduced?
2 In what ways is it different to the procedures outlined in the 1981 Education Act?

A staged approach

A staged approach to special educational needs might be as follows:

■ *Stage 1* – The child's teacher *identifies* and *records* their concerns Discussions take place with parents and action is taken in class

■ *Stage 2* - The *Special Educational Needs Co-ordinator (SENCO)* becomes involved, and an **Individual Education Plan (IEP)** is drawn up after consultation with the child's parents

■ *Stage 3* – *Specialist advice* may be sought at this stage, and new individual education plans may be produced. *Review meetings* will be held. A decision will be made about whether to ask the LEA to make a statutory assessment

■ *Stage 4* – The LEA is consulted, and a **multi-professional assessment** may be carried out

■ *Stage 5* – The LEA considers the information gathered from the assessment, and draws up a Statement of Special Educational Needs on the basis of the information.

These stages are not seen as a one-way-street. Most children's needs will be fully met at Stages 1, 2 or 3, without the need for a Statement.

Once their problems have been identified and overcome, children are expected to drop back down the ladder. Only a small proportion will progress to Stages 4 and 5.

School policies and procedures

Schools must consider what the Code of Practice says when drawing up their policies for children with special educational needs. The school's policy will outline:

■ the name of the teacher who is responsible for children with special educational needs (often called the Special Educational Needs Co-ordinator)

■ the school's arrangements for deciding which children need special help, stage by stage

■ how the school plan to work closely with parents.

> **Individual Education Plan (IEP)**
> An outline of short- and long-term aims and objectives with targets for achievement of goals by children with special educational needs

> **multi-professional assessment**
> A measuring of the childs performance by professional from different backgrounds, e.g. health care, social work, psychology, etc.

Do this! 20.4

In your work placement in an educational setting, identify the Special Educational Needs Co-ordinator and ask how the Special Educational Needs Code of Practice operates in the school. Ask how many children there are in the school at each of the five stages in the process.

Think about it

1 Why may the staged process mean that some children do not receive the specialist support they need as early as possible?

2 Why are reviews so crucial to children with special educational needs?

The Code of Practice and parents

The Code of Practice gives new rights to parents, whose role is now seen as being much more central than it was before. Schools and other agencies must work in partnership with parents, and parents have the right of access to a new, independent tribunal if they feel the assessment or the provision made available by the LEA is flawed

 Progress check

1 Describe the staged process laid down by the Code of Practice for identifying and managing the needs of all children.
2 What should be drawn up at Stage 2?
3 At what stage would outside specialist professionals be involved?
4 How can parents appeal against the assessment process or the provision made by the LEA?

Do this! 20.5

Design an information leaflet for parent/carers about your workplace policies and procedures for disabled children.

Key terms

You need to know what these words and phrases mean. Go back through the chapter and find out.

accommodation away
    from home
advocacy
congenital deformity
domiciliary services
Individual Education
    Plan (IEP)
legislation
multi-professional
    assessment
National Curriculum
Portage Home
    Teaching scheme
psychological
Statement of Special
    Educational Needs
statutory duty

Now try these questions

1 Outline the main requirements regarding children with special educational needs in the Education Act 1988.

2 Describe, in your own words, the underlying principles of the Children Act concerning disabled children.

3 What services may be required by families with a disabled child?

4 Describe the procedure in a school if a member of staff thinks a child in their class has special educational needs.

5 How has recent legislation safeguarded the welfare of disabled children?

6 How has recent legislation promoted partnership with parents of disabled children?

21 *Providing inclusive care and education*

This chapter includes:
- **Principles of good practice**
- **Access**
- **Alternative provision of care**

Recent legislation encourages the involvement of disabled children in **mainstream settings**, both in education and care. It is therefore now more likely that disabled children will be in nursery classes, schools, day nurseries, family centres or residential establishments. Consideration of the needs of all children will be necessary if these settings are to be truly inclusive.

If settings adopt the social model of disability they will want to review their provision to ensure that the environment, attitudes, and practices do not disable children with identified conditions or impairments.

You may find it helpful to read this chapter in conjunction with:

- **Book 1, Chapter 17**   Understanding disability
- **Book 1, Chapter 18**   Conditions and impairments
- **Book 1, Chapter 19**   The needs of disabled children and their families
- **Book 1, Chapter 20**   The legal framework
- **Book 1, Chapter 22**   The role of professionals

mainstream setting
Not special provision for disabled children but what is available for *all* children

Recent legislation encourages the involvement of disabled children in mainstream settings

Principles of good practice

Language

As with issues of race and gender, the setting should have a clear policy about the use of language to describe disabled children. This policy should be clearly explained to all users of the setting.

Images

marginalise
To categorise and put to one side

Everything learned about images of other **marginalised** or minority groups applies to disabled children. In the past, nearly all images of disabled people were produced by non-disabled people, often on behalf of charities. Their aim was to evoke sympathy, pity, fear and guilt. This was justified as necessary to raise money for disabled people.

It is very difficult to find positive images of disabled children. Children's books have few disabled characters. The books available often focus entirely on the impairment, with titles such as *Mary Has a Hearing Loss* or *I Have Cerebral Palsy*. Rarely are disabled people portrayed as ordinary people. However, Letterbox Library now market some texts portraying positive images of disabled children and including disabled characters alongside their non-disabled peers.

Think about it

How could you introduce play equipment in a child-care setting to include disabled children's way of life?

Play equipment and toys

Play equipment and toys that include the daily stuff of disabled children's lives such as wheelchairs, hearing aids, splints or glasses are rare, but invaluable. It may be possible, with permission, to use actual equipment belonging to disabled children.

Activities

Organised, directed activities should always seek to be inclusive. The needs of disabled children in the group should be considered at the planning stage. If a child cannot do something in the same way as most children, they may be consulted about what they could do instead.

In educational settings, teachers will aim to use differentiation in the tasks set. This means that individual or groups of children are given different tasks related to the aim of the lesson, at a level that provides a manageable challenge to them. This involves careful planning if disabled children are not to be segregated from the class. Special needs support assistants may be involved in this process at the planning and implementation stage (see Chapter 22, page 367).

Think about it

How could you encourage the involvement of disabled adults in your work setting?

Do this!   21.3

1 Design and produce a game to include a blind child alongside their peers.
2 Differentiate a task set by staff in your work setting and make it accessible to a child in the group with moderate learning difficulties.
3 Find out about the role of a special needs support assistant. What is involved in this role? Does this role appeal to you?

The involvement of disabled adults can provide positive role models for disabled children

Role models

The involvement of disabled adults, of all ages and at all levels, in care and education settings can provide positive role models for disabled children. Disabled adults can also help to raise the level of disability awareness in the setting.

Do this!   21.4

Make up a simple story (suitable for a 6-year-old) including a disabled person that does not focus on their condition or impairment. The story could include disabled people involved in everyday activities alongside non-disabled people.

Progress check

1 Where have most images of disabled people come from in the past? What were they produced for?
2 What play equipment should be available in an inclusive setting?
3 What is differentiation?
4 How can the involvement of disabled adults benefit any educational setting?

Access

For an establishment to include disabled children, certain aspects need to be considered. Detailed information and training on inclusion of disabled children is available from condition- or impairment-specific voluntary organisations and self-help groups, but outlines of general principles for good practice are listed above. Establishments including disabled children need to provide:

- equipment that all children can use; much equipment produced for disabled people is inclusive: ramps, lifts, adjustable tables, automatic doors, long-handled taps, touch-sensitive controls, large print and grab rails can be used by all children
- a range of options such as tapes, braille and print versions of documents
- a range of seat and table sizes and shapes
- empty floor space that is kept uncluttered
- flexible, adjustable equipment, for example a sand tray that comes off the stand, high chairs with removable trays
- sturdy versions of 'ordinary' toys and furniture
- a range of scissors, knives and other implements
- soft play areas for activities such as crawling, jumping, climbing
- extra adult supervision to facilitate integration
- some equipment for individual children to facilitate integration; there should be discussions with the child and full-time carers about what to buy before expensive purchases are made
- spacious toilet facilities designed for wheelchair users that can then be used by all children
- private age-appropriate toilet or changing area
- disability awareness and equality training for all staff.

Think about it

How inclusive is your work setting?

Do this!	21.5

Consider your own workplace and write a list of physical changes that would need to be made to include:
a) a blind child
b) a child who uses a wheelchair.
What other aspects would need to be considered?

Access for children with sensory impairments

Children with impaired sight

The following aspects need to be considered in order to include blind and partially sighted children. Establishments will need to provide:

- opportunities to explore the environment and people using touch, smell, hearing and any residual sight
- the opportunity for children to **orientate** themselves physically (this may involve visiting the setting when few people are present)
- stability and order, a place for everything and everything in its place; the child will need to be informed and shown any changes
- plenty of light
- a hazard-free environment, or an indication of hazardous things such as steps or sharp corners
- information about other children's needs, for example a child with a hearing loss who may not respond to them
- some specific items such as books in **braille**, toys or board games which are especially designed to be inclusive.

Children with impaired hearing

The following points need to be considered by an establishment including deaf and hearing-impaired children.

- Hearing impairment is largely invisible; even a mild hearing loss is significant in a noisy crowded room.
- A child with impaired hearing cannot tell you what they missed!
- Hearing aids are not a replacement for hearing and may be of little use to some children.
- Deaf children's greatest special need is access to language and communication; complete access can only come about through universal use of language and communication accessible to deaf children. This will often mean British Sign Language, which will need to be used by everyone in the setting.
- Deaf children need to communicate with other children as well as adults.
- Deaf children have a range of intellectual ability as all children do; if we deny them access to language we create a learning difficulty for them.

---

orientate
To determine the position of things

---

braille
A system of printing in relief (raised dots in combination) for use by people with impaired sight.

Think about it

How does your workplace measure up to the list above? How difficult would it be to ensure it did? What may prevent it happening?

Think about it

1 How is equipment produced specifically for disabled people beneficial to all children?
2 How may we deny deaf children access to language?
3 Think of four measures that could be taken to ensure the full involvement of:
    a) a 2-year-old-child with Down's syndrome in a private day nursery
    b) a 6-year-old-child with muscular dystrophy in an infant class
    c) a 4-year-old-child with diabetes in a nursery class.

Case study: Inclusive education

Lake View Primary School's brochure states that they provide education for all children in the locality aged 3–7 years. I don't think they realised what a challenge it would be, when they offered my daughter, Emily, a place in the nursery.

Before Emily started, we went to visit for a session. The other children were curious and asked me why Emily had a funny face and couldn't talk properly. After our visit, the staff decided to prepare the children before Emily started properly. They had to search hard for suitable books to read to the children, but finally found Letterbox Library. The staff were willing to learn; they asked me questions about Emily and had a couple of sessions with a disability equality trainer.

Emily was very clingy and demanding at first. Staff couldn't manage her with 35 other children, so the school employed a special needs support assistant for part of the time, to help Emily integrate with the other children. They approached the local college and a student with learning difficulties came to the school on work placement. Emily latched on to him and it seemed to increase his self-confidence, as well as Emily's.

Whenever the children ask what is wrong with Emily, staff explain that she has Down's syndrome. They always answer the children's questions honestly, even when they are funny, like 'Is it catching?'

The nursery staff say they have learned so much from having Emily and now do some things differently for all the children.

1 Why did Emily's parent want her to go to the local school?
2 How did the nursery staff prepare for Emily's admission?
3 Why did staff explain Emily's condition using the proper name?
4 Why did staff seek out a student with learning difficulties to help in the nursery?

 ## Progress check

1 In what formats should written documents/information be produced to ensure their accessibility to parents/carers who may themselves be disabled?
2 What will be needed to facilitate children's integration in the setting?
3 How should a setting decide what to purchase to support a disabled child?
4 What should be provided for all staff?
5 What creates a learning difficulty for deaf children?

Alternative provision of care

Residential care

Recent legislation confirms that the best place for a disabled child to be brought up is within their own family. For many reasons, however, this may not be possible. Some disabled children need medical care and for this reason are accommodated in health service establishments. Some attend residential special schools where they may be weekly or termly boarders.

Disabled children in residential care are particularly vulnerable. There have been many incidents, some recorded in the biographies of disabled people, of long-term mistreatment in residential institutions. The Children Act 1989 aims to provide safeguards concerning the welfare of disabled children accommodated away from home.

Generally speaking, children should not be accommodated long-term in National Health Service hospital settings. The intention of the Children Act is that disabled children in residential care, including independent schools, should not be forgotten and that social services departments should assess the quality of child care offered.

Think about it

1 Why may it be impossible for a child to be brought up within their own family?
2 Why is it generally undesirable for disabled children to spend long periods of time in hospital settings?

Accommodation away from home

Think about it

1 Why are disabled children in residential accommodation particularly vulnerable?
2 Why is foster care preferable to residential care?

If a child has to be accommodated away from home, their residential homes must be registered and regulated. Social services departments are empowered to enter a care home in order to find out if children's welfare is being satisfactorily safeguarded and promoted.

Foster placements

There has been an increase in the number of successful foster placements for disabled children over the last ten years. Some national voluntary organisations provide specialist fostering programmes for disabled children.

Foster carers have to be willing to be involved in their disabled child's educational learning programmes, where appropriate, in assessments and reviews, and be willing to encourage the disabled child to make friends in the community.

Respite care

Caring for a disabled child, though often rewarding, can be exhausting. If the best place for a disabled child to be brought up is within their own family, the family is likely to need support and encouragement to enable them to go on caring. Respite care provides one way of offering such support and encouragement.

There are four main types of respite care:
- residential care
- family-based care
- care in the child's own home
- holiday schemes.

These services are offered by different agencies, both statutory and voluntary, and groups of parents who have banded together for the purpose. The service may be provided by a voluntary organisation, while the cost is met by social services. Each service offers parents or carers time off and has advantages and disadvantages. Rarely are all available to the parents or carers of disabled children; occasionally none is available.

Residential respite care

The disabled child goes to stay in approved accommodation for an agreed period of time. This accommodation is usually provided by an institution such as a hospital ward, a children's home or a boarding school.

The disadvantage is that it is usually **institutionalised care**, a complete contrast to family life at home. The advantages include the possibility of it becoming familiar to the child and that it does not depend on any one person offering the service.

Family-based respite care

The family of a disabled child is linked to another family (or single person), who are willing to take the disabled child into their home for periods of time. Such schemes are usually managed by social services or a voluntary organisation.

Respite care in a child's own home

This type of care is a specialised child-sitting service. It may be an extension of a home-help service except that the 'family aid' cares for the child rather than the home.

> **Think about it**
>
> Why may some families be reluctant to accept respite care?

> **institutionalised care**
> Care where the needs of the institution and carers are more important than the needs of the individuals being cared for within it

> **Think about it**
>
> 1 Are you aware of any establishments in your area that offer respite care? What training and qualifications do the staff have? What will their work be like?
> 2 What advantages does family-based respite care have?

Respite holiday schemes

There are holiday schemes for disabled children. Some provide for children only, others for the whole family. They are organised by a number of voluntary organisations and take a number of different forms, for example adventure holidays, foreign trips. Often parents or carers have to pay for this service.

Think about it

1 What are the disadvantages of respite care in a child's own home?
2 Do you know of any voluntary organisations that provide holiday schemes?

 Progress check

1 Where is usually the best place for a disabled child to be brought up?
2 Which Act aims to safeguard the welfare of disabled children accommodated away from home?
3 What must foster carers of disabled children be willing to do?
4 Identify four types of respite care.

Do this!   21.6

1 List the advantages and disadvantages of four types of respite care.

2 Research your local area and find out about the respite care on offer to parents of disabled children. Design an information leaflet for parents of disabled children, outlining these alternatives.

3 Visit a residential establishment for disabled children.

Key terms

You need to know what these words and phrases mean. Go back through the chapter and find out.
mainstream setting
marginalise
orientate
braille
institutionalised care

Now try these questions

1 What are the principles of good practice when including disabled children in mainstream settings?

2 What do establishments need to provide to include disabled children?

3 Why is it important for disabled children to have contact with disabled adults?

4 How does the Children Act seek to safeguard the welfare of disabled children and encourage support for parent/carers to care for their disabled child in their own home?

5 How can disabled children and their families benefit from respite care?

22 The role of professionals

This chapter includes:

- Health service professionals
- Education service professionals
- Social service professionals
- Social Security Benefits Agency
- Voluntary organisations
- Learning and therapy programmes

There seems to be a baffling array of professionals involved with disabled children and their families. Their titles change from time to time. It is important that child-care workers can find their way around the statutory, voluntary and private sectors, and act as a signpost to disabled children and their families. They will need to have a basic knowledge and understanding of the roles of significant professionals.

For simplicity, the professionals described in this chapter have been identified as working within either health, education, social services or voluntary organisations. Of course, some may work for more than one. In some areas, a service that is provided by, for example, social services will, in another area, be provided by a voluntary organisation, on behalf of social services.

The information in this chapter should be used to support information you are able to find locally.

You may find it helpful to read this chapter in conjunction with:

- ▶ **Book 1, Chapter 17**   Understanding disability
- ▶ **Book 1, Chapter 18**   Conditions and impairments
- ▶ **Book 1, Chapter 19**   The needs of disabled children and their families
- ▶ **Book 1, Chapter 20**   The legal framework
- ▶ **Book 1, Chapter 21**   Providing inclusive care and education

Health service professionals

Paediatricians

Paediatricians are doctors specialising in the diagnosis of conditions and impairments in children, and the medical care of children with these conditions and impairments. They may be the first health service professional to become involved with a disabled child in the maternity unit, the children's ward or out-patient department.

Health visitors

Every child under the age of 5 has a health visitor. Health visitors are qualified nurses with additional training. They work in the community attached to a clinic or general practice and usually undertake the routine developmental checks. The health visitor is often the health-care professional most closely involved with the family at home. They are able to provide a link with, and between, other professionals and services.

Physiotherapists

Physiotherapists assess children's motor development and skills, and assess how well they can move and balance. They may work in schools as well as hospital clinics. They may demonstrate exercises and activities that parents and other carers will carry out themselves.

Occupational therapists

independent life skills
Skills needed to live and care for oneself

Occupational therapists seek to encourage **independent life skills**, such as dressing, eating and moving around independently. For this reason they may assess a child's fine motor skills. They can advise about any special equipment that may be helpful and arrange for it to be supplied. This may be out in the community as well as in hospital clinics.

Speech and language therapists

Speech and language therapists seek to develop all aspects of children's expressive and receptive communication skills and language development. As well as assessing speech, they also assess tongue and mouth movements and their effects on eating and swallowing. Speech therapists will work out programmes of activities and exercises to help children to acquire language, understand concepts and use speech. Parents or carers may be involved in carrying these programmes out. Speech therapists may be based in schools, hospital clinics or in the community.

Clinical psychologists

Clinical psychologists are mainly concerned with children's emotional, social and intellectual development. Their assessment of children covers all aspects of their circumstances. They will have discussions with their families and other carers as well as making direct observations of children's behaviour.

School nurses

School nurses often check children's weight, height, eyesight and hearing in school. They may pick up difficulties in any of these areas. They may be based full-time in special schools where they supervise the routine medical care of disabled children.

Play therapists

Play therapists use play to help children handle particular feelings or experiences that may be hindering their development. The therapists need to have been trained for and supported in this task, as they are likely to be dealing with powerful emotions.

Play workers

Play workers are usually trained nursery nurses, employed in some hospitals to play with children, both those visiting clinics and those admitted to the wards. They represent a non-threatening adult in a setting that may provoke anxiety for children. They may be involved in raising awareness and preparing children for a possible stay in hospital.

> **Think about it**
>
> Which health service professional is likely to have most contact with a disabled child and their family?

> **Progress check**
>
> 1 Why may an occupational therapist assess children's fine motor skills?
> 2 Which professional may explain a disabled child's condition or impairment to parents following diagnosis?
> 3 What do speech therapists do to encourage children's language development?
> 4 What is the difference between a play therapist and a play worker?

Education service professionals

Educational psychologists

Educational psychologists advise the local education authority about the education of individual children. They will be involved in the educational assessment of disabled children, including the assessment that may lead to a statement of special educational needs. They may advise the professionals who are working directly with a disabled child about learning and behaviour modification programmes.

Special needs support teachers

Special needs support teachers, sometimes called specialist teachers or support teachers, are teachers who often have additional training and experience; they are often **peripatetic** and visit disabled children in different schools. They may specialise in one particular impairment, for example hearing loss or visual impairment. They are involved in the direct teaching of individual children, as well as in advising staff and parents of ways to maximise children's learning potential.

Pre-school support teachers

They are special needs support teachers who work with disabled children and families before a child starts school. They visit children in their own home and devise small steps teaching programmes for parent/carers to follow with their child.

Special needs support assistants

Special needs support assistants have many different labels, for example special assistants, education care officers, classroom assistants or special needs nursery nurses. They may be qualified nursery nurses or child-care workers, or they may have no formal child-care training.

They adopt a variety of different roles depending on the school or nursery and the children they are employed to support. Some work with individual children who have a statement of special educational need, others with groups of children with a variety of additional needs. The main focus of their work may be to provide medical or learning support. They may be involved in observing and monitoring children, liaising with other professionals and working under their direction. They may have regular contact with parents and carers.

Special needs advisers

Special needs advisers focus on the curriculum, teaching methods, materials, schemes and equipment used in schools. They have a role as inspectors to ensure provision of the National Curriculum.

Think about it

Why is the phrase 'special needs' in some of the titles of education service professionals?

Education welfare officers

Education welfare officers undertake welfare duties on behalf of children and their parents or carers. They will be involved with children whose attendance is irregular. They may arrange transport for disabled children to school.

Progress check

1 Who will be involved in the statutory assessment procedure for children with special educational needs?
2 What does it mean to be peripatetic?
3 Describe the role of a special needs support assistant.
4 How may an education welfare officer be involved with disabled children and their families?

Social service professionals

Social workers

statutory child protection
Those aspects of protecting children that are covered by legislation

Social workers may be based in hospitals or in local area offices. Their work with disabled children includes **statutory child protection** duties. They may advise on the availability of all services in the area: health, education, welfare benefits or care, or they may put families in touch with appropriate agencies.

They may advocate on behalf of disabled children, for example enabling them to obtain the services to which they are entitled. Social workers may be involved in assessment for referral to day care, respite care, home helps and other domiciliary care under the heading of family aids.

Specialist social workers and technical officers

Specialist social workers and technical officers may have additional training and experience to work with people with particular conditions or impairments, for example deaf or blind people.

Nursery officers

Nursery officers work in day nurseries and family centres. They may also visit family homes to liaise between home and nursery.

Family aids

Family aids provide practical support for families in their own home. The helpers may be involved in domestic duties, child care and other family needs.

Residential child care workers

Residential child care workers may work in long- or short-stay residential accommodation for disabled children. The officer may be a key worker for a disabled child accommodated away from home by the local authority.

Think about it

How do your think the training of social services professionals differs from that of educational services professionals?

Do this!   **22.1**

1 Choose a professional role, and do some further research to increase your understanding of that role.

2 Seek to shadow a professional involved with disabled children and their families.

 Progress check

1 What statuory duties do social workers carry out?
2 In what capacity do nursery nurses work for social services?

Social Security Benefits Agency

Think about it

What is the difference between social services and social security?

The main role of the Social Security Benefit Agency is the provision of welfare benefits. There is a range of benefits available to disabled children and their families. These are frequently subject to change. The Citizens' Advice Bureau provides up-to-date advice and information about welfare benefits.

 Progress check

1 What is the function of the Social Security Benefits Agency?
2 Which voluntary organisation can give advice about social security benefits?

Voluntary organisations

Collectively, voluntary organisations provide every conceivable type of support for disabled children and their families. Some are national organisations and others local. It is beyond the scope of this book to provide information about the services they offer, but information is available from local libraries.

In recent years, there has been an increase in the role and extent of involvement by voluntary organisations in the lives of disabled children. Many of these organisations work in a highly professional and pioneering way. Much of the innovative work with and on behalf of disabled people is done through voluntary organisations and self-help groups.

Think about it

What pioneering work that has been done by a voluntary organisation are you aware of?

Do this! 22.2

Research a voluntary organisation concerned with the needs of disabled children and their families. What do they see as their role? How do they raise funds? Which professionals work for them? Are they a self-help organisation?

 Progress check

What are the roles and functions of voluntary organisations who are concerned with disabled children and their families?

Learning and therapy programmes

Portage Home Teaching scheme

The Portage Guide to Early Education was originally developed in a rural area centred on the town of Portage in Wisconsin, USA. The schemes devised are used with children with moderate and severe learning difficulties, behaviour problems and developmental delay. Weekly home visits of one to two hours are made by a Portage Home Visitor. Home visitors come from a range of professions.

Most approaches have found that a short training programme is all that is initially required. The purpose of each visit is to help the parent or carer to select and set short-term goals for the child, expected to be achieved in one or two weeks, and to devise an appropriate way for the carer to teach these.

As well as short-term goals, each Portage Home Visitor sets, with the parent or carer, long-term goals for the child to work towards, so that the weekly visits and short-term goals can be seen as steps in a general progression towards the desired objective.

Workers are trained to use a developmental checklist which covers development from birth to 6 years in the areas of socialisation and language, cognitive, self-help and motor skills.

One of the aims of Portage is that parents and carers will become sufficiently skilled to enable the role of the Portage Home Visitor to change to consultant and supporter. The Portage method aims to enable parents and carers to become independent of the Home Visitor eventually, and to become the main worker with the child. Unfortunately, because of limited financial resources, some local authorities may see Portage as a relatively cheap solution to the needs of disabled children and their families, rather than as a service to offer alongside other services.

Bobath technique

The Bobath technique is a form of physiotherapy developed by Professor Bobath and his wife, aimed at enabling the best possible posture and mobility for children with cerebral palsy. It is important that skills are transferred from the therapist to the parents or carers and from them to anyone caring for the child. Treatment begins with an initial assessment at the Bobath Centre in London.

Doman-Delacato therapy (patterning)

Doman-Delacato therapy claims that it is possible to treat the brain itself. Undamaged portions of the brain are taught to take over the function of the damaged part. The basic assumption behind the therapy is that mobility can be achieved through movement. This movement cannot occur spontaneously and must be initiated from the outside by other people. Movement must be frequent, intense and repetitive. Teams of volunteers put the child through a set of movements for between three and eight hours a day. Not surprisingly the child often protests at this and Doman-Delacato is consequently a controversial therapy.

Conductive education

motor-impaired
An impairment of a function of movement

According to Dr Mari Hari, a leading supporter of conductive education, it is 'a method of enabling "the **motor impaired**" to function in society without requiring special apparatus such as wheelchairs, ramps or other artificial aids'. It is based on the theory that, under the right conditions, the central nervous system will restructure itself.

orthofunction
A teaching method that involves the whole person physically and mentally and 'instils in children the ability to function as members of society, and to participate in normal social settings appropriate to their age'

Conductors (therapists) use **orthofunction**, a teaching method that involves the whole person physically and mentally and 'instils in children the ability to function as members of society, and to participate in normal social settings appropriate to their age'.

Conductive education offers a positive approach to a clear set of goals. It has produced results beyond the expectations of professionals and parents of children with cerebral palsy and spina bifida. It should be remembered, however, that the treatment places emphasis on adapting individuals rather than environments. It follows a medical, not a social, model of disability.

Think about it

What are the advantages and disadvantages of the learning and therapy programmes described above?

Do this! 22.3

Research one of the learning and therapy programmes described in this chapter. Write a case study about one disabled child and their family who have benefited from the programme

Progress check

Give brief explanations of the following learning and therapy programmes:
a) Portage
b) Bobath technique
c) Doman-Delacato therapy
d) conductive education.

Key terms

You need to know what these words and phrases mean. Go back through the chapter and find out
**independent life skills
motor-impaired
orthofunction
peripatetic
statutory child
   protection**

Now try these questions

1 Chose either health, education or social services. Outline the roles and responsibilities of three professionals in that service.

2 Explain what is meant by conductive education.

3 Explain the aims and objectives of Portage home teaching.

4 What are the advantages and disadvantages of learning and therapy programmes?

Glossary

ABC of behaviour The pattern of all behaviour: *Antecedent* – what happens before the behaviour occurs; *Behaviour* – the resulting behaviour, acceptable or unacceptable; *Consequence* – the result of the behaviour, positive or negative

absolute poverty Not having enough provision to maintain health and working efficiency

accessible Easy to reach or approach

accident An unexpected and unforeseen event

accident book Legal documen-tation of all accidents and injuries occurring in any establishment

accommodation away from home A placement with a foster carer or in a residential setting arranged by the local authority social services department

achievement The emotional need for the satisfaction gained from success

active immunity The body's ability to resist a disease that has been acquired by having the disease or by having a specific immuni-sation

advocacy Speaking on behalf of, or in favour of disabled people

affection The emotional need to feel loved by parents, carers, family, friends and the wider social community

AIDS Acquired Immune Deficiency Syndrome, results from infection with Human Immunodeficiency Virus (HIV) and damages the immune system

amino acid A part of protein

amniocentesis A sample of amniotic fluid is taken via a needle inserted into the uterus through the abdominal wall; used to detect chromosomal abnormalities

amnion The membranes that make up the sac containing the developing baby

anaemia A condition in which the blood lacks adequate amounts of haemoglobin

anatomically correct dolls Dolls with accurately reproduced body parts including sexual organs

animism The belief that everything that exists has a consciousness

anoxia A deficiency of oxygen

antecedent *See* **ABC of behaviour**

antenatal The period of time from conception until the baby is born

antenatal care Care of the pregnant mother and developing fetus during pregnancy

anterior fontanelle A diamond-shaped area of membrane at the front of the baby's head. It closes between 12 and 18 months of age

antibody A substance made by white cells to attack pathogens

anti-convulsant A drug that is given to prevent fits

anti-discriminatory practice Practice that encourages a positive view of difference and opposes negative attitudes and practices that lead to unfavourable treatment of people

Apgar score A method of assessing the newborn baby's condition by observing the vital signs

Area Child Protection Committee (ACPC) Writes, monitors and reviews the child protection procedures for its area, and promotes co-ordination and communication between all workers

artificial ventilation Mouth-to-mouth breathing to get oxygen into the lungs of the casualty

associative play Play with other children; intermittent interactions and/or involvement in the same activity although their play may remain personal

asthma Difficulty in breathing when the airways in the lungs become narrowed; triggered by allergies, infections, exercise, emotional upset

attainment targets Different elements of a curriculum area. For example, the attainment targets for English are speaking, reading and writing

audiometry A method of testing hearing using sound produced by a machine called an audiometer

autism Difficulty in relating to other people and making sense of the social world

average A medium, a standard or a 'norm'

baseline assessment An assessment of a child's capabilities on entry to school at 5 years

bedtime routine A consistent approach to putting children to bed which encourages sleep by increasing security

behaviour Acting or reacting in a specific way, both unacceptably and acceptably

behaviourists Psychologists whose work demonstrates that learning takes place because actions are reinforced positively, through reward, or negatively, by punishment

behaviour modification Techniques used to bring about changes in unacceptable behaviour so that it becomes acceptable

belonging The emotional need to feel wanted by a group

bilingual Speaking two languages

biological theories Our temperament, sociability, emotional responses and intelligence are determined by what we inherit genetically from our biological parents

birth asphyxia Failure of the baby to establish spontaneous respiration a birth

bond of attachment An affectionate two-way relationship that develops between an infant and an adult

booking clinic The first visit to the hospital antenatal clinic

booster An additional dose of a vaccine given after the initial dose

braille A system of printing in relief (raised dots in combination) for use by people with impaired sight.

British Sign Language (BSL) The visual, gestural language of the British deaf community

bronchitis A chest infection caused by infection of the main airways

bronchodilator A drug that helps the airways to expand, used to treat asthma

Caesarian Delivery of the fetus via an abdominal incision

calorie A unit of energy

capillaries Very small blood vessels

cardiopulmonary resuscitation (CPR) Chest compressions and artificial ventilation to get oxygen circulating around the body

central nervous system The brain, spinal cord and nerves

cerebral palsy A disorder of movement and posture; part of the brain that controls movement and posture is damaged or fails to develop

cerebro-spinal fluid The fluid surrounding the brain and spinal cord

cervix The narrow entrance to the uterus from the vagina

child-centred With the child at the centre, taking into account the perspective of the child

child protection register Lists all the children in an area who are considered to be at risk of abuse or neglect

children in need A child is 'in need' if they are unlikely to achieve or maintain a reasonable standard of health or development without the provision of services, or if they are disabled

chorionic villus sampling (CVS) A small sample of placental tissue is removed via the vagina; used to detect chromosomal and other abnormalities

chromosome Long threads of DNA carrying hundreds of genes present in every human cell

chronological age The age of a child in years and months

cleft lip or palate A structural impairment of the top lip, palate or both

coeliac condition A metabolic disorder involving sensitivity to gluten; there is difficulty in digesting food

cognitive development The development of thinking and understanding, which includes problem-solving, reasoning, concentration, memory, imagination and creativity; *also called* intellectual development

coherent self-image and self-concept A view of themselves that fits together and makes a complete whole

colostrum The first breast milk containing a high proportion of protein and antibodies

compensatory education A programme or initiative that is offered to those who might be likely to experience disadvantage in the education system

complementary feeds Additional feeds as well as breast feeds

complete protein A protein containing all the essential amino acids; *also called* first-class proteins

concentration The skill of focusing all your attention on one task

concept The way in which a range of knowledge and experiences can be organised, understood and referred to. Concepts can be simple, for example *wet, long, red*, or complex and abstract, such as *love, freedom, justice*

conception Occurs when sperm fertilises a ripe ovum

condition Medically-defined illness

conductive deafness Deafness caused by an interruption to the process of sounds passing through the eardrum and the middle ear

conductive education A teaching method aimed at enabling motor-impaired children to function in society; *see* **orthofunction**

congenital A disease or disorder which occurs during pregnancy and is present from birth

congenital deformity A term used in the Children Act 1989; a disability evident at the time of birth

congenital dislocation of the hip The hip joint is unstable or dislocated because it fails to develop properly before birth

conscience The faculty by which we know right from wrong

conscientious objections Not to do something on the grounds of belief

consequence *See* **ABC of behaviour**

conservation In Piaget's concrete operations stage, an understanding that the quantity of a substance remains the same if nothing is added or taken away, even though it may appear different

consistency The emotional need to

feel that things are predictable

contract In the context of unacceptable behaviour, an agreement between an adult and child with the aim of modifying behaviour

contraction Involuntary, intermittent muscular tightenings of the uterus

co-operation card A record of pregnancy carried by the mother and used at each antenatal appointment

co-operative play Children play together co-operatively; able to adopt a role within the group and to take account of others' needs and actions

cradle cap A scaly, dry crust on the scalp and/or forehead

creativity The expression of ideas in a personal and unique way, using the imagination

critical or sensitive period A period of time vital for the achievement of a particular skill

cultural background The way of life of the family in which a person is brought up

culture The way of life, the language and the behaviour that is acceptable and appropriate to the society in which a person lives

curiosity An inquisitive interest

curriculum The content and methods that comprise a course of study

customs Special guidelines for behaviour which are followed by particular groups of people

cystic fibrosis An hereditary, life-treatening condition affecting the lungs and digestive tract

day care The provision of care during the day in a variety of settings outside people's own homes with people other than close relatives, either full- or part-time

decentre Being able to see things from another's point of view

demand feeding Feeding babies when they are hungry in preference to feeding by the clock

dental caries Tooth decay

deep relaxing sleep (DRS) Periods of inconsciousness during the sleep cycle

designated member of staff The person identified in an establishment to whom allegations or suspicions of child abuse should be reported

Desirable Outcomes Curriculum The curriculum that must be provided by all centres receiving government funding for the education of 4-year-olds

development centile charts A way of recording development so that the child's performance can be seen visually

developmentalists Psychologists whose work demonstrates that learning is linked to clearly defined stages of development and that children proceed through these at varying speeds

diabetes A condition in which the body cannot metabolise carbohydrates, resulting in high levels of sugar in the blood and urine

differentiate To distinguish and classify as different

differentiation (in biology) The term used to describe how cells in the body develop and take on different functions

differentiation (in education) The matching of provision to the individual needs and develop-mental level of the child

diffuse bruising Bruising that is spread out

digestion The process of breaking down food so that it can be absorbed and used by the body

disability The disadvantage or restriction of activity caused by society which takes litle or no account of people who have physical or mental impairments and thus excludes them from the mainstream of social activities. According to the social model, disability is defined as 'socially imposed restriction' Oliver (1981)

disclosure (of abuse) When a child tells someone (they have been abused)

discrimination Behaviour based on prejudice which results in someone being treated unfairly

distraction test A hearing test carried out at about 7 months

distress syndrome The pattern of behaviour shown by the children who experience loss of a familiar carer with no one to take their place

DNA (deoxyribonucleic acid) A chemical messenger containing genetic information found in the nucleus of every cell

domiciliary services Services provided in the home

dominant gene A powerful gene which dominates other genes at fertilisation

dose The prescribed amount of medicine to be taken

Down's syndrome A condition caused by an abnormal chromosome, which affects a person's appearance and development

eczema An irritating dry skin rash often caused by an allergy

egocentric Self-centred, from the words *ego* meaning self and *centric* meaning centred on; seeing things only from one's own viewpoint

embryo The term used to describe the developing baby from conception until eight weeks after conception

Emergency Protection Order A court order which enables a child to be removed to safe accommodation or kept in a safe place

emergent writing An approach to writing that encourages children to write independently; *also known as* developmental writing

emotional development The growth of the ability to feel and express an increasing range of emotions appropriately, including those about oneself

empathy An understanding of how other people feel

empower To enable children to take part in the world

encopresis Deliberate soiling into the pants, onto the floor or other area after bowel control has been established

endocrine gland A ductless gland which produces and stores hormones, releasing them directly into the bloodstream

endometrium The lining of the uterus

enquiry (into suspected abuse) A local authority has a duty to carry out an enquiry if there are reasonable grounds to suspect that a child is suffering or is likely to suffer significant harm

E number A number given to an additive approved by the European Union

enuresis Involuntary bedwetting during sleep

environmental aids and adaptations For example, a flashing light doorbell for deaf people, modified utensils and eating tools, bathing aids, etc.

enzyme A substance that helps to digest food

epidural Anaesthetic injected into the epidural space in the spine to numb the area from the waist down

epilepsy Recurrent attacks of temporary disturbance of the brain function

episiotomy A cut to the perineun to assist the delivery of the fetus

equal opportunities All people participating in society to the best of their abilities, regardless of race, religion, disability, gender or social background

equal opportunities policies Policies designed to provide opportunities for all people to achieve according to their efforts and abilities

ethnic group A group of people who share a common culture

ethnic minority group A group (of people with a common culture) which is smaller than the majority group in their society

ethologist A person who studies human nature, intellect and character systematically

experiential Achieving through experience

extended family A family grouping which includes other family members who live either together or very close to each other and are in frequent contact with each other

failure to thrive Failing to grow normally for no organic reason

family of origin The family a child is born into

fat-soluble vitamin A vitamin that can be stored by the body, so it need not be included in the diet every day

febrile convulsion A fit or seizure that occurs as a result of a raised body temperature

femur The long bone in the thigh

fetal alcohol syndrome A condition affecting babies whose mothers are alcoholic or 'binge' drinkers in pregnancy

fetal distress A condition of the fetus resulting from lack of oxygen, usually occurring during labour

fetus The term used to describe the baby from the eighth week after conception until birth

fine motor skills Small finger movements, manipulative skills and hand–eye co-ordination

flammable Material which burns easily

fluoride A mineral which helps to prevent dental decay

fontanelles The areas on the baby's head where the skull bones have not joined together

food allergies Reactions to certain foods in the diet

forceps Spoon-shaped implements to protect the head and assist in the delivery of the fetus

frenulum The web of skin joining the gum and the lip

frozen awareness/frozen watchfulness Constantly looking around, alert and aware (vigilant), while remaining physically inactive (passive), demonstrating a lack of trust in adults

functions of the family The things the family does for its members

gender Being either male or female

gene Detailed unit of inheritance carrying genetic information which is responsible for passing characteristics from generation to generation

genetic counselling Specialist service to provide advice and support for parents who may carry genetically inherited conditions

genital Sexual organs

glue ear Where infected material builds up in the middle ear following repeated infections

gluten A protein found in wheat, rye, barley and oats

grant-maintained status Schools which receive their money (grant) directly from the government, not from their local authority

grief Feelings of deep sorrow at the loss, through death, of a loved person

gross motor skills Whole body and limb movements, co-ordination and balance

guardian *ad litem* Person appointed by the courts to safeguard and promote the interests and welfare of children during court proceedings

Guthrie test On the sixth day after birth, sample of the baby's blood is taken, usually by pricking the heel, to test for phenylketonuria, cystic fibrosis and cretinism

haemoglobin A red oxygen-carrying protein containing iron present in the red blood cells

haemophilia An inherited blood disorder where there is a defect in one of the clotting factors

head lag The baby's head falls back when pulled to sit

health visitor A trained nurse who specialises in child health promotion

hearing impairment Either conductive deafness or nerve deafness; ranges from slight hearing difficulty to profound deafness

hearsay What you are told by others

heat rash Pin-point red skin rash

heredity The transmission of characteristics from one generation to the next

hidden curriculum Messages, often unintended, that are communicated to children as a consequence of the attitudes and values of the adults who deliver the curriculum

HIV Human immunodeficiency virus; *see* **AIDS**

hormones Chemical messengers produced in endocrine glands and carried in the bloodstream to their target organ to stimulate a specific action

housing associations Non-profit-making organisations that exist to provide homes for people in need of housing from a variety of social and cultural backgrounds

Human chorionic gonadaotrophin (HCG) A hormone produced by the implanted embryo, which is excreted in the mother's urine; its presence confirms pregnancy

hydrocephalus A condition involving an increase in the fluid surrounding the brain, often associated with spina bifida

hygiene The study of the principles of health

hypertension High blood pressure

hypoglycaemia Low levels of glucose in the blood

hypothermia A body temperature of less than 35° C

hypothesis The provisional explanation or solution to a problem reached by assessment of the observed facts.

identification Making oneself the same as those who are significant to us

imagination The ability to form mental images, or concepts of objects not present or that do not exist

imitate To copy closely, take as a model

immunity The presence of antibodies which protect the body against infectious disease; *see* **active immunity**; **passive immunity**

impairment Lacking part or all of a limb, or having altered or reduced function in a limb, organ or mechanism of the body. According to the social model, impairment is defined as 'individual limitation' (Oliver 1981)

implantation Occurs when the fertilised ovum settles into the lining of the uterus; *see* **ovum**

imprinting An attachment that forms rapidly

inclusive Organised in a way that enables all to take a full and active part; meeting the needs of all children

incomplete protein A protein containing some essential amino acids; *also called* second-class proteins

incubation period The time from when pathogens enter the body until the first signs of infection appear

incubator An enclosed cot which regulates temperature and humidity

independence The development of skills that lead to less reliance on other people for help or support; the emotional need to feel you are managing and directing your own life

independent life skills Skills needed to live and care for oneself

indicators Signs and symptoms

Individual Education Plan (IEP) An outline of short- and long-term aims and objectives with targets for achievement of goals by children with special educational needs

induction Starting labour by artificial means, for example by breaking the waters or giving hormones to stimulate contractions

infant mortality rate The number of deaths in the first year of life calculated per 1,000 live births

inherit The passing of a characteristic or set of characteristics from one generation to the next

initial child protection conference Brings together the family, professionals concerned with the child and other specialists to exchange information and make decisions

innate Existing from birth

innate ability Natural ability

instincts Patterns of behaviour that are not learned

institutionalised care Care where the needs of the institution and carers are more important than the needs of the individuals being cared for within it

institutionalised discrimination Unfavourable treatment occurring as a consequence of the procedures and systems of an organisation

institutional oppression The power of organisations brought to bear on an individual to keep them in their place

insulin A hormone produced in the pancreas to metabolise carbohydrate in the bloodstream and regulate glucose

intellectual development *See* **cognitive development**

internalise To understand the things that adults think are important and begin to believe and behave similarly

jargon Terminology that is specific to a particular professional background

jaundice Yellowing of the skin and whites of the eyes as a result of too much bilirubin in the blood

Job Seekers' Allowance Benefits paid to people who are registered as unemployed

ketones Excreted in the urine as a result of the breakdown of body cells to provide energy

key worker Works with, and is concerned with the care and assessment of, particular children

labelling Giving a reputation (or label) to someone based upon a small part of their behaviour. For example, a child who is very noisy may be labelled as disruptive. This creates a prejudiced view of the child

labour The process by which the fetus, placenta and membranes are expelled from the birth canal

lacerations Tears in the skin

Language Acquisition Device (LAD) The name Chomsky gives to our innate physical and intellectual abilities that enable us to acquire and use language

language development The development of communication skills, which includes non-verbal communication, reading nd writing skills, as well as spoken language; *also called* linguistic development

lanugo The fine hair found on the body of the fetus before birth andon the newborn infant; mainly associated with pre-term babies

layette First clothes for a baby

learning theories Children develop as they do because they have contact with other people and learn from them

legislation Laws that have been made

lethargy Lacking energy, tired and unresponsive

light-for-dates A baby who is smaller than expected for the length of pregnancy (gestation)

line manager The person to whom you are responsible in the organisation

linguistic development *See* **language development**

listeriosis A disease resulting from infection with the listeria virus which may damage the fetus

literacy The aspects of language concerned with reading and writing

localising Searching for and locating the source of a sound

local management of schools (LMS) Enables a head teacher and the governors of a school to decide how to spend their money and staff a school

locomotion The developing ability to move from one place to another, usually by crawling, walking, running

look and say An approach to reading that relies on recognition of the shape or pattern of a word

low birth-weight Babies born prematurely (pre-term) or below the 10th centile for their gestation, usually weighing less than 2.5 kg at birth

mainstream setting *Not* special provision for disabled children but what is available for *all* children

Makaton A system of simple signs used with people who have limited language skills

marginalise To categorise and put to one side

maternal deprivation 'The prolonged deprivation of young children of maternal care' (Bowlby)

maternal mortality rate The number of women who die as a result of pregnancy within a year of the birth

matriarchal family A family in which women are important and dominant

maturity Complete in natural and expected development for age; being fully developed and capable of self-control

means test An assessment of a person's income and savings, made by completing a form (test) about their income (means) to determine whether they are eligible to receive certain benefits

meconium The first stool passed by the newborn infant – a soft black/green motion which is present in the fetal bowel from about the sixteenth week of pregnancy

medical model A view of disability as requiring medical intervention

melanocytes Pigmented cells

memory The part of the brain where information is stored and retrieved from

menstrual cycle The process of ovulation and menstruation in sexually mature, non-pregnant women

metabolic Related to the process of digesting, absorbing and using food

migration The movement either to or from a country

milestones Important skills which the average child should have accomplished within a specified time

milia 'Milk spots' – small white spots on the nose of newborn babies caused by blocked sebacious glands

milk teeth The first 20 (deciduous) teeth

mongolian blue spot Smooth, bluish grey to purple skin patches consisting of an excess of pigmented skin cells

moral conscience An understanding of right and wrong

motor development The process of muscular movements becoming more complex

motor-impaired An impairment of a function of movement

moulding The process during birth where the shape of the baby's head is changed to make the birth easier

multiability society A society where people have a variety of differing abilities and disabilities

multicultural society A society whose members have a variety of cultural and ethnic backgrounds

multi-disciplinary Made up of different professionals

multilingual Speaking many languages

multiple deprivation The concentration of social problems in one area

multi-professional assessment A measuring of the child's performance by professional from different backgrounds, e.g. health care, social work, psychology, etc.

muscular dystrophy; Duchenne A condition involving progressive destruction of muscle tissue, which only affects boys

nappy rash Soreness of the skin in the nappy area

narrative A piece of factual writing

National Childcare Strategy A strategy introduced by the UK government in May 1998 to ensure good quality, accessible, affordable child care for children aged up to 14

National Curriculum A course of study, laid down by government, that all children between 5 and 16 in state schools in the UK must follow

nature–nurture debate Discussion as to whether genetic factors (nature) or environmental factors (nurture) are more important in influencing behaviour and achievement

negative self-image A view of oneself as not worthwhile or valuable

neonate A newborn baby

nerve deafness Deafness caused by damage to the inner ear, or to the nerves, or hearing centres in the brain

neural tube Cells in the embryo that will develop into the baby's spinal cord

non-judgemental Not taking a fixed position on an issue

non-verbal communication Non-spoken communication, for example, bodily movements, eye contact, gestures and facial expression; sometimes used to enhance or replace speech

norm Developmental skill achieved within an average time-scale

normative measurements An average or norm against which any individual child's development can be measured

norms The rules and guidelines that turn values into action

nuclear family A family grouping where parents live with their children and form a small group with no other family members living near to them

nutrient A substance that provides essential nourishment

object permanence An understanding that objects continue to exist when not in view

oedema Swelling of the tissues with fluid

oestrogen A hormone produced by the ovaries

orientate To determine the position of things

orthofunction A teaching method used in conductive education that involves the whole person physically and mentally and 'instils in children the ability to function as members of society, and to participate in normal social settings appropriate to their age'

ossification The process by which the bones become hardened

otitis media An infection of the middle ear

over-compliant Too easily changed in response to the wishes of others

ovum Egg produced by the ovary

palmar grasp Whole-hand grasp

pancreas A gland that secretes insulin and enzymes that aid digestion; *see* **enzyme**; **insulin**

parasite Lives on and obtains its food from humans

parallel play A child plays side-by-side with another child, but without interacting; their play activities remain separate

paramount Of first importance

parental responsibility The duties, rights and authority that parents have towrds their children

partnership with parents A way of working with parents that recognises their needs and their entitlement to be involved in decisions affecting their children

passive immunity The body's ability to resist a disease, acquired from antibodies given directly into the body, for example the antibodies passed on in breast milk.

pathogen Germs such as bacteria and viruses

patriarchal family A family in which men are dominant and make the important decisions

peer group (or **peers**) A child's equals, i.e. other children

pelvis The bones that make up the hip girdle

percentile charts/centile charts Specially prepared charts that are used to record measurements of a child's growth. There are centile charts for weight, height and head circumference.

perinatal The period of time during birth

peripatetic Travelling to see those they work with

personal identity (or **self-identity**) One's own individuality, the characteristics that make us separate and different from others, our personality

personality *See* **personal identity**

personal continuity A sense of having a past, a present and a future

phagocytosis The process by which white cells absorb pathogens and destroy them

phenylketonuria (PKU) A metabolic impairment that prevents the normal digestion of protein; recessively inherited

phonics An approach to reading that is based on recognition of sounds

physical development The development of bodily movement and control

pincer grasp Thumb and first finger grasp

pinpoint haemorrhages Small areas of bleeding under the surface

placenta The structure that supports the baby as it develops in the uterus

placental barrier The placenta's function in allowing the exchange of materials between mother and fetus

Portage Home Teaching scheme A scheme to help parents/carers to teach their children with learning difficulties in their own homes, by setting short-term, achievable goals

positive action Taking steps to ensure that a particular individual or groups has an equal chance to succeed

positive image The representation of a cross-section of a whole variety of roles and everyday situations, to challenge stereotypes and to extend and increase expectations

positive self-image A view of oneself as worthwhile and valuable

postnatal Describes the period of time after the birth

posture Position of parts of the body

poverty trap Experienced by people if they are receiving state benefits and they find that by earning a small amount more they lose most of their benefits and become worse off

preconceptual The time between a couple deciding they would like to have a baby and when the baby is conceived

preconceptual care Attention to health before pregnancy begins

predisposing factors Factors that make abuse or neglect more likely to occur – usually the result of a number of these factors occurring together

pre-eclampsia *See* **toxaemia of pregnancy**

prejudice An opinion, usually unfavourable, about someone or something, based on incomplete facts

premature A baby born before 36 completed weeks of pregnancy; also referred to as pre-term

prescribed roles Duties laid down by others

pre-term A baby born before 36 completed weeks of pregnancy; also referred to as premature

primary health care team A group of professionals who are concerned with the delivery of first-line health care and health promotion

primitive reflex An automatic response to a particular stimulus in a neonate

primitive tripod grasp Thumb and two finger grasp

principle A basic truth which underpins an activity

private sector *See* **private services**

private services Services provided by individuals, groups of people, or companies to meet a demand, provide a service, and make a financial profit; *also known as* the private sector

problem-solving The ability to draw together, and assess information about a situation in order to find a solution

procedure A pre-set agreed way of doing something

process A continuous series of events which leads to an outcome

professional approach How workers deal with and relate to people – they must not allow personal responses to affect their work

progesterone A hormone produced by the ovaries

prone Lying face down

psychoanalytical theory A mixture of biological and learning theories, involving the idea that a child's development can be badly affected if at any stage their needs are not met appropriately

psychological From the study of the mind

psychopathic events Actions by people who are unable to put themselves in another person's place and empathise with how that person might feel

pyloric stenosis A thickening of the muscle at the outlet of the stomach to the small intestine – milk cannot pass through the narrowed outlet into the small intestine

rapid eye movements (REM) Periods of dream sleep

ratio The numerical relationship or proportion of one quantity to another

recessive gene The weaker gene of a pair at fertilisation

reconstituted family A family grouping in which the adults and children who have previously been part of a different family

recovery position Safe position to place an unconscious casualty in if they are breathing and have a pulse

referral The process by which suspected abuse is reported by one person to someone who can take action if necessary

reflective practitioners Workers who think about what they have done/said with a view to improving practice

reflex An involuntary response to a stimulus

regression Responding in a way that is appropriate to an earlier stage of development

regulations Formal rules that must be followed

reinforcement Responding to an action or behaviour so that a particular consequence – a reward or punishment – is associated with the action and it is repeated (positive reinforcement) or not (negative reinforcement)

relative poverty Occurs when people's resources fall seriously short of the resources commanded by the average individual or family in the community

residential care The provision of care both during the day and the night outside people's homes with people other than close relatives

respite care Short-term care for a child to receive training and assessment and/or to allow their family to have a break

Rhesus factor A specific factor in the blood of about 85 per cent of humans

rights of children The expectations that all children should have regarding how they are treated within their families and in society; *see* **universal needs of children**

rights of parents To bring up their children and make decisions on their behalf, but they also have duties and responsibilities towards their children; *see* **parental responsibility**

rituals Sets of activities

role model A person whose behaviour is used as an example by someone else as the right way to behave

role-play Acting out a role as someone else

rubella German measles, a mild viral infection which damages the fetus in the first 12 weeks of pregnancy

sacrum Base of the spine

safety legislation Laws which are created to prevent accidents and promote safety

sanction A negative outcome attached to a specific behaviour

saturated fats Solid at room temperature and come mainly from animal fats

schema Piaget's term for all the ideas, memories and information that a child might have about a concept or experience

screening Checking the whole population of children at specific ages for particular abnormalities

sebum An oily substance which lubricates the skin, it is produced by the sebaceous glands and secreted through the hair shaft

Section 8 Orders Passed by a court when there is a dispute about whom a child should live with, who they can have contact with, and some of the steps and decisions adults can take about them

self-acceptance Approving of oneself, not constantly striving to change oneself

self-advocacy Putting forward one's own viewpoint

self-approval Being pleased with oneself

self-awareness A knowledge and understanding of oneself

self-concept See **self-image and self-concept**

self-esteem Liking and valuing oneself; *also referred to as* self-respect

self-identity See **personal identity**

self-image and self-concept The picture we have of ourselves and the way we think other people see us

self-reliance The ability to depend on oneself to manage

self-worth Thinking of oneself as having value and worth

sensory impairment Hearing or sight loss

separation distress Infants becoming upset when separated from the person to whom they are attached

sequence The order in which a series of milestones occur

serum alpha-fetoprotein (SAFP) A protein found in the maternal blood during pregnancy; a high level requires further investigation

sex-linked disorders Characteristics and diseases inherited via the X (female) chromosome

sickle cell anaemia An inherited condition of haemoglobin formation

skill An ability that has been practised

social approval When a person's conduct and efforts are approved of by others

social creation Brought about by society

social development The growth of the ability to relate to others appropriately and become independent, within a social framework

social emotions Empathy with the feelings of others; the ability to understand how others feel

socialisation The process by which children learn the culture (or way of life) of the society into which they are born

socially deviant behaviour Behaviour that is socially different and does not follow the rules of the dominant group in a society

social mobility The movement of a person from one social group (class) to another

social model A view of disability as a problem within society

social role A position in society that is associated with particular group of expected behaviours

social status The value that a society puts on people in particular roles in society

socio-economic group Grouping of people according to their status in society, based on their occupation, which is closely related to their wealth/income; another way of referring to someone's social class

solitary play A child plays alone

spatial awareness A developing knowledge of how things move and the effects of movement

special educational needs Learning difficulties requiring special educational provision to be made

specific learning difficulties Difficulties learning to read, write or spell or in doing mathematics, not related to generalised learning difficulties

specific therapeutic goals Identified objectives to counteract the effects of the condition or impairment

sperm (spermatozoa) The mature male sex cell

spina bifida A condition in which the spine fails to develop properly before birth

spinal cord Nerve tissue which carries messages from the brain to the rest of the body, and vice versa

spiritual beliefs What a person believes about the non-material world

Statement of Special Educational Needs A written report setting out a disabled child's needs and the resources needed to meet these needs

statutory child protection Those aspects of protecting children that are covered by legislation

statutory duty Duty required by law

statutory school age The age at which a child legally has to receive education: from the beginning of the term after their fifth birthday, until the end of the school year in which they have their sixteenth birthday

statutory sector Care establishments provided by the state; *also known as* the state sector

statutory service A service provided by the government after a law (or statute) has been passed in parliament; *also referred to as* the state sector

stereotyped roles Pre-determined, fixed ideas that individuals are expected to conform to

stereotyping When people think that all the members of a group have the same characteristics as each other; often applied on the basis of race, gender or disability

sticky eyes A discharge from the eyes in the first three weeks of life

stimulus Something that arouses a reaction

stools Faeces, the product of digested food

stranger anxiety Fear of strangers

subconscious Thoughts and feelings that a person is not fully aware of

subdural haematoma Bleeding into the brain

substitute care The care given to children during periods of separation from their main carers

sudden infant death syndrome (SIDS) The unexpected and usually unexplained death of a young baby

suffocation Stopping respiration

supine Lying on the back

sweat Liquid produced in the sweat glands and secreted through the pores onto the surface of the skin

talipes An abnormal position of the foot caused by the contraction of certain muscles or tendons

term Between the 38th and 42nd week of pregnancy

theories of development Ideas about how and why development occurs

threshold of acceptability The behaviour towards children that is believed to be acceptable by a society at a certain time

thrush A fungal infection of the mouth and/or nappy area

tokenistic A superficial representation of minority or disadvantaged groups, for example including a single black child in a school brochure, a single woman on a board of directors

toilet training Teaching young children the socially acceptable means of emptying the bladder and bowels into a potty and/or toilet

toxaemia of pregnancy A serious condition which only occurs in pregnancy and may damage the health of the fetus and the mother, also known as pre-eclampsia or, in its severe form, as eclampsia

toxin A poisonous substance produced by pathogens

transcutaneous nerve stimulation (TENS) An electronic device to control pain in labour

transition In the context of child care, the movement of a child from one care situation to another

trial-and-error learning The earliest stage in problem-solving. Young children randomly try out solutions to a problem, often making errors, until finding a solution or giving up

triple test An antenatal blood test to measure levels of serum alpha-fetoprotein (SAFP), human chorionic gonadotrophin (HCG) and oestriol

ultrasound scan A check made during pregnancy using an echo-sounding device to monitor the growth and development of the fetus

umbilical cord Contains the blood vessels that connect the developing baby to the placenta

unconscious Showing no response to external stimulation

undescended testicles When the testes remain located in the body instead of coming down into the scrotum

universal needs of children All children have certain needs, whatever their culture, ethnic origin, social class or family background, and are entitled to have them met

unsaturated fats Liquid at room temperature and come mainly from vegetable and fish oils

uterus Part of the female reproductive tract; the womb

vaccine A preparation used to stimulate the production of antibodies and provide immunity against one or several diseases

values Beliefs that certain things are important and to be valued, for example a person's right to their own belongings

vascular Well supplied with blood vessels

ventouse A suction cup applied to the fetal head to assist delivery

ventral suspension When the baby is held in the air, face down

vernix caseosa White creamy substance found on the skin of the fetus, in the skin creases of mature babies and on the trunk of pre-term infants

viable Capable of surviving outside the uterus

villi Finger-like projections of the placenta that fit into the wall of the uterus

visual impairment Impairment of sight, ranging from blindness to partial sight

voluntary action An intentional act that a child chooses to do

voluntary sector Care establishments provided by voluntary organisations

voluntary services Services provided by voluntary organisations which are founded by people who want to help certain groups of people they believe are in need of support; *also referred to as* the voluntary sector

weals Streaks left on the flesh

weaning The transition from milk feeds to solid foods

womb *See* **uterus**

zone of proximal development Vygotsky's term for the range of learning that the child is incapable of achieving alone but that is possible with assistance

Index

Page references in blue are to this book; those in black refer to Book 2. Page references in italic indicate illustrations or tables.